"This book interrogates the crucial topic of 'Ethnicity' in Africa, a continent where the vicissitudes of colonial division had meant that 'identity' connotations have reverberating consequences on the complexities of intergroup relations. In discussing the topic, the book goes beyond the platitudinous explanations to offer fresh discussions that advance intellectual debate. Indeed, the uniqueness of the book lies as much on the diversity of the themes it covers, as with the quality of the analysis it offers. The contributors provide absorbing analysis and penetrating insights, thus bringing eloquence and clarity to the complexities of diversity in Africa. The collective thinking in the book is at the cutting edge of application, and it stands out from a mass of recent books on the subject. Undeniably, no one who wants to find his or her way through the political and economic minefield of Africa in the next decade would have a better guide, as it is a book from which every academic and practitioner would benefit for its accessible arguments and its succinct overview of current thinking on the subject. This is indeed a fascinating and immensely readable book that comes highly recommended."

Abiodun Alao, *Professor of African Studies, King's College London, UK*

"[T]his work takes a fascinating and nuanced approach to how ethnicity interacts with development. Okediji offers groundbreaking insights into how ethnic fragmentation manifests not only in the halls of power but also in the workforce. What makes this work exceptional and an important contribution to economics and African studies is that Okediji does not settle for a singular simple answer. Rather he leans into the complexity of underdevelopment through a rigorous multidisciplinary methodology that approaches the problem from different disciplinary angles. [. . .] This is an important work for anyone who wants to understand the roots of underdevelopment and the role of ethnicity in African civil society."

Jacob K. Olupona, *Professor of African Religious Traditions and African and African American Studies, Harvard University, USA*

"The relationship among identity, inequality, and economic development is central to understanding the challenges faced by sub-Saharan African polities. This edited volume poignantly and intensely demonstrates the crushing effects of the intersection of ethnicity and inequality on economic development, as well as why a critical analysis of this intersection is vital for our understanding of the choices confronting the state, as well as political and civil society, on the continent. Students of African states and societies, particularly in development economics, as well as policymakers, will find this book helpful for their reflections."

Wale Adebanwi, *Presidential Penn Compact Professor of Africana Studies and Director, Center for Africana Studies, University of Pennsylvania, USA*

ETHNICITY, INEQUALITY, AND ECONOMIC DEVELOPMENT IN SUB-SAHARAN AFRICA

This book uses a multidisciplinary approach to explore the links between ethnicity, inequality, and economic development in sub-Saharan Africa.

This book shows how ethnic identity influences all aspects of life in African societies, defining access to political institutions and economic resources, resulting in horizontal or structural inequalities. It demonstrates that ethnicity operates both directly and indirectly through political and economic institutions in which the dynamics of ethnic engagement serve as a basis for resource allocation. Drawing on a blend of micro and macro perspectives, this book assesses the economic, cultural, legal, and sociological connections among ethnicity, inequality, and economic development in sub-Saharan Africa. Chapters provide a critical framework that grounds ethnic fragmentation as a central agency of underdevelopment and principally focus on three key areas:

- The origins and dynamics of ethnicity in sub-Saharan Africa
- Socioeconomic inequality in sub-Saharan Africa and its link to ethnic identity
- The relationship between governance networks and ethnic identity

A distinctive contribution to development literature, this book will be of interest to students and scholars of economics, development studies, geography, anthropology, political science, sociology, and African studies.

Tade O. Okediji is a professor in the Department of African American and African Studies and in the Department of Applied Economics at the University of Minnesota Twin Cities in Minneapolis, Minnesota, USA. He has published extensively on the effects of ethnic diversity on long-term economic performance in sub-Saharan Africa.

Routledge Studies in African Development

Transformative Innovation for Sustainable Human Settlements
A South African Context
Edited by Andrew Emmanuel Okem, Sithembiso Lindelihle Myeni and Tshepang Mosiea

Basic Income for Disasters and Climate Change in Africa
Agrarian Risk Reduction and Adaptation
Sara Bernardo

Children's Lived Experience of Poverty and Vulnerability in Kenya
Going Beyond Multi-dimensionality
Elizabeth Ngutuku

African Values and Development
Rethinking Agenda 2063
Edited By Ezra Chitando and Eunice Kamaara

Chinese Development Aid and Africa
What, How, and Why
Edited by Elling Tjønneland

Ethnicity, Inequality, and Economic Development in Sub-Saharan Africa
Edited by Tade O. Okediji

For more information about this series, please visit: www.routledge.com/Routledge-Studies-in-African-Development/book-series/RSAD

ETHNICITY, INEQUALITY, AND ECONOMIC DEVELOPMENT IN SUB-SAHARAN AFRICA

Edited by Tade O. Okediji

Routledge
Taylor & Francis Group
LONDON AND NEW YORK

Designed cover image: Alamy

First published 2026
by Routledge
4 Park Square, Milton Park, Abingdon, Oxon OX14 4RN

and by Routledge
605 Third Avenue, New York, NY 10158

Routledge is an imprint of the Taylor & Francis Group, an informa business

British Library Cataloguing-in-Publication Data
A catalogue record for this book is available from the British Library

ISBN: 9781032412535 (hbk)
ISBN: 9781032412511 (pbk)
ISBN: 9781003357025 (ebk)

DOI: 10.4324/9781003357025

Typeset in Times New Roman
by codeMantra

CONTENTS

FIGURES

TABLES

BOXES

CONTRIBUTORS

Adebowale M. Adeleke is Lecturer in the Economics Department at the University of Ibadan in Ibadan, Nigeria. He has published articles on international trade and finance and on energy and growth empirics in Nigeria.

Adigun Agbaje is Professor of Political Science at the University of Ibadan. One of Nigeria's most prolific political scientists, he is the author of *The Nigerian Press, Hegemony and the Social Construction of Legitimacy, 1960–83* (1992).

Emmanuel R. Aiyede is Professor of Political Institutions, Governance, and Public Policy in the Political Science Department at the University of Ibadan. He has published numerous peer-reviewed articles, book chapters, and edited books on politics in Africa generally and in Nigeria specifically.

Olayinka Akanle is Sociology Professor at the University of Ibadan and a senior research associate in the Sociology Department at the University of Johannesburg in South Africa. He has published extensively on the link between micro and macro migration processes with an emphasis on human mobility and socioeconomic development.

Olufunmilayo B. Arewa is Professor in the Antonin Scalia Law School at George Mason University in Fairfax, Virginia, United States, and a leading scholar in business law, technology, and entrepreneurship. Her book *Disrupting Africa: Technology, Law, and Development* (2021) won the International Studies Association's STAIR Book Award.

Dauda A. Busari is Senior Lecturer in the Sociology Department at the University of Ibadan. His research employs a multidisciplinary approach to explore the dynamics of democratization in Nigeria, and culture, society, and economic development. He has held a visiting position at Northwestern University in Evanston, Illinois, United States.

Promise M. Hlungwani is Lecturer at Marondera University of Agricultural Sciences and Technology in Marondera, Zimbabwe. His research interests are in public policy, poverty, and development economics, and his work has appeared in several academic journals.

Tolulope Rachael Jerumeh is a research fellow at the Nigerian Institute of Social and Economic Research in Ibadan, Nigeria. She holds her PhD in Agricultural Economics from the University of Ibadan. Her research interests include agricultural policy, food security, and poverty-related issues.

Peter Mukarumbwa is a Yorkshire and Humber Policy Engagement and Research Network policy fellow at the University of Bradford in Bradford, England. His research interests include policy research, evaluation of development programs, and urban food security. He holds a PhD in agricultural economics.

Abbyssinia Mushunje is Professor and former Head of the Agricultural Economics and Extension Department at the University of Fort Hare in South Africa. He is a prominent researcher and has published widely on issues including land reform, climate change, farm efficiency, and food security in South Africa and Zimbabwe.

Saul Ngarava holds his PhD in Agricultural Economics and is a research associate in the University of Lincoln's School of Natural Sciences in Lincoln, United Kingdom. His work on rural development, climate change, agricultural economics, and disaster risk management in South Africa has appeared in multiple international publications.

E. Olawale Ogunkola is Economics Professor at the University of Ibadan and Director of the university's Trade Policy Research and Training Programme. A senior research fellow at the Centre for Econometrics and Allied Research in Ibadan, Nigeria, he has published widely on trade and regional integration in Africa.

Tade O. Okediji is Professor in the Department of African American and African Studies and in the Department of Applied Economics at the University of Minnesota Twin Cities in Minneapolis, Minnesota, United States. He has published extensively on the effects of ethnic diversity on long-term economic performance in sub-Saharan Africa.

Victor Olusegun Okoruwa is Professor of Agricultural Economics at the University of Ibadan. A distinguished fellow of the African Association of Agricultural Economists and a fellow of the Nigerian Association of Agricultural Economists, he is a renowned scholar on resource economics, agricultural policy, and rural development in Africa.

Akinpelu O. Olutayo is Professor in the Department of Sociology at the University of Ibadan. His work on the sociology of development in Africa and Nigeria, globalization in Africa, and Indigenous politics in Africa has appeared in numerous books and international academic journals.

Ayokunle O. Omobowale is Professor in the Sociology Department at the University of Ibadan. The author of *The* Tokunbo *Phenomenon and the Second-Hand Economy in Nigeria* (2013), he has published extensively on sociology and development, including urban development, in Nigeria and across Africa.

Aderonke Mary Omotola holds her PhD in Agricultural Economics and is currently a researcher at the Community Revolution, a sustainable development nonprofit organization in Nottingham, England. Her research interests include welfare-related issues, gender studies, and impact evaluation.

Titiloye Ademola Oyejide is Emeritus Professor of economics at the University of Ibadan and chairperson of the Centre for Trade and Development Initiative in Ibadan, Nigeria. A former member of the World Trade Organization' advisory panel, he has published widely on trade, trade policy, and regional integration in Africa.

Olugboyega A. Oyeranti is Professor in the Economics Department at the University of Ibadan. His work on the intersection of economic growth and social dynamics in Nigeria has appeared in several international journals. He also works on the effects of trade, employment, and rural poverty reduction in Nigeria.

Simbarashe Tatsvarei is Senior Lecturer in the Department of Agricultural Business Development and Economics at the University of Zimbabwe in Harare, Zimbabwe. He has published articles on land governance, impact evaluation, agricultural value chains, and policy analysis in Zimbabwe.

James Siguru Wahutu is Assistant Professor in the Department of Sociology and Council on African Studies at Yale University in New Haven, Connecticut, United States, and a faculty associate at Harvard University's Berkman Klein Center for Internet and Society in Cambridge, Massachusetts, United States.

PREFACE

The quest for sustained development and economic growth in sub-Saharan Africa remains daunting. Despite notable strides in many countries, a discernible path toward sustainable development largely eludes the subcontinent. Notwithstanding myriad economic policies to address economic underperformance recommended or imposed by international financial institutions or implemented by domestic governments, dire poverty, and chronic structural inequality remain entrenched. Scholars from various disciplines continue to investigate and advance theories to explain the tragedy of sub-Saharan Africa's post-independence development.

Ethnicity is a major factor in—and impediment to—Africa's development and growth. Its impact is evident at every level, including political power dynamics, access to socioeconomic and political institutions, distribution of social services, and resource allocation, resulting in dramatic structural inequalities. Economic development literature widely recognizes that ethnic diversity adversely affects countries' prospects for long-term economic performance. However, these studies lack the critical framework that grounds ethnic fragmentation as a central agent for underdevelopment. Ethnic diversity in Africa affects socioeconomic inequality—and development more broadly—through both direct and indirect channels; those indirect channels have yet to be fully explored.

Understanding ethnicity's effects on African development requires a vigorous examination with a multidisciplinary emphasis. To that end, this volume delves into Africa's economic development conundrum from a coordinated cross-social sciences perspective. Its original contributions from the fields of economic theory, agricultural and applied economics, law, political science, and sociology seek to clarify the links between ethnicity, inequality, and economic development. Its interdisciplinary focus takes a holistic approach to studying ethnicity, its multifarious manifestations and implications, and its outsized impact on Africa's development.

The chapters herein concentrate principally on three broad areas: the dynamics of ethnicity in sub-Saharan Africa; socioeconomic inequality in sub-Saharan Africa and its correlation to ethnic identity; and the relationship between sub-Saharan African governance networks and ethnic identity. In Chapter 1, "Ethnopolitical and Economic Development in Sub-Saharan Africa: A Review," volume editor Tade Okediji outlines the history and evolution of ethnic diversity as a subject of inquiry in development economics, with a focus on African development. He highlights the examples of Nigeria and Kenya to illustrate the indirect mechanisms through which ethnicity affects economic performance—for example, how ethnicity influences economic development via political development.

In Chapter 2, "Elitism, Ethnicity, and Development in Nigeria," Akinpelu Olutayo, Ayokunle Omobowale, Olayinka Akanle, and Dauda Busari investigate the role of elites in manipulating colonial-era conceptions of ethnic identity and the allegiances constructed around them to explain Nigeria's persistent inequality and underdevelopment. Through the lens of the country's prospects for sustainable, long-term development, the authors interrogate the forces of colonialism and post-colonial ethnic identity politics and the legacy of indirect rule to spotlight the contemporary interplay of elitism, governance, inequality, and poverty. They conclude that until these relationships are fully understood—and systemic policy approaches are adopted to address the long-standing dynamics and societal ills that underlie them—sustainable development in Nigeria will remain elusive.

Ethnoregional inequality and poverty foster intense political competition, deep distrust, and prolonged conflict, all major impediments to development. In Chapter 3, "Ethnoregional Inequality and Poverty: Social Policy as an Imperative to Stability and Inclusive Development in Sub-Saharan Africa," Emmanuel Aiyede and Adigun Agbaje examine various dimensions of inequality and ethnicity to unravel the drivers of inequality, exclusion, and social instability. They then turn to social policy as a means to mitigate inequality and poverty in ethnically fragmented societies and evaluate successes and failures across the continent, with a particular focus on the African Union's Social Policy Framework for Africa and its potential to transform Africa's development landscape. The authors advocate the adoption of the framework to effect changes to economic and social structures that perpetuate vulnerabilities and to promote economic and political empowerment among marginalized ethnic groups.

In Chapter 4, "The Sociopolitical Ascendancy of the Kikuyu in Post-Independence Kenya: The Colonial Legacy of Ethnic Inequality," Tade Okediji traces the political and economic rise of Kenya's largest ethnic group since the end of the colonial period. This chapter's economic history analysis illustrates how deeply ethnicity is ingrained in modern-day politics in Kenya. This embeddedness dates back to the British establishment of the East Africa Protectorate in 1895, at which point ethnicity became an integral part of the dialogue—and ultimately the predominant factor in Kenya's post-independence socioeconomic and political life and public policy decision-making. Although constitutional reforms in 2010 sought to redress these inequalities by devolving power from the central government, this chapter contends that the results have been mixed at best: In large part, the de rigueur rent-seeking and ethnic patronage that have characterized Kenyan politics since independence has simply migrated to the regional and county levels, essentially localizing the pernicious behavior and its ill effects. As the saying goes, nothing changes if nothing changes; until meaningful reforms can succeed at unwinding the colonial legacy and addressing the extreme socioeconomic and ethnic inequalities that it wrought, the prospects for ordinary Kenyans—and for the country's development writ large—will remain under its shadow.

A pertinent aspect of the discourse on ethnicity and inequality in Africa is its impact on gender disparities. In Chapter 5, "Gendered Ethnicity: Compounding Inequality in Resource Distribution and Decision-Making for Women in Sub-Saharan Africa," Abbyssinia Mushunje, Saul Ngarava, Simbarashe Tatsvarei, and Peter Mukarumbwa document how gendered ethnicity influences resource distribution and decision-making. They apply intersectionality theory to dissect the interlinkages between gender, ethnicity, and inequality to demonstrate how ethnicity, as a social institution, shapes gender inequality by reinforcing cultural and social norms that preserve existing gender gaps. Noting that existing scholarship insufficiently explores these overlapping social identity categories (and the norms and practices constructed around them) and how they factor into women's access to resources and opportunities for decision-making agency across the subcontinent, they conclude that sub-Saharan Africa's prospects for sustainable, inclusive development depend on policies that target ethnic and gender inequalities in tandem.

In Chapter 6, "Ethnic Inequality and Agricultural Resource Allocation and Distribution in Nigeria: The Need for Inclusive Growth," Victor Olusegun Okoruwa, Tolulope Rachael Jerumeh, and Aderonke Mary Omotola illuminate how entrenched ethnic inequality stemming from ethnic favoritism has historically been the basis for allocating and distributing federal funds in Nigeria. Their study employs waves (or phases) of the World Bank's General Household Survey to analyze agricultural input supply and the extent of equity and inclusiveness in its allocation and distribution across different geopolitical zones in Nigeria. This chapter covers the time span between 2010 and 2018, during which two different presidential administrations were in power: President Goodluck Jonathan from 2010 to 2015 and President Muhammadu Buhari between 2015 and 2018. Jonathan and Buhari hailed from different ethnic groups and adopted differentially inclusive policies. The contrasts presented in this chapter illustrate the influence of ethnopolitics in public policy decision-making, and ultimately in economic development—specifically, how ethnicity is employed as a basis for economic policy choices and resource distribution, thereby exacerbating ethnic divides.

At the core of development planning in post-independence Africa are strategies to reduce poverty and inequality and to unlock the continent's development and growth potential. Trade is an indispensable component of economic growth, and economics literature often proffers poverty reduction as a potential benefit of trade. In Chapter 7, "Regional Trade Performance and Poverty: An Assessment of the Economic Growth Linkage in Nigeria," E. Olawale Ogunkola and Olugboyega Oyeranti use a fully modified ordinary least squares (FM-OLS) estimation to analyze the effects of regional trade in Africa between 1981 and 2019 on the poverty level in Nigeria. They evaluate how sectoral economic growth correlates to poverty across twenty-five sectors, and their results indicate that regional trade in Africa positively affects overall growth in Nigeria. This study has important implications for identifying sectors for poverty reduction in light of the African Continental Free Trade Area agreement's adoption in 2019. The authors recommend macroeconomic strategies to promote private-sector development and access to finance to stimulate investment in lagging sectors.

Quite the contrarian in Chapter 8, "Not Everything Is About Ethnicity: Conflict and the Politics of Belonging in Africa," James Siguru Wahutu offers a somewhat divergent but nevertheless insightful view on the ethnicity, inequality, conflict, and development discourse. His nuanced analysis examines so-called *naming* and *claiming* paradigms to situate ethnicity in Africa. The former frames ethnicity as primordial, static, and essentialist, wherein ethnic identity is prescribed by external forces or agents. The latter, by contrast, views ethnic identity as malleable, straddling multiple forms of identity and belonging; it captures the lived experience of Africans and the fluid nature of origin and identity as a selective process, situating African agency at the center of knowledge. Unlike naming, which flattens identity into singular ethnolinguistic/regional/religious groups, claiming allows identity to be intersectional and formed from a matrix of identities based on an individual or group context. Wahutu asserts that a more polysemic and polydimensional understanding of ethnicity, informed by both intersectional and sociology of knowledge methodologies, will foster better strategies to address ethnic inequality, promote economic development, and mitigate conflict in Africa.

The work of the United Nations and other international agencies centers around eliminating inequality, poverty, and social exclusion in African countries—most notably through the Sustainable Development Goals (SDGs). In Chapter 9, "Socioeconomic Inequality in Sub-Saharan Africa and Its Links to Governance Systems," Promise Hlungwani, Abbyssinia Mushunje, Simbarashe Tatsvarei, Peter Mukarumbwa, and Saul Ngarava propose that SDG attainment depends on realigning governance systems to address the persistent and worsening problem of socioeconomic inequality on the subcontinent. Using measures including the World Bank's Worldwide Governance Indicators and the Gini index, the chapter outlines the ways in which poor governance causes and complicates inequality. After establishing that good governance plays an essential role in reducing socioeconomic inequalities, the authors recommend policies that cultivate transparency in availing economic opportunities, foster gender-equal access to land and resources, equalize workers' pay, encourage labor-intensive industries, close tax loopholes that benefit the rich, and introduce stronger social protection programs in order to set sub-Saharan Africa on a path to sustainable long-term development.

In Chapter 10, "Ethnic Diversity, Socioeconomic Inequality, and Conflict in Nigeria: The Case for Political and Financial Restructuring," T. Ademola Oyejide and Adebowale Adeleke point to the ongoing Boko Haram insurgency and the intractable conflict between nomadic herders and sedentary farmers (along with other lower-order conflicts) as strong evidence that most if not all conflicts in Nigeria—regardless of their putative roots—either have ethnic or ethnoreligious undertones or are presented as such by their instigators so as to garner support for their cause. The authors scrutinize various socioeconomic indicators to demonstrate that conflict, whether ostensibly or actually ethnic or ethnoreligious in nature exacerbates Nigerian socioeconomic inequality, in the process hindering economic growth and causing manifold social harms. While acknowledging that political and financial restructuring are not a panacea and can yield unintended consequences, they conclude that Nigerian federalism can only overcome the socioeconomic and political inequalities that continue to incite ethnic and ethnoreligious conflict and stifle the country's development by overhauling the political structure and financial allocation formula to reduce state governments' reliance on the federal government, address regional and ethnic disparities, foster social cohesion and a strong national identity, and promote lasting stability and economic growth.

The chapters in this volume confront colonialism as an inescapable theme in African development studies. Whereas colonial rule did not create ethnic identity or groups, it did intensify ethnic cleavages and rivalries by amalgamating disparate ethnic groups and subsuming them under an exploitative political structure to facilitate colonial control. In Chapter 11, "Identity, Inequality, and Colonial Overhang: Law and Continuing Legacies of Divide and Rule in Nigeria," Olufunmilayo Arewa examines the nexus of colonialism, identity, inequality, and law to demonstrate how Nigeria's colonial legacy deeply ingrained ethnic divisions in law, and how patterns and policies established during British rule have amplified those divisions, fostered pervasive inequality, and depressed economic growth and development. Arewa unpacks the hybrid legal framework established during the colonial period, which borrowed elements from both English statutory law and African customary law but failed to reconcile divergent and often conflicting elements of each, thus embedding a differential system of ethnic identification and jurisdiction limited to particular customary boundaries. In short, Nigerian jurisprudence was fragmented from the outset, which entrenched ethnically driven social and political schisms that endure today.

Development experts and practitioners have touted Africa as the next major frontier in the globalized economy. Yet deconstructing how African economies function—and how the complex interrelationships between socioeconomic and cultural variables dynamically affect African development—presents a complex challenge. Analyzing the reasons for sub-Saharan Africa's dismal economic performance requires a holistic approach primarily because the subcontinent's societies are built on informal networks in which kinship ties and ethnic identity exert powerful influence in local markets, social relations, and political alliances.

Implementing policies to reduce systemic inequality and induce growth requires formal institutions to coordinate with those informal networks; it also requires a deeper understanding of how informal networks influence the design and structure of formal ones.

The chapters in this volume reflect a diversity of methodological approaches and perspectives previously lacking in the field of African development studies. The analytical and empirical inquiries in these pages, with their focus on the economic, cultural, sociological, and legal connections between ethnicity, inequality, and economic development in sub-Saharan Africa, represent a distinctive and much-needed contribution to the literature. This multidisciplinary approach is critical for designing effective and sustainable development strategies for the African subcontinent in a rapidly changing world.

ACKNOWLEDGMENTS

This book would not have come to fruition without the encouragement and support of several individuals.

First and foremost, I express my deepest gratitude to the Lord, whose divine inspiration guided the creation of this book and its execution.

Thanks to each contributing author's commitment to the research project and the vibrant conversation during the initial workshop, which was held under the auspices of the University of Minnesota's African American & African Studies and Applied Economics Departments in Lagos, Nigeria, in August 2019.

I am deeply appreciative of the undergraduate and graduate students who, through their engagement in my course on African development, sparked the idea for this book.

I also thank Professors Abiodun Alao, Rodney Smith, Donald Liu, Jacob Olupona, John Wright, and Wale Adebanwi who took the time to discuss various ideas and topics related to this book's theme and enriched its overall content. Jovin Lasaway provided invaluable assistance at various stages of the completion of the manuscript for which I am enormously grateful. Tomas Felcman provided excellent editorial assistance.

I am also grateful to Professor Germano Mwabu, who organized and hosted my visit to the Department of Economics at Kenyatta University, where I researched Chapter 4 of the volume. Additionally, I am grateful to Professor Martin Etyang at Kenyatta University for his comments and suggestions on earlier versions of Chapter 4.

I am indebted to Daniel Smith, Professor of Anthropology and Director of the Africa Initiative at Brown University's Watson Institute for International and

Public Affairs, for hosting me during my sabbatical at Brown in 2021–22, during which I revised portions of this book manuscript.

Finally, I am profoundly grateful to my wife, Professor Ruth Okediji, for her encouragement, support, and patience in listening to my thoughts and ideas about various aspects of the manuscript. Her unwavering support has been a continuous source of inspiration.

ACRONYMS

ACCORD	African Centre for the Constructive Resolution of Disputes
ACGSF	Agricultural Credit Guarantee Scheme Fund (Nigeria)
ACN	Action Congress of Nigeria (Nigeria)
ADB	Asian Development Bank
ADF	augmented Dickey-Fuller test
AfCFTA	African Continental Free Trade Area
AfDB	African Development Bank
AG	Action Group (Nigeria)
AgPER	agriculture public expenditure review
AGRA	Alliance for a Green Revolution in Africa
AIAE	African Institute for Applied Economics
AIC	Akaike information criterion
ANC	Amani National Congress (Kenya)
ANPP	All Nigeria People's Party (Nigeria)
APC	All Progressives Congress (Nigeria)
APC	Arewa People's Congress (Nigeria)
APGA	All Progressives Grand Alliance (Nigeria)
ATA	Agricultural Transformation Agenda (Nigeria)
AU	African Union
AUSPF	Social Policy Framework for Africa (African Union)
BBC	British Broadcasting Corporation
CBN	Central Bank of Nigeria
CCM	Chama Cha Mashinani (Kenya)
CGE	computable general equilibrium modeling
CIA	Central Intelligence Agency
CIGI	Centre for International Governance Innovation

CKRC	Constitution of Kenya Review Commission
CODESRIA	Council for the Development of Social Science Research in Africa
COMESA	Common Market for Eastern and Southern Africa
CORD	Coalition for Reforms and Democracy (Kenya)
COVID-19	coronavirus disease of 2019
CPC	Congress for Progressive Change (Nigeria)
CRPD	Centre for Research on Peace and Development
CRS	constant returns to scale
CSAE	Centre for the Study of African Economies
DRC	Democratic Republic of the Congo
EAC	East African Community
ELDS	educationally less developed state (Nigeria)
ELF	ethnolinguistic fractionalization index
EOI	equity opportunity index
FAO	Food and Agriculture Organization (United Nations)
FCT	Federal Capital Territory (Nigeria)
FIW	Forschungsschwerpunkt Internationale Wirtschaft [Research Focus on International Economics]
FM-OLS	fully modified ordinary least squares estimation
FMSP	Fertilizer Market Stabilization Program (Nigeria)
FORD–Kenya	Forum for the Restoration of Democracy
FTC	Federal Capital Territory (Nigeria)
GAD	gender and development
GDI	Global Development Institute
GDP	gross domestic product
GEMA	Gikuyu, Embu, and Meru Association (Kenya)
GESS	Growth Enhancement Support Scheme (Nigeria)
GHS	Generalized Household Survey (World Bank)
GII	gender inequality index
GLO	Global Labor Organization
GMM	generalized method of moments method
GNPP	Great Nigeria People's Party (Nigeria)
GTAP	Global Trade Analysis Project (Purdue University)
HIV	human immunodeficiency virus
IDI	inclusive development index
IDPs	internally displaced persons
IDS	Institute of Development Studies
IEBC	Independent Electoral and Boundaries Commission (Kenya)
IESE	Instituto de Estudos Sociais e Económicos [Institute of Social and Economic Studies]
IGR	internally generated revenue

ILO	International Labour Organization
IMF	International Monetary Fund
IPC	Igbo People's Congress (Nigeria)
IPOB	Indigenous People of Biafra (Nigeria)
IYC	Ijaw Youth Council (Nigeria)
KADU	Kenya African Democratic Union
KANU	Kenya African National Union
KAU	Kenya African Union
KCA	Kikuyu Central Association (Kenya)
KIM	Kenya Independence Movement
KLFA	Kenya Land and Freedom Army
LCR	land consolidation and registration program (Kenya)
LDCs	least developed countries
LDP	Liberal Democratic Party (Kenya)
MASSOB	Movement for the Actualization of the Sovereign State of Biafra (Nigeria)
MDGs	Millennium Development Goals (United Nations)
MDRII	multidimensional regional integration index
MENA	Middle East and North Africa
MEND	Movement for the Emancipation of the Niger Delta (Nigeria)
MFIs	microfinance institutions
ML	maximum likelihood estimation
MOSOP	Movement for the Survival of the Ogoni People (Nigeria)
MPI	Multidimensional Poverty Index
MSMEs	micro, small, and medium enterprises
NAK	National Alliance of Kenya
NARC	National Rainbow Coalition (Kenya)
NASA	National Super Alliance (Kenya)
NCC	National Constitutional Conference (Kenya)
NCNC	National Council of Nigerian Citizens/National Council of Nigeria and the Cameroons
NDA	Niger Delta Avengers (Nigeria)
NDP	National Development Party (Kenya)
NDPVF	Niger Delta People's Volunteer Force (Nigeria)
NPC	Northern People's Congress (Nigeria)
NPN	National Party of Nigeria
NPP	Nigerian People's Party
OAU	Organization of African Unity
OCHA	United Nations Office for the Coordination of Humanitarian Affairs
ODM	Orange Democratic Movement (Kenya)
OECD	Organization for Economic Co-operation and Development

OI	opportunity index
OLS	ordinary least squares regression
OPC	O'odua People's Congress (Nigeria)
OPHI	Oxford Poverty and Human Development Initiative
PDP	People's Democratic Party (Nigeria)
PNU	Party of National Unity (Kenya)
PPPs	purchasing power parities
PREG	politically relevant ethnic groups index
PSFS	public spending on fertilizer subsidy
RUGA	rural grazing area policy (Nigeria)
SADC	Southern African Development Community
SAM	social accounting matrix
SBC	Schwarz Bayesian criterion
SDGs	Sustainable Development Goals (United Nations)
SDI	social diversity index
SMEs	small and medium enterprises
SOF	social opportunity function
UBEC	Universal Basic Education Commission (Nigeria)
UDA	United Democratic Party (Kenya)
UN	United Nations
UNCTAD	UN Trade and Development
UNDP	United Nations Development Programme
UNECA	United Nations Economic Commission for Africa
UNESCO	United Nations Educational, Scientific and Cultural Organization
UNICEF	United Nations Children's Fund
UNRISD	United Nations Research Institute for Social Development
UNU-WIDER	United Nations University World Institute for Development Economics Research
UPN	Unity Party of Nigeria
URP	United Republican Party (Kenya)
USAID	United States Agency for International Development
WAD	women and development
WDIs	World Development Indicators (World Bank)
WDM	Wiper Democratic Movement (Kenya)
WEF	World Economic Forum
WHO	World Health Organization
WID	women in development
WJP	World Justice Project
ZANU–PF	Zimbabwe African National Union–Patriotic Front

PART 1

Perspectives on Ethnicity in Sub-Saharan Africa

1

ETHNOPOLITICAL AND ECONOMIC DEVELOPMENT IN SUB-SAHARAN AFRICA

A Review

Tade O. Okediji

Introduction

The study of how socioeconomic and cultural variables influence economic development dates back to the classical school of economics, and particularly to Karl Marx's postulation linking economic development to political and social institutions (Marx, 1954).[1] Specifically, Marx inferred that changes in economic performance are inextricably linked to political and social institutions; he suggested a causal relationship among the relevant variables, with the causality running from social and political institutions to economic development (Dorfman, 1991).

The end of World War II coincided with decolonization and the emergence of newly independent countries and economies referred to as the *third world* (though that label has largely been discarded in favor of *developing world*). The quest to understand the economic, political, and social challenges confronting those newly independent states, the majority of them in Africa, led to a resurgence of the subdiscipline of development economics, along with a renewed focus on the role of non-economic factors in determining long-term economic performance. This research resided predominantly in the realm of institutional economics, pioneered by scholars such as Thorstein Veblen and Gunnar Myrdal (Veblen, 1912; Myrdal, 1968). However, the preeminence of neoclassical and Keynesian economics as the mainstream orthodoxies overshadowed institutional economics. Economists in the postwar period deemed neoclassical and Keynesian approaches more applicable to the pressing economic issues in developing economies, like business cycles and income distribution (Hermann, 2018).

Douglass North's 1993 Nobel Prize in Economics for his work on applying economics and history to explain economic growth and institutional change rekindled the focus on institutional economics. In his acceptance speech, North opined that

DOI: 10.4324/9781003357025-2

the lack of progress in economic development post–World War II derived from a poor understanding of the role that institutions and institutional factors play in economic performance (North, 1994). Thereafter, mainstream economics began to recognize that neoclassical and Keynesian methodologies are insufficient to explain economic development and growth in developing countries. This renaissance of institutional economics sparked fresh research on institutions, both formal and informal, and their interactions with socioeconomic and cultural variables. These new insights capture more precisely the realities of African countries mired in extreme poverty and inequality since their independence.

Africa in the 1990s was still reeling from the effects of its worst decade in terms of economic growth, often referred to as the lost decade, during which some countries even had negative growth rates (Collier & Gunning, 1999). Questions persisted about the continent's perpetual state of underdevelopment and stymied growth, but this new research avenue established the link between institutions and long-term economic growth. Because African societies are mostly informal economies, understanding how informal institutions influence economic performance is essential to understanding African development. In other words, examining institutions in the context of neoclassical and Keynesian methodologies offers a better explanation for the process of and path to economic development.

Empirical studies on African development and growth have focused primarily on three themes as reasons for the continent's dismal growth performance: identifying sources of meager growth in Africa, understanding Africa's growth dynamics relative to other regions, and explaining Africa's growth from a structural perspective (Chitonge, 2016).[2] Growth studies tend to employ proxies—such as political stability indexes (estimated using variables like the number of assassinations, coups, or civil wars) and years of schooling for human capital—as estimates for qualitative variables. Proxies for informal institutions include social capital or social cohesion and trust indexes. A seminal paper by William Easterly and Ross Levine titled "Africa's Growth Tragedy" uses an ethnic diversity index, the ethnolinguistic fractionalization (ELF) index, as a proxy for social capital, revealing that ethnic diversity accounts for more than 30 percent of the growth differential between Africa and the rest of the world (Easterly & Levine, 1997).[3] Their work suggests that ethnically fragmented societies are less likely to agree on macroeconomic policies to promote long-term growth due to competitive rent-seeking behavior, which itself is inimical to growth. Two years prior, Paolo Mauro was the first to introduce ethnic diversity to empirical growth studies. Also employing the ELF index, his work concluded that greater ethnic diversity begets a higher likelihood of political instability, which in turn impedes economic development and growth (Mauro, 1995).

The Easterly and Levine paper opened a new vista of research in development economics, especially pertaining to African development. It was the first study to use a proxy for social dynamics or social capital in growth regressions. A number of related studies have broadly supported its conclusion that ethnic fragmentation leads to inadequate provision of public services due to competition among ethnic groups for the provision of public goods, resulting in insufficient development policies (Easterly & Levine, 1997). For instance, Anthony Annett shows that ethnic fragmentation leads to higher levels of government consumption and diverts resources from macroeconomic variables needed for development (Annett, 2001). Rafael La Porta et al. demonstrate that ethnic diversity considerably influences the quality of government (La Porta et al., 1999). Robert Barro suggests that competition for limited resources makes sustaining a democracy more difficult in ethnically diverse societies (Barro, 1999). Alberto Alesina et al. posit that various expressions of ELF are important determinants of economic success (Alesina et al., 2003). And José Montalvo and Marta Reynal-Querol illustrate that ELF has direct negative effects on growth (Montalvo & Reynal-Querol, 2005).

These conclusions notwithstanding, other studies indicate that ethnic fragmentation has a statistically insignificant impact on growth (Block, 2001; Sachs & Warner, 1997). Jean-Louis Arcand, Patrick Guillaumont, and Sylviane Guillaumont Jeanneney, for example, suggest that Easterly and Levine's results as to the channels through which ethnic diversity impacts economic growth are unconvincing (Arcand, Guillaumont, & Jeanneney, 2000; Easterly & Levine, 1997). Theirs and other contrary works support the need for a deeper inquiry into how ethnicity—and more specifically ethnic diversity and fragmentation—leads to lower growth in Africa.

Ethnic Diversity in Sub-Saharan Africa: Concept and Measurement

Perhaps the most widely used measure of ethnic diversity is the ELF index, which derives from data in the *Atlas narodov mira* (Atlas of the peoples of the world) and engenders different indexes and computations that measure ethnic fragmentation.[4] As a singular measure of ethnic diversity in cross-national studies on economic growth, the ELF index infers ethnicity as a primary cause of lackluster growth and dismal economic performance in post-independence African states. In their study of ethnopolitics and democratic sustainability in Africa, James Scarritt and Shaheen Mozaffar classify ethnopolitical groups in sub-Saharan African countries using data from the 1993 *Minorities at Risk* dataset and from the 1972 primer *Black Africa: A Comparative Handbook* (Scarritt & Mozaffar, 1999). Scarritt and Mozaffar's work codifies ethnopolitical groups in a three-tier scheme: national dichotomy, middle-level aggregation, and lower-level aggregation. Countries in the first tier have highly politicized ethnic groups. The second tier consists of coalitions of ethnic groups that align politically but have not led to a partitioning of the country's population. In the third tier are coalitions within middle-level groups in which two or more groups (neither of which have national significance) are in opposition to each other or seek to differentiate themselves from other groups (Scarritt

& Mozaffar, 1999; Gurr, 1993; Morrison, Mitchell, & Paden, 1972). Though not irrelevant, ethnopolitics as a basis for ethnic fragmentation in sub-Saharan Africa seems an attenuated approach to understanding the formation of ethnic groups.

Alesina et al. compute three separate ethnic fragmentation measures—linguistic, ethnic, and religious—using data derived primarily from *Encyclopedia Britannica*, and also from the 2000 CIA *World Factbook*, from David Levinson's 1998 handbook *Ethnic Groups Worldwide*, and from Minority Rights Group International's 1997 *World Directory of Minorities* (Alesina et al., 2003; CIA, 2000; Levinson, 1998; Minority Rights Group International, 1997). Again, these singular measures are proxies for ethnic diversity. Although their granularity is a significant improvement over the ELF index, as James Fearon points out, neither Alesina et al.'s discussion of ethnicity nor their subsequent computation distinguishes between the variables *ethnic* and *linguistic* (Alesina et al., 2003). Fearon computes two indexes of ethnic diversity: a fractionalization index based on measures of ethnicity other than just linguistic (as in the ELF index) and an index of cultural diversity (a measure of cultural distance between groups and a modification beyond the fractionalization index). Fearon's sources include Barbara Grimes's 1996 *Ethnologue: Languages of the World*, the 2000 CIA *World Factbook*, *Encyclopedia Britannica*, and various Library of Congress Country Studies (Fearon, 2003; CIA, 2000; Grimes, 1996). Compared with the ELF index, Fearon's indexes are significantly more germane to ethnic dynamics and realities in sub-Saharan Africa, where ethnicity is a complex amalgam of attributes that inform identity. That said, both Alesina et al.'s and Fearon's measures of ethnic diversity are singular measures attempting to represent multifarious expressions and manifestations of ethnicity.

Daniel Posner's fractionalization index of politically relevant ethnic groups (PREGs) is designed to be a more appropriate and robust measure of ethnic fragmentation in sub-Saharan Africa. Posner aptly notes, however, that PREG suffers the same shortcomings as ELF, in that it only encompasses ethnic groups that are politically relevant—in other words, ethnic groups vying for control over public policy decisions (Posner, 2004). Public policy formulation occurs at the national level and coincides with national development planning. To the extent that public policy decisions involve access to and distribution of national resources, they incentivize members of different ethnic groups to jockey for political positions in order to participate in public policy decision-making to benefit their respective ethnic constituencies. The PREG index falls short in this sense: Determining ethnic configurations based on differing public policy issues does not accurately depict ethnic diversity in Africa because it narrows the definition of measuring ethnic fragmentation. Yet one of the PREG index's unique features is its time variant: Ethnic groups contending for participation in or control over public policymaking can change over time, depending on the particular public policy matter.

A 2005 article by Tade Okediji titled "The Dynamics of Ethnic Fragmentation" introduces an ethnic fragmentation measure called the social diversity index (SDI).

A composite measure of linguistic, religious, and racial composition among 133 countries, the SDI is the first measure that fully captures multiple ethnic ascriptions in a singular index—which is especially pertinent here given the numerous and overlapping identities in sub-Saharan Africa (Okediji, 2005). The motivation behind this approach is to highlight the heterogeneous nature of ethnic identity, which in turn accentuates the inadequacy of a singular index as a proxy for ethnic fragmentation. The cross-cutting nature of ethnic identity, which the SDI reflects, epitomizes ethnicity in sub-Saharan Africa. The SDI draws its computations from data in the 2001 *World Christian Encyclopedia*, the 1999 CIA *World Factbook*, and the 1972 *World Handbook of Political and Social Indicators* (Okediji, 2005; Barrett, Kurian, & Johnson, 2001; CIA, 1999; Taylor & Hudson, 1972). An advantage of the *World Christian Encyclopedia* over other data sources is that it contains the most detailed compendium of the world's religious groups. Inasmuch as the SDI captures the overlapping nature of ethnic identity/fragmentation, it suffers from a similar shortcoming to the other indexes in that it does not identify the exact expression of ethnic diversity. Rather, it suggests that ethnic diversity has multiple expressions.

African Ethnicity and African Development: An Institutional Perspective

Africa is arguably the most ethnically diverse continent in the world. It is thus unsurprising that cross-national studies reveal a correlation between growth and ethnic fragmentation. African ethnicity involves a dynamic, wide-ranging, and complex interplay of expressions, including language, geography, religion, cultural norms, and traditions. Unlike other regions of the world—like Europe or the United States, where ethnic ascriptions are generally defined and fixed—ethnicity in Africa is multifaceted and involves many overlapping identities (Okediji, 2005; Fearon, 2003). Conceptualizations of ethnicity include primordialist, constructivist, and instrumentalist approaches.

Primordialists believe that ethnic identity is biological, based on blood ties, language, and race, and essentially immutable. Take, for instance, the Yoruba, the largest ethnic group in southwestern Nigeria. Yoruba is an intra-ethnic identity, denoting both a cultural group and a dominant language with varied dialects; it expresses unique cultural and traditional values and practices, serving as a basis for bonding and group identity. The same holds true with the Igbo, southeastern Nigeria's largest ethnic group. Igbo, too, is both a cultural identity and a language with numerous dialects spread across several states (Abia, Anambra, Ebonyi, Enugu, and Imo), geographically divided by the Niger River; before colonial rule, these states were politically fragmented communities that operated as independent republics. The Kikuyu (also called the Gikuyu), the largest ethnic group in Kenya, is yet another example: Kikuyu is both a language and a cultural group—an intra-ethnic identity that simultaneously embodies a language group and an ethnolinguistic identity. These three intra-ethnic groups and many others like them have immutable characteristics that inform their members' identities and sense of uniqueness.

By contrast, the constructivist approach views ethnic identity as a social construction. Constructivists hold that individuals possess multiple ethnic identities and attributes that they can activate depending on particular political or economic contexts or outcomes, and that ethnic identity is fluid and can change endogenously over time (Chandra, 2012).[5] Instrumentalists, meanwhile, consider ethnicity a social or political construct strategically employed for political advantage or capital by appealing to such ethnic sentiments as religion, language, or other cultural traits. According to the instrumentalist frame, elites competing for political dominance or power often employ ethnicity as a tool for mass mobilization for their advantage. It is the instrumentalist approach that best describes the various indirect ways that ethnic identity can influence economic development in sub-Saharan Africa, as the rest of this chapter describes. To that effect, Nigeria and Kenya, both in their experiences with colonialism and their respective post-independence aftereffects, offer cogent examples of ethnicity becoming entwined in a country's politics and the reverberatory effects on economic development.

Nigeria

Nigeria is Africa's most populous nation and its largest economy, and the instrumental use of ethnicity is deeply embedded in its sociopolitical economy. The amalgamation in 1914 of Nigeria's northern and southern protectorates (formally, the Northern Nigeria Protectorate and the Colony and Protectorate of Southern Nigeria), along with subsequent tactics of *divide and rule* that typified British colonial rule, set the stage for the ethnicization of governance—that is, the calculated use of ethnicity as an instrument and a basis for allocating resources, whether infrastructure, land, or political power.[6] These two distinct, independent societies with dramatic political, economic, religious, and social differences became an ostensibly unified Nigeria in 1960, cementing the country's fragile post-independence sociopolitical arrangement and creating a fervent and enduring power struggle between the Muslim north and the Christian south. Since independence, Nigeria's various democratic, military, and autocratic regimes have perpetually jostled for power as the dominant Hausa/Fulani, Igbo, and Yoruba ethnic groups sought control over the country's governance.

Historically, political parties in Nigeria have evolved along strong ethnic and regional lines. At the inception of independence and the first republic (1963–66), the major ethnic groups dominated the three major political parties: The Yoruba in the southwest headed the Action Group, the Hausa/Fulani in the north ran the Northern People's Congress, and the Igbo in the southeast ran the National Council of Nigerian Citizens/National Council of Nigeria and the Cameroons. Again, during the Second Republic (1979–83), the major political parties had a similar orientation: The Yoruba dominated the Unity Party of Nigeria, the Nigerian People's Party had its stronghold in Igbo land, and the National Party of Nigeria and the Great Nigeria People's Party had a strong Hausa/Fulani base and bias in the north. Currently, two dominant political parties typically vie for the presidency: the powerful People's Democratic Party (PDP) and the All Progressives Congress (APC). The APC is a merger of four parties: the Action Congress of Nigeria (ACN), the All Progressives Grand Alliance, the All Nigeria People's Party (ANPP), and the Congress for Progressive Change (CPC). More importantly, the APC is a confederation of anti-PDP politicians seeking to countervail PDP dominance at the polls (Okeke, 2016). Although neither political party exhibits a strong ethnic or regional bias, there was a tacit agreement within the PDP that the presidency would rotate between the Muslim north and the Christian south. The country's religious dichotomy further compounds the North-South political power struggle: Nigeria is the only African nation in which the Muslim share of the population is roughly the same as the Christian.

Ethnopolitical tensions stemming from this contestation for political control continue to pose a challenge to Nigeria's fragile unification. These tensions have mobilized ethnic groups around their grievances, led to electoral violence, and even fostered separatist movements, as later chapters describe in detail. The Nigerian case also illustrates an important yet somewhat overlooked perspective on the variegated nature of ethnicity in sub-Saharan Africa—namely, that the continent's ethnic heterogeneity contributes to a mismatch between concept, context, and measurement criteria. As a phenomenon, ethnicity (and specifically ethnic diversity) does not necessarily hinder economic development. Prior to colonial rule, the stateless African societies coexisted through informal networks and other forms of intra- and inter-ethnic governance systems. Colonialism erased these informal networks by coalescing ethnic groups into states and imposing a foreign system of governance. In Nigeria, a system of *indirect rule*—wherein Indigenous chiefs were co-opted to serve as political intermediaries within the colonial administration—perverted traditional Indigenous power structures. The resulting sociopolitical power structure essentially made traditional rulers into agents of the colonial administration, which was antithetical to Indigenous norms of governance (Siollun, 2021).

In southeastern Nigeria, the consequences of indirect rule were particularly pernicious to the preexisting Indigenous networks. Before colonial rule, these communities operated as politically autonomous societies; colonial administrators deposed some of the traditional rulers and instituted a new power structure in the form of the *warrant chief* system.[7] This newly imposed system of governance had two effects: It inverted the traditional power structure by destroying Indigenous institutions, and it spawned a new class of new ruling elites who had access to financial resources through taxation. This paradigm shift set the stage for a new class of political elites and a system of fractious elite rule that has dominated Nigeria's post-independence sociopolitical economy. The ethnicization of governance and the identity politics that it fostered endure today. It is in this context that ethnic identity is detrimental to development and growth in Nigeria.

Kenya

Since Kenya's inauguration as an independent nation in 1963, ethnicity has been deeply entrenched in national politics. Presidential candidates and successive presidents, starting with Jomo Kenyatta, consolidated their rule through ethnic chauvinism, patronage, and rent-seeking. A case in point is the 2007 presidential election, contested between the incumbent Mwai Kibaki, a Kikuyu representing the National Rainbow Coalition (NARC), and Raila Odinga, a Luo at the time representing the Orange Democratic Movement (ODM). The use of incendiary language during the presidential campaign and the appeal to old ethnic hatreds became the politicians' rallying cry to instigate ethnic othering. To underscore the Kikuyu domination of the government, Odinga's camp called the Kibaki regime the "Mount Kenya mafia," a reference to the inveterate ethnic clientelism that dominated the latter's government, and Odinga vowed to end Kenya's "economic apartheid" if elected (Lynch, 2008; Kagwanja & Southall, 2009). Kibaki, meanwhile, framed his campaign as a contest of "forty-one tribes against one"—in essence, as Kenya against the Kikuyu (Chege, 2008).[8]

The ethnicization of the 2007 election campaign and the use of inflammatory rhetoric exacerbated existing distrust in the election process among Kenyan citizens. After the electoral commission declared Kibaki the winner and Odinga challenged the election results, the ensuing electoral crisis erupted into ethnic violence that killed more than twelve hundred people over a three-month period. The Luo and the Kalenjin targeted the Kikuyu, which in turn prompted Kikuyu retaliation. The violence persisted until Odinga and Kibaki came to a power-sharing arrangement, brokered by former United Nations Secretary-General Kofi Annan. The 2008 National Accord and Reconciliation Act established a coalition government that included the office of the prime minister; Kibaki would remain as president and Odinga would serve as prime minister. This consociational government stemmed the ethnic electoral violence, and it also paved the way for a long-sought constitutional overhaul in 2010 (Berman, Cottrell, & Ghai, 2009). Nevertheless, Kenyan politics remain deeply ethnicized.

Kenya is another example of how British colonial rule (i.e., indirect rule) effectuated ethnopolitical competition that continues to dominate post-independence politics and governance—and of the instrumental use of ethnicity in politics—today. Land reform featured prominently during the negotiations for political independence. Tade Okediji and Wahutu Siguru have shown how the formation of ethnopolitical parties in post-independence Kenya dates back to two key moments in Kenyan history: the displacement of the Kikuyu, the Kalenjin, and the Maasai from their lands in the Central, Rift Valley, and Coast Provinces and the subsequent unequal distribution of land during colonial rule; and the preferential redistribution of the land to Kikuyu elites by Kenya's founding president, Jomo Kenyatta—himself a Kikuyu—at independence. (The Kalenjin and other ethnic groups displaced from their land in the so-called White Highlands during the colonial period had expected that the Kenyatta regime would redistribute, as promised, the confiscated land back to its original owners.) (Okediji & Siguru, 2017).[9]

In the years leading up to Kenya's independence in 1963, two major pseudo-ethnopolitical parties vied for control: the Kenya African National Union (KANU) and the Kenya African Democratic Union (KADU). KANU comprised the two largest ethnic groups, the Kikuyu and the Luo, as well as the Kamba, the Embu, the Meru, and the Gusii. KADU was composed of numerous smaller ethnic groups, including the Giriama, the Kalenjin, the Luhya, and the Maasai, along with resident Asians and Europeans who perceived their interests as better protected under the covering of KADU (Sanger & Nottingham, 1964). Jomo Kenyatta was the leader of KANU (whose predecessor, the Kenya African Union, or KAU, had been formed in 1944 in response to grievances against the British colonial administration). KADU's founders—Daniel arap Moi (a Kalenjin), Ronald Ngala (a Giriama), and Masinde Muliro (a Luhya)—were former members of KANU, but they differed with Kenyatta on political ideology: Whereas Kenyatta favored centralization of government, Ngala, Moi, and Muliro favored decentralization.

Moi, Ngala, and Muliro (and their respective coethnics) were also apprehensive of Kikuyu and Luo domination. As such, when Kenyatta (a Kikuyu), along with Jaramogi Odinga Odinga and Tom Mboya (both Luo), founded KANU in 1960, Moi, Ngala, and Muliro formed KADU, whose slogan during the first presidential campaign in 1963 was a promise that the land in the White Highlands occupied by the colonial state would return to the local population after independence. After losing to KANU, KADU dissolved and merged with KANU in 1964 to form a one-party state under Kenyatta (Throup & Hornsby, 1998; Ahluwalia, 1996; Gibbon, 1995; Harbeson, 2012).[10] Contrary to the conditions of the merger, however, the Kenyatta government redistributed the land in the central region and the Rift Valley only to Kikuyu settlers and not to the other original inhabitants, the Kalenjin and the Maasai (Minorities at Risk Project, 2010; Branch & Cheeseman, 2009). (Moi, for his part, would later become Kenya's longest-serving president, ruling from 1978 to 2002, during which time he more than matched Kenyatta's land settlement, ethnic patronage, and cronyism in the Rift Valley in particular (Boone, 2021).) The resulting ethnoregional land dispute became a permanent theme in Kenyan politics, enrooting ethnicity, power contestation, and resource distribution in contemporary politics (Kanyinga, 2009). In other words, through governance and ethnic elite coalition-building, ethnicity became a public policy tool.

The above discussion illustrates the paradox of ethnicity in sub-Saharan Africa with regard to political and economic development. Although ethnic groups predated colonial rule, their amalgamation into political units by the colonial administrators—and the subsequent dismantling of established Indigenous institutions through the imposed system of governance—created sociopolitical units with ethnic fragmentation, intrinsic internal competition, and the potential for strife built in. Indirect rule was inimical to sustained economic progress as it reinvented ethnic groups as ethnic competitors and intensified ethnic divisions within countries. But the prevailing perception in development literature that ethnic diversity *per se* is deleterious to African economic development skews how we conceptualize diversity's impact on the prospects for long-term economic performance in Africa. A more fitting approach is one that identifies ethnic groups and their various experiences and conceptions to determine the channels through which those experiences and conceptions affect African development and, ultimately, to assess the full nature and extent of their influence on African economic performance.

Political Elites and Ethnic Fragmentation: Do Ethnic Elite Coalitions Supersede Ethnicity?

This section presents an alternative view of the dynamics of ethnicity that is especially relevant to sub-Saharan Africa. In considering the instrumentalist perspective on ethnicity as a sociopolitical construct strategically employed for political or personal gain (or both), one cannot discount the role of political competition among elites for resources, or the frequent tactic of appealing to group characteristics and expressions such as language and dialect, religion, and other cultural traits for the purpose of mass mobilization. In sub-Saharan Africa (as elsewhere), national politics provides an entrée to power and access to state resources for distributive and redistributive purposes, as well as a vehicle for ethnic patronage and wealth accumulation: Whosoever controls the political levers controls the spoils (Nnoli, 1980). Yet political elites do not always intend to serve the interests of their constituents; some seek power for personal gain or aggrandizement.

As the post-independence sociopolitical economies in Nigeria and Kenya exemplify, ethnic elite coalitions are the principal mechanism through which ethnicity is instrumentalized and politicized in sub-Saharan Africa. Those in power habitually use their amassed ethnic patronage for political advantage to mobilize constituents and vie for influence and power among the club of elites. Quite often, they do so in concert with political elites from other ethnic groups in order to expand their base and consolidate their power. The viability of these coalitions derives from the respective political power bases of the individual leaders—that is, individual politicians' ability to coalesce members of a group (be they coethnics or members of other ethnic groups) around a common cause or interest by appealing to ethnic instincts or impulses. It is common to see political alliances and elite ethnic groupings shifting with political tides, a dynamic that stems from the colonial-era legacies of inter-ethnic rivalries and resource contestation. This is where the fluid nature of ethnic elite coalitions in sub-Saharan Africa—and the corollary effects on economic growth and development—comes into play.

Elite capture of the post-colonial state dominates the political landscape in post-independence sub-Saharan Africa, and inter-ethnic competition and political elitism remain an endemic quality of national politics. The formation of political parties and alliances in Nigeria and Kenya offers an example of this phenomenon. In post-independence Nigeria, for example, political parties have historically evolved along ethnoregional lines, but the last two decades have seen a shift in political alliances. Although ethnicity (and indeed coethnicity) continues to feature prominently in national politics, coalitions among elites across ethnicities have become prevalent. Since the onset of the Fourth Republic in Nigeria in 1999, two political parties have dominated the national scene: the PDP and the APC. The PDP was a party of bigwigs and was in power from 1999 to 2015. The APC, on the other hand, is a coalition of three opposition parties: the ACN, the CPC, and the ANPP. The sole intent of the merger that created the APC was to defeat the PDP, which it succeeded in doing in the 2015 presidential election, ending the PDP's sixteen-year dominance of national politics (Okeke, 2016).

The complex interplay of ethnopolitics is perhaps even more evident in Kenya, where political elitism and a deep-rooted ethnicization have dominated at the national level. Chapter 4 provides a more in-depth examination of Kenya's post-independence sociopolitical economy, but an overview of the last two decades offers a glimpse into the interconnectedness of ethnicity, inequality, and development in Kenya's neopatrimonial political system (Berman, Cottrell, & Ghai, 2009; Murunga & Nasong'o, 2006). As founding president, Jomo Kenyatta instituted a single-party state in 1964 that dominated national politics until 1991, when KANU agreed to institute a multiparty system and to introduce term limits. This ostensible political liberalization, however, only proceeded in the context of pressure from international aid donors (and, to a lesser extent, domestic calls for political change) (Harbeson, 2012; Richburg, 1991; Nasong'o, 2007). As Shadrack Wanjala Nasong'o notes, "the Moi regime had been so oppressive that the mere legalization of opposition political parties was received as a major act of political liberalization" (Nasong'o, 2007).[11]

Even so, the shift to multipartyism did usher in a new era of political coalitions among elites, for whom ethnopolitical wheeling and dealing had long since become a permanent fixture. Political parties formed around ethnic constituencies provided a powerful bargaining chip for elites, enabling them to jostle for high-ranking political appointments. For instance, in 2002, Daniel arap Moi (a Kalenjin, though since 1964 a member of the Kikuyu-dominated KANU) successfully enticed Raila Odinga (a Luo and then leader of the National Development Party, or NDP) to merge his party with KANU and assume the role of general secretary of the united party. This merger was short-lived, however: Moi, having agreed to term limits in 1991 and nearing the end of his final term, had reportedly agreed to endorse Odinga as KANU's presidential candidate but instead handpicked Uhuru Kenyatta (a Kikuyu like his father, Jomo). Odinga and his followers thus left KANU to join the Liberal Democratic Party (LDP), which subsequently united with the National Alliance of Kenya (NAK) and the Forum for the Restoration of Democracy (FORD)–Kenya (along with several smaller political parties) to form the NARC. NARC went on to defeat KANU in the 2002 presidential election, when Mwai Kibaki (a Kikuyu) won the presidency. Yet like the KANU merger, NARC too collapsed when Kibaki failed to honor a power-sharing arrangement between his NARC faction (NAK) and Odinga's (LDP)—instead resorting to ethnic patronage and chauvinism (in the form of the aforementioned Mount Kenya mafia cabal of friends and associates) (Murunga & Nasong'o, 2006).[12]

A rift over the proposed distribution of powers between the president and prime minister was ultimately NARC's death knell. Tensions had emerged within the party over the power-sharing arrangement because Kibaki supported an arrangement that ensured a strong presidency and a weak prime minister. In a 2005 referendum presented to the public, his proposal was resoundingly defeated. In response, Kibaki sacked the cabinet ministers who voted against the referendum, which led to NARC's demise and the formation of the ODM (Berman, Cottrell, & Ghai, 2009). The failed constitutional reforms over the issue degenerated precipitously into an ethnicized public rancor between Kikuyu and Luo politicians, with the latter decrying the effort—which weakened the prime minister's powers while bolstering the president's—as Kikuyu hegemony. Although the referendum failed in a national vote (a major defeat for Kibaki's government), the campaign process effectively destroyed the coalition. Odinga's LDP faction, along with several KANU members of parliament and Uhuru Kenyatta, formed the ODM, while Kibaki formed the Party of National Unity (PNU). The irony of Odinga forming an alliance with Uhuru Kenyatta is noteworthy, both having been members of KANU during the Moi era, and Odinga having split from the party because Moi handpicked Kenyatta as his successor.

This latest split set the stage, in 2007, for one of the most contentious presidential contests in post-independence Kenya. The campaigns were fraught with visceral ethnic hatreds hurled between the opposing camps, with each side accusing the other of voter fraud, intimidation, and rigging. In the election, Kibaki and the PNU dominated among the Kikuyu, Embu, and Meru of the Central Province and among the Kamba in the Eastern Province, while Odinga and the ODM secured major victories among the Luhya in the Western Province and the Kalenjin in the Rift Valley region and among other smaller ethnic communities (Berman, Cottrell, & Ghai, 2009). Both sides declared victory, but as the incumbent, Kibaki had the power of the presidency behind him. When the electoral commission declared Kibaki the winner, Odinga disputed the election results, plunging the country into a violent ethnoregional crisis that killed more than twelve hundred people. The eventual power-sharing agreement that ended the crisis and established the Kibaki-Odinga coalition government was yet another example of political wheeling and dealing among elites.

The 2013 presidential campaign saw another round of political jockeying by elites. It was the first election since the ratification of the new constitution in 2010, the outcome of a national referendum following the 2007 post-election violence (Kramon & Posner, 2011).[13] Constitutional limits prevented Kibaki from running for reelection. Odinga once again sought the presidency, running under the umbrella of the newly formed Coalition for Reforms and Democracy, which included the ODM along with several other parties. The other candidate was Uhuru Kenyatta, who ran under the banner of the Jubilee Alliance. Kenyatta chose William Ruto (a Kalenjin) as his running mate. Dubbed the "Uhuruto" ticket, theirs was a union of unlikely allies given the Kalenjins' long-standing grievance against the Kikuyu, dating back to the Jomo Kenyatta era, over their native lands. Historically, in multiparty elections, the Kalenjin had almost always voted against the Kikuyu candidate in national elections—instead supporting KADU (in 1963), KANU (in 1992, 1997, and 2002), and the ODM (in 2007); this swing in 2013 illustrates the shifting alliances and the fluid nature of coalitions (Lynch, 2014).[14] Ruto himself had supported Odinga in his 2007 presidential bid under the ODM banner (Lynch, 2014).[15] Indeed, Kenyatta's choice of Ruto as a running mate was shrewdly strategic—and successful: Kenyatta defeated Odinga to win the presidency. The "Uhuruto" union created an inter-ethnic coalition that successfully galvanized the Kalenjin in the Rift Valley region to support the Jubilee Alliance, again demonstrating the fluidity—and efficacy—of elite coalitions in the pursuit of political power and economic resources.

In 2017, Uhuru Kenyatta and Raila Odinga faced off again for the presidency, Kenyatta on the new Jubilee Party's ticket and Odinga on the ODM's. When the Independent Electoral and Boundaries Commission (IEBC) declared Kenyatta the victor, Odinga refused to concede and contested the results on the grounds of electoral fraud. He took his case all the way to the Supreme Court and prevailed: The court annulled the presidential election and ordered a subsequent election within sixty days. Kenyatta won the runoff, although Odinga withdrew from the race prior to election day, refusing to participate without "adequate reforms" on the part of the IEBC to ensure a free and fair election (BBC, 2017). In the end, to ease the political tensions and ethnic rancor that surrounded the election and runoff, Kenyatta and Odinga called a political truce, famously shaking hands in March 2018. It was a gesture, after months of political brinksmanship and angry demonstrations, to restore the legitimacy of the presidency and a sense of political order (Cheeseman et al., 2019). Some also saw the reconciliatory handshake as a tacit understanding of a later transfer of power, though it was William Ruto, not Raila Odinga, who won the 2022 presidential election. Regardless of the handshake's intent—or the ultimate outcome of any agreement it was meant to signify—it was a conspicuous display of suprapartisan politicking between two powerful, often opposing political elites from dominant rival ethnic groups, further illustrating how deeply embedded ethnicity and informal institutions are in contemporary Kenyan political life.

The preceding discussion elucidates how informal networks are an essential feature of formal institutions of governance—and in particular how the quest for political power and access to state resources (whether for personal aggrandizement, accumulation of wealth, ethnic patronage, or possibly even bona fide public service) drives ethnic elite coalitions and strategic political alliances. The viability of these inter-ethnic coalitions derives from their political power base, which in turn emanates from an appeal to ethnic and other cultural expressions and characteristics that coalesce ethnic groups around a common purpose or ideology. In this way, elite inter-ethnic coalitions are an expression of the instrumentalist approach to ethnicity and the manner in which ethnic identity can affect economic and political outcomes.

Conclusion

Ethnic identity continues to play a salient role in socioeconomic and political development in sub-Saharan Africa, and the effects of that role have proved detrimental to African development and growth. Although African societies are primarily informal economies, the entrenchment of cultural attributes such as ethnic identity impacts formal institutions and outcomes. The now-famous post-election handshake between Uhuru Kenyatta and Raila Odinga in 2017—and the near-instantaneous easing of the electoral crisis that precipitated it—is a case in point (Cheeseman et al., 2019).[16]

As this chapter has outlined, ethnic identity is multidimensional in sub-Saharan Africa. The instrumentalist perspective on ethnicity describes the various indirect ways that ethnic identity can influence economic development via political development. The origins of this link date back to European contact with Indigenous Africans and subsequent colonization. Before the colonial period, Indigenous rule was a bottom-up system of governance. British indirect rule co-opted and formalized the existing Indigenous governance structures by appointing local chiefs as proxy leaders, creating a layered system of political elitism and channeling preferred ethnicities into governance roles. In effect, this exploitative system destroyed the Indigenous institutions that served as the bedrock of African societies, providing social cohesion and trust in governance.

To the extent that colonialism had an ethnoregional dimension, it further intensified inter-ethnic divisions and rivalries, setting sub-Saharan Africa on an uneven development path that has persisted since independence. Colonial rule also enmeshed ethnicity in political and economic development in Africa by altering resource allocation—including land ownership and access to formal education—among ethnic groups. The imposed pyramidal system of indirect rule instilled ethnic consciousness and elitism in African politics and governance, breeding structural inequalities that linger today.

In the most basic sense, politics is what people do to achieve and hold onto power; governance is what they do with that power once realized. That ethnic consciousness and elitism became embedded in African national politics and governance is self-evident, as the experiences of Nigeria and Kenya recounted above amply demonstrate. Across sub-Saharan Africa, rather than attempting to reform the deleterious colonial structures that bifurcated Indigenous rule and impoverished societies, leaders of the post-colonial African states often sought ways to reinforce this pernicious system by issuing authoritarian decrees and establishing institutions that amounted to the same divide-and-rule strategy that they vehemently opposed during the struggle for independence. Ethnicity became a potent and exploitative instrument for political mobilization in the democratic experiment, and ethnic mobilization became a mechanism for contestation in a subverted, winner-takes-all system of democracy. In Nigeria, for example, the initial post-independence democratic experiment was short-lived due to deeply entrenched ethnoregional resentments that date back to the amalgamation of the northern and southern protectorates. These divisions are readily apparent in the formation of Nigerian political parties (Agbu, 2016).

Inasmuch as the impetus for political competition is access to and control over the distribution of state economic resources, the examples of Nigeria and Kenya illuminate the ways in which ethnicity is employed as an instrument for mobilization in political systems. As Abner Cohen expounded in 1974, ethnicity can be viewed as a political mechanism for competing interest groups (Cohen, 1974). In post-independence sub-Saharan Africa, control over and access to political power have become means to redress the ethnic and ethnoregional inequalities that colonialism created. As the Nigerian and Kenyan cases illustrate, the resulting ethnic chauvinism and patronage are rampant in national governance on the subcontinent, as are the dire repercussions in the economic development sphere that continue to reverberate today.

Notes

1 Along with Marx, the notable proponents of the classical school included Adam Smith, Robert Malthus, Jean-Baptiste Say, and John Stuart Mill. See Robert Dorfman, "Review Article: Economic Development from the Beginning to Rostow," *Journal of Economic Literature* 29, no. 2 (June 1991): 578.

2 Horman Chitonge, *Economic Growth and Development in Africa: Understanding Trends and Prospects* (London, UK: Routledge, 2016), 115.

3 Soviet social scientists developed the concept of ethnolinguistic fractionalization in 1964 in an attempt to measure the ethnolinguistic diversity of the world's population (Bruk et al., 1964).

4 The ELF index, developed by Charles Taylor and Michael Hudson, is loosely defined as the probability that two randomly selected individuals in a country will belong to the same ethnolinguistic group. The ELF index is computed as follows:

$$\text{ELF} = 1 - \sum_{i=1}^{I} \left(\frac{n_i}{N} \right)^2, 1, \ldots I$$

where n_i represents the number of people in the ith group, N is the total population, and I is the number of ethnolinguistic groups in a country. Higher ELF values correspond to greater levels of diversity. The index takes on a value between zero and one, where zero indicates high ethnic homogeneity and one indicates high ethnic heterogeneity (Taylor & Hudson, 1972; see also Bruk et al., 1964).

5 Kanchan Chandra, ed. *Constructivist Theories of Ethnic Politics* (New York, NY: Oxford University Press, 2012), 5.

6 *Divide and rule* refers to the ubiquitous colonial strategy of adopting policies that intentionally weakened Indigenous power structures and institutions, such that native populations would be less able to mount effective opposition to colonial authority (Cambridge Advanced Learner's Dictionary and Thesaurus, 2024).

7 The *warrant chief* system instituted during British colonial rule facilitated indirect rule by appointing Indigenous Africans thought to be influential or presumed to have leadership qualities as local chiefs on an ad hoc basis. These individuals were issued warrants giving them certain authorities, including oversight over tax collection as well as judicial powers, over the local population (Siollun, 2021).

8 Michael Chege, "Kenya: Back from the Brink?," *Journal of Democracy* 19, no. 4 (October 2008): 133; Peter Kagwanja and Roger Southall, "Kenya—A Democracy in Retreat?," *Journal of Contemporary African Studies* 27, no. 3 (2009): 265.

9 The importance of land displacement in Kenya's history cannot be overstated. Chapter 4 explores the history and politics of land in Kenya, which center around the area in the central, coast, and Rift Valley regions dubbed the White Highlands (named for the British policy giving European settlers exclusive rights to prime agricultural land previously inhabited by members of the Kikuyu, Kalenjin, and Maasai ethnic groups) (Morgan, 1963).

10 David Throup and Charles Hornsby, *Multi-Party Politics in Kenya: The Kenyatta and Moi States and the Triumph of the System in the 1992 Election* (Oxford, UK: James Currey, 1998), 12; Davinder Pal Ahluwalia, *Post-Colonialism and the Politics of Kenya* (New York, NY: Nova Science, 1996), 35; Peter Gibbon, ed., *Markets, Civil Society and Democracy in Kenya* (Uppsala, Sweden: Nordiska Afrikainstitutet, 1995), 15; John W. Harbeson, "Land and the Quest for a Democratic State in Kenya: Bringing Citizens Back In," *African Studies Review* 55, no. 1 (April 2012): 23.

11 Shadrack Wanjala Nasong'o, "Political Transition Without Transformation: The Dialectic of Liberalization Without Democratization in Kenya and Zambia," *African Studies Review* 50, no. 1 (April 2007): 96.

12 Godwin R. Murunga and Shadrack Wanjala Nasong'o, "Bent on Self-Destruction: The Kibaki Regime in Kenya," *Journal of Contemporary African Studies* 24, no. 1 (2006): 9–10.

13 The 2010 constitutional referendum, in which Kenyans overwhelmingly voted to adopt a new constitution, sought to decentralize government and devolve power from the presidency. The new constitution created Kenya's current forty-seven counties out of the original eight provinces, each with its own independent government. It also established the Independent Electoral and Boundaries Commission "to conduct transparent, efficient, and impartial elections" and to "undertake boundary delimitation for equitable representation and sustainable democracy" (Independent Electoral and Boundaries Commission, 2023).

14 Gabrielle Lynch, "Electing the 'Alliance of the Accused': The Success of the Jubilee Alliance in Kenya's Rift Valley," *Journal of Eastern African Studies* 8, no. 1 (2014): 95.
15 Lynch, "Electing the 'Alliance of the Accused'," 96.
16 Nic Cheeseman et al., "Kenya's 2017 Elections: Winner-Takes-All Politics as Usual?," *Journal of Eastern African Studies* 13, no. 2 (2019): 217.

Bibliography

Agbu, Osita. "An Overview of Party Formation in Nigeria, 1960–1999." In *Elections and Governance in Nigeria's Fourth Republic*, edited by Osita Agbu, 27–36. Dakar, Senegal: CODESRIA Books, 2016.

Ahluwalia, Davinder Pal. *Post-Colonialism and the Politics of Kenya*. New York, NY: Nova Science, 1996.

Alesina, Alberto, et al. "Fractionalization." *Journal of Economic Growth* 8, no. 2 (June 2003): 155–94, https://doi.org/10.1023/A:1024471506938.

Annett, Anthony. "Social Fractionalization, Political Instability, and the Size of Government." *IMF Staff Papers* 48, no. 3 (2001): 561–92. Previous version published as Annett, Anthony. "Social Fractionalization, Political Instability, and the Size of Government." IMF Working Paper No. WP/00/82. Washington, DC: International Monetary Fund, April 2000, https://www.imf.org/external/pubs/ft/wp/2000/wp0082.pdf.

Arcand, Jean-Louis, Patrick Guillaumont, and Sylviane Guillaumont Jeanneney. "How to Make a Tragedy: On the Alleged Effect of Ethnicity on Growth." *Journal of International Development* 12, no. 7 (October 2000): 925–38, https://doi.org/10.1002/1099-1328(200010)12:7%3C925::AID-JID667%3E3.0.CO;2–Y.

Barrett, David B., George T. Kurian, and Todd M. Johnson, eds. *World Christian Encyclopedia*. New York, NY: Oxford University Press, 2001.

Barro, Robert J. "Determinants of Democracy." *Journal of Political Economy* 107, no. S6 (December 1999): S158–83.

Berman, Bruce J., Jill Cottrell, and Yash Ghai. "Patrons, Clients, and Constitutions: Ethnic Politics and Political Reform in Kenya." *Canadian Journal of African Studies* 43, no. 3 (2009): 462–506, https://doi.org/10.1080/00083968.2010.9707567.

Block, Steven A. "Does Africa Grow Differently?" *Journal of Development Economics* 65, no. 2 (August 2001): 443–67.

Boone, Catherine, Fibian Lukalo, and Sandra F. Joireman. "Promised Land: Settlement Schemes in Kenya, 1962 to 2016." *Political Geography* 89 (August 2021): 102393, https://doi.org/10.1016/j.polgeo.2021.102393.

Branch, Daniel, and Nic Cheeseman. "Democratization, Sequencing, and State Failure in Africa: Lessons from Kenya." *African Affairs* 108, no. 430 (January 2009): 1–26, https://doi.org/10.1093/afraf/adn065.

British Broadcasting Corporation (BBC). "Kenya's Raila Odinga Quits Election Re-Run." *BBC News*, October 10, 2017, https://www.bbc.com/news/world-africa-41572128.

Bruk, Solomon Il'ich, et al. *Atlas narodov mira*. Moscow, USSR: Akademija Nauk SSSR, 1964.

Cambridge Advanced Learner's Dictionary and Thesaurus, s.v. "Divide and Rule," accessed May 13, 2024, https://dictionary.cambridge.org/us/dictionary/english/divide-and-rule.

Central Intelligence Agency (CIA). *The World Factbook*. Washington, DC: U.S. Government Printing Office, 1999, https://www.cia.gov/the-world-factbook/about/archives.

CIA. *The World Factbook*. Washington, DC: U.S. Government Printing Office, 2000, https://www.cia.gov/the-world-factbook/about/archives.

Chandra, Kanchan, ed. *Constructivist Theories of Ethnic Politics*. New York, NY: Oxford University Press, 2012.

Cheeseman, Nic, et al. "Kenya's 2017 Elections: Winner-Takes-All Politics as Usual?" *Journal of Eastern African Studies* 13, no. 2 (2019): 215–34, https://doi.org/10.1080/17531055.2019.1594072.

Chege, Michael. "Kenya: Back from the Brink?" *Journal of Democracy* 19, no. 4 (October 2008): 125–39, https://doi.org/10.1353/jod.0.0026.

Chitonge, Horman. *Economic Growth and Development in Africa: Understanding Trends and Prospects*. London, UK: Routledge, 2016.

Cohen, Abner, ed. *Urban Ethnicity*. London, UK: Routledge, 1974.

Collier, Paul, and Jan Willem Gunning. "Why Has Africa Grown Slowly?" *Journal of Economic Perspectives* 13, no. 3 (Summer 1999): 3–22, https://doi.org/10.1257/jep.13.3.3.

Dorfman, Robert. "Review Article: Economic Development from the Beginning to Rostow." *Journal of Economic Literature* 29, no. 2 (June 1991): 573–91, https://www.jstor.org/stable/2727524.

Easterly, William, and Ross Levine. "Africa's Growth Tragedy: Policies and Ethnic Divisions." *The Quarterly Journal of Economics* 112, no. 4 (November 1997): 1203–50, https://doi.org/10.1162/003355300555466.

Fearon, James D. "Ethnic and Cultural Diversity by Country." *Journal of Economic Growth* 8, no. 2 (June 2003): 195–222, https://doi.org/10.1023/A:1024419522867.

Gibbon, Peter, ed. *Markets, Civil Society and Democracy in Kenya*. Uppsala, Sweden: Nordiska Afrikainstitutet, 1995.

Grimes, Barbara F. *Ethnologue: Languages of the World*. Vol. 13. Dallas, TX: Summer Institute of Linguistics, 1996.

Gurr, Ted Robert. *Minorities at Risk: A Global View of Ethnopolitical Conflicts*. Washington, DC: United States Institute of Peace, 1993.

Harbeson, John W. "Land and the Quest for a Democratic State in Kenya: Bringing Citizens Back In." *African Studies Review* 55, no. 1 (April 2012): 15–30, https://doi.org/10.1353/arw.2012.0025.

Hermann, Arturo. "The Decline of the 'Original Institutional Economics' in the Post-World War II Period and The Perspectives of Today." *Economic Thought* 7, no. 1 (2018): 63–68.

Independent Electoral and Boundaries Commission, "Our Mission," accessed August 25, 2023, https://www.iebc.or.ke/iebc/?vission.

Kagwanja, Peter, and Roger Southall. "Kenya—A Democracy in Retreat?" *Journal of Contemporary African Studies* 27, no. 3 (2009): 259–77, https://doi.org/10.1080/02589000903216930.

Kanyinga, Karuti. "The Legacy of the White Highlands: Land Rights, Ethnicity, and Post-2007 Election Violence in Kenya." *Journal of Contemporary African Studies* 27, no. 3 (2009): 325–44, https://doi.org/10.1080/02589000903154834.

Kramon, Eric, and Daniel N. Posner. "Kenya's New Constitution." *Journal of Democracy* 22, no. 2 (April 2011): 89–103, https://doi.org/10.1353/jod.2011.0026.

La Porta, Rafael, Florencio López-de-Silanes, Andrei Shleifer, and Robert W. Vishny. "The Quality of Government." *The Journal of Law, Economics, and Organization* 15, no. 1 (March 1999): 222–79, https://doi.org/10.1093/jleo/15.1.222.

Levinson, David. *Ethnic Groups Worldwide: A Ready Reference Handbook*. Phoenix, AZ: Oryx Press, 1998.

Lynch, Gabrielle. "Courting the Kalenjin: The Failure of Dynasticism and the Strength of the ODM Wave in Kenya's Rift Valley Province." *African Affairs* 107, no. 429 (October 2008): 541–68, https://doi.org/10.1093/afraf/adn060.

Lynch, Gabrielle. "Electing the 'Alliance of the Accused': The Success of the Jubilee Alliance in Kenya's Rift Valley." *Journal of Eastern African Studies* 8, no. 1 (2014): 93–114, https://doi.org/10.1080/17531055.2013.844438.

Marx, Karl. *Capital. Vols.* I - III. Moscow: Foreign Languages Publishing House, 1954.

Marx, Karl. *Capital: A Critique of Political Economy*. Vols. 1–3. Moscow, USSR: Foreign Languages Publishing House, 1957–62. First published 1867–94.

Mauro, Paolo. "Corruption and Growth." *The Quarterly Journal of Economics* 110, no. 3 (August 1995): 681–712, https://doi.org/10.2307/2946696.

Minorities at Risk Project, "Chronology for Kikuyu in Kenya," last updated July 16, 2010, https://www.mar.umd.edu/chronology.asp?groupId=50103.

Minority Rights Group International. *World Directory of Minorities*. London, UK: Minority Rights Group International, 1997, https://minorityrights.org/app/uploads/2023/12/1997-directory.pdf.

Montalvo, José G., and Marta Reynal-Querol. "Ethnic Polarization, Potential Conflict, and Civil Wars." *American Economic Review* 95, no. 3 (June 2005): 796–816, https://doi.org/10.1257/0002828054201468.

Morgan, William Thomas Wilson. "The 'White Highlands' of Kenya." *The Geographical Journal* 129, no. 2 (June 1963): 140–55, https://doi.org/10.2307/1792632.

Morrison, Donald George, Robert Cameron Mitchell, and John Naber Paden. *Black Africa: A Comparative Handbook*. New York, NY: Free Press, 1972.

Murunga, Godwin R., and Shadrack Wanjala Nasong'o. "Bent on Self-Destruction: The Kibaki Regime in Kenya." *Journal of Contemporary African Studies* 24, no. 1 (2006): 1–28, https://doi.org/10.1080/02589000500513713.

Myrdal, Gunnar. *Asian Drama: An Inquiry into the Poverty of Nations*. Vols. 1–3. New York, NY: Pantheon, 1968.

Nasong'o, Shadrack Wanjala. "Political Transition Without Transformation: The Dialectic of Liberalization Without Democratization in Kenya and Zambia." *African Studies Review* 50, no. 1 (April 2007): 83–107, https://doi.org/10.1353/arw.2005.0126.

Nnoli, Okwudiba. *Ethnic Politics in Nigeria*. Enugu, Nigeria: Fourth Dimension, 1980.

North, Douglass C. "Economic Performance Through Time." *American Economic Review* 84, no. 3 (June 1994): 359–68, https://www.jstor.org/stable/2118057.

Okediji, Tade O. "The Dynamics of Ethnic Fragmentation: A Proposal for an Expanded Measurement Index." *The American Journal of Economics and Sociology* 64, no. 2 (April 2005): 637–62, https://doi.org/10.1111/j.1536-7150.2005.00382.x.

Okediji, Tade O., and Wahutu J. Siguru. "The Role of Ethnicity in Political Formation in Kenya: 1963–2007." In *Dissent, Protest and Dispute in Africa*, edited by Toyin Falola and Emmanuel M. Mbah, 133–51. New York, NY: Routledge, 2017.

Okeke, Remi Chukwudi. "Dominant Political Parties, Struggling for Survival in Nigeria: The Narrative of Decapitated Sleaze and Crusade of Anti-Corruption Legacy." *International Letters of Social and Humanistic Sciences* 67 (2016): 78–84, https://d-nb.info/1190996286/34.

Posner, Daniel N. "Measuring Ethnic Fractionalization in Africa." *American Journal of Political Science* 48, no. 4 (October 2004): 849–63, https://doi.org/10.1111/j.0092-5853.2004.00105.x.

Richburg, Keith B. "Kenyan Leader Opts for Multi-Party Rule." *The Washington Post*, December 2, 1991, https://www.washingtonpost.com/archive/politics/1991/12/03/kenyan-leader-opts-for-multi-party-rule/4e0fb998-a0d7-434c-bc75-efa43c626c0c.

Sachs, Jeffrey D., and Andrew M. Warner. "Sources of Slow Growth in African Economies." *Journal of African Economies* 6, no. 3 (October 1997): 335–76, https://doi.org/10.1093/oxfordjournals.jae.a020932.

Sanger, Clyde, and John Nottingham. "The Kenya General Election of 1963." *The Journal of Modern African Studies* 2, no. 1 (March 1964): 1–40, https://doi.org/10.1017/S0022278X00003645.

Scarritt, James R., and Shaheen Mozaffar. "The Specification of Ethnic Cleavages and Ethnopolitical Groups for the Analysis of Democratic Competition in Contemporary Africa." *Nationalism and Ethnic Politics* 5, no. 1 (1999): 82–117, https://doi.org/10.1080/13537119908428555.

Siollun, Max. *What Britain Did to Nigeria: A Short History of Conquest and Rule*. London, UK: Hurst, 2021.

Taylor, Charles Lewis, and Michael C. Hudson. *World Handbook of Political and Social Indicators*. New Haven, CT: Yale University Press, 1972.

Throup, David, and Charles Hornsby. *Multi-Party Politics in Kenya: The Kenyatta and Moi States and the Triumph of the System in the 1992 Election*. Oxford, UK: James Currey, 1998.

Veblen, Thorstein. *The Theory of Leisure and Class: An Economic Study of Institutions*. New York, NY: Macmillan, 1912.

2

ELITISM, ETHNICITY, AND DEVELOPMENT IN NIGERIA

Akinpelu O. Olutayo, Ayokunle O. Omobowale, Olayinka Akanle, and Dauda A. Busari

Introduction

Historians have long observed that modern-day Nigeria is a result of "paper protectorates" fastened together by colonial fiat (Alubo, 2004). The local chieftains who signed those papers, which amalgamated the future country's various ethnic groups into two colonial protectorates (northern and southern) and later into the Colony and Protectorate of Nigeria, did so under duress and often threat of force. Such was the "scramble for Africa" by the European powers, the sole purpose of which was to secure access to the raw materials needed for the colonialist enterprise (Frankema, Williamson, & Woltjer, 2018). The colonialist powers that be undertook every effort to ensure the unfettered flow of trade between the colonies and the colonial headquarters back home. One such effort to that effect was to inaugurate a class of new elites to represent the Crown's interests in the colonized territories. This manufactured identity was a complicated one, requiring a foreign outlook and orientation; it can best be understood in terms of the dichotomy between the "primitive" and the "modern" man: The latter were those who craved the colonialists' way of life, while the former were the local indigenes wedded to their traditional governance structures, customs, and beliefs (Markus, 1994; Berman, 1998; Ayandele, 1974). Those who sought to emulate and embrace the colonialists' ways eventually emerged as the new elites.

Indeed, the entire colonial venture can be explained using the logic of binary opposites—modernity versus tradition—not just at the theoretical level but empirically and practically as well. It is therefore not surprising that what we call the glued paper protectorate model continues to experience tethering challenges. It would be difficult to classify the colonial experiment as capitalist without a nod to Marxist thought, but suffice it to say, in British colonial Africa at least,

DOI: 10.4324/9781003357025-3

what was termed *modern* was ineluctably *capitalist*, oriented with individualistic entrepreneurial values.

In colonial Nigeria, such values were instilled and reinforced through the educational institutions established in the colonized territories in what was termed "modernization by design" (Morse et al., 1969). Entry into such institutions required members of the various Indigenous ethnic groups to support their coethnics with the hope that those who succeeded would turn around and help their communities by securing access to the benefits of development and progress (the proverbial "good things in life") through patronage—namely, by helping their compatriots gain preferential access to schools and positions in government or business (Ekeh, 1983; Omobowale & Olutayo, 2010). Indigenous knowledge came to be perceived as inferior to colonialist education. In this vein, scholarships were awarded to teach European ideas and customs to students in order to supplant the local ways of life, which were considered substandard (Olutayo, 2009a, 2009b, 2010; Omobowale & Olutayo, 2009). In colonial Nigeria, this educational model set the stage for a new brand of elitism that centered on modernity as the precondition for economic development and growth and was built around colonialist constructions of ethnicity that stood in stark contrast to the realities that predated British rule. This chapter explores the interplay of elitism, ethnicity, and development in Nigeria wrought by these colonial-era paradigm shifts.

The rally around ethnic sentiment during Nigeria's push for independence was fallout from the *indirect rule* system imposed by the British, wherein colonial authorities employed Indigenous authorities (or chiefs) as political intermediaries, essentially turning traditional rulers into agents of the colonial administration (Omobowale & Olutayo, 2010; Siollun, 2021). The perpetuation of ethnicity as the overarching principle and identity category at independence was a direct result of this framework. The educated local elites, many of whom had become successful in business ventures, became leaders whose authority derived from the colonial structure, and whose governance modeled it. These leaders—the political elites who rose to prominence under indirect rule—hailed principally from the emerging country's three major ethnic groups: the Hausa-Fulani, the Yoruba, and Igbo.[1] In fomenting Nigeria's independence movement, they whipped up sentiments around ethnic identities both in political party formulations and in the general governance ideology.

This ethnicization concretized regional governments as the basis for development activities, with the regions being somewhat autonomous from federal authority. For example, in the western region, the Yoruba-dominated Action Group (AG), under the leadership of Obafemi Awolowo, implemented progressive policies such as free universal primary education and free health care for children (Jackson, 1972). However, ethnicization also aligned ethnic groups against one another. Even within each ethnic identity, stratified configurations began to appear as people from different subethnic groups achieved success in business and educational attainment (Ugbem, Omobowale, & Olutayo, 2014, 2019; Ugbem, 2014; Igwe & Omobowale,

2018). These individuals began to vie for supremacy among themselves, employing ethnic identity in much the same way as the colonialists had in instrumentalizing ethnic identification. Alignments and loyalties were malleable, orienting and reorienting around fluid notions of identity defined by particular desired objectives (Osaghae, 1991). In this landscape, ethnic identity came to determine the course of governance and development in Nigeria.

As described above, a colonialist worldview underpinned the nascent political elites' concept of development. Central to this orientation was a bent toward economistic reductionism that framed development in quantitative terms, derived from the need to make raw materials from the colonized territories available to industries in the colonizing nations (especially during the world wars). Trade, as such, was assiduously encouraged. Couched under the law of comparative advantage, the colonized territories were to exchange raw materials for finished goods, the prices of both being determined by the colonizers. To advance this trade juggernaut, transport infrastructures were created to move goods from the hinterland to the ports. Colonial agents, foreign missionaries, and multinational corporations helped to ensure that nothing hindered the flow of trade abroad. Where these people settled became the urban areas, with amenities like pipe-borne water, electricity, educational institutions, and so on provided to make life comfortable for the foreigners (and, by extension, to the burgeoning local corps d'elite). Ambitious and motivated Indigenous new elites set out to emulate the colonialists as they prepared to take over from them.

The elites representing different ethnic groups after independence, their power devolved from the colonialist apparatus, did not depart from this development orientation: They envisioned economic prosperity's benefits trickling down preferentially to those they chose to assist by way of education and positions in government and industry. This chapter investigates the role of elites and the politics of identity and ethnicity through this prism to explain Nigeria's persistent inequality, pervasive poverty, and lackluster development. It first delves into the colonial roots of ethnic construction in Nigeria to illuminate how those identities carried over into the post-independence era, reflecting elitist political arrangements and ethnic identity politics that defined the country's social, economic, and governance structures at independence and continue to dominate them today. Bearing in mind the development perspective that underlies those colonial-era sentiments, we posit that what elites term *development* today in fact connotes *under*development, and that the post-independence class of elites—having thus enrooted itself by way of the colonial juggernaut—is more concerned with maintaining its dominance in society than with bestowing "the good things in life" upon the masses.

This chapter then examines how elites manipulate post-colonial ethnic identity constructs to negotiate and realign allegiances and contest for power and access. Such identity constructions and alignments are intricately tied to governance and politics and are rarely if ever inclusive; all too often, they lead to unequal access, disproportionate representation, poverty, and social strife. Ultimately, this chapter concludes that the ethnic, political, and socioeconomic stratification wrought by colonialist configurations of identity—and the inequality, poverty, and social unrest that these conditions bred—have created a development emergency in Nigeria. Until these intersectionalities are fully understood and systemic policy approaches are adopted to mitigate their deleterious effects, sustained economic development and growth in Nigeria will remain out of reach.

Colonialism and Post-Colonial Ethnic Identities in Nigeria

Nigeria's colonial administration saddled the country with deep-seated identity politics and lasting inter-ethnic rivalries, and the ambitions of the Nigerian political elites have allowed the problem to fester (Albeely, Mahmoud, & Yahaya, 2018; Abdulwaheed, Adebiyi, & Bakare, 2018). Yahaya Yakubu has argued that after sixty-plus years of independence and more than two decades of uninterrupted (if tenuous) democracy, ethnic roots still hold stronger allegiance for Nigerian citizens than national loyalty (Yakubu, 2017). The 1914 amalgamation of the northern and southern protectorates laid the groundwork for the ethnic schism that has plagued the country since independence. Lord Frederick Lugard, the governor of both the Northern Nigeria Protectorate and the Colony and Protectorate of Southern Nigeria, sought to administer the territory as a single whole for practical reasons: Uniting the ethnically distinct, hitherto independent nations reconstituted as "tribes" by the colonialists under one banner was an administrative strategy whose motive was largely economic. As a result, Nigeria's budding educated and economic elites forged a lasting understanding of the inchoate state along ethnic lines at this early stage (Omobowale, 2018).

Sir Arthur Richards, the British governor general of Nigeria from 1943 to 1948, remarked that ethnic antagonism heightened after the merger of the northern and southern protectorates, describing the amalgamation as an "accident of British suzerainty." Contemporary Nigeria was "still far from being one country or one nation socially or even economically . . .. Socially and politically there are deep differences between the major tribal groups." Richards also problematized the reality that Nigeria's multifarious ethnic groups spoke different languages and had "highly divergent customs and ways of life." Perhaps somewhat ironically, it was his establishment of Nigeria's three regions in 1946–47, detailed in the next section, that solidified the foundation for the regionalism and ethnicization in Nigerian politics that persists today (Ojukwu, 2009).[2]

Foundations of Nigeria's Ethnic Identity Politics

The coalescence of African peoples, kingdoms, and nations into ethnoregional groupings is one of the major outcomes of colonialism. In Nigeria, the British regarded the indigenes as "primitive" and "tribal," "heathens" whose civilization and development were circumscribed by weak governance and social structures, inferior technical and intellectual knowledge, and debauchery (all terms ascribed by colonial anthropologists) (Omobowale, 2015; Derricourt, 2011). Such constructions overtly rationalized colonization to obscure the true intent: the exploitation of resources for the benefit of the homeland. The colonization project fused Nigeria into a pair of protectorates and later a single colony consisting of the major ethnic groups—the Hausa-Fulani in the north, the Yoruba in the west, and the Igbo in the east—and numerous minority tribes (Omobowale, 2018; Bourne, 2015). The colonialists viewed the Fulani as the most sophisticated, describing them as "Mohammedans" with a structured political system headed by a sultan. The Hausa, whose Habe kingship system the Fulani had overthrown, were their subjects, and that conglomeration informed the integration of the two ethnicities into the Hausa-Fulani. The Yoruba had a semi-structured *oba* (kingship) political system, while the Igbo were purported to be fluidly republican, guided by a council of community elders. The colonialists characterized the other groups as largely unorganized and animists (Ugbem, Omobowale, & Olutayo, 2019; Bourne, 2015). These classifications were the genesis from which Nigerian ethnic identity politics arose; the contention for space, power, and supremacy among the three fueled both ethnoreligious conflicts and political alliances, usually between the northern Hausa-Fulani and either the Yoruba or the Igbo to the south (Omobowale, 2018).

The 1950s, the preparatory eve for Nigeria's independence, saw the incipient nation's minority ethnic groups largely subsumed into that trifecta of rival major ethnicities. These inter-regional and inter-ethnic political power dynamics persisted well beyond the colonial period—many of them enduring into the present day. Nigeria's emergent political leaders were acutely aware of these divisions. As Obafemi Awolowo, the prominent nationalist politician, said in 1947,

> Nigeria is not a nation; it is a mere geographical expression. There are no "Nigerians" in the same sense as there are "English" or "Welsh" or "French." The word Nigeria is merely a distinctive appellation to distinguish those who live within the boundaries of Nigeria from those who do not.
>
> *(Awolowo, 1947)*[3]

That same year, Abubakar Tafawa Balewa (who later became the country's first and only prime minister) observed that the territory called Nigeria lacked a vital criterion of nationhood, in that it shared only a common government and territory; its union, he stated, was not voluntary, and its diverse people did not share a common culture, identity, language, or history. "Since the amalgamation of Southern and Northern provinces in 1914 Nigeria has existed as one country only on paper," he opined. ". . . It is still far from being united" (Babatunde, 2015).[4] Statements credited to Awolowo, Balewa, and Ahmadu Bello (all considered among the country's founding fathers) reflected the positions of the educated and economic elites who took the reins of the newly independent state in 1960: Nigeria's path forward as a nation—in governance, social structure, and development—would be forged based on ethnicity.

Upon independence, the Hausa-Fulani-dominated Northern People's Congress (NPC), led by Ahmadu Bello, formed an alliance with the Igbo-led National Council of Nigeria and the Cameroons (NCNC), led by Nnamdi Azikiwe. Obafemi Awolowo's AG was the opposition faction in the new state's parliamentary government (Adebanwi, 2019). The first six years of post-independence governance were thus the Hausa-Fulani and Igbo elites against the Yoruba. It was a period of political upheavals in western Nigeria, with Awolowo and Samuel Ladoke Akintola (also a Yoruba), the western region premier chief, at loggerheads over political strategies. Awolowo preferred political autonomy for the AG in the western region, insisting that the Yoruba had little to gain from the center, while Akintola favored a coalition with the central government to secure access to federal funds. Akintola asserted his power as the region's chief executive and resisted overarching control by Awolowo's AG, instead aligning the Yoruba with the NPC–NCNC power bloc (i.e., with the Hausa-Fulani and the Igbo) to empower his region and his party, ultimately succeeding in gaining federal support against Awolowo and political control over the western region. In the heat of the imbroglio between the two men, Awolowo's stiff opposition to the NPC-led federal government led to sedition charges. Although he was convicted in 1963 and sent to prison for ten years (Balogun, 2013; Adebanwi, 2008), western Nigeria remained in turmoil, especially following the 1964 parliamentary election.

Meanwhile, a growing rift had soured relations between the Igbo and the Hausa-Fulani. In response to widespread resentment over northern political dominance and rampant corruption among senior-ranking federal officials, a group of junior Igbo military officers headed by Major Chukwuma "Kaduna" Nzeogwu led a failed coup d'état on January 15, 1966 (Sklar, 1967). No Igbo leaders or ranking military officers died in the conflict, but Akintola, Balewa (then the prime minister), Bello (then the northern region premier chief), and a host of Hausa-Fulani and Yoruba military officers were killed (Ikpe, 2000). Major General Johnson Aguiyi-Ironsi, an Igbo and head of the Nigerian army at the time of the uprising, outwitted a coupist sent to arrest or kill him and took over as the military head of state, thus ending civilian rule (Albin-Lackey & Rawlence, 2007). Ironsi's government did not prosecute arrested coupists despite demands from Hausa-Fulani members of the military. The new government also signed into law a decree replacing the federal system with the unitary one, doing away with regional governments, banning political parties, and appropriating greater powers to the head of state. The Hausa-Fulani and the Yoruba condemned the Nzeogwu coup as an Igbo attempt to assert political dominance at the federal level. Ironsi was killed in a countercoup on July 29, 1966, along with many Igbo officers. Targeted violence against the

Igbo in northern Nigeria prompted a secession declaration of the eastern region, the Igbos' native land, as the independent state of Biafra in 1967, with the eastern region's governor, Lieutenant Colonel Odumegwu Ojukwu, as the de facto head of state (Maiangwa, 2016).

Roughly seven years after Nigeria gained independence from the British, the country descended into a brutal, two-and-a-half-year-long civil war. Although accounts of the actual human death toll vary widely, at least one million Nigerians died during the war, untold numbers of them from famine and disease resulting from the federal government's naval blockade of Biafra, which was designed to "starv[e] the secessionists into submission" (Bradley, 2023; Nwaubani, 2020). The hostilities and their aftermath shifted the previous Hausa-Fulani–Igbo political power structure, pitting the northern Hausa-Fulani and the western Yoruba against the predominantly Igbo eastern region. The war ended with Biafra's capitulation on January 15, 1970, marking a termination of the hostilities between the Hausa-Fulani and Igbo that Nzeogwu's coup had ignited. The federal government commenced a process of reintegration, rehabilitation, and reconstruction of eastern Nigeria immediately after the war, but the whole ugly chapter had the opposite effect to that which the Igbo had hoped: It cemented an informal Hausa-Fulani–Yoruba alliance that endures today, more than five decades later. Moreover, claims of Igbo marginalization in southeastern Nigeria persist, as does a sense of stigmatization dating back to the civil war. Many Igbo contend that they have never fully reintegrated into Nigerian society, citing exclusion from federal appointments, barriers to high-ranking positions in the armed forces, and inequitable resource-sharing (Atata, 2019; Atata & Omobowale, 2018; Maiangwa, 2016; Nsoedo, 2019; Okwuosa, Nwaoga, & Uroko, 2021).

Ethnicity over Nationality: The Federal Character Principle

The preceding chronology of the major events from 1957 to 1970 offers a quick reflection on the historical foundations of ethnic contentions in Nigeria. Prior to independence, the British had worked out an arrangement to divide Nigeria into three regions: the north, dominated by the Hausa-Fulani; the southwest (or west), dominated by the Yoruba; and the southeast (or east), dominated by the Igbo. In 1963, the first restructuring of the federal system carved out a fourth midwestern region from the original western region (see Chapter 10) (Osaghae, 1991; Komolafe, 2023). Two months before the civil war broke out in July 1967, in order to weaken the influence of the Ojukwu government in eastern Nigeria and isolate the Igbo secessionists—and also to address the demands of the minority ethnic groups by diluting the hegemony of the larger ones—General Yakubu Gowon split Nigeria's four regions into twelve states. Gowon, a Christian from the Middle Belt who had served as General Ironsi's chief of staff during the January 1966 coup, had been installed as head of state in August of that year.

Gowon's immediate goal upon the Biafran surrender was to rehabilitate the fragile nation and foster a sense of unity and stability by addressing the long-standing (and lingering) sentiments that fueled the civil war while promoting economic development. His very first act as ruler, in 1966, had been to reinstate the federal system that Ironsi had abrogated months before, arguably lighting the fuse that ignited the war. As Nigeria's longest-serving head of state, Gowon's government initiated a number of nation-building initiatives and major infrastructural projects that, along with the spike in oil production in the Niger Delta, yielded some of the country's highest growth years on record. (For more on the oil boom, along with its far-reaching consequences, see Chapter 10.) Nevertheless, he, too, was ousted by a coup in July 1975, just three days shy of nine years in office (Osaghae, 1992; Directorate of Intelligence, 1970; Johnson, 1975; Macrotrends, 2025). The new federal military government headed by General Murtala Muhammed, a northerner and a Hausa, convened a constitutional drafting committee, promising a return to democratic civilian rule by 1979 (ostensibly the reason for Gowon's ouster) (Olawale, 2017). Indeed, Nigeria's new constitution went into effect in 1979, though Muhammed did not live to see it: He was assassinated during a failed military coup in 1976. But his deputy, Olusegun Obasanjo, was appointed head of state, and he committed to returning the country to civilian rule. Obasanjo lifted General Ironsi's 1966 ban on political parties in 1978, and the country transitioned to presidential democracy in 1979 after fourteen years of military rule (Osaghae, 1992; Read, 1979).

The 1979 constitution introduced the principle of *federal character*, emphasizing by design Indigenous origin over nationality (Adamolekun, Erero, & Oshionebo, 1991; Dibua, 2011). The principle was born out of a desire to prevent the domination of any ethnic or religious group or region in the country's governance and to foster a sense of national unity after the disastrous civil war. Specifically, it sought to promote equity, fairness, inclusion, and representation in appointments to public service positions by addressing horizontal inequality and ensuring that access to public service appointments "fairly reflect[s] the linguistic, ethnic, religious, and geographic diversity of the country" (Adamolekun, Erero, & Oshionebo, 1991; Odinakachukwu & Obidimma, 2021; Ogunniran, 2018; Suberu, 2022).[5] The provision reflects an overarching ethos that being Nigerian—and thus having access to state resources—is predicated on ethnic identification over and above national citizenship.

Then and now, ethnicity is widely considered the most basic and politically salient identity. A 2000 study by Afrobarometer on Nigerians' attitudes toward democracy and markets found that ethnicity "is demonstrably the most conspicuous group identity": Almost one-half (48.2 percent) of Nigerians surveyed preferred to self-label by ethnicity, while less than one-third (28.4 percent) chose class identity and only one-fifth (21 percent) chose religious affiliation (Lewis & Bratton, 2000).[6] The country's three principal ethnic identities (Hausa-Fulani, Yoruba, and Igbo) correspond to the colonial regions at the time of independence (Osaghae, 1986), which has allowed strong regional identities to be consolidated in the post-colonial period. A pervasive regionalist attitude has accompanied Hausa-Fulani, Yoruba, and Igbo contestations for dominance, especially in their respective regions (Suleiman & Maiangwa, 2023).

Needless to say, this ethos has profound implications across the board. In the context of economic growth and development, the primacy of ethnic and regional association over national identity ipso facto impedes Nigeria's advancement. The fact that access (and non-access) to state resources is largely based on ethnic affiliation means that contestations among different ethnic groups are inevitable. Case in point: Nigeria's affirmative representative system, which is discussed below, exemplifies a mechanism through which ethnic contentions have hindered the country's development progress. Based on a quota system and the federal character principle, affirmative action aims to distribute resources and grant opportunities to the citizenry based on ethnic, state, and regional considerations—meaning that development projects are awarded based on ethnic and political interests rather than on merit and efficient resource allocation. In short, Nigeria runs unequivocally on the platform of ethnicities (Dibua, 2011; Adamolekun, Erero, & Oshionebo, 1991).

Consciously and unconsciously, Nigerians are socialized to prioritize ethnic affiliations over social and civic relations. Although inter-ethnic relations in everyday interactions proceed with the normalcy of the mundane in workplaces, market spaces, and neighborhoods throughout the country, volatility lurks beneath the surface. Even a disagreement between coworkers or neighbors of different ethnicities has the potential to spark violence, as it did in a market in Ibadan in 2021: What started as a disagreement between a Yoruba trader and a Hausa porter quickly degenerated into inter-ethnic violence that killed more than twenty people and left massive property destruction in its wake (Kabir, 2021).

The reality that ethnic and regional affiliations predominate in the hearts and minds of Nigerians over other group identities and national associations pervades the country's institutions. Politics revolves around ethnicity and indigeneity—and particularly along the north–south divide—at the federal and state levels. If the president is from the north, then a vice president from the south is customary; the same tacit understanding applies to legislative and judicial positions. Media outlets frequently comment on the ethnicity of justices and judges, and the public oftentimes attributes judicial pronouncements and judgments (especially on political and constitutional matters) to a presiding judge's ethnicity. The ethnicities of military and police figureheads, too, often elicit public concern vis-à-vis the president's ethnic identity. As a result of this preeminence of ethnic identity, unsurprisingly, allocation and distribution of resources continue to be contentious along ethnoregional lines in Nigeria (Suberu, 2001). Despite the federal character mandate, the general perception is that politicians favor their regions in resource allocation and other policy considerations. In particular, because the north lags behind the south in economic development, northern politicians favor redistribution of resources to benefit the northern states (Demarest & Langer, 2023). For example, during the administration of Muhammadu Buhari (2015–23), who hailed from the northern region, the general perception in society was that key cabinet positions and high-ranking military appointments were lopsided in favor of individuals from the north (Ogunniran, 2018).

Ethnoregional concerns also affect the education sector. Nigeria's Universal Basic Education Commission (UBEC) is a federal agency funded by the government and the World Bank and tasked with providing education policy recommendations, resources, infrastructure, and funding across the country (Magashi, 2015). It has faced allegations that it preferentially supports the north over the south (Onyekwena et al., 2017; Igenegbai, 2016). The UBEC, for its part, claims that many southern states lack access to UBEC funds due to failure to provide "counterpart funding" (which refers to the matching funds—generally 50 percent—required for states to receive federal grants), or for other administrative reasons (Igenegbai, 2016). Contentions also abound over access to primary education (and particularly access to UBEC funds therefor) and *unity schools*—federal government–owned colleges or secondary schools. As the name implies, unity schools (of which there were 115 across northern and southern Nigeria as of 2024) aim to foster cross-ethnic unity among Nigerians. Until the reintroduction of private secondary schools in the mid-1990s, unity schools were upheld as a model of ethnic integration, representing the country's best secondary schools (Abdullahi, 2023; Lawal et al., 2021).[7]

Unity school admission is not based solely on merit; different states have differing admission standards. Over the years, candidates in the south have performed better on entrance examinations than candidates in the north, ostensibly due to the south's superior educational infrastructure and resources. In response, the Federal Character Act of 1996 codified a quota-based affirmative action system to level the playing field and enhance access to publicly funded secondary education for candidates from educationally disadvantaged states. The affirmative action provision applies to unity school admissions across the country's thirty-six states and the Federal Capital Territory (FCT), effectively applying a lower admission standard for candidates from the north. Federal universities use a similar system in applying admission criteria. Per the Joint Admissions and Matriculation Board for tertiary education, nearly all of Nigeria's federal universities have "catchment" and "educationally less developed state" clauses in their admission policies; the Universities of Ibadan and Abuja are the only ones with universal or national admission policies. The board deems twenty-three states educationally disadvantaged, the majority of them in the country's north.[8] These policies seek to democratize and expand access to tertiary education in disadvantaged regions. However, perhaps unsurprisingly, critics (particularly in the south) view such policies through an ethnic lens as an agenda to give northern students an undue advantage in unity school and federal university admissions.

Their origins notwithstanding, Nigeria's modern ethnic, regional, and political identities evolved from the ethnoregional structures of the colonial period and the immediate post-colonial federation, from which the modern Nigerian state's ideologies and institutions took their shape (Henry et al., 2018). Ethnoregional identity constructions have formalized ethnicity as a form of political currency. Ethnically underpinned and often discriminatory practices in contestations for access, influence, and power, through which certain groups are shut out or denied opportunities, privileges, or equal societal rights, have become commonplace. As the next section describes, the resulting system of ethnic stratification, hierarchical access, and ranked citizenship has created a class of Nigerian elites that dominates politics and governance at every level.

Elites, Ethnicity, and Underdevelopment

Governance describes the ways in which countries and societies manage their affairs politically, and the manners in which governing groups exercise power and authority, particularly at the macro level. Good governance, per the World Bank, is essential for development: "It helps countries improve economic growth, build human capital, and strengthen social cohesion" (World Bank, Worldwide Governance Indicators: Overview, 2024). In developing countries especially, governance is typically the realm of the elites. As such, because governance is the process of politically managing the state's affairs, understanding the intricate and often problematic linkages between elitism and governance is key to understanding development—and development challenges. For a society's poorest and most vulnerable, the difference between good and bad governance profoundly affects their daily lives. An inability of government institutions to prevent conflict, provide security, or furnish basic services and resources can have dire consequences. Moreover, lack of opportunity can prevent generations of poor families from lifting themselves out of poverty and contributing to economic growth. Good governance, therefore, is central to achieving development.

Politics in Nigeria, as elsewhere, is the domain of the elites. They are the privileged few, the rich, often the more educated, and they have huge social networks and vast social capital. Given these advantages, the elites are able to dominate national politics and governance, making strategic decisions that influence resource allocation, investment, and growth and shaping policies that impact development. In doing so, they routinely appeal to constructs of ethnic identity and allegiances thereof (be they primordial or relics of colonialism) to negotiate access—or non-access—to state power and resources. Ethnoregional affiliations are the structural base from which elites orchestrate and maintain power and relevance. Ethnicity thus becomes paramount in contestations for national and regional resources.

Language, geography, and history are major elements and proxy representations of identities. These proxies and the identities they represent are highly visible in

Nigeria and are integral to people's concepts of belonging and place within the state and its institutions. Nigerians consider ethnic identity the essential coalescence of these proxies. As this chapter has demonstrated, most Nigerians self-describe along ethnic identity lines over national identity or other group identities, and the hundreds of ethnic identities in the country all vie for a piece of the proverbial pie. Although socioeconomic class is at times also a unifying identity for the purposes of this contestation, ethnic identity informs socioeconomic status, political culture, and voting behaviors above all else (Akanle, 2017, February 2012). And ultimately, it is the ethnic configuration of the elite ruling class that drives the manners and processes by which these competing identities constellate, shift, divide, and contend (Akanle, 2012). As loyalties and alliances shift, the elites are central to and strategic in managing these ebbs and flows in ways that suit their desired ends. As they manipulate and exploit the masses for solipsistic gains, the resulting power dynamics inherently breed inequality and poverty, fomenting regional and national underdevelopment.

Historical records suggest that autonomous ethnolinguistically and geographically distinct groups (or "tribes," in the colonialists' parlance) in the region that would become Nigeria jostled among one another for resources, power, and position just as pre-modern peoples did elsewhere in the world. Even in these precolonial societies in Africa, people contended with problems of inequality, elitism, and inter-group competition (Akanle & Olorunlana, 2014). Yet, as previously discussed, issues of inter-group contestations, inequality, and the role of the elites in Nigeria were dramatically exacerbated by colonial-era ruling constructs and identity constructions (Akanle, 2011). Over the years since independence, competition among Nigeria's ethnic groups has contributed to numerous regional reconfigurations and bifurcations. Specifically, as discussed above, before the outbreak of the Biafran War in 1967, the federal military government divided the country's then four regions into twelve states. In the immediate sense, the move was aimed at avoiding the eastern region's secession and averting the civil war. But it also sought to address the demands of minority ethnic groups, erstwhile subsumed throughout the four regions under the hegemony of the majority groups, who were demanding more access to power and federal resources in lieu of relying on the majority groups' political parties for representation (Osaghae, 1991). More states were created over the years; at present, the country has thirty-six states along with the FCT and 774 local governments (National Bureau of Statistics, 2025).

Yet given the sheer number of minority ethnic groups (representing a full 30 percent of the population) (Suberu, 2021), the creation of these administrative territories has not lessened inter-ethnic contentions. Rather, it has only broadened the opportunities extended to the elite class. The elites continue to dominate Nigerian social, economic, and political institutions primarily because education remains the major determinant of access to state resources and positions of power. Inescapably, then, elitism shapes politics, and politics in turn shapes development, especially when politics is laden with negotiations (and manipulations) of traditional ethnoregional identity constructs and the alliances built around them. Rounding out the vicious circle, those manipulations inevitably perpetuate inequality and underdevelopment. In Nigeria, as in any system where elitism is a driving political force, more inclusive, egalitarian, and accountable governance is the only way to break the cycle, reduce inequality, and drive sustainable development.

Nigerian elites (often called the "cabal" in Nigerian political lexicon (Godson, 2024)) enjoy preferential access to state resources and development planning, and the country suffers from a large measure of elitist state capture. Political elites often play the ethnic identity card to legitimize state capture under the guise of representing the interests of particular ethnic groups. By way of this strategic, quasi-legitimized corruption—and of their outsized influence on the national stage more broadly—the elites become the puppeteers in the theater of identity-driven inter-group contestations for power and influence, and ultimately the producers of systemic inequality. Furthermore, as in much of post-independence sub-Saharan Africa, political elitism and ethnic patronage in Nigeria go hand in hand. The ruling elites' role in fostering inter-ethnic realignments and contestations serves as a political ploy to preserve their own dominance, entrenching inequality and poverty among the masses for their own advantage. The end result, in addition to untold social harm,[9] is a kleptocratic system that stymies economic growth and prospects for long-term development (Chijioke, 2022).

Politics provides elites with a powerful mechanism with which to manipulate ethnic associations and instigate class warfare to achieve their objectives (Bolarinwa & Osuji, 2022). The post-independence machinations of the Hausa-Fulani-led NPC and the Igbo-dominated NCNC seeking to erode the AG (Yoruba) political power base are a poignant example (Jackson, 1972). Ethnoregional elite competition has fueled inter-ethnic agitations more recently as well. For example, elites in the Niger Delta belonging to the Ijaw and Ogoni ethnic groups have clamored for more control over the region's oil revenues, prompting attacks on oil installations by militia groups. Tensions eased somewhat during the presidency of Goodluck Jonathan (a member of the Ijaw minority ethnic group) but flared again when Jonathan lost the presidential election to Buhari (a Hausa-Fulani) in 2015. Meanwhile, Igbo elites have persisted in their protests of marginalization by other ethnic groups and, concerningly (given the origins of Nigeria's devastating civil war), have renewed demands for autonomy, most notably through the secessionist Movement for the Actualization of the Sovereign State of Biafra and Indigenous People of Biafra. Some Yoruba elites, too, have agitated for self-determination, calling for the establishment of the "Oduduwa Republic" (Ogunniran, 2018). Although these campaigns are perceived as mass mobilizations, they are susceptible to manipulation by ethnic elites (Babalola & Onapajo, 2019).[10]

Social cohesion, economic well-being, equitable access and representation, and a sense of belonging are all requisite for the peace and security of people and states (Adesina, 2011). And elite-driven contestation for resources, status, and power is universal. In sub-Saharan Africa (and Nigeria in particular), the effects of identity-based negotiating and maneuvering for primacy and the resulting political exclusions, disproportionate access to resources, and socioeconomic inequality affect the state and its people in dynamic and critical ways. If not properly managed, these conditions can destabilize nations, hinder governance, and frustrate growth and development (Akanle, Olorunlana, & Shittu, 2017). Inasmuch as Nigerian elites play a crucial role in governance and societal outcomes, they are driving the country's development in the wrong direction.

Poverty is a central indicator for the first of the United Nations Sustainable Development Goals—"ending poverty in all its forms everywhere." The World Bank already ranks Nigeria among the world's poorest nations, second only to India as of 2023 (UNDESA, 2024; World Bank, The World Bank in Nigeria: Overview, 2024; World Bank, World Development Indicators: Poverty and Inequality, 2024). (According to the Brookings Institution, Nigeria actually surpassed India as the nation with the highest number of people living in extreme poverty as of 2018 [Kharas, Hamel, & Hofer, 2018].) As of 2019, Nigerian Bureau of Statistics estimates put more than eighty-seven million Nigerians living below the poverty line, with an average of six people falling into poverty every minute (Onu et al., 2019). And as of 2022, the bureau listed 133 million people in Nigeria (or 63 percent of the population) as multidimensionally poor, as measured by the United Nations Development Programme's Multidimensional Poverty Index (Ichedi, 2022).[11] Worse yet, poverty is increasing rather than decreasing—the World Bank in 2023 projected that thirteen million more Nigerians would fall below the poverty line by 2025 (Sulaimon, 2023). Successive governments have failed to reverse these trends; scant access to health care, education, and basic goods and services sustains these conditions, which the ruling elites do little or nothing to alleviate.

Poverty and exclusionary identity politics are inimical to sustainable short- and long-term development. Paradoxically, poverty and inequality are not just consequences of but causes of underdevelopment, with elitism facilitating the relationship in both directions. Political elites in developing countries can and all too often do create class structures and governance frameworks that increase the vulnerability of the impoverished in a way that employs ethnicity and religious affiliation to reinforce and protect their own self-interest. Because the elites wield considerable influence in society and power over governance, they can easily manipulate economic and political insecurities and identity contestations among disparate groups as tools for exclusionary politics (Bolarinwa & Osuji, 2022).[12] They are then free to create and perpetuate poverty and inequality by capturing political and economic resources to maintain their power and influence and fund their patronage base. An elitist system is thus exclusionary by definition; any appearance of inclusivity (during elections, for example) is almost invariably either empty political rhetoric or shady political maneuvering. In reality, in Nigeria and other developing countries alike, exploitation of the poor by the elite ruling class is de rigueur.

As described above, negotiations for power and access around colonial-era ethnic identity constructs are often the instruments of this exploitation in Nigeria. Primordial norms, values, identities, and traditions factor into the equation, as does run-of-the-mill corrupt politics, but a unique political culture of *godfatherism* in Nigeria further entrenches the cycle.[13] All these mechanisms serve to legitimate the state capture by the political elites. The uneven social and power relations between the ethnic majority political elites and the minority groups they marginalize create an indelible cycle of poverty and inequality, political instability, state fragility, and violence. Underdevelopment is the inevitable result.

Conclusion

This chapter examined how the dynamics of elitism and ethnic identity politics in Nigerian governance and society contribute to the country's rampant inequality, widespread poverty, and chronic underdevelopment. It argues that the social structures, identities, and attitudes carried over into the post-independence era continue to perpetuate elitism, and that elitism in turn thrives by negotiating and manipulating colonial constructs of ethnicity and identity and the allegiances built around them. That the nexus of elitism and ethnicity in Nigeria impedes development is abundantly clear. That it also provokes violent conflict across the country—which then exacerbates the social and political ills that prevent inclusive governance and economic growth in the first place—is a tragic and vicious cycle. Aiding and abetting this national affliction is the fact, enshrined in the constitution, that ethnic identities and loyalties eclipse a Nigerian national consciousness, to the pronounced detriment of national unity. As a result, principles like federal character and affirmative action that are intended to address horizontal inequality and foster equitable access and representation are instead viewed as partial and patrimonialist, sowing ethnic rancor and elevating the deep societal divisions that thwart socioeconomic progress and sustained development and growth.

Although the intersectionalities of elitism, ethnic identity, and inequality in Africa have always presented challenges, one inherent (though rarely acknowledged) positive is that they often elevate discourses around equality as an imperative, and around how elites can address inequality and poverty by extending benefits to the socially and economically challenged. They can do so either through official channels (such as the federal character constitutional provision and its policy outgrowths) or unofficially through patronage and benevolence. Issues that arise around elitism, inequality, and inter-ethnic contestation provide platforms for continuous interrogation of the status quo and for discussions, policies, and efforts toward building more inclusive societies primed for growth and sustainable development in the long run.

Notes

1 According to the CIA *World Factbook*, in addition to being Africa's most populous nation, Nigeria is composed of more than 250 distinct ethnic groups; the Wilson Center puts that number at more than 300. In addition to the Hausa, who comprise 30 percent of the population, the Yoruba (15.5 percent), the Igbo (15.2 percent), and the Fulani (6 percent), the major minority ethnic groups include the Tiv (2.4 percent), the Kanuri/Beriberi (2.4 percent), the Ibibio (1.8 percent), and the Ijaw/Izon (1.8 percent). The remaining quarter of the population comprises myriad smaller ethnic groups (Numbers are current as of 2018.) (CIA, 2023; Green, 2023).

2 Chris C. Ojukwu, "Igbo Nation, Modern Statecraft and the Geopolitics of National Survival in a Multiethnic Nigeria," *African Journal of Political Science and International Relations* 3, no. 5 (May 2009): 183.

3 Obafemi Awolowo, *Path to Nigerian Freedom* (London, UK: Faber & Faber, 1947), 47–48.

4 Osabiya Babatunde, "Nigeria's Federalism, Unity and Development," *Global Journal of Management and Business Research* 15, no. 2 (2015): 2.

5 Notwithstanding the centrality of the doctrine, recent administrations have been criticized for violating the spirit of the federal character principle, fueling secessionist movements and militias (such as the Niger Delta militias in the south-south zone, the Oduduwa People's Congress in the southwest, the Arewa Consultative Forum in the north, and the People of Biafra in the southeast). See Ogunniran (2018). See also Chapters 6 and 10 for more on Nigeria's geopolitical zones.

6 Peter Mark Lewis and Michael Bratton, "Attitudes to Democracy and Markets in Nigeria," Afrobarometer Paper No. 3, MSU Working Papers on Political Reform in Africa, ed. Michael Bratton, E. Gyimah-Boadi, and Robert Mattes (Accra, Ghana: Afrobarometer, April 2000), 24–25, 27.

7 Private secondary schools started in Nigeria in 1842; most of them were mission schools started by Christian missionaries. The state assumed their ownership and administration during the period of military governance in the 1970s following the civil war (Ezegwu & Okoye, 2024). In September 2024, the Federal Ministry of Education announced plans to transition Nigeria's 115 federal unity colleges into "basic and secondary schools," although no specific timeline was given (Ogwo, 2024).

8 The states deemed educationally disadvantaged by the Joint Admissions and Matriculation Board are Adamawa, Bauchi, Benue, Borno, Gombe, Jigawa, Kaduna, Kano, Katsina, Kebbi, Kogi, Kwara, Nasarawa, Niger, Plateau, Sokoto, Taraba, Yobe, and Zamfara in the north and Bayelsa, Cross River, Ebonyi, and Rivers in the south (Willott, 2011).

9 The highly controversial Almajiri system in northern Nigeria (and its consequences) is both a poignant example of the harm resulting from rampant poverty and impotent economic growth resulting from failed economic policies and a symptom of the problem. *Almajiri*, which translates to "child student," is a system of education wherein poor, often rural parents unable to afford formal schooling send their young boys to an itinerant teacher (or *mallam*) for an Islamic education centered on learning the Qur'an. Unfortunately, this system has led to child neglect, destitution, exploitation, and outright abuse. With many of the mallams acting in loco parentis reliant on charity themselves, the boys under their tutelage often resort to begging and other servile tasks. The widespread disassociation and restiveness of Nigerian youths today owes in part to the Almajiri system (Magashi, 2015; Abubakar, 2013; Ifijeh & Iwu-James, 2012; Akanle, 2019).

10 Dele Babalola and Hakeem Onapajo, "New Clamour for 'Restructuring' in Nigeria: Elite Politics, Contradictions, and Good Governance," *African Studies Quarterly* 18, no. 4 (October 2019): 46.

11 According to the World Bank, the MPI is "a means to capture the complexity of poverty that considers dimensions of well-being beyond just monetary poverty." It measures the percentage of households in a given country that are deprived along three

dimensions—monetary poverty, education, and basic infrastructure services—in order to convey "a more complete picture of poverty" (World Bank, Multidimensional Poverty Measure, 2024).

12 Oluwasegunota F. O. Bolarinwa and Ucheoma C. Osuji, "Political Elitism in Nigeria: Challenges, Threats and the Future of Citizenship," *Open Journal of Philosophy* 12, no. 1 (February 2022): 110, 113.

13 The *Oxford Dictionary of African Politics* defines *godfatherism* as "a term used primarily in Nigeria to refer to wealthy and powerful figures who exert political influence behind the scenes while often remaining out of the limelight. A classic 'godfather' will have earned their money through government contracts or access to the country's oil wealth and will have used their largesse to establish a network through which they can influence political developments. A successful godfather, for example, will be able to shape not only who is nominated to contest elections but also who wins" (Cheeseman, Bertrand, & Husaini, 2019).

Bibliography

Abdullahi, Bolaji. "Back to the Basics: How to Fix UBE and Public Basic Education in Nigeria." *Agora Policy Memorandum*, August 8, 2023, https://agorapolicy.org/research/policy-memo/90-back-to-the-basics-how-to-fix-ube-and-public-basic-education-in-nigeria.html.

Abdulwaheed, Atanda, Oluwashina Moruf Adebiyi, and Adebola Rafiu Bakare. "Ethnicity and Election Outcomes in Nigeria: Interrogating the 2015 Presidential Election." *Journal of African Elections* 17, no. 1 (June 2018): 117–40, https://hdl.handle.net/10520/EJC-fbe52a36a.

Abubakar, Sanusi. "Almajirci: Some Home Truths (I), (II)." *Daily Trust* (Abuja, Nigeria), November 5, 2013, https://dailytrust.com/almajirci-some-home-truths-i and https://dailytrust.com/almajirci-some-home-truths-ii.

Adamolekun, Ladipo, John Erero, and Basil Oshionebo. "'Federal Character' and Management of the Federal Civil Service and the Military." *Publius: The Journal of Federalism* 21, no. 4 (Fall 1991): 75–88, https://doi.org/10.1093/oxfordjournals.pubjof.a037980.

Adebanwi, Wale. "Contesting Multiculturalism: Federalism and Unitarism in Late Colonial Nigeria." In *Multiculturalism in the British Commonwealth: Comparative Perspectives on Theory and Practice*, edited by Richard T. Ashcroft and Mark Bevir, 167–90. Oakland: University of California Press, 2019.

Adebanwi, Wale. "The Cult of Awo: The Political Life of a Dead Leader." *The Journal of Modern African Studies* 46, no. 3 (September 2008): 335–60, https://doi.org/10.1017/S0022278X08003339.

Adesina, Jimi O. "Beyond the Social Protection Paradigm: Social Policy in Africa's Development." *Canadian Journal of Development Studies* 32, no. 4 (December 2011): 454–70, https://doi.org/10.1080/02255189.2011.647441.

Akanle, Olayinka. "Kinship Support Orientations and Class Dynamics of Nigerian International Migrants." *International Review of Modern Sociology* 38, no. 1 (February 2012): 131–53, https://www.jstor.org/stable/43499873.

Akanle, Olayinka. "The Nigerian State." In *Peoples and Cultures of Nigeria*, edited by Ayodele Sanuel Jegede, Akinpelu Olanrewaju Olutayo, Femi O. Omololu, and Bernard E. Owumi, 21–34. Ibadan, Nigeria: University of Ibadan Department of Sociology, 2012.

Akanle, Olayinka. "Post-Colonial Nation Building, Global Governance, Globalisation, and Development in Nigeria and Africa." *Africa Insight* 41, no. 3 (2011): 1–15, https://hdl.handle.net/10520/EJC17715.

Akanle, Olayinka. Review of *The Rise of Africa's Middle Class: Myths, Realities and Critical Engagements*, by Henning Melber. *African Studies Quarterly* 17, no. 3 (November 2017): 109–11, https://journals.flvc.org/ASQ/article/view/136073/140519.

Akanle, Olayinka. "Youth Restiveness, National Security and Development in Nigeria." In *Security and Society in Nigeria*, edited by Ifeanyi P. Onyeonoru and Adewole A. Atere, 1–14. Ibadan, Nigeria: Ibadan University Press, 2019.

Akanle, Olayinka, and Adetayo Olorunlana. "Christianity and Disability in Post-Colonial South-Western Nigeria." *Journal of Environment and Culture* 11, no. 2 (March 2014): 30–44, https://www.researchgate.net/publication/315715577.

Akanle, Olayinka, Adetayo Olorunlana, and Olamide Sarafadeen Shittu. "Culture, Suicide-Terrorism and Security in Nigeria." In *Terrorism and Counter Terrorism War in Nigeria*, edited by Pius Adejoh and Waziri Adisa, 138–49. Lagos, Nigeria: University of Lagos Press, 2017.

Albeely, Tayfour Sidahmed, Ahmed Tanimu Mahmoud, and Aliyu Yahaya. "Ethnicity, Tribalism, and Racism and Its Major Doctrines in Nigeria." *Dirasa Ifriqiyya* 59 (2018): 29–46.

Albin-Lackey, Chris, and Ben Rawlence. *Criminal Politics: Violence, 'Godfathers' and Corruption in Nigeria*. New York, NY: Human Rights Watch, October 2007, https://www.hrw.org/reports/2007/nigeria1007/nigeria1007webwcover.pdf.

Alubo, Ogoh. "Citizenship and Nation Making in Nigeria: New Challenges and Contestations." *Identity, Culture and Politics: An Afro-Asian Dialogue* 5, nos. 1 and 2 (January 2004): 135–61, https://doi.org/10.1017/S0022050718000128.

Atata, Scholastica Ngozi. "Biafra Renaissance Among the Igbo of South-East Nigeria." Ph.D. diss., University of Ibadan, Nigeria, 2019.

Atata, Scholastica Ngozi, and Ayokunle Olumuyiwa Omobowale. "The Social Symbolism of Biafra Protest Songs in South-Eastern Nigeria." *The Nigerian Journal of Sociology and Anthropology* 16, no. 1 (July 2018): 1–11, https://doi.org/10.36108/NJSA/8102/61(0110).

Awolowo, Obafemi. *Path to Nigerian Freedom*. London, UK: Faber & Faber, 1947.

Ayandele, Emmanuel Ayankanmi. *The Educated Elite in the Nigerian Society*. Ibadan, Nigeria: Ibadan University Press, 1974.

Babalola, Dele, and Hakeem Onapajo. "New Clamour for 'Restructuring' in Nigeria: Elite Politics, Contradictions, and Good Governance." *African Studies Quarterly* 18, no. 4 (October 2019): 41–56, https://asq.africa.ufl.edu/wp-content/uploads/sites/168/vi18i4a03.pdf.

Babatunde, Osabiya. "Nigeria's Federalism, Unity and Development." *Global Journal of Management and Business Research* 15, no. 2 (2015): 1–7, https://journalofbusiness.org/index.php/GJMBR/article/view/1604/1-Nigerias-Federalism-Unity_JATS_NLM_xml.

Balogun, Amusa Saheed. "An Assessment of the Partisan Role of the Nigeria Police Force in the 1962 Action Group Crisis." *Journal of the Historical Society of Nigeria* 22 (2013): 33–62, https://www.jstor.org/stable/24768916.

Berman, Bruce J. "Ethnicity, Patronage and the African State: The Politics of Uncivil Nationalism." *African Affairs* 97, no. 388 (July 1998): 305–41, https://doi.org/10.1093/oxfordjournals.afraf.a007947.

Bolarinwa, Oluwasegunota F. O., and Ucheoma C. Osuji. "Political Elitism in Nigeria: Challenges, Threats and the Future of Citizenship." *Open Journal of Philosophy* 12, no. 1 (February 2022): 105–22, https://doi.org/10.4236/ojpp.2022.121007.

Bourne, Richard. *Nigeria: A New History of a Turbulent Century*. London, UK: Zed Books, 2015.

Bradley, Miriam. "Nigerian Civil War, 1967–1970." In *The Politics and Everyday Practice of International Humanitarianism*, edited by Miriam Bradley, 27–44. Oxford, UK: Oxford University Press, 2023.

Central Intelligence Agency (CIA). *The World Factbook*. Washington, DC: U.S. Government Printing Office, 1962–, last updated December 19, 2023, https://www.cia.gov/the-world-factbook/countries/nigeria.

Cheeseman, Nic, Eloïse Bertrand, and Sa'eed Husaini, eds. *Oxford Dictionary of African Politics*. Oxford, UK: Oxford University Press, 2019.

Chijioke, Onah Celestine, Asadu Ikechukwu, and Amujiri Benjamin. "Politico-Administrative Elite Corruption: The Bane of Nigeria's Underdevelopment." *African Renaissance* 19, no. 1 (March 2022): 79–100, https://journals.co.za/doi/abs/10.31920/2516-5305/2022/19n1a4.

Demarest, Leila, and Arnim Langer. "Managing Diversity in Nigeria's Fourth Republic National Assembly: Integrated Parties Versus Ethno-Regional Balancing." *Publius: The Journal of Federalism* 53, no. 4 (Fall 2023): 593–617, https://doi.org/10.1093/publius/pjad010.

Derricourt, Robin. *Inventing Africa: History, Archaeology and Ideas*. New York, NY: Pluto Press, 2011.

Dibua, Jeremiah I. "Ethnic Citizenship, Federal Character and Inter-Group Relations in Postcolonial Nigeria." *Journal of the Historical Society of Nigeria* 20 (2011): 1–25, https://www.jstor.org/stable/41857172.

Directorate of Intelligence. "Special Report: Nigeria After the War." *Central Intelligence Agency*, May 28, 1970. Declassified, issued by the U.S. Department of State, Washington, DC, April 21, 2005, https://static.history.state.gov/frus/frus1969-76ve05p1/pdf/d194.pdf.

Ekeh, Peter P. *Colonialism and Social Structure: An Inaugural Lecture Delivered at the University of Ibadan on 5 June 1980*. Ibadan, Nigeria: University of Ibadan, 1983.

Ezegwu, Chidi, and Dozie Okoye. "Political Bargaining, Religion, and Educational Development: The Nigerian Experience from the Takeover of Schools from Christian Missions." *International Journal of Educational Development* 106 (April 2024): 1–10, https://www.sciencedirect.com/science/article/pii/S0738059324000221.

Frankema, Ewout, Jeffrey Williamson, and Pieter Woltjer. "An Economic Rationale for the West African Scramble? The Commercial Transition and the Commodity Price Boom of 1835–1885." *Journal of Economic History* 78, no. 1 (March 2018): 231–67, https://doi.org/10.1017/S0022050718000128.

Godson, Ezomo. "The 'Cabal' Theory: Who Truly Controls Nigeria's Government?" *Applied Worldwide Nigeria* (blog), October 14, 2024, https://nigeria.appliedworldwide.com/the-cabal-theory-who-truly-controls-nigerias-government.

Green, Mark A. "Nigeria Has More than 500 Languages, 300 Ethnic Groups . . . and Critically Important Elections." The Wilson Center, February 21, 2023, https://www.wilsoncenter.org/blog-post/nigeria-has-more-500-languages-300-ethnic-groups-and-critically-important-elections.

Henry, Jacob Uche, Kenneth I. Nwokike, Amiara Solomon Amiara, and Chijioke Eze. "Ethnicity, Conflict and Issues of Political Balancing in Nigeria, 1954–2015." *EBSU Journal of Social Sciences and Humanities* 8, no. 1 (2018): 41–62.

Ichedi, Sunday Joel. "Nigeria Launches Its Most Extensive National Measure of Multidimensional Poverty," *National Bureau of Statistics News Release, Federal Government of Nigeria*, November 17, 2022, https://www.nigerianstat.gov.ng/news/78.

Ifijeh, Goodluck, and Juliana Iwu-James. "Provision of Formal Education to Almajiris: The Role of Libraries." *European Scientific Journal* 8, no. (July 2012): 97–108, https://test.eujournal.org/index.php/esj/article/view/233.

Igenegbai, Philip. "Education Counterpart Funding Scheme in Nigeria: The Journey So Far." *Benin Journal of Education Studies* 24, nos. 1 and 2 (2016): 9–17, https://beninjes.com/index.php/bjes/article/view/21/17.

Igwe, Dickson O., and Ayokunle Olumuyiwa Omobowale. "Identity Politics, Land Conflict and the Deepening Development Challenges in Ezillo Community, Ebonyi State, South-East Nigeria." *KASU Journal of Social Sciences* 9, no. 1 (2018): 47–62.

Ikpe, Ukana B. "Patrimonialism and Military Regimes in Nigeria." *African Journal of Political Science* 5 no. 1 (2000): 146–62, https://doi.org/10.4314/ajps.v5i1.27318.

Jackson, Larry R. "Nigeria: The Politics of the First Republic." *Journal of Black Studies* 2, no. 3 (March 1972): 277–302, https://doi.org/10.1177/002193477200200302.

Johnson, Thomas A. "Nigeria Plans Growth Based on Oil Funds." *The New York Times*, February 11, 1975, https://www.nytimes.com/1975/02/11/archives/nigeria-plans-growth-based-on-oil-funds.html.

Kabir, Adejumo. "Inside Story: How Artisans' Fight Led to Ethnic Violence in Oyo." *Premium Times* (Abuja, Nigeria), February 14, 2021, https://www.premiumtimesng.com/news/headlines/442757-inside-story-how-artisans-fight-led-to-ethnic-violence-in-oyo.html.

Kharas, Homi, Kristofer Hamel, and Martin Hofer. "The Start of a New Poverty Narrative." *Future Development* (blog), Brookings Institution, June 19, 2018, https://www.brookings.edu/articles/the-start-of-a-new-poverty-narrative.

Komolafe, Kayode. "The Arrival of Midwest." *ThisDay* (Lagos, Nigeria), August 30, 2023, https://www.thisdaylive.com/index.php/2023/08/30/the-arrival-of-midwest.

Lawal, Iyabo, Lawrence Njoku, Charles Ogugbuaja, Uzoma Nzeagwu, and Ann Godwin. "Nigeria's Unity Schools, from Glory to Ordinary." *The Guardian* (Lagos, Nigeria), June 14, 2021, https://guardian.ng/features/education/nigerias-unity-schools-from-glory-to-ordinary.

Lewis, Peter M., and Michael Bratton. "Attitudes to Democracy and Markets in Nigeria." Afrobarometer Paper No. 3. MSU Working Papers on Political Reform in Africa. edited by Michael Bratton, Emmanuel Gyimah-Boadi, and Robert Mattes. Accra, Ghana: Afrobarometer, April 2000, https://www.afrobarometer.org/wp-content/uploads/2022/02/AfropaperNo3_0.pdf.

Macrotrends, "Nigeria Economic Growth 1960–2025," accessed March 8, 2025, https://www.macrotrends.net/global-metrics/countries/nga/nigeria/economic-growth-rate.

Magashi, Salim Bashir. "Education and the Right to Development of the Child in Northern Nigeria: A Proposal for Reforming the *Almajiri* Institution." *Africa Today* 61, no. 3 (Spring 2015): 65–83, https://doi.org/10.2979/africatoday.61.3.65.

Maiangwa, Benjamin. "Revisiting the Nigeria-Biafra War: The Intangibles of Post-War Reconciliation." *International Journal on World Peace* 33, no. 4 (December 2016): 39–67, https://resolver.scholarsportal.info/resolve/07423640/v33i0004/39_rtnwtigopr.xml.

Markus, György. "A Society of Culture: The Constitution of Modernity." In *Rethinking Imagination: Culture and Creativity*, edited by Gillian Robinson and John Rundell, 15–29. London, UK: Routledge, 1994.

Morse, Chandler, Douglas E. Ashford, Fredrick T. Bent, William H. Friedland, John W. Lewis, and David B. Macklin, eds. *Modernization by Design: Social Change in the Twentieth Century*. Ithaca, NY: Cornell University Press, 1969.

National Bureau of Statistics, Federal Government of Nigeria. "About Us," accessed March 9, 2025, https://www.nigerianstat.gov.ng/page/about-us.

Nsoedo, Ezeakukwu E. "The Marginalization of the Igbo People in Nigeria's Political and Economic Sectors: What Is the Way Forward?" *Open Journal of Social Sciences* 7, no. 7 (July 2019): 427–37, https://doi.org/10.4236/jss.2019.77035.

Nwaubani, Adaobi Tricia. "Remembering Nigeria's Biafra War That Many Prefer to Forget." *British Broadcasting Corporation (BBC)*, January 14, 2020, https://www.bbc.com/news/world-africa-51094093.

Odinakachukwu, Emmanuel Okeke, and Obidimma, Emmanuel Chukwudebere. "The Federal Character of Nigeria: A Delicate Bedrock for National Unity and Loyalty." *Nnamdi Azikiwe University Journal of International Law and Jurisprudence* 12, no. 2 (2021): 9–19, https://www.ajol.info/index.php/naujilj/article/view/215301.

Ogunniran, Iyabode. "In Search of a Viable Federalism: The Federal Character Principle in the Nigerian Constitution." *IACL-AIDC Blog*, International Association of Constitutional Law, September 11, 2018, https://blog-iacl-aidc.org/blog/2018/9/10/in-search-of-a-viable-federalism-the-federal-character-principle-in-the-nigerian-constitution.

Ogwo, Charles. "FG to Unbundle 115 Unity Colleges into Basic, Secondary Schools." *Business Day* (Lagos, Nigeria), September 18, 2024, https://businessday.ng/news/article/fg-to-unbundle-115-unity-colleges-into-basic-secondary-schools.

Ojukwu, Chris C. "Igbo Nation, Modern Statecraft and the Geopolitics of National Survival in a Multiethnic Nigeria." *African Journal of Political Science and International Relations* 3, no. 5 (May 2009): 181–90, https://www.internationalscholarsjournals.com/articles/igbo-nation-modern-statecraft-and-the-geopolitics-of-national-survival-in-a-multiethnic-nigeria.pdf.

Okwuosa, Lawrence, Chinyere T. Nwaoga, and Favour Uroko. "The Post-War Era in Nigeria and the Resilience of Igbo Communal System." *Jàmbá: Journal of Disaster Risk Studies* 13, no. 1 (2021): 55–67, https://doi.org/10.4102/jamba.v13i1.867.

Olawale, Gabriel. "Why We Overthrew Gowon—Obasanjo." *Vanguard* (Lagos, Nigeria), August 6, 2017, https://www.vanguardngr.com/2017/08/why-we-overthrew-gowon-obasanjo.

Olutayo, Akinpelu Olanrewaju. "Education Infrastructure and Unsustainable Development." *Human Affairs* 20, no. 2 (June 2010): 183–98, https://doi.org/10.2478/v10023-010-0018-8.

Olutayo, Akinpelu Olanrewaju. "The Irony of Knowledge in Africa's Development." Department of Sociology Monograph No. 5, University of Ibadan, 2009a.

Olutayo, Akinpelu Olanrewaju. "Social Construction of Statehood in Nigeria." In *State and Civil Society Relations in Nigeria*, edited by Akinpelu Olanrewaju Olutayo, Ilufoye S. Ogundiya, and Jimot Amzat, 70–84. Ibadan, Nigeria: Hope Publications, 2009b.

Omobowale, Ayokunle Olumuyiwa. "The Roots of Division, Activism, and Civil Society in Nigeria." *International Sociology* 33, no. 5 (September 2018): 558–67, https://doi.org/10.1177/0268580918791968.

Omobowale, Ayokunle Olumuyiwa. "Stories of the 'Dark' Continent: Crude Constructions, Diasporic Identity, and International Aid to Africa." *International Sociology* 30, no. 2 (March 2015): 108–18, https://doi.org/10.1177/0268580915571796.

Omobowale, Ayokunle Olumuyiwa, and Akinpelu Olanrewaju Olutayo. "Political Clientelism and Rural Development in South-Western Nigeria." *Africa* 80, no. 3 (August 2010): 453–72, https://doi.org/10.3366/afr.2010.0305.

Omobowale, Ayokunle Olumuyiwa, and Akinpelu Olanrewaju Olutayo. "Social Capital and Human Development in Nigeria: The Case of Lalupon Community, Ibadan, Oyo

State." *African Identities* 7, no. 1 (February 2009): 71–82, https://doi.org/10.1080/14725840802583348.

Onu, Emele, Pauline Bax, Mustapha Adamu, and Yinka Ibukun. "Six People Fall into Extreme Poverty in This Nation Every Minute." *Bloomberg*, February 22, 2019, https://www.bloomberg.com/news/articles/2019-02-22/six-people-fall-into-extreme-poverty-in-this-nation-every-minute.

Onyekwena, Chukwuka, Muhammed Adekunle, Nduka Eleanya, and Olumide Taiwo. "Improving Basic Education Outcomes in Nigeria: Effectiveness, Accountability and Equity Issues." Abuja, Nigeria: Centre for the Study of the Economies of Africa, 2017, https://report.educationcommission.org/wp-content/uploads/2017/01/Improving-Basic-Education-Outcomes-in-Nigeria.pdf.

Osaghae, Eghosa A. "Ethnic Minorities and Federalism in Nigeria." *African Affairs* 90, no. 359 (1991): 237–58.

Osaghae, Eghosa E. "Federalism, Local Politics and Ethnicity in Nigeria: Do Ethnic Minorities Still Exist in Nigeria?" *The Journal of Commonwealth and Comparative Politics* 24, no. 2 (1986): 151–68, https://doi.org/10.1080/14662048608447492.

Osaghae, Eghosa E. "Government and Politics." In *Nigeria: A Country Study*, edited by Helen Chapin Metz, 203–51. Washington, DC: U.S. Government Printing Office, 1992, https://www.marines.mil/Portals/1/Publications/Nigeria%20Study_3.pdf.

Osaghae, Eghosa E. "A Re-Examination of the Conception of the Ethnicity in Africa as an Ideology of Inter-Elite Competition." *African Study Monographs* 12, no. 1 (1991): 43–60, https://doi.org/10.14989/68070.

Read, James S. "The New Constitution of Nigeria, 1979: 'The Washington Model'"? *Journal of African Law* 23, no. 2 (Autumn 1979): 131–74, https://doi.org/10.1017/S0021855300010810.

Siollun, Max. *What Britain Did to Nigeria: A Short History of Conquest and Rule*. London, UK: Hurst, 2021.

Sklar, Richard L. "Nigerian Politics in Perspective." *Government and Opposition* 2, no. 4 (1967): 524–39, https://doi.org/10.1111/j.1477-7053.1967.tb01183.x.

Suberu, Rotimi T. "Ethnic Inequality, the Federal Character Principle, and the Reform of Nigeria's Presidential Federalism." WIDER Working Paper No. 2022/113. Helsinki, Finland: United Nations University World Institute for Development Economics Research (UNU-WIDER), October 2022, https://doi.org/10.35188/UNU-WIDER/2022/247-8.

Suberu, Rotimi T. *Federalism and Ethnic Conflict in Nigeria*. Washington, DC: United States Institute of Peace, 2001.

Suberu, Rotimi Timothy. "Nigeria: A Model of Federalist Ethnic Conflict Management or Federalist Illusion?" In *Teaching Federalism: Multidimensional Approaches*, edited by John Kincaid and John Wesley Leckrone, 242–53. Cheltenham, UK: Edward Elgar, 2021.

Sulaimon, Olanrewaju. "World Bank Projects 13mln More Nigerians Will Fall Below Poverty Line by 2025." *Nigerian Tribune*, April 24, 2023, https://www.zawya.com/en/economy/africa/world-bank-projects-13mln-more-nigerians-will-fall-below-poverty-line-by-2025-luwq683k.

Suleiman, Muhammad Dan, and Benjamin Maiangwa. "Nigeria at 63: Four Reasons for Persistent Disunity Six Decades On." *The Conversation* (Waltham, MA), September 30, 2023, https://theconversation.com/nigeria-at-63-four-reasons-for-persistent-disunity-six-decades-on-214675.

Ugbem, Comfort Erima. "The Dynamics of Identity Construction Among Ethnic Groups in Benue State, Nigeria." Ph.D. diss., University of Ibadan, Nigeria, 2014, https://repository.ui.edu.ng/server/api/core/bitstreams/38dbe277-8ed2-4893-94e1-97eb2208adef/content.

Ugbem, Comfort Erima, Ayokunle Olumuyiwa Omobowale, and Akinpelu Olanrewaju Olutayo. "Agba Performance and Igede Nationalism in North-Central Nigeria." *Journal of Environment and Culture* 11, no. 1 (June 2014): 14–29, https://www.researchgate.net/publication/334431989.

Ugbem, Comfort Erima, Ayokunle Olumuyiwa Omobowale, and Akinpelu Olanrewaju Olutayo. "Racial Politics and Hausa-Fulani Dominant Identity in Colonial and Post-Colonial Northern Nigeria." *The Nigerian Journal of Sociology and Anthropology* 17, no. 1 (June 2019): 85–100, https://doi.org/10.36108/NJSA/9102/71(0160).

United Nations Department of Economic and Social Affairs (UNDESA), Sustainable Development Goal No. 1, accessed February 4, 2024, https://sdgs.un.org/goals/goal1.

Willott, Chris. "'Get to the Bridge and I Will Help You to Cross': Merit, Personal Connections and Money in Access to Nigerian Higher Education." *African Spectrum* 46, no. 1 (April 2011): 85–108, https://doi.org/10.1177/000203971104600104.

World Bank, "Multidimensional Poverty Measure," *Poverty and Equity Brief*, last updated October 2024, https://www.worldbank.org/en/topic/poverty/brief/multidimensional-poverty-measure.

World Bank, "The World Bank in Nigeria: Overview," last updated October 14, 2024, https://www.worldbank.org/en/country/nigeria/overview.

World Bank, "World Development Indicators: Poverty and Inequality," accessed February 4, 2024, https://datatopics.worldbank.org/world-development-indicators/themes/poverty-and-inequality.html.

World Bank, "Worldwide Governance Indicators: Overview," accessed February 7, 2024, https://www.worldbank.org/en/publication/worldwide-governance-indicators.

Yakubu, Yahaya. "Ethnicity, Federal Character Principle and National Development in Nigeria: A Critical Evaluation." *Journal of Nation-Building and Policy Studies* 1, nos. 1 and 2 (June and November 2017): 7–23, https://doi.org/10.31920/2516-3132/2017/v1_2n1a1.

3

ETHNOREGIONAL INEQUALITY AND POVERTY

Social Policy as an Imperative to Stability and Inclusive Development in Sub-Saharan Africa

Emmanuel R. Aiyede and Adigun Agbaje

Introduction

Poverty and inequality have reached dire levels across the African subcontinent. As of 2019, World Bank data indicated that 41 percent of people in sub-Saharan Africa were living below the poverty line "in absolute destitution," according to Oxfam International. If current economic trends continue, World Bank estimates predict that 87 percent of the global poor will be concentrated in sub-Saharan Africa by 2030 (Seery, Okanda, & Lawson, 2019; World Bank, 2018). Furthermore, according to the United Nations Development Programme (UNDP), ten of the nineteen most unequal countries in the world are in sub-Saharan Africa, and southern Africa has the highest level of income inequality in the world (Odusola et al., 2017).[1] A 2019 Oxfam briefing paper emphasized that inequality has also reached a crisis point in West Africa, where the wealthiest 1 percent own more than everyone else in the region combined. As an example, the collective wealth of Nigeria's five richest individuals (US$29.9 billion) exceeded the federal government's 2017 budget; the wealthiest net roughly 150,000 times more from their wealth alone than the poorest 10 percent of Nigerians spend on their basic consumption in a year (Hallum & Obeng, 2019). According to Oxfam, governments in the region have done little to address these gross disparities.

The United States Agency for International Development (USAID) defines *inclusive development* as "an equitable development approach built on the understanding that every individual and community, of all diverse identities and experiences, is instrumental in the transformation of their own societies" (USAID, 2024).[2] Inclusive development has received increasing attention in the literature and discourse across disciplines, particularly as an underlying theme in the United

DOI: 10.4324/9781003357025-4

Nations *2030 Agenda for Sustainable Development*. But, as Joyeeta Gupta and Courtney Vegelin observed in a paper published in 2016,

> Achieving sustainable development has been hampered by trade-offs in favour of economic growth over social well-being and ecological viability, which may also affect the [SDGs]. . .. In contrast, the concept of inclusive development emphasizes the social, ecological and political dimensions of development.
>
> *(Gupta & Vegelin, 2016)*

Moreover, according to a 2016 United Nations report, "awareness of the importance of inclusion. . . has not yet been translated into political commitment or the necessary normative shifts that are imperative for inclusive development" (UN-DESA, 2016).

In an effort to conceptualize and quantify inclusive development, the World Economic Forum (WEF) developed the inclusive development index (IDI) in 2017 as part of its System Initiative on Shaping the Future of Economic Progress (Cann, 2018). The IDI was a composite global index designed to be "a more integrated and holistic" measure of a country's economic growth and development than gross domestic product (GDP) per capita (WEF, 2017).[3] In a study published in 2023, Oleksandr Dluhopolskyi and Alina Zhukovska showed an inverse relationship between the IDI and the Gini index (broadly, a summary measure of inequality) in developed countries but not in developing countries, proposing strategies to ensure that inclusive development can reduce economic inequality (Dluhopolskyi & Zhukovska, 2023).[4]

Extreme inequality and poverty hinder economic growth and stifle social mobility and political agency while also fueling instability and violent conflict. "Inequality is a catalyst for social tensions within communities," Oxfam warns, "with citizens' frustrations spilling to increase. . . violence in various forms" (Mayah et al., 2017).[5] Yet the news is not all bad. According to Matthew Martin, international director of Development Finance International,

> Extreme inequality is not inevitable, and you don't have to be a wealthy country to do something about it. We know that policies such as free public healthcare, safety nets for people who can't work, decent wages and a fair tax system have been proven to fight inequality. Failure to implement them is a political choice. . . with catastrophic economic and human costs.
>
> *(Whiting, 2020)*

Equity and inclusivity are threads woven throughout the *2030 Agenda for Sustainable Development* and the Sustainable Development Goals (SDGs) set forth therein. In addition to explicit pledges to "end poverty in all its forms everywhere" and to "reduce inequality within and among countries," the ideals of inclusivity, social stability, and equal access to resources and opportunity perfuse the SDGs (UN, 2015). Written between the lines is the reality that social policy lies at the heart of this collective global project.

Against the background of the subcontinent's pervasive horizontal and vertical inequalities, this chapter explores the literature on inequality in Africa as it relates to ethnicity and social policy to unravel linkages and obstacles to sustainable inclusive development. It examines the types of inequality—namely, horizontal (i.e., inequality *between* different societal groups) and vertical (i.e., inequality *within* certain groups, or among individuals within a society as a whole), each of which has both objective and subjective dimensions—along with the drivers of inequality and exclusion. Ample evidence suggests that inequalities among groups within a society may be a stronger impetus for conflict than inequalities among individuals. This linkage implicates not just social stability but prospects for inclusive development as well (Hillesund et al., 2018). This chapter argues that policies to address vertical inequality do not necessarily address horizontal inequality, and vice versa. Indeed, measures to ameliorate horizontal inequality may in fact serve to deepen vertical inequality (in either its objective or subjective forms).

We then investigate the interplay of horizontal inequality, social policy, and inclusive development, particularly in the context of the Social Policy Framework for Africa (AUSPF)—a promising methodology outlined by the African Union (AU) in 2009. For countries that chose to implement its policy prescriptions, the AUSPF could prove transformative to the social and economic structures that perpetuate inequalities by serving as a model for transcending the dominance of ethnic elites and promoting the economic and political empowerment of disadvantaged and marginalized populations in meaningful, practical ways. This chapter reviews the uptake—or lack thereof—of the AUSPF policy framework in African countries and finds that prevailing practices continue to reinforce the elites' economic and political power without addressing the needs and concerns of the poor and disempowered. It also finds that several African states have not sufficiently committed to reducing inequality and poverty. Although the AUSPF is not binding, we argue that states should be encouraged to adopt its normative foundations and policy guidelines that seek to break Africa's long-standing poverty and inequality cycles and usher in an era of inclusive development.

To achieve the urgently needed social protections that the AUSPF envisages, countries and leaders must renew commitments to social policy—and especially social investment—that have fallen by the wayside since the 1990s, when structural adjustment programs made World Bank and International Monetary Fund (IMF) loans conditional on economic and social reforms (Nsouli, 1989; Helleiner, 1992). These renewed commitments are imperative to change the wayward course of sub-Saharan Africa's economic and social development and to ensure long-term peace and stability, and they will require a continental approach that encompasses collaboration and sharing of experiences, successes, and challenges. Perhaps most importantly, to achieve the social progress that is encapsulated in the AUSPF—and that is essential for peace and stability on the continent—horizontal and vertical inequalities must be addressed in tandem.

Ethnicity and Inequality

Sociopolitical discourse on ethnoregional inequality considers ethnicity as a social difference or a politicization of difference and views the attendant challenges posed for political and social stability through that prism. Ethnically heterogeneous societies in which inequality coincides with group differences are often plagued by distrust, suspicion, marginalization, discrimination, and sometimes by ethnophobia and violent conflicts. Yet the relationship between ethnicity and the ethnic group on the one hand and inequality and social policy on the other is understudied, particularly in the context of discussions about fostering social stability, preventing conflict, and cultivating inclusive development.

Ethnicity analyses follow various pathways. One of the common ones scrutinizes ethnicity as a problem of politics and economy—specifically, of political competition (by elites, generally, for access to public offices or positions in government) or socioeconomic competition (among citizens, as members of subgroups of a larger society, for access to social amenities such as health and education services and resources). Both facets of this competition for access suggest struggles for inclusion: for dominance over or protection of (often exclusive) access to opportunities, whether they be social, economic, or political. This chapter explores the correlations between ethnicity, inequality, and social policy from these broader perspectives.

The concepts of the ethnic group and ethnicity attracted intellectual attention from scholars of African politics and development in the 1960s and 1970s. Efforts to define and clarify their meaning in the African context centered around the terms *tribe* and *tribalism*—as co-opted by the settler colonialist enterprise—as synonymous. To wit, what would be classified as *ethnic* in advanced Western countries was labeled *tribal* in Africa. In this usage, *tribal* connoted a strong ethnic identification with an implicit primitivity and insinuated a challenge to national integration and the legitimacy of the state. The presumption is that this version of ethnic consciousness will give way to national identification as a society modernizes and its social interactions become more rationalized. In other words, the primordial notion of ethnicity is seen as competing with or upstaging identification with the state, but the pursuit of national integration and the promotion of state legitimacy will gradually deepen national identity and supplant ethnic identification as primary (Osaghae, 1994).

However, the inability of some states to overcome the steadfastness of ethnic identity breeds the perception of a weak state or a backward civilization. States in which ethnic identification strengthens over time—a hallmark of deeply divided societies—are regarded as troubled states at risk of disintegration (Osaghae, 1994). Debates around these concepts have produced differing perspectives on ethnicity. In general, an ethnic group refers to a community of people or a group with a common culture, tradition, and sense of identity. Elements of this identity include shared language, customs, and rituals along with a collective consciousness of self, based on kin, in relation to the general *other* (Githongo, 2006).[6] That being said, African colonialism's arbitrary amalgamations of peoples into states, forcing multiple identities to coexist and compete. (Chapter 2 talks about the ramifications of this phenomenon in Nigeria.) Within these fabricated nationhoods, some groups invariably eclipsed others (Githongo, 2006).

Questions of how and how much group consciousness plays into the dynamics of ethnicity in the pursuit of public relevance, social and economic dominance, and political agency have given rise to two interpretations of ethnicity: primordialist and instrumentalist. The primordialist interpretation suggests that ethnic boundaries are natural, constituting an unchanging legacy acquired by individuals at birth that predates social interaction. This ethnic expression falls outside the framework of the consciousness of difference in relation to social, economic, or political competition. Conversely, the instrumentalist interpretation defines ethnic identity as voluntary, functional, and context-specific—a pragmatic response to socioeconomic and political pressures and "a basis for group action." It holds that ethnic groups exist and mutate, and that their potency is often situational (although instrumentalists would argue that the durability of ethnic boundaries belies this mutation) (Osaghae, 1994).[7] Yet both perspectives allow for ethnic groups to be exclusionary, to advance discriminatory practices, and to be mobilized against the state, or to act as a force for progress and accountability. Hence, ethnicity takes center stage in numerous realms that directly impact a nation's prospects for sustainable, inclusive development: distributive pressures and competition for access to resources and position; the quest for social capital and social justice; and state stability. Understanding the challenges of managing ethnic heterogeneity while harnessing its benefits therefore becomes crucial.

Dimensions of Inequality

African states have experienced an upsurge in vertical inequality (Nel, 2018). More often than not, levels of poverty and inequality coincide with regional, religious, or ethnic differences, and all these factors have been implicated in intra-state conflicts in Africa—including the many twenty-first-century conflicts over elections in Africa, notably in Côte d'Ivoire, Kenya, and Nigeria. Multidimensional inequalities relating to differences in urbanization, access to infrastructures and social resources (including water, electricity, hospitals, and schools), access to land, and access to public office and government employment also abound across regions and ethnic groups in most African countries. At the same time, ethnicity exemplifies that inequality is not purely a vertical phenomenon. In terms of income level gradations among common citizens of a state, inequalities and resulting inter-group tensions also exist between culturally and regionally distinct identity groups. This type of *horizontal* inequality differs from typical (or *vertical*) inequality. Horizontal inequality ties more closely to the instrumentalist view of ethnicity, in which the ethnic group is socially constructed around identity traits such as ancestry, language, religion, and region of origin. As social constructs, per the instrumentalist approach, ethnic group boundaries are malleable and fluid. However, they are costly to reshape, and, as such, they tend to have continuity over time (Stewart, 2005, 2010). Thus, horizontal inequality refers to inequalities between groups of people distinguishable by each one's common ancestral, regional, racial, religious, cultural, or linguistic identity markers. As we discuss below, inequality in its various dimensions can be the basis of centrifugal mobilization; taken to extremes, it can enflame societal tensions to the point that they erupt into violent conflict or even civil war.

Both horizontal and vertical inequality have two dimensions (or subdimensions, if you will): objective (or actual) and subjective (or perceived). The former refers to empirical measures of inequality, whereas the latter refers to the perception that inequality exists regardless of reality. Arnim Langer and Saturo Mikami have observed that objective and subjective horizontal inequality do not always coincide. In a study of five sub-Saharan African countries (Ghana, Kenya, Nigeria, Uganda, and Zimbabwe), they identified several factors that account for discrepancies between actual and perceived horizontal inequality. They found that people's individual socioeconomic circumstances tend to distort their perceptions of their group's situation and relative position, and that people's perceptions of inter-group political inequality color their perceptions of prevailing socioeconomic inequalities. Other factors that influence the mismatch between objective and subjective horizontal inequality include a lack of objective data (or misleading comparisons); manipulation of perceptions by elites or group leaders; inaccurate media reporting; inefficient access to information; misjudgment of group size; and cross-dimensional contamination resulting from political exclusion or marginalization.[8]

Horizontal inequality is inherently multifaceted, encompassing the economic, the social, the cultural, and the political. Moreover, one group may be advantaged in one regard and disadvantaged in another. Economic horizontal inequalities include unequal access to or possession of financial, human, and natural resource–based assets, along with disparities in income levels and employment opportunities (which in turn depend on such assets, along with general economic conditions). Social horizontal inequality entails access to social services, such as health care, education, and housing, while cultural horizontal inequality relates to the recognition and standings of different groups' languages, customs, norms, and practices within the national milieu. Political horizontal inequality refers to the distribution of political opportunities and power among groups (including control over the presidency, the cabinet, parliamentary assemblies, the bureaucracy, local and regional governments, and the armed forces), and to people's ability to participate politically, to express their needs, and to have those needs met by the state (Fukuda-Purr, Langer, & Mine, 2013).[9]

Drivers of Inequality and Exclusion in Sub-Saharan Africa

Drivers of inequality on the subcontinent are diverse, and they vary from country to country. Some derive from historical factors such as settler colonialism or geographic factors such as post-colonial land reforms (Chancel et al., 2023). Others materialize out of policy approaches taken by governments. Although the root causes of inequality are rarely the same from country to country, common culprits include restricted (often patrimonialist) access to land, capital, and markets; inequitable tax systems; corruption; and vulnerability to unfavorable global markets. A 2017 UNDP report identified three basic structural drivers of inequality in sub-Saharan Africa. The first is a highly dualistic economic structure characterized by limited, preferential employment of a burgeoning labor elite in the government, multinational company, and resource sectors, while the majority of laborers earn low wages in the informal and subsistence sectors. The second is a high concentration of human capital and land among certain groups and regions—more so in eastern and southern Africa (especially in Kenya, Zimbabwe, and South Africa) than elsewhere on the continent. The third is the limited distributive capacity of the state, which is often linked to the so-called natural resource curse, an urban bias in public policy, and ethnic and gender inequalities. In terms of public policy and state redistributive capacity, inequality is due to "regressive taxes, unresponsive wage structures and inadequate investment in education, health and social protection for vulnerable and marginalised groups" (Odusola et al., 2017).[10]

Any discussion of horizontal inequality in Africa must note that the formation of identity groups dates back to and even before colonial times. In many sub-Saharan African states, regional, ethnic, and religious differences emerged over generations, heavily influenced by colonial land settlement schemes and modes of colonial governance that treated regions and ethnic groups separately and disparately. Colonialist policies also shifted ethnic group configurations by arbitrarily amalgamating distinct groups into discrete administrative units, which in turn benefitted from different levels of access to infrastructure, resources, education, and employment (Stewart, Mkandawire, & Katayanagi, 2013). The exploitative practices and institutions forced on the continent during colonial rule further exacerbated ethnic group differences by concentrating political and economic power in the hands of the few—the burgeoning elites who became the dominant socioeconomic and political classes in their respective nations after independence. See Chapters 1 and 2 for more detail on how these policies and practices played out in Kenya and Nigeria.

Geography was also a factor. The ethnic groups inhabiting the central bureaucratic structure in West Africa, for instance, were mostly those that were situated close to the coast or the capital cities. Having had more interaction with the colonial authorities and earlier access to Western education, they became the employees of choice in state institutions, the civil service, and state-owned enterprises. In some instances, the colonial authorities privileged particular groups or subgroups, thereby creating artificial hierarchies within ethnolinguistic or ethnoreligious groups—and effectively inaugurating guilds of elites that would become the ruling classes after independence. On the colonial bias of education in Nigeria, for example, Sonia Graham has observed that "it was during colonialism that regional differences manifested in the sphere of education," which then had "a knock-on effect on the regional formation of human capital and general economic development" (Graham, 1966).[11] Abdul Raufu Mustapha has attributed the dramatic inequality between Nigeria's eastern and western regions and the country's north partly to the gap in educational attainment (again, a direct result of colonial administrative policies) and partly to geographic access and natural economic endowments. In spite of the federal character/affirmative action principle that has been in place since the 1970s and the rotation of offices, Mustapha has observed that inequalities in Nigeria have deepened rather than decreased in some significant areas (Mustapha, 2006).[12]

In Nigeria and elsewhere, geoeconomic considerations compounded colonial-era horizontal inequalities. Groups in the hinterlands have historically suffered from infrastructure and communication deficits. In many countries, outside of capital cities (which grew around the original colonial headquarters), transportation infrastructure was constructed with the primary (if not sole) purpose of moving agricultural products and other goods from the outlands to the seaports for export. In most countries, government policies after independence did little to mitigate these disadvantages. Education and health expenditures, too, often heavily favored the capitals and were biased in favor of elites. Hospitals and medical facilities tended to cater to the needs of the rich rather than providing preventive health care for the masses. And secondary and tertiary educational institutions prioritized elite students over those from less affluent backgrounds.

Much has been written about urban bias as a driver of regional inequalities, especially between north and south, in Ghana, Nigeria, and Côte d'Ivoire (Langer & Mikami, 2013; Mustapha, 2006). Urban bias describes the ramifications of colonialist infrastructure concentration in areas inhabited by settlers; those areas became the post-colonial urban centers, and their populations have enjoyed disproportionate access to resources, institutions, and modernity relative to outlying areas (Odusola et al., 2017; Kimenyi, 2013). In the case of Nigeria, colonial concentration in the southeast and southwest led to significant infrastructural development (in the form of schools, hospitals, roads, and other resources), but the northern part of the country had no such influx of resources. As Western education and Christianity spread rapidly in southern Nigeria, with it came infrastructural development; by contrast, Muslim leaders in the north resisted Western education proffered by Christian missionaries, setting the stage for the north-south development disparity and the significant regional inequalities evident today (Afigbo, 1991; Okonwo, 2023). (For more on the north-south divide in Nigeria as a legacy of colonialism, see Chapters 2 and 11.)

Clientelism and corruption also serve to increase horizontal inequality. Elites in sub-Saharan African countries in particular are notorious for using the powers of the state for personal enrichment and empowerment (van de Walle, 2009). Clientelism commonly manifests through ethnic patronage, which worsens horizontal inequality by excluding certain ethnic groups from access to political power. This ethnic patronage erodes public trust and perpetuates colonial-era identity politics. While some leaders, including those in Nigeria and Côte d'Ivoire, have introduced various affirmative action measures and ethnic quotas to foster equitability among different regions and ethnic groups, those policies have had limited success and tend to be controversial. More often, post-independence African leaders have simply entrenched their own ethnic groups' dominance. In some countries (Kenya and Nigeria, for example), politicians have even promoted violence as a means to win multiparty elections and preserve or gain power (Kimenyi, 2013; Onwudiwe & Berwind-Dart, 2010).

Horizontal Inequality, Social Stability, and Inclusive Development

Conventional wisdom holds that alleviating group-based inequality in Africa, whether subjective or objective, is critical for social stability and conflict prevention—and ultimately for sustainable inclusive development. To this effect, any inquiry into the linkages between horizontal inequality and conflict must examine the various dimensions of group-based inequalities. Any such inquiry must also look at how institutional political processes manage horizontal inequality to ensure peace—or fail to do so, thus worsening societal divisions that can escalate into violent conflicts and even civil wars. Recent research on sources of violent conflicts has found uneven group access to political power and economic resources to be one of the most salient underlying causes of social instability. Severe horizontal inequalities invoke frustration and discontent that can instigate group mobilization to violence along ethnic, religious, or regional lines (Stewart, 2000, 2005).

A common political practice among African leaders is to focus on ameliorating grievances and threats from elites who perceive or proclaim inequality (be it objective or subjective) and have the capacity to challenge the government by leveraging ethnicity at a mass scale (whether by patronage or incorporation of their and/or other groups' political bases). Such ameliorative measures can take the form of quotas, elite inclusion in government, or rotation of public offices across ethnic groups or regions. These types of initiatives are often ad hoc, situational approaches that reflect political strategies—short-term fixes to avert conflict and provide a sense, if not always a reality, of commitment to inclusion. Limited in their reach and duration, they typically expire upon changes in leadership. When government neglects or discontinues such distributive measures, whether institutionalized (such as policies around Nigeria's federal character principle described in Chapter 2) or non-institutionalized (such as the situational approaches described above), the resulting anger and frustration can foment inter-ethnic tension and conflict.

Meaningful policy prescriptions targeting horizontal inequality in a divided society must acknowledge ethnic heterogeneity, if not as a root cause, then as a primary causal factor, and they must do so systemically. A federalist formula, both for conflict management and for harnessing the benefits of diversity, is one such approach. Federalism uniquely supports the idea of unity in diversity. It furnishes a divided society with a sphere of collaboration and centralized governance and, at the same time, provides a degree of autonomy for the constitutive units. Multiple layers of governance enable cooperation, competition, and experimentation that dynamize government while creating platforms for interaction and negotiation over common concerns, thereby strengthening the state (and, albeit indirectly, sustaining its territorial integrity) (Kincaid, 2001; Aiyede, 2009). Federalism recognizes disparity among groups and the necessity of protecting each group's distinct needs through state institutions. For instance, most federal states have bicameral national legislatures in which one assembly comprises equal representation of the federation's component states or territories, while the other's membership is determined based on population (Tsebelis & Money, 1997).

Frances Stewart has identified two distinct policy methodologies typically employed to address horizontal inequalities. The first is a direct (or affirmative action) model, which targets deprived groups in various ways to give preferential treatment in areas like employment, education, or political representation (Stewart, 2005, 2010). Affirmative action seeks to actively dismantle institutionalized or informal cultural norms and systems that perpetuate group-based disadvantages and the inequalities that those norms and systems breed. It builds on the ideals of democracy, integration, and pluralism to promote inclusiveness by leveling the playing field among people based on particular identity categories (such as ethnicity, race, religion, geographic location, gender, sexual orientation, and physical disability). The goal is to change the distribution of or access to jobs, education, health, wealth, or other social goods in order to reduce inequality among groups. Affirmative action measures are a fairly common practice in federations (Sowell, 2004). The second policy strategy to address group-based inequalities engages indirect "universal policies," which by design benefit poorer groups disproportionately. Stewart explains, "Where poorer groups are regionally concentrated, policies to promote the development of poorer regions generally reduce horizontal inequality. Progressive taxation and policies targeting resources towards lower-income individuals" do so as well. Stewart notes that anti-discrimination legislation is another form of indirect policy, though one that requires a strong legal system for enforcement (Stewart, 2005, 2010).

Reducing horizontal inequality often calls for a combination of direct and indirect policies. Yet measures to address vertical inequality do not necessarily address horizontal inequality, and vice versa. Indeed, those aimed at alleviating horizontal inequality may serve to deepen vertical inequality in its objective or subjective forms.[13] Elites, in turn, can manipulate subjective perceptions of vertical inequality to mobilize citizens either to pressure the government for change or to generate uprisings that they (the elites) can then exploit for political purposes—ends that frequently serve to reinforce horizontal inequality. To reiterate, subjective inequality does not always coincide with objective inequality. Perception matters: One group may consider itself disadvantaged relative to other groups in terms of access to economic resources, for example, when in fact it is better off than other groups. This perceptual disconnect may be owed to a particular group's relative non-visibility in political echelons relative to another's.

Yoichi Mine, Frances Stewart, Sakiko Fukuda-Parr, and Thandika Mkandawire have investigated how political institutions interact with objective and subjective inequalities, and how those interactions influence social stability. Focusing on power-dispersing institutions, power-concentrating institutions, and dimensions of centralization versus decentralization, they argue that political exclusion and the ways in which people perceive their positions in a political system matter for stability. Their study shows that power-sharing through cooperative or coalition government and decentralization of power to regions or districts both serve to reduce the likelihood of conflict. They further suggest that violent conflicts are more likely to arise in regions or countries where economic, social, political, and cultural status inequalities exist concurrently and in which some groups are disadvantaged across every dimension. They maintain that the simultaneous presence of severe political and socioeconomic horizontal inequalities makes for an extremely volatile sociopolitical environment: Not only do the excluded political elites have a strong incentive to mobilize their supporters to violence along ethnic lines, but they are also likely to find it relatively easy to gain support among their ethnic constituencies (Mine et al., 2013).

Clearly, then, initiatives to address both objective and subjective inequality are essential to fostering stability and reducing the likelihood of conflict, which makes the state's capacity for (and commitment to) reducing inequality and promoting shared prosperity—at the individual and group levels alike—crucial to development. Put simply, sustainable inclusive development requires implementing policies to reduce vertical and horizontal inequality, a central fact that underscores the criticality of social policy in Africa. Unfortunately, African states have largely withdrawn from social expenditure commitments prescribed in the structural adjustment programs of the 1990s. Making matters worse, the widespread influence of neoliberal approaches to economic development has positioned social expenditure as a trade-off to growth. Neoliberalism sacrifices social development for economic development and equity for efficiency. Yet reducing both horizontal and vertical inequalities calls for measures that "enhance social rights and empowerment, protect citizens from social contingencies and poverty—and ultimately enable them to strive towards their life goals" (Hujo & Yi, 2015).[14] Inasmuch as the objective of development is to improve the quality of life for individuals in a society, development strategies must integrate measures to ensure that people's well-being is paramount. As such, social expenditure is vastly more than merely payment for social consumption that reduces savings and investment: It is a vital form of social investment that complements—and in reality buttresses—economic development (Townsend, 2004).

Studies have shown that rising inequality has negative effects on productivity and long-term economic growth, and on many indicators of individual and group well-being (Boushey, 2019; Wilkinson & Pickett, 2018; Voitchovsky, 2011; IMF, 2014). On the other hand, countries that invest in expanding education, infrastructure, productivity, and social mobility to poorer regions grow faster because they can draw upon more of their workforce, more effectively match people to the right jobs, and generally improve output—all while reducing inequality and building fairness and inclusivity into the system (Shafik, 2018).[15] Market and state activities can mutually reinforce equity, inclusiveness, and growth. And countries that adopt social welfare policies are far better situated to achieve the goals, set forth in the UN's *2030 Agenda for Sustainable Development*, of universally reducing poverty and inequality and leaving no one behind (Barr, 2018; UN, 2015; UNSDG, 2019).

Social Policy Performance among African States

Africa is the second-most unequal continent in the world and is rapidly becoming the global epicenter of extreme poverty. According to Oxfam International, the number of people in Africa living on less than $1.90 a day (the World Bank's benchmark for extreme poverty, based on purchasing power parity [PPP] for 2011) is rising, and the richest 0.0001 percent own 40 percent of the entire continent's wealth.[16] As of 2019, Oxfam reported that 41 percent of the people in sub-Saharan Africa were living in "absolute destitution" (Seery, Okanda, & Lawson, 2019; Hallum & Obeng, 2019). As of 2023—in part due to the COVID-19 pandemic—35.4 percent of people in sub-Saharan Africa were living below the poverty line of $2.15 (based on PPP for 2017) (Baah et al., 2023). The World Bank predicts that by 2030, 87 percent of the global poor will reside in Africa if current economic trends continue (Seery, Okanda, & Lawson, 2019; Hallum & Obeng, 2019).

Many states in Africa have the capacity to transform institutions that can work to alleviate horizontal and vertical inequalities. Governments can use social policy mechanisms such as courting greater investment to transform health and educational institutions, for example. They can also implement economic policies targeted at the poor and at marginalized groups. Yet most have not done so. No African country ranks in the top ten of those *most* committed to reducing inequality, although several have demonstrated commitments to doing so and have made progress. In 2019, Oxfam identified Ethiopia and Namibia as having made significant strides in reducing inequality, largely by increasing social spending in the education and health sectors. Between 2005 and 2015, for example, Ethiopia brought an additional fifteen million children into school and employed more than four hundred thousand primary school teachers (Seery, Okanda, & Lawson, 2019; Martin et al., 2020). Naturally, statistics like these also bode well for reducing poverty.

Conversely, however, the Oxfam Commitment to Reducing Inequality Index in 2020 ranked Nigeria and South Sudan second-to-last and last, respectively, among the 158 countries least committed to fighting inequality. Based on data from the World Poverty Clock, which gives real-time estimates through 2030 for almost every country in the world, the Brookings Institution announced in 2018 that Nigeria had overtaken India as the nation with the highest number of people living in extreme poverty: In India, 73 million out of India's population of 1.324 billion (or 5.5 percent) were living in conditions of extreme poverty; in Nigeria, that figure was 87 million out of 200 million (or 43.5 percent). Moreover, while poverty rates in India continue to fall, extreme poverty in Nigeria is growing at a rate of six people every minute (Kharas, 2018). The 2019 global Multidimensional Poverty Index (MPI) found that the number of "multidimensionally poor" Nigerians increased from 86 million to 98 million between 2007 and 2017; in the 2022 MPI, that number rose to 133 million, or 63 percent of the population (UNDP, 2019).[17] As elsewhere in Africa, poverty in Nigeria has strong regional and ethnic correlations. In Nigeria, Ghana, and Côte d'Ivoire, for instance, clear divisions in terms of the distribution of poverty exist between north and south (Ukiwo, 2013; Langer & Mikami, 2013). In Kenya, access to health care, piped water, and electricity are widely disparate across provinces (Githongo, 2006; Kimenyi, 2013).

Given these and many other dire statistics, it is not at all surprising that social protections in many African countries are anemic at best. A 2017 report by the International Labour Organization (ILO) that analyzed coverage, benefits, and public expenditures on social protection for children, working-age women and men, and older persons around the world found that Africa—"where human needs are largest"—has the largest proportion of its population lacking access to social protection (ILO, 2017).[18] Many African countries' national constitutions, including those of Nigeria, Kenya, and Ghana, refer to social protection as a right that the state is duty-bound to uphold, but this right is not always enforceable. Some countries have given effect to this right by codifying social assistance programs derived from international law or the doctrines that inform it (such as the 1948 Universal Declaration of Human Rights and the 1981 African Charter on Human and People's Rights). Even so, these top-down laws must be accompanied by social accountability mechanisms and bottom-up initiatives that can empower citizens to ensure that governments deliver social assistance and other services effectively and fairly (UNDP, 2019).[19]

Stephen Devereux notes that most African countries have ratified international social protection treaties such as the Universal Declaration of Human Rights, the International Covenant on Economic, Social and Cultural Rights (1966), the Convention on the Elimination of All Forms of Discrimination Against Women (1979), the Convention on the Rights of the Child (1989), and the Convention on the Rights of Persons with Disabilities (2006) (Devereux, 2020). However, as of this volume's publication, only fourteen countries had ratified the ILO's Minimum Standards of Social Security Convention (1952), which advocates for a rights-based package that guarantees access to health care for all, as well as income security for children, people of working age, and older persons (ILO, 2022). Low-income countries have relied on donors to develop national social protection policies and to fund social assistance programs, and few African countries operate government-run social assistance programs on a national scale. While most countries in eastern and southern Africa lack national social protection policies, they have longer histories of delivering social assistance to their citizens relative to their western African counterparts. State-run social assistance programs are more common in middle-income countries that have the technical and financial capacity to design and implement social programs without requiring advice or support from donor agencies or international financial institutions. For most donor-driven social assistance programs, sustainability questions remain should donors withdraw financial or technical assistance (Devereux, 2020) (Table 3.1).

According to an International Social Security Association joint survey, as of 2019, only seven countries—Botswana, Eswatini, Kenya, Lesotho, Namibia, Mauritius, and Seychelles—had universal mandatory old-age income security programs. Most countries do have an old-age income security program related to contributory earnings, although such programs are often confined to the formal sector and thus limited in coverage. Only ten countries had any form of unemployment security as of 2019 (ISSA & USSSA, 2019).

The Way Forward

Inequality, poverty, and social polarization have been on the rise for at least the last two decades in Africa (Amponsah, Agbola, & Mahmood, 2023), and these trends make efforts to augment social inclusion and alleviate inequality and poverty all the more critical as development objectives for sub-Saharan Africa. Tackling horizontal and vertical inequalities will require African states and their leadership to change their social protection orientation. An important step in the right direction came in 2008, when the African Union Conference of Ministers in Charge of Social Development ratified the AUSPF—"an overarching policy structure to assist African Union Member States to strengthen and give increasing priority to

TABLE 3.1 National Social Protection Policies or Strategies in Africa by Region, 2019

Region	*Countries with a National Social Protection Policy or Strategy*	*Countries with No National Social Protection Policy or Strategy*
West Africa	Burkina Faso, Cabo Verde, Côte d'Ivoire, Gambia, Ghana, Liberia, Mali, Nigeria, Senegal, Sierra Leone	Benin, Guinea, Guinea-Bissau, Togo
Central Africa	Burundi, Central African Republic, Chad, Democratic Republic of Congo, Gabon, São Tomé and Príncipe	Cameroon, Congo, Equatorial Guinea
East Africa	Comoros, Djibouti, Ethiopia, Kenya, Madagascar, Rwanda, Somalia, Tanzania (mainland + Zanzibar), Uganda	Eritrea, Mauritius, Seychelles, South Sudan, Sudan
Southern Africa	Eswatini, Lesotho, Malawi, Mozambique, Namibia, Zambia, Zimbabwe	Angola, Botswana, South Africa
North Africa	Mauritania	Algeria, Egypt, Libya, Morocco, Tunisia, Western Sahara

Source: Stephen Devereux "Policy Pollination: A Brief History of Social Protection's Brief History in Africa," IDS Working Paper No. 543 (Brighton, UK: Institute of Development Studies, December 2020), 39.

their national social policies and hence promote human empowerment and development" (African Union, 2008).[20] The AUSPF provides ample guidance for the type of transformative social protection policy needed to reverse course in Africa. The challenge that remains is to achieve widespread implementation, taking into account the varying contexts across countries.

As a construct, social policy refers to "collective interventions in the economy to influence access to and the incidence of adequate and secure livelihoods and income" (Mkandawire, 2004).[21] It plays redistributive, protective, and developmental roles in society and is central to building capabilities and social capital (and ultimately, agency), deepening democracy, and fostering sustainable inclusive development (Mkandawire, 2008). According to the AU, a continent-wide approach to social policy will yield substantial gains—including the reduction of inequality (African Union, 2015). In short, social policy is the way forward.

In post-independence Africa, individual governments were largely left to their own devices to grapple with social policy until the 2000s. In 2004, the newly launched AU, the successor organization to the post-independence era Organisation of African Unity, oversaw the first in a series of continent-level meetings and initiatives intended to assist AU member states in formulating and implementing national social policies. There, in Ouagadougou, Burkina Faso, member states committed to strengthening social protection schemes and extending them to previously excluded workers and their families. In 2006, the Livingstone and Yaoundé Calls for Action went a step further, calling on governments to include social protection programs in their national development plans and budgets. The eleventh African regional meeting of the ILO in 2007 and subsequent regional meetings in 2008 on investing in social protection in Africa culminated in the AUSPF (African Union, 2008). After an extensive consultation process, all AU member states endorsed the AUSPF in January 2009.

The AUSPF draws on the United Nations ideal of enhancing human capabilities and ensuring minimum standards of well-being and dignity for all. The framework ties directly into the AU's vision of "an integrated, prosperous and peaceful Africa. . . driven and managed by its own citizens and representing a dynamic force in the international arena." According to the AUSPF, this vision requires "build[ing] human capital, break[ing] the intergenerational poverty cycle and reduc[ing] the growing inequalities that constrain Africa's economic and social development." The framework provides an operational definition of social protection that is instrumental, pragmatic, and comprehensive and highlights linkages to other social sectors. It conceptualizes social protection as "responses by the state and society to protect citizens from risks, vulnerabilities and deprivations" and to ensure "a minimum standard of livelihood" for all people in a given country—specifically, measures to ensure education and health care, social welfare, livelihood, and access to employment and stable income. The AUSPF goes beyond social protections as mechanisms for providing assistance against economic risks and livelihood shocks to address social risks, including "social exclusion, discrimination, and violations of minority rights." It aims to provide a model for governments to combine employment and income distribution policies to reduce poverty, with the overarching objective of facilitating "sustainable social development focusing on social integration with access to basic social services" (African Union, 2008; Devereux & Sabates-Wheeler, 2004; SCCRRC, 2005).

In order to generate economic growth, increase participation from all levels of society, and ensure that people across the socioeconomic spectrum benefit equally, the AUSPF outlines eighteen thematic social issues with significant interlinkages: population and development; labor and employment; social protection; health; infectious diseases; migration; education; agriculture, food, and nutrition; the family; children, adolescents, and youth; aging; disability; gender equality and women's empowerment; culture; urban development; environmental sustainability; the impact of globalization and trade liberalization; and good governance, anti-corruption, and the rule of law (African Union, 2008). More broadly, the framework lays out four functions of social policy for achieving progressive development: reproduction, production, redistribution, and social protection. Importantly, the AUSPF does not segregate economic measures from social transformation measures; it seeks to replace the tendency to see social policy as consumption, instead taking a strategic view of social policy as investment.

In terms of production and reproduction, the framework takes a life-cycle approach that addresses the requisites for achieving safe birth of wanted and healthy babies of both sexes; their nurture, health care, and basic and continuing education; and their empowerment to contribute to the economy and society. It also addresses responsible family life; support for the temporarily or permanently incapacitated; and dignity and care for the elderly and terminally ill. The AUSPF recognizes that production and growth depend on social relationships between a range of producers and service providers and their access to resources; on their rights and obligations in the contexts of association and contract, including commercial and professional associations, trade unions, civil society, and political and administrative organizations; and on their governance, responsiveness, and accountability. Furthermore, it defines the relationships between basic resources, capital, and labor to ensure sustainability of their mutual use, including adaptation and resilience in the face of climate change and other exogenous shocks. The production approach visualizes an Africa that balances the requirements for growth with the ability to negotiate with external forces on equal terms. This new paradigm will develop African economies' productive capacities by shifting from low employment generation and natural resource extraction to high employment in labor-intensive manufacturing, the agro-industry, and service provision. The AUSPF acknowledges that this shift will require adequate investment in both infrastructure and human capital as well as increased productivity and incomes in the informal sector (African Union, 2010).

Redistribution involves the role of government in ensuring equitable opportunities and outcomes through development strategies that benefit society. In this sense, protective policies and interventions enhance the capacity of the poor and marginalized to escape from poverty and enable them to manage risks and shocks. Further, the AUSPF calls for a commitment to a national "social protection floor" that provides access to basic services (including health care, nutrition, education, and housing) and basic income for all. Not only will this universal access offer a way to break the poverty cycle, but it will also afford those trapped in that cycle the chance to live with dignity. And it emphasizes "the need to strengthen existing national social protection systems and to implement new ones to ensure that all the vulnerable groups are included in mainstream development" (African Union, 2010).

The AUSPF implementation plan provides guidelines to support national governments in formulating and implementing progressive social policies, to assist AU member states when country-specific social challenges and situations arise, and to harmonize country-level plans to honor preexisting commitments by member states (African Union, 2010). In addition, in 2022, the AU adopted into its charter an additional protocol on the rights of citizens to social protection and social security. The charter reaffirms that "the right to social protection is a human right," and that signatories to the protocol "have the obligation to ensure that social protection is available, accessible, adequate, affordable and transparent" (African Union, 2022). All fifty-four AU member states have ratified the AU charter (ACHPR, 2024).

Conclusion

African societies remain mired in escalating horizontal and vertical inequality in its subjective and objective forms. Policymakers and academic researchers should prioritize horizontal inequalities, as research has shown group-based inequality coinciding with identity categories such as region, religion, and ethnicity to be a major factor in the intense political competition, distrust, frustration, and conflict that continue to destabilize sub-Saharan African states and render them fragile.[22] Many countries have taken steps to cultivate inclusion by deconcentrating and dispersing power through power-sharing frameworks and affirmative action. However, these measures are often limited and only effective in the short term. Strategies that address horizontal inequalities—including targeted and universal social protection initiatives—will strengthen these policies. The goal is to establish social protection floors that guarantee universal access to basic services and basic income for all.

The AUSPF offers a road map to achieve this goal. Yet many sub-Saharan African states have not adequately committed to reducing inequality or to implementing the kinds of inclusive social policies that are needed. Although the AUSPF is not binding, efforts must be made to proselytize its normative foundations and its doctrine of social policy, encompassing production, reproduction, redistribution, and social protection, as vital elements of any national social protection architecture. Power-sharing and affirmative action measures should be proportional with government policies to promote progressive taxation, boost social spending, strengthen labor market protection, invest in agriculture, and bolster land rights for smallholder farmers. Additionally, policymakers must ensure women's access to land; reverse urban bias in services and economic opportunities; promote labor-intensive industries; set and uphold minimum wages; strengthen capacities to keep the wealthy from evading taxes; introduce strong social protection programs; and end all forms of exclusion (Seery, Okanda, & Lawson, 2019).

To end the cycles of inequality that subjugate many and perpetuate poverty in sub-Saharan Africa, leaders must work to change the culture of governance and break from policies and norms that sustain the concentration of wealth, income, and power among elites. Doing so will require governments to adopt a broader approach to social policy that recognizes its multiple facets and hinges on the principle of solidarity, which holds that societal benefits and obligations should be shared fairly, equally, and justly among members of the society (Jalsenjak, 2020). As the United Nations *World Social Report 2020* noted,

> Rising inequality is not inevitable. Inequality levels and trends differ among countries that are at similar levels of development and equally exposed to trade,

technological innovation and even the effects of climate change. National policies and institutions do matter.

(UNDESA, 2020)[23]

Measures to address horizontal inequality that coincide with regional, religious, and ethnic divides yet only focus on incorporating elites—and therefore fail to respond to persistent vertical inequality—are insufficient for longer-term stability and sustainable inclusive development. Ethnic mobilization can be used both to preserve privilege and to sue for inclusion. Notwithstanding the urgency of addressing horizontal inequality to foster stability and inclusive development, policies must also be targeted at vertical inequality (namely, raising the incomes of the poor and providing basic needs such as food, health care, education, and transportation) to ensure resilience and bolster social cohesion. Addressing vertical inequality will make it easier to address subjective horizontal inequality; it will also go a long way toward reducing the mismatch between subjective and objective inequality. Such efforts to ensure that all Africans are able to live productive and fulfilling lives should be guided by the UN's SDGs pledge to "leave no one behind" (UNSDG, 2019).[24] And they should be driven by the overarching principles of inclusive development: the fair, equitable, and just distribution of socioeconomic and political benefits across ethnic, religious, and social strata in order to ameliorate inequalities and empower all—including the marginalized—as global citizens.

Notes

1 Ayodele Odusola et al., eds., *Income Inequality Trends in Sub-Saharan Africa: Divergence, Determinants and Consequences* (New York, NY: United Nations Development Programme, 2017), iii, 2. These figures are derived from the Gini index. See World Bank DataBank, 2024.

2 Editor's note: Although the USAID website was unavailable as of publication due to the U.S. political situation, USAID's definition of inclusive development appears elsewhere, including in the annual program statement for a USAID/Nigeria initiative called Partnerships for Progress. See USAID/Nigeria, 2024. Unfortunately, the future of that program, along with countless others funded through USAID, is uncertain as of this writing.

3 World Economic Forum, *The Inclusive Growth and Development Report 2017* (Geneva, Switzerland: World Economic Forum, 2017), v.

4 Oleksandr Dluhopolskyi and Alina Zhukovska, "Inclusive Development as an Instrument to Overcome Economic Inequality and Discrimination," *Economics—Innovative and Economics Research Journal* 11, no. 1 (2023): 24. According to the World Bank, the Gini index measures "the extent to which the distribution of income or consumption among individuals or households within an economy deviates from a perfectly equal distribution" (World Bank DataBank, 2024).

5 Emmanuel Mayah et al., "Inequality in Nigeria: Exploring the Drivers," Oxfam Policy Paper (Oxford, UK: Oxfam International, May 2017), 5.

6 John Githongo, "Inequality, Ethnicity and the Fight Against Corruption in Africa: A Kenyan Perspective," *Economic Affairs* 26, no. 4 (December 2006): 19.

7 Eghosa E. Osaghae, "Ethnicity in Africa or African Ethnicity: The Search for a Contextual Understanding," in *African Perspectives on Development: Controversies, Dilemmas and Openings*, ed. Ulf Himmelstrand, Kabiru Kinyanjui, and Edward Mburugu (Kampala, Uganda: Fountain Press, 1994), 139.

8 Cross-dimensional contamination refers to individuals who perceive their ethnic group to be economically disadvantaged (or advantaged) compared with other ethnic groups; people who belong to a group that sees itself as politically excluded are more likely to view their ethnic group as economically disadvantaged relative to other ethnic groups (Langer & Smedts, 2013). See also Arnim Langer and Saturo Mikami, "The Relationship Between Objective and Subjective Horizontal Inequalities: Evidence from Five African Countries," in *Preventing Violent Conflict in Africa: Inequalities, Perceptions and Institutions*, eds. Yoichi Mine et al., (New York, NY: Palgrave Macmillan, 2013), 245–46.

9 Sakiko Fukuda-Purr, Arnim Langer, and Yoichi Mine, "Disentangling the Linkages Between Horizontal Inequalities and Political Institutions," in *Preventing Violent Conflict in Africa: Inequalities, Perceptions and Institutions*, eds. Yoichi Mine et al. (New York, NY: Palgrave Macmillan, 2013), 3–4.

10 The natural resource curse refers to the paradox of countries rich in natural resources that struggle to harness that wealth to boost their economies and consequently suffer from lower economic growth than countries without abundant natural resources (Ross, 1999).

11 Sonia F. Graham, *Government and Mission Education in Northern Nigeria, 1900–1919* (Ibadan, Nigeria: Ibadan University Press, 1966), 136.

12 For more on the federal character principle in Nigeria, see Chapter 2.

13 For example, the quota system in tertiary education, rooted in the federal character principle, aims to address disparities in access to education by giving preference to students from less developed or educationally disadvantaged states. However, religion and culture preclude girls from attending school in certain parts of the country. Their lack of access to education lowers their income potential in the labor market, thereby deepening vertical inequality in households that have boys versus girls (Dauda & Oyeleke, 2021).

14 Katja Hujo and Ilcheong Yi, *Social Policy and Inclusive Development*, UNRISD Classics, Vol. 1 (Geneva, Switzerland: United Nations Research Institute for Social Development, 2015), 3.

15 Nemat Shafik, "A New Social Contract," *Finance and Development* 55, no. 4 (December 2018): 7.

16 In September 2022, the World Bank updated the international poverty line to $2.15 per person per day, based on 2017 PPPs (World Bank, 2022).

17 According to the World Bank, the MPI is "a means to capture the complexity of poverty that considers dimensions of well-being beyond just monetary poverty." It measures the percentage of households in a given country that are deprived along three dimensions—monetary poverty, education, and basic infrastructure services—in order to convey "a more complete picture of poverty" (World Bank, 2024; Ichedi, 2022).

18 ILO, *Universal Social Protection to Achieve the Sustainable Development Goals*, ILO World Social Protection Report, 2017–19 (Geneva, Switzerland: International Labour Organization, 2017), 121.

19 UNDP, *The State of Social Assistance in Africa 2019* (New York, NY: United Nations Development Programme, 2019), 46–47.

20 African Union, *Social Policy Framework for Africa* (Addis Ababa, Ethiopia: African Union, 2008), 17.

21 Thandika Mkandawire, "Introduction," in *Social Policy in a Development Context*, ed. Thandika Mkandawire (New York, NY: Palgrave Macmillan/United Nations Research Institute for Social Development, 2004), 1.

22 State fragility is generally assessed based on "the combination of exposure to risk and insufficient coping capacities of the state, system and/or communities to manage, absorb or mitigate those risks" (OECD, 2024).
23 UNDESA, *World Social Report 2020: Inequality in a Rapidly Changing World* (New York, NY: United Nations, 2020), 5.
24 UNSDG, *United Nations Sustainable Development Cooperative Framework* (New York, NY: United Nations, 2019).

Bibliography

Afigbo, Adiele E. "Background to Nigerian Federalism: Federal Features in the Colonial State." *Publius: The Journal of Federalism* 21, no. 4 (Fall 1991): 13–29, https://doi.org/10.1093/oxfordjournals.pubjof.a037965.

African Commission on Human and Peoples' Rights (ACHPR), "State Parties to the African Charter," accessed October 24, 2024, https://achpr.au.int/en/states.

African Union. *Agenda 2063: The Africa We Want*. Addis Ababa, Ethiopia: African Union Commission, 2015, https://au.int/Agenda2063/popular_version.

African Union. "Protocol to the African Charter on Human and Peoples' Rights on the Rights of Citizens to Social Protection and Social Security." Adopted by the Thirty-Fifth Ordinary Session of the Assembly of Heads of State and Government of the African Union, Addis Ababa, Ethiopia, February 6, 2022, https://au.int/en/treaties/protocol-african-charter-human-and-peoples-rights-rights-citizens-social-protection-and.

African Union. *Social Policy Framework for Africa*. Addis Ababa, Ethiopia: African Union, 2008, https://www.un.org/esa/socdev/egms/docs/2009/Ghana/au2.pdf.

African Union. "Social Policy Framework for Africa—Implementation Strategy Proposal." Drafted at the Second Session of the African Union Conference of Ministers in Charge of Social Development, Khartoum, Sudan, November 21–25, 2010, https://www.acts-consultancy.com/docs/AU%20Social%20Policy%20Framework%20-%20Implementation%20Strategy%20-%20revised%204-11-10.pdf.

Aiyede, Emmanuel Remi. "The Political Economy of Fiscal Federalism and the Dilemma of Constructing a Developmental State in Nigeria." *International Political Science Review* 30, no. 3 (June 2009): 249–69, https://doi.org/10.1177/0192512109105636.

Amponsah, Mary, Frank Agbola, and Amir Mahmood. "The Relationship Between Poverty, Income Inequality and Inclusive Growth in Sub-Saharan Africa." *Economic Modelling* 126 (September 2023): 1–20, https://doi.org/10.1016/j.econmod.2023.106415.

Baah, Samuel Kofi Tetteh, et al. "September 2023 Global Poverty Update from the World Bank: New Data on Poverty During the Pandemic in Asia." *World Bank Data Blog*, September 20, 2023, https://blogs.worldbank.org/en/opendata/september-2023-global-poverty-update-world-bank-new-data-poverty-during-pandemic-asia.

Barr, Nicholas. "Shifting Tides: Dramatic Social Changes Mean the Welfare State Is More Necessary than Ever." *Finance and Development* 55, no. 4 (December 2018): 16–19, https://www.imf.org/en/publications/fandd/issues/2018/12/redesigning-the-welfare-state-barr.

Boushey, Heather. *Unbound: How Inequality Constricts Our Economy and What We Can Do About It*. Cambridge, MA: Harvard University Press, 2019.

Cann, Oliver. "Focus on GDP Fuelling Inequality and Short-Termism." *World Economic Forum*, January 22, 2018, https://www.weforum.org/press/2018/01/focus-on-gdp-fuelling-inequality-and-short-termism.

Chancel, Lucas, et al. "Income Inequality in Africa, 1990–2019: Measurement, Patterns, Determinants." *World Development* 163 (March 2023): 106162, https://doi.org/10.1016/j.worlddev.2022.106162.

Dauda, Rasaki Stephen, and Olusola Joel Oyeleke. "Poverty and Inequality: The Challenges to Sustainable Development in Nigeria." *Ilorin Journal of Economic Policy* 8, no. 2 (2021): 1–16, https://www.ajol.info/index.php/ijep/article/view/278803.

Devereux, Stephen. "Policy Pollination: A Brief History of Social Protection's Brief History in Africa." IDS Working Paper No. 543. Brighton, UK: Institute of Development Studies, December 2020, https://doi.org/10.19088/IDS.2020.004.

Devereux, Stephen, and Rachel Sabates-Wheeler. "Transformative Social Protection." IDS Working Paper No. 232. Brighton, UK: Institute of Development Studies, October 2004, https://www.ids.ac.uk/download.php?file=files/dmfile/Wp232.pdf.

Dluhopolskyi, Oleksandr, and Alina Zhukovska. "Inclusive Development as an Instrument to Overcome Economic Inequality and Discrimination." *Economics—Innovative and Economics Research Journal* 11, no. 1 (2023): 11–27, https://doi.org/10.2478/eoik-2023-0016.

Fukuda-Purr, Sakiko, Arnim Langer, and Yoichi Mine. "Disentangling the Linkages Between Horizontal Inequalities and Political Institutions." In *Preventing Violent Conflict in Africa: Inequalities, Perceptions and Institutions*, edited by Yoichi Mine et al., 1–9. New York, NY: Palgrave Macmillan, 2013.

Githongo, John. "Inequality, Ethnicity and the Fight Against Corruption in Africa: A Kenyan Perspective." *Economic Affairs* 26, no. 4 (December 2006): 19–23, https://doi.org/10.1111/j.1468-0270.2006.00664.x.

Graham, Sonia F. *Government and Mission Education in Northern Nigeria, 1900–1919*. Ibadan, Nigeria: Ibadan University Press, 1966.

Gupta, Joyeeta and Vegelin, Courtney. "Sustainable Development Goals and Inclusive Development." *International Environmental Agreements* 16 (June 2016): 433–48, https://doi.org/10.1007/s10784-016-9323-z.

Hallum, Christian, and Kwesi W. Obeng. "The West Africa Inequality Crisis: How West African Governments Are Failing to Reduce Inequality, and What Should Be Done About It." Oxfam Briefing Paper. Oxford, UK: Oxfam International, July 2019, https://hdl.handle.net/10546/620837.

Helleiner, Gerald Karl. "The IMF, the World Bank and Africa's Adjustment and External Debt Problems: An Unofficial Overview." *World Development* 20, no. 6 (June 1992): 779–92, https://doi.org/10.1016/0305-750X(92)90051-V.

Hillesund, Solveig, et al. "Horizontal Inequality and Armed Conflict: A Comprehensive Literature Review." *Canadian Journal of Development Studies* 39, no. 4 (2018): 463–80, https://doi.org/10.1080/02255189.2018.1517641.

Hujo, Katja, and Ilcheong Yi. *Social Policy and Inclusive Development*. UNRISD Classics, vol. 1. Geneva, Switzerland: United Nations Research Institute for Social Development, 2015, https://cdn.unrisd.org/assets/library/books/pdf-files/i-social-policy-and-inclusive-development.pdf.

Ichedi, Sunday Joel. "Nigeria Launches Its Most Extensive National Measure of Multidimensional Poverty." *National Bureau of Statistics news release, Federal Government of Nigeria*, November 17, 2022, https://nigerianstat.gov.ng/news/78.

International Labour Organization (ILO). *Universal Social Protection to Achieve the Sustainable Development Goals*. ILO World Social Protection Report, 2017–19. Geneva, Switzerland: ILO, 2017, https://www.social-protection.org/gini/gess/ShowWiki.action?id=594.

ILO. *Workers' Guide to ILO Conventions Concerning Minimum Standards of Social Security*. Geneva, Switzerland: ILO, 2022.

International Monetary Fund (IMF). "Sustaining Long-Run Growth and Macroeconomic Stability in Low-Income Countries: The Role of Structural Transformation and Diversification." IMF Policy Paper. Washington, DC: IMF, March 2014, https://www.imf.org/external/np/pp/eng/2014/030514a.pdf.

International Social Security Association (ISSA) and United States Social Security Administration (USSSA). *Social Security Programs Throughout the World: Africa, 2019*. Washington, DC: Social Security Administration, 2019.

Jalsenjak, Borna. "Principle of Solidarity." In *Encyclopedia of Sustainable Management*, edited by Samuel Idowu, René Schmidpeter, Nicholas Capaldi, Liangrong Zu, Mara Del Baldo, and Rute Abreu, 1–3. Cham, Switzerland: Springer Cham, 2020, https://doi.org/10.1007/978-3-030-02006-4.

Kharas, Homi, Kristofer Hamel, and Martin Hofer. "The Start of a New Poverty Narrative." *Future Development* (blog), Brookings Institution, June 19, 2018, https://www.brookings.edu/articles/the-start-of-a-new-poverty-narrative.

Kimenyi, Mwangi S. "The Politics of Identity, Horizontal Inequalities and Conflict in Kenya." In *Preventing Violent Conflict in Africa: Inequalities, Perceptions and Institutions*, edited by Yoichi Mine et al., 153–77. London, UK: Palgrave Macmillan, 2013.

Kincaid, John. "Economic Policy-Making: Advantages and Disadvantages of the Federal Model." *International Social Science Journal* 53, no. 167 (March 2001): 85–92, https://doi.org/10.1111/1468-2451.00296.

Langer, Arnim, and Saturo Mikami. "The Relationship Between Objective and Subjective Horizontal Inequalities: Evidence from Five African Countries." In *Preventing Violent Conflict in Africa: Inequalities, Perceptions and Institutions*, edited by Yoichi Mine et al., 208–51. New York, NY: Palgrave Macmillan, 2013.

Langer, Arnim, and Kristien Smedts. "Seeing Is Not Believing: Perceptions of Horizontal Inequalities in Africa." CRPD Working Paper No. 16. Leuven, Belgium: Centre for Research on Peace and Development, August 2013, https://soc.kuleuven.be/crpd/files/working-papers/wp16.pdf.

Martin, Matthew, et al. *Fighting Inequality in the Time of COVID-19: The Commitment to Reducing Inequality Index 2020*. Development Finance and Oxfam Research Report. Oxford, UK: Oxfam International, October 2020, https://hdl.handle.net/10546/621061.

Mayah, Emmanuel, et al. "Inequality in Nigeria: Exploring the Drivers." Oxfam Policy Paper. Oxford, UK: Oxfam International, May 2017, https://www.oxfam.org/en/research/inequality-nigeria-exploring-drivers.

Mine, Yoichi, et al., eds. *Preventing Violent Conflict in Africa: Inequalities, Perceptions and Institutions*. New York, NY: Palgrave Macmillan, 2013.

Mkandawire, Thandika. "Introduction." In *Social Policy in a Development Context*, edited by Thandika Mkandawire, 1–33. New York, NY: Palgrave Macmillan/United Nations Research Institute for Social Development, 2004.

Mkandawire, Thandika. "Social Development Policies: New Challenges for the Social Sciences." *International Social Science Journal* 58, no. 189 (2008): 395–404, https://doi.org/10.1111/j.1468-2451.2007.00637.x.

Mustapha, Abdul Raufu. "Ethnic Structure, Inequality and Governance of the Public Sector in Nigeria." Democracy, Governance and Human Rights Programme Paper No. 24. Geneva, Switzerland: United Nations Research Institute for Social Development, November 2006, https://assets.publishing.service.gov.uk/media/57a08c97ed915d3cfd0014aa/wp18.pdf.

Nel, Philip. "Inequality in Africa." In *The Routledge Handbook of African Development*, edited by Tony Binns, Kenneth Lynch, and Etienne Nel, Chapter 8, 104–119. New York, NY: Routledge, 2018.

Nsouli, Saleh M. "Structural Adjustment in Sub-Saharan Africa: The Policy Issues and Challenges for the 1990s." *Finance & Development* 26, no. 3 (September 1989): 30–33, https://doi.org/10.5089/9781451952032.022.

Odusola, Ayodele, Giovanni Andrea Cornia, Haroon Bhorat, and Pedro Conceição, eds. *Income Inequality Trends in Sub-Saharan Africa: Divergence, Determinants and Consequences*. New York, NY: United Nations Development Programme, 2017, https://doi.org/10.18356/542cba95-en.

Okonwo, Ogechukwu. "The Making of Modern Nigeria: British Imperialism and the Political Evolution of Nigeria." *The Republic* (Lagos, Nigeria), September 29, 2023, https://republic.com.ng/october-november-2023/the-making-of-nigeria.

Onwudiwe, Ebere, and Chloe Berwind-Dart. *Breaking the Cycle of Electoral Violence in Nigeria*. USIP Special Report No. 263. Washington, DC: United States Institute of Peace, December 2010, https://www.files.ethz.ch/isn/127382/SR263-Breaking_the_Cycle_of_Electoral_Violence_in_Nigeria.pdf.

Organization for Economic Co-operation and Development (OECD), "What Is Fragility?," accessed April 14, 2024, https://www.oecd.org/en/blogs/2022/09/what-is-fragility.html.

Osaghae, Eghosa E. "Ethnicity in Africa or African Ethnicity: The Search for a Contextual Understanding." In *African Perspectives on Development: Controversies, Dilemmas and Openings*, edited by Ulf Himmelstrand, Kabiru Kinyanjui, and Edward Mburugu, 137–51. Kampala, Uganda: Fountain Press, 1994.

Ross, Michael L. "The Political Economy of the Resource Curse." *World Politics* 51, no. 2 (January 1999): 297–322, https://doi.org/10.1017/S0043887100008200.

Save the Children's Child Rights Resource Centre (SCCRRC), "Draft Social Policy Framework for Africa," April 2005, https://resourcecentre.savethechildren.net/pdf/6762.pdf.

Seery, Emma, Joab Okanda, and Max Lawson. "A Tale of Two Continents: Fighting Inequality in Africa." Oxfam Briefing Paper. Oxford, UK. Oxfam International, September 2019, https://hdl.handle.net/10546/620856.

Shafik, Nemat. "A New Social Contract." *Finance and Development* 55, no. 4 (December 2018): 4–8, https://doi.org/Downloads/lse-a-new-social-contract-shafik.pdf.

Sowell, Thomas. *Affirmative Action Around the World: An Empirical Study*. New Haven, CT: Yale University Press, 2004.

Stewart, Frances. "Crisis Prevention: Tackling Horizontal Inequalities." *Oxford Development Studies* 28, no. 3 (October 2000): 245–62, https://doi.org/10.1080/713688319.

Stewart, Frances. "Horizontal Inequalities as a Cause of Conflict: A Review of CRISE Findings." World Development Report 2011 Background Paper. Oxford, UK: Centre for Research on Inequality, Human Security and Ethnicity, August 2010, https://hdl.handle.net/10986/9126.

Stewart, Frances. "Horizontal Inequalities: A Neglected Dimension of Development." In *Wider Perspectives on Global Development*, edited by United Nations University World Institute for Development Economics Research, 101–35. London, UK: Palgrave Macmillan, 2005.

Stewart, Frances, Thandika Mkandawire, and Mari Katayanagi. "Findings and Implications: The Role of Development Cooperation." In *Preventing Violent Conflict in Africa: Inequalities, Perceptions and Institutions*, edited by Yoichi Mine et al., 252–74. London, UK: Palgrave Macmillan, 2013.

Townsend, Peter. "From Universalism to Safety Nets: The Rise and Fall of Keynesian Influence on Social Development." In *Social Policy in a Development Context*, edited by Thandika Mkandawire, 37–62. New York, NY: Palgrave Macmillan/United Nations Research Institute for Social Development, 2004.

Tsebelis, George, and Jeannette Money. *Bicameralism*. Cambridge, UK: Cambridge University Press, 1997.

Ukiwo, Ukoha. "Managing Horizontal Inequalities and Violent Conflicts in Nigeria." In *Preventing Violent Conflict in Africa: Inequalities, Perceptions and Institutions*, edited by Yoichi Mine et al., 178–207. New York, NY: Palgrave Macmillan, 2013.

United Nations (UN). *Transforming Our World: The 2030 Agenda for Sustainable Development*. New York, NY: United Nations, 2015, https://sdgs.un.org/2030agenda.

United Nations Department of Economic and Social Affairs (UNDESA). *Leaving No One Behind: The Imperative of Inclusive Development—Report on the World Social Situation 2016*. New York, NY: United Nations, 2016, https://www.un.org/esa/socdev/rwss/2016/full-report.pdf.

UNDESA. *World Social Report 2020: Inequality in a Rapidly Changing World*. New York, NY: United Nations, 2020, https://desapublications.un.org/publications/world-social-report-2020-inequality-rapidly-changing-world.

United Nations Development Programme (UNDP). "MPI—More Nigerians Are Multidimensionally Poor than a Decade Before 2017." *UNDP News Release*, July 10, 2019, https://www.undp.org/nigeria/press-releases/mpi-more-nigerians-are-multidimensionally-poor-decade-2017.

UNDP. *The State of Social Assistance in Africa 2019*. New York, NY: United Nations Development Programme, 2019, https://www.undp.org/africa/publications/state-social-assistance-africa-report.

United Nations Sustainable Development Group (UNSDG). *United Nations Sustainable Development Cooperative Framework*. New York, NY: United Nations, 2019, https://unsdg.un.org/download/1512/687.

United States Agency for International Development (USAID), "Inclusive Development," last accessed November 28, 2024, en_inclusive-develop_print.pdf.

USAID/Nigeria, U.S. Agency for International Development Partnerships for Progress Annual Program Statement, APS No. 72062024APS00001, December 13, 2024, https://govtribe.com/file/government-file/aps-no-72062024aps00001-partnerships-for-progress-dot-pdf.

van de Walle, Nicolas. "The Institutional Origins of Inequality in Sub-Saharan Africa." *Annual Review of Political Science* 12 (2009): 307–27, https://doi.org/10.1146/annurev.polisci.11.063006.092318.

Voitchovsky, Sarah. "Inequality and Economic Growth." In *The Oxford Handbook of Economic Inequality*, edited by Brian Nolan, Wiemer Salverda, and Timothy M. Smeeding, 549–74. Oxford, UK: Oxford University Press, 2011.

Whiting, Kate. "These Countries Were Doing Best at Tackling Inequality Before COVID-19." *World Economic Forum*, October 8, 2020, https://www.weforum.org/agenda/2020/10/inequality-oxfam-covid-19-poverty-reduction.

Wilkinson, Richard, and Kate Pickett. *The Inner Level: How More Equal Societies Reduce Stress, Restore Sanity and Improve Everyone's Well-Being*. London, UK: Penguin Books, 2018.

World Bank, "Fact Sheet: An Adjustment to Global Poverty Lines," last updated September 14, 2022, https://www.worldbank.org/en/news/factsheet/2022/05/02/fact-sheet-an-adjustment-to-global-poverty-lines.

World Bank, "Multidimensional Poverty Measure," *Poverty and Equity Brief*, last updated October 2024, https://www.worldbank.org/en/topic/poverty/brief/multidimensional-poverty-measure.

World Bank. *Poverty and Shared Prosperity 2018: Piecing Together the Poverty Puzzle.* Washington, DC: World Bank Group, 2018, https://hdl.handle.net/10986/30418.

World Bank DataBank, *Metadata Glossary*, s.v. "Gini index," accessed February 8, 2024, https://databank.worldbank.org/metadataglossary/world-development-indicators/series/si.pov.gini.

World Economic Forum (WEF). *The Inclusive Growth and Development Report 2017*. Geneva, Switzerland: World Economic Forum, 2017, https://www3.weforum.org/docs/WEF_Forum_IncGrwth_2017.pdf.

PART 2

Socioeconomic Inequality and Ethnic Identity in Sub-Saharan Africa

4

THE SOCIOPOLITICAL ASCENDANCY OF THE KIKUYU IN POST-INDEPENDENCE KENYA

The Colonial Legacy of Ethnic Inequality

Tade O. Okediji

Introduction

Kenya is the largest economy in East Africa and the third largest economy on the continent, after Nigeria and South Africa. The Anglo-German Agreement of 1886 declared much of eastern Africa a British sphere of influence; the Crown proclaimed the territory that comprises modern Kenya as the East Africa Protectorate in 1895, and the Colony of Kenya—named for Mount Kenya—in 1920 (Mutua, 2008).[1] Modern-day Kenya is a union of formerly independent ethnic communities merged together to enable the British to administer the colonial state and exert economic control (Berman, Contrell, & Ghai, 2009).

Kenya gained its independence from the United Kingdom in 1963. Per the most recent census in 2019, the country has a population of about 47.5 million. Agriculture represents the largest share of gross domestic product (GDP) at 34 percent, followed by manufacturing at 16 percent (KNBS, 2020). The World Bank classifies the Kenyan economy as "lower middle income," with a gross national income per capita of $1,460.00 (KNBS, 2020). With roughly seventy different ethnic nationalities, Kenya is quite ethnically diverse. The largest ethnic groups are the Kikuyu (17 percent), the Luhya (14 percent), the Luo (11 percent), the Kamba (10 percent), the Kalenjin (13 percent), the Meru (4 percent), and the Gusii (6 percent). The Kikuyu primarily reside in the central region, the Luo in the Nyanza region in the country's southwest, the Luhya in the western region, the Kamba mainly in the southeastern lowlands, and the Kalenjin in the Rift Valley region. Ethnicity defines contemporary Kenyan life, including day-to-day interactions, diet, employment, and land ownership. Different ethnic groups engage in distinct economic activities, mostly determined by their respective regions within the country. For example, the Kikuyu are primarily agriculturists; land ownership—considered the only

DOI: 10.4324/9781003357025-6

means of production and supply of resources—is the bedrock of their economic life (Kenyatta, 1965).

The colonial administration divided Kenya geographically into provinces (Central, Coast, Eastern, Nairobi, North Eastern, Nyanza, Rift Valley, and Western), and those demarcations remained in place until 2010, when a constitutional reform subdivided the provinces into forty-six districts (excluding Nairobi) (Mueller, 2014). The central region—the Kikuyu heartland, much of it encompassing the so-called White Highlands settled by the British during colonization—became the heart of the Kenyan economy. (See Chapter 1 for a detailed discussion of the colonial-era displacement of the Kikuyu and other ethnic groups from their land and the long-standing ethnic rivalries and conflicts bred by this legacy.) The region's infrastructural advantages—particularly schools, roads, and health facilities first established during the colonial period, along with a substantial allocation of state resources since independence—have made it the country's most economically developed region (Berg-Schlosser & Siegler, 1990).[2] This edge firmly embedded Kikuyu hegemony, which has persisted throughout Kenya's post-independence political history. The resulting ethnic clientelism transcended democratization, becoming an endemic aspect of political life.

Ethnicity in Kenya is inextricably linked to an enduring colonial and post-colonial legacy that forged uneven regional development. During the negotiations for political independence, ethnic consciousness became an integral part of the political dialogue in Kenyan society (Zaleza, 2014). The uneven pattern of colonial capitalist intrusion and penetration in Kenya corresponded to regional, ethnic, and class forces and contributed to Kenya's post-independence ethnopolitical conundrum. More specifically, the Kikuyus' extensive contact with colonial settler capitalism in the central region proved a significant advantage relative to ethnic groups in other regions in terms of educational attainment, business acumen, land acquisition, and access to resources (Ajulu, 2002). In addition to being Kenya's largest ethnic group, the Kikuyu constitute a clear majority across the central region and a majority in ten out of seventy-six constituencies, two out of fourteen of those in the Rift Valley region (Lynch, 2014).[3] Due to their considerable contact with colonial settler capitalism—as in, because they were forced to participate in the exploitative colonial capitalist arrangement—the Kikuyu residing in the Central Province enjoyed rapid economic development. After independence, with Kenya's assimilation of pro-Western capitalism, their prior exposure to the capitalist economic system virtually guaranteed the Kikuyus' place as the largest petty bourgeoisie in the country (Ajulu, 2002).

This chapter analyzes the relationship between the Kikuyu as an ethnic group (or nation)—encompassing the Kikuyu in Kiambu, Muranga, Kirinyaga, Nyeri, and Nyandarua Counties and their close cousins the Meru and the Embu, who occupy Meru, Embu, and Tharaka-Nithi Counties—and the other major Kenyan ethnic groups.[4] A fundamental premise of this exposition is that the socioeconomic and political contestations among ethnic nationalities in Kenya is a lasting legacy of British colonial rule, prior to which the various ethnic nationalities coexisted amicably under Indigenous structures of governance, as the next section describes. The modern-day iteration of political elitism in Kenya has its roots in the elitist British colonial structure: British colonialism—and specifically the colonial administrative structure—created ethnic hierarchies that remain entrenched in Kenyan politics and society today. Furthermore, this discussion presupposes that ethnicity (as in ethnic identity) as a form of cultural expression is innocuous: It merely informs an individual's heritage, expressed through language, social interaction, and traditional beliefs. However, when ethnic identity becomes a basis for ownership and access to economic resources, distribution of public goods, and political representation, the likely outcomes are inequality, competition, and protracted conflict. Such is the case in post-independence Kenya, where the politicization of ethnicity gave rise to a social-economic-political hierarchy among ethnic groups for access to public resources and political power.

This chapter proceeds with a brief discussion of the history of the Kikuyu people, followed by an in-depth look at the role of the Kikuyu in the political regimes in post-independence Kenya. The next section examines the country's successive presidential regimes to illustrate the symbiotic relationship between ethnicity and national politics in contemporary Kenyan society. The last section looks at the deeply rooted ethnic socioeconomic inequalities since independence, their roots in the legacy of British indirect rule and their ramifications on Kenya's sociopolitical economy, and efforts to curb the ethnic patronage and chauvinism that resulted.

History of the Kikuyu People

The Kikuyu originated from West Africa, along with other Bantu ethnolinguistic groups.[5] They ultimately settled in the Mount Kenya region in present day central Kenya and began farming the highlands south and west of the mountain. The Kikuyu are historically a very cohesive group. Individualism is traditionally discouraged in favor of collectivism (July, 1998). They developed an egalitarian system of governance that relied heavily on group discussion and consensus in decision-making, for example, in cultivating land, planting, and harvesting (Kenyatta, 1965). Although the Kikuyu family structure is patrilineal and polygamous, women have always featured prominently in the social and political structure. For instance, during the Mau Mau insurrection, Kikuyu women played a crucial role in providing forest fighters with supplies and military information and occasionally joined ranks with combat soldiers (July, 1998).

Colonialism dramatically altered the sociopolitical economy and ethnic relations in Kenya. The Kikuyu model of landholding was based on the principles of *githaka* (or individual ownership) and *mbari* (or family ownership) (Kilson Jr., 1955),[6] which provided a sense of economic and psychological security. However, colonial legislation and decrees, most notably the 1915 amendment to the Crown Lands Ordinance, gave the colonial governor control over land ownership and sale—effectively dispossessing the Kikuyu (as well as the Kalenjin and the Maasai) of their land and rendering them "tenants at will of the Crown with no more than temporary occupancy rights to land" (Good, 1976; Kameri-Mbote, 2009). Policies like the 1915 ordinance that allowed the confiscation of Indigenous lands engendered a loss of socioeconomic stability, breeding discontent that would ultimately lead to the Mau Mau uprising (Klopp, 2002).

In response to their dissatisfaction over losing their land, the Kikuyu began to form protest organizations in the 1920s to prevent further encroachment on their land and to challenge British authority in Kenya, including the Kikuyu Association, the East African Association, and the Young Kikuyu Association, a branch of the East African Association. The latter disbanded in 1922, after fatal clashes with police during protests over British rule generally and occupation of their land specifically, but some of its members and leaders regrouped and formed the Kikuyu Central Association (KCA) in 1924. One of the newly reconstituted association's first recruits was Jomo Kenyatta, who would become the first prime minister and later president of independent Kenya.

This long history of political mobilization fostered a political shrewdness in the Kikuyu, who have been at the forefront of mobilizing efforts for political development and social change in Kenya since the colonial era. Historically, their impetus for political galvanization was colonial domination and displacement from their land, seeking the eradication of British rule and Kenyans' right to self-governance. The Kikuyu-led Kenya African Union (KAU), which was formed in 1944, was the first nationalist movement established (and the predecessor of the Kenya African National Union, or KANU).

The Mau Mau uprising, which began in 1952, was a major turning point in Kenyan history. The confrontation between Kenya Land and Freedom Army (KLFA) soldiers, also known as the Mau Mau, on one side and the British Army (aided by African loyalists who sided with the colonial government) on the other was the culmination of decades of grievances with settler colonialism and British rule. It was also arguably the catalyst for Kenyan independence. Although the Mau Mau were predominantly ethnic Kikuyus, Merus, and Embus, units of Kamba and Maasai fighters also fought during insurrection, seeking to regain their lands and drive out the English settlers. After several attempts to negotiate with the British had failed, the Mau Mau became more defiant and the colonial authorities declared a state of emergency in October 1952, at which point British forces were deployed to suppress the rebellion. In 1953, the colonial administration banned the KAU and jailed its leaders, including Jomo Kenyatta. The British defeated the revolt in 1956, but not before eleven thousand KLFA fighters had been killed, including the Mau Mau leader, Dedan Kimathi. Despite the Mau Maus' defeat, the rebellion—and the fact that the state of emergency remained in place until December 1959—almost certainly expedited Kenya's path to independence by inciting broader and more fervent political mobilization against the colonial regime (Githuku, 2016; Klopp, 2002).

Kikuyu Sociopolitical Structure and Influence

For the most part, the political structure in Kenya today is based on informal power relations, ethnic identities, and cultural values and practices coupled with the distribution of wealth that emerged during the colonial period through interactions with formal state and market institutions (Berman, Contrell, & Ghai, 2009). As discussed above, the Kikuyu tradition of forming political organizations and wielding political influence dates back to the 1920s. That history, along with the Kikuyus' close contact with colonial settler capitalism and consequent introduction to a monetary economy, gave the Kikuyu a significant advantage over other ethnic groups in Kenya both before and after independence.

On a more granular level, the Kikuyu benefitted disproportionately from land tenure policies that enabled them to amass private landholdings under the colonial administration. Between the 1930s and the 1960s, the British instituted various policies allocating prime farmland taken from the Kalenjin and the Maasai to the Kikuyu, thanks at least in part to Jomo Kenyatta and the KCA's lobbying efforts (Minorities at Risk Project, 2010). One such policy, known as the million-acre settlement scheme, carved out large parcels of land in the Rift Valley region, which the Maasai regarded as their historic patrimony, for Kikuyu settlement. Another, the land consolidation and registration (LCR) program instituted by the colonial government after the Mau Mau rebellion, in effect also privileged the Kikuyu. The LCR, which effectively validated traditional Kikuyu inheritance practices, established a freehold tenure system by consolidating land into single holdings and distributing those holdings to individual landholders. The LCR set the foundation for a subsequent program—the Swynnerton plan, which provided low-cost development loans to individuals who had secured a land title via the LCR by using their assets (i.e., that land) as collateral (Harbeson, 2012).

As the principal beneficiaries of these land policies, the Kikuyus' accumulation of wealth economically empowered them and contributed to their comparatively accelerated socioeconomic advancement and modernization (Harbeson, 2012). Consequently, after independence, the Kikuyu found themselves far better situated than other ethnic groups to adapt to a modern economy as Kenya adopted a capitalist orientation (Ajulu, 2002). Although colonial administrators intended the Swynnerton plan and the LCR to serve as "the basis for a multi-racial alternative to African nationalism," the undue economic edge and influence enjoyed by the Kikuyu—and especially their preferential colonial-era land allocations and transactions, given the importance and value of land in Kenya—served to heighten tensions between the Kikuyu and other ethnic groups (Ajulu, 2002; Harbeson, 2012).

The Kenya African National Union was formed in 1960 out of two pseudo-ethnic political parties: the former KAU, which the colonial government had banned during the Mau Mau rebellion, and the Kenya Independence Movement (KIM). KANU's political leadership represented an alliance between the Kikuyu and the Luo, the two largest ethnic groups at the time, both of which sought to expand their land claims into Kalenjin homelands and espoused a free market in land (Gibbon, 1995).[7] Jomo Kenyatta (a Kikuyu), Jaramogi Odinga Odinga (a Luo), and Tom Mboya (also a Luo and the former head of the KIM) were KANU's founders. Meanwhile, the Kalenjin formed an alliance with the Luhya, the Kenya African Democratic Union (KADU), to represent the ethnic minorities of the Rift Valley and Coastal Provinces. Led by Ronald Ngala (a Giriama), Daniel arap Moi (a Kalenjin who would become Kenya's longest-serving president), and Masinde Muliro (a Luhya), KADU advocated *majimboism* (regionalism) to counteract the more powerful Kikuyu-dominated KANU; it sought to create semiautonomous regions based on ethnicity, along with strong regional authorities to regulate access to land (Gibbon, 1995; Harbeson, 2012; Minorities at Risk Project, 2010).

In the multiparty elections in 1963, KANU defeated KADU, Jomo Kenyatta was elected prime minister, and, in December, the newly independent Commonwealth realm of Kenya was born. Subsequently, in 1964, when Kenya became a republic and Kenyatta became president, he appointed Odinga as his vice president (a presidential privilege until the constitutional reforms of 2010). Kenyatta undermined KADU by enticing its members with financial favors and beneficial budget appropriations for their constituencies (Berman, Contrell, & Ghai, 2009; Omolo, 2002). For instance, when a dispute over land in the Rift Valley erupted between the Luhya and the Kalenjin within the soon-to-be-defunct KADU, Kenyatta resolved the dispute in favor of the Kalenjin. The strategic move was a condition of the KANU-KADU merger that created a one-party state and government consistent with KANU's ideology. Ultimately, however, the Kenyatta government redistributed the land in the Rift Valley, Coast, and Central Provinces (the former White Highlands) only to Kikuyu settlers and not to the Kalenjin or the Maasai, who also lost their land there during the colonial period (Oucho, 2010; Mueller, 2008; Minorities at Risk Project, 2010; Branch & Cheeseman, 2009). As described in Chapter 1, this ethnoregional land dispute—and the ethnic entrenchment that it gave rise to—became a fixture in Kenyan politics that endures today.

Kenyan Presidential Regimes

Jomo Kenyatta: 1963–78

At independence in 1963, Kenya found itself at a crossroads between the centralized, authoritarian structures of governance that characterized colonial rule and its nascent, purportedly democratic political system (Ahluwalia, 1996).[8] This dualism set the stage for the tumultuous and often acrimonious politics and governance that have persisted in post-independence Kenya. The country's post-colonial political power dynamics have evolved along strictly ethnic lines—a direct result of the legacy of *indirect rule*, which co-opted local chiefs as agents of the colonial state, and the ethnopolitical competition it fostered (Siollun, 2021).[9] (See Chapters 1 and 2 for more on indirect rule.)

The independent Kenyan state emerged as a parliamentary democracy with a multiparty political system. The newly elected Jomo Kenyatta appeared to promote the democratic ideal of inclusion, forging a broad, ethnically diverse coalition. But the veneer of democratic principles faded quickly: Kikuyu hegemony permeated all aspects of society during the Kenyatta regime, which essentially proved to be little more than an extension of colonial-era policy. The Kikuyu elites effectively colonized the state and came to dominate Kenya's politics, commerce, and civil service. This rent-seeking scheme altered the sociopolitical landscape by intensifying ethnic polarization in modern-day Kenya (Omolo, 2002).

Kenyatta quickly formed a cabal of close Kikuyu associates who became the political elite, amassing political and economic power and wealth and exerting considerable influence over the state. He centralized power by passing numerous constitutional amendments strengthening the office of the presidency and ensuring presidential control over the civil service and the local governments (Mueller, 2014; Nasong'o, 2007a). He worked diligently to eliminate political opposition, perfecting the art of cronyism by giving his cabal land appropriations and employment in high-ranking civil service positions. Judicial appointments and influential government positions—including the head of the central bank and the head of the civil service—became the domain of the Kikuyu (Omolo, 2002). He exacerbated ethnic inequalities and discontent by consolidating Kikuyu, Embu, and Meru domination of the country's economy, notably through the establishment of the Gikuyu, Embu, and Meru Association (GEMA) in 1971 (Omolo, 2002). The Kikuyu enjoyed easier access to bank credit for business ventures during his rule, with some amassing sizable wealth and land as a result. Favors for loyalty, undergirded by ethnic chauvinism, became the norm—a practice akin to the colonial administration's indirect rule policy. In these myriad ways, Kenyatta effectively created a neopatrimonial state (Omolo, 2002; Berman, Contrell, & Ghai, 2009).

Daniel arap Moi: 1978–2002

Daniel arap Moi's rise to the presidency in 1978 ushered in an authoritarian era in Kenyan politics that altered the balance of ethnopolitical power. Although himself a Kalenjin, Moi had shrewdly aligned himself with the Kikuyu and KANU after KADU's 1963 electoral defeat and had served as Kenyatta's vice president from 1966 to 1978 (Harbeson, 1998).[10] Shortly before Kenyatta's death, in an effort to maintain Kikuyu political hegemony, elite Kikuyu politicians (in GEMA) sought to block Moi's presidency through a constitutional challenge. Kenyatta himself opposed the move, believing that Kikuyu political and economic dominance would be better preserved with Moi as president (Omolo, 2002; Throup & Hornsby, 1998). In the end, the attorney general, Charles Njonjo, upheld Moi's constitutional right to be president and foiled the plot, and Moi ascended to the presidency upon Kenyatta's death (Mutua, 2008; Ajulu, 2002; Karimi & Ochieng, 1980).

Once in power, Moi initially sought to maintain the Kikuyu political elite in his inner circle. He placed Charles Njonjo and Mwai Kibaki, both Kikuyus (and the latter a future president), in positions of power and influence. However, this strategy shifted after the first few years as he began to chip away at Kikuyu dominance in the civil service and other high-ranking government institutions, including the military ranks. Over the course of his twenty-four-year reign, he repeatedly reshuffled his cabinet and replaced Kikuyus with Kalenjins. He also employed divide-and-conquer tactics to exploit tensions among competing factions within the Kikuyu body politic in order to consolidate his power and elevate his Kalenjin cabal. Although the Kikuyu are the largest ethnic group in Kenya, they are not necessarily monolithic—and they certainly were not during the Moi era. Broadly, there were three camps: the Mau Mau group, the Kenyatta loyalists, and the Kikuyu masses. Moi adroitly exploited the discordance among them. Said tensions were most evident between the rural Kikuyu masses and the Kikuyu elites, for whom Kenyatta's rule had been a boon. The Kenyatta period also benefitted some of the Mau Mau, but a vast majority of former Mau Mau fighters remained poor and landless, breeding disenchantment among them as well (Harbeson, 1998; Branch & Cheeseman, 2009; Throup & Hornsby, 1998).[11]

Needless to say, the Kikuyu elites saw Moi's erosion of their power and influence as a threat. Their diminished primacy in the Kenyan political economy stymied their long-established rent-seeking scheme. The impetus for a failed military coup d'état in 1982 is widely thought to have been the disrupted status quo and waning power status of the Kikuyu political elite, military brass, and top police officials. Although military officers from the Luo ethnic group were among those seeking to oust Moi, most of the coup plotters were Kikuyu senior-ranking officers. Regardless, the plan backfired, and Moi deftly used the thwarted coup to purge the army of senior-ranking Kikuyu officers and to remove prominent Kikuyu politicians from key cabinet positions. For instance, in a cabinet reshuffle following the foiled coup, he demoted Mwai Kibaki—who had served as one of his closest advisers in the early days of his presidency—from the powerful Kenyatta-appointed position of finance minister to minister of home affairs (though Kibaki remained Moi's vice president until 1988).[12] Moi became even more wary of his erstwhile ally, Charles Njonjo, a possible presidential challenger, whom he sought to discredit and remove as attorney general (Throup & Hornsby, 1998).[13] In addition, he purged the Kikuyu from the upper echelons of the military and replaced them with Kalenjin loyalists; he even reassigned the prominent Kikuyu army commander (General John Musomba) who had personally overseen his safe return to Nairobi following the coup attempt to a diplomatic post and replaced him with a Kalenjin (General Jon Sawe) (Throup & Hornsby, 1998).[14]

Moi's increasingly ruthless political maneuvering cemented his authoritarian government. He passed numerous laws to consolidate his power and ultimately, in 1982, amended the constitution to institute de jure what Kenyatta had instituted de facto: a one-party state (Adar & Munyae, 2001; Ajulu, 2002; Mueller, 2014;

Harbeson, 1998; Branch & Cheeseman, 2009).[15] By the mid-1980s, he had created a predatory, neopatrimonial state that heavily favored his Kalenjin constituency by concentrating public and private infrastructure in the Kalenjin-dominated Rift Valley Region (Ajulu, 2002).[16] Moi's policies of political centralization dismantled the Kikuyu ethnic patronage networks created during the Kenyatta era. Ministers and cabinet officials were centrally appointed and routinely demoted unceremoniously; between 1988 and 1991, nine cabinet ministers were dismissed from office (Throup & Hornsby, 1998).[17] He rewarded loyalists and routinely surveilled and detained people who criticized his government, including politicians, lawyers, university lecturers, and students. In the words of Susanne Mueller, his initial populism was a mask for a far more draconian and repressive regime than that of his predecessor (Mueller, 2014).[18]

Under increasing internal and international pressure for multipartyism, Moi agreed to multiparty elections in 1992 (Nasong'o, 2007b).[19] A number of politicians defected from KANU to form opposition parties, such as the Forum for the Restoration of Democracy (FORD–Kenya) (Mueller, 2014; Throup & Hornsby, 1998).[20] Moi won the presidential elections in 1992 and 1997 nevertheless, albeit amid widespread accusations of voting irregularities (McKinley Jr., 1997). He was constitutionally barred from running in 2002, but, as discussed in Chapter 1, he lured Raila Odinga (a Luo and the son of Jaramogi Odinga Odinga) and his National Development Party into a merger with KANU with a promised endorsement as his successor. He instead endorsed Uhuru Kenyatta (a Kikuyu, the son of Jomo Kenyatta), yet neither Odinga nor Kenyatta prevailed: Former KANU member (and Moi vice president and cabinet official) Mwai Kibaki and the newly formed National Rainbow Coalition (NARC) won the 2002 contest (Mueller, 2014).[21]

The 2002 presidential election brought an end to the most repressive regime in Kenyan political history, during which Daniel arap Moi systematically transformed the country's political economy and power structure from a neopatrimonial state to a centralized, autocratic one. In doing so, he methodically eroded the political dominance that the Kikuyu had exerted in national politics since independence. He also cemented the ethnically divisive Kenyan politics of the twenty-first century.

Mwai Kibaki: 2002–13

After Moi's two-and-a-half-decade dismantling of Kikuyu hegemony, Mwai Kibaki (a Kikuyu) was elected president in 2002, defeating KANU candidate Uhuru Kenyatta. Kibaki's victory was the first for a non-KANU presidential candidate in Kenya's four-decade post-independence history. His win was undergirded by NARC, an alliance forged between three major political parties—the Liberal Democratic Party (LDP), the National Alliance of Kenya (NAK), and FORD–Kenya—along with ten smaller ones (Nasong'o & Murunga, 2007; Berman, Contrell, & Ghai, 2009). The coalition augured a paradigm shift in Kenya's national politics: "a new political era of dialogue, consensus and power sharing," in the words of

Shadrack Nasong'o and Godwin Murunga. The new Kibaki government promised to rout government corruption and institute constitutional reforms reducing "the overwhelming powers of the presidency" within one hundred days of taking office (Nasong'o & Murunga, 2007).[22]

Kibaki's rise to power created a groundswell of optimism after the despotic Moi era. Sadly, this ray of hope was fleeting, as the Kibaki regime quickly backslid into the déjà vu politics of ethnic chauvinism and patronage that dominated the Kenyatta and Moi presidencies. Kibaki appointed his Kikuyu cronies to cabinet positions, thus failing to honor the NARC power-sharing agreement that helped usher him to power. His inner circle of friends and associates came to be called the "Mount Kenya mafia" (Berman, Contrell, & Ghai, 2009).[23] He structured his regime on a patronage system that engendered vast corruption and rent-seeking among senior government officials, most of whom were part of that inner circle (Nasong'o & Murunga, 2007).[24] Notwithstanding his election on an anti-corruption platform (Bachelard, 2010), his government came to symbolize unconstrained elites plundering state resources for personal gain. Despite revelations of widespread corruption by John Githongo, the anti-corruption czar—including a massive government procurement scandal that implicated the president himself—the Kibaki regime refused to quell the pervasive rogue behavior by government officials (Bachelard, 2010; Berman, Contrell, & Ghai, 2009).

Between 2002 and 2005, an intensive constitutional reform initiative undertaken by the newly established Constitution of Kenya Review Commission (CKRC) again revealed ethnicity's deep entrenchment in Kenyan politics.[25] The referendum was an attempt to curtail the power of professional politicians engaged in rampant corruption and abuse of office that were eroding Kenya's sociopolitical fabric and badly undermining public trust in government. The CKRC solicited input from Kenyan citizens across the country in 2002; in 2003, the National Constitutional Conference convened and ultimately endorsed what came to be known as the Bomas draft.[26] In essence, the Bomas constitution would have transferred much of the presidency's vast power to the prime minister—an office that had ceased to exist in 1964 when Kenya became a republic (Ghai, Sep. 2020). A core aspect of the Bomas proposal was the sovereignty of the citizenry: It devolved power to the people by enhancing democracy and attempting to avoid ethnic tensions. It also aimed to foster nation-building and to make politicians more accountable to the public (Ghai, Aug. 2020).

In 2004, Kibaki rejected the Bomas draft, amid outcry from both KANU and the LDP (IRIN News, 2004; Chitere et al., 2006). The collapse of the Bomas process set the LDP and the NAK at odds, creating a rift within NARC. Despite intense KANU and LDP opposition, the government's alternative draft constitution, which rejected the prime minister as head of state and preserved a strong presidency, passed in parliament in July 2005 (Cutler, 2010). In November, however, voters roundly rejected the so-called Wako draft, named for then Attorney General Amos Wako. The next day, Kibaki dismissed his entire cabinet (IRIN News, 2005).

The issue of power-sharing between the offices of the president and the prime minister brought NARC to its knees, pitting Kibaki and his NAK supporters against Odinga and his LDP faction.[27] More broadly, it pitted the Kikuyu against the Luo.[28] The political rancor quickly degenerated to an ethnicized feud, once again illustrating the deep ethnicization of Kenyan politics. Unsurprisingly, the Kikuyu had largely favored the Wako draft's diminished role for the prime minister, whereas the Luo saw the Wako version of the referendum as a Kikuyu ploy to preserve their own political power and influence while sidelining everyone else (Berman, Contrell, & Ghai, 2009).

The ethnic divide intensified during the 2007 presidential election between the incumbent Kibaki (backed, incidentally, by his predecessor, Moi) and the challenger Odinga, culminating in a political showdown and a national electoral crisis. More than 90 percent of the Kikuyu and Meru around Mount Kenya reportedly voted for Kibaki, while Odinga secured enormous support among the Luhya and Luo in the western region, the Kalenjin in the Rift Valley region, the smaller ethnic groups in the Coast Province, and the country's Muslim population; he also secured the northeastern region, which is predominately ethnic Somali (Berman, Contrell, & Ghai, 2009). But the results were extremely close and highly contested: Although the press reported that Odinga was leading by three hundred seventy thousand votes with 90 percent of the electorate accounted for, Kibaki pressured the electoral commission to declare him the winner by two hundred thousand votes out of nine million cast, igniting an already tense electoral process (Berman, Contrell, & Ghai, 2009).

Mass violence erupted along ethnic lines, forcing groups to flee from regions where they were ethnic minorities to their ancestral homelands. The electoral schism between primarily Luo and Kalenjin Odinga supporters and Kikuyu, Embu, and Meru Kibaki loyalists rapidly descended into one over long-standing land and social injustices (Sievers & Peters, 2008). Kalenjins in the western Rift Valley targeted Kikuyus, who had lived on land the Kalenjin viewed as theirs for more than fifty years, while Kalenjins fled from the eastern regions of the Rift Valley and central Kenya to traditional Kalenjin heartlands. Between December 2007 and February 2008, more than twelve hundred people lost their lives, and nearly seven hundred thousand were displaced (Cheeseman, Lynch, & Willis, 2016; Lynch, 2014).[29]

To resolve the impasse and restore order, Kibaki and Odinga agreed to a power-sharing arrangement brokered by former United Nations Secretary-General Kofi Annan, the 2008 National Accord and Reconciliation Act, whereby Odinga would serve as prime minister while Kibaki remained president (Sievers & Peters, 2008). Although it did fulfill the Bonas commission's aspiration to establish the office of the prime minister, the agreement expanded the executive cabinet to include members of minority parties alongside Kibaki's new Party of National Unity and Odinga's Orange Democratic Movement (ODM), which originated during the constitutional referendum in 2005. This new structure was referred to as the grand coalition cabinet, or the government of national unity (Cheeseman & Tendi, 2010; Berman, Contrell, & Ghai, 2009; Cheeseman et al., 2019). The new power-sharing arrangement also established commissions to investigate the 2007 electoral crisis and the impetus behind the post-election violence, and it renewed calls for a constitutional overhaul (Berman, Contrell, & Ghai, 2009).

In 2010, during Kibaki's second term in office, Kenya finally ratified a new constitution. Kibaki was in a much weaker position because his government was a consociational arrangement forged in the wake of the post-election crisis in 2007–08, and he was also halfway through his second and final term as president, term limits having been imposed by his predecessor Moi in 1991. Kibaki's support for the referendum may have been borne out of concern for his political legitimacy and an eye toward his legacy (Cheeseman, Lynch, & Willis, 2016).[30] But for the country, the referendum stood for promoting inclusion and fair representation, fostering a greater sense of national unity, and advancing democracy. The new constitution, which passed with nearly 70 percent of the vote, substantially decentralized governance by devolving power from the central government into two tiers—the national government and forty-seven independent county governments headed by governors (Kramon & Posner, 2011; Bassett, 2017).

It also changed the electoral framework in Kenya. Previously, a winning candidate had to secure at least 25 percent of the vote in a minimum of 50 percent of Kenya's provinces; failure to attain this threshold necessitated a runoff. Under the new constitution, a winning presidential candidate needs an absolute majority of the popular vote—50 percent plus one—or a runoff is held (Cheeseman et al., 2019). Other new provisions included the Supreme Court's exclusive authority to serve as the arbiter of presidential election petitions and the creation of the Kenya Independent Electoral and Boundaries Commission (KIEBC) (KIEBC, 2023). Additionally, the 2010 constitution established the office of the deputy president for the presidential candidate's running mate; prior to the 2010 referendum, the vice president served at the discretion of the president, and being a presidential running mate did not guarantee being vice president (Berman, Contrell, & Ghai, 2009).

Despite these reforms to foster a more inclusive civil society, the ethnicization of politics remains deeply entrenched in Kenya, primarily because politicians still employ ethnic patronage as a galvanizing mechanism to bolster their political positions and use access to resources—especially land—as leverage (Cheeseman et al., 2019). Informal institutions and power relations remain an integral part of the electoral process (not just in Kenya, but in other African countries as well). These informal norms provide stability to ethnic groups by establishing codes of conduct. Additionally, the political system in Kenya is structured on informal power relations, ethnic identities, cultural values and practices, and wealth distribution, all of which evolved from relations with formal state and market institutions during the colonial period.[31]

Uhuru Kenyatta: 2013–22

The 2013 presidential election was the first national election under the new constitutional framework. Uhuru Kenyatta (a Kikuyu) had staunchly supported the referendum to decentralize the federal government—a strategic move, as he and the Kikuyu elites feared losing their grip on power (Dickovick & Riedl, 2014). A repeat of the electoral violence that resulted from the disputed 2007 presidential election between Kibaki and Odinga would threaten the political elite establishment and Kikuyu dominance; decentralization gave the appearance of a power-sharing agenda among the ethnic groups.

As in previous years, the 2013 presidential election was an ethnically divisive contest, this time between Raila Odinga and his newly formed Coalition for Reform and Democracy (CORD)—which comprised the ODM, the Wiper Democratic Movement, and FORD–Kenya—and the Jubilee Alliance of Uhuru Kenyatta and William Ruto, the latter a Kalenjin and former KANU member (during the Moi regime). Ruto had supported Kenyatta's unsuccessful run against Kibaki to become Moi's successor. After Kenyatta, as KANU's flagbearer, had lost the 2002 presidential race to Kibaki (under NARC's banner), Ruto had joined Odinga's ODM (following the latter's split from Kibaki). He parted ways with Odinga after the 2007 election but remained in the grand coalition government in a ministerial capacity (Lynch, 2014). In 2013, under the newly launched United Republican Party, Ruto formed a coalition with Kenyatta's National Alliance to form the Jubilee Alliance (colloquially called the "Uhuruto" ticket) to run as the deputy presidential candidate (Lynch, 2014).[32]

The 2013 presidential election was bitterly contested. According to the KIEBC, Kenyatta won with 50.51 percent of the vote, whereas Odinga received 43.7 percent (Cheeseman, Lynch, & Willis, 2016). The election was also fraught with irregularities. Odinga and his supporters believed that Kenyatta, the incumbent, unfairly benefitted by using state resources to further his campaign, and that he manipulated the polls during the campaign and afterward (Cheeseman et al., 2019).[33] However, unlike the mass violence that followed the 2007 presidential election, 2013 did not plunge Kenya into ethnic violence and chaos. This outcome was in part because the coalitions that formed the national political parties were weak and loosely organized. As a result, political loyalties, alignments, and leaders did not garner strong party support, and local alliances and rivalries did not manifest as explosively along ethnic lines (Cheeseman, Lynch, & Willis, 2016).

The 2017 presidential election again saw Kenyatta and the new Jubilee Party facing off against Odinga, who now represented the National Super Alliance, an expanded coalition of CORD that also included the Amani National Congress and Chama Cha Mashinani. As in 2013, it was a heated battle plagued with accusations of voter fraud on both sides. Although Kenyatta won the majority vote (with 54 percent of the vote compared with Odinga's 45 percent), Odinga petitioned the Supreme Court to challenge the election results, as allowed by the 2010 constitution, on the grounds of voting irregularities. The court agreed with Odinga and annulled the election, but Kenyatta prevailed in the revote (albeit with a rather apathetic voter turnout of about 39 percent) (Cheeseman et al., 2019; Carter Center, 2018).

Like so many before it, the 2017 election evoked ethnic sentiments, confirming that the ethnic divide in Kenyan national politics is alive and well. In particular, because Odinga and his supporters believed that he won the election, they perpetuated the narrative that the Kikuyu did not want to relinquish their hold on the presidency and would incite violence to further their interests (Lynch, 2014). And indeed, there were reports of violence against Odinga supporters by pro-establishment actors (Bakumenko, 2022). However, unlike previous presidential elections that fomented lingering acrimony, in a demonstration of political chivalry, the presidential rivals famously shook hands in March 2018, putting aside their bitterness in a public display of unity clearly intended to convey political legitimacy, order, and stability.[34]

Due to term limits, Kenyatta was ineligible to run for a third term in 2022. In 2020, Ruto left the Jubilee Party and announced his alliance with the United Democratic Party. Leading up to the 2022 presidential election, Kenyatta publicly supported his former rival, Odinga, who joined the Azimio La Umoja party (Swahili for "Resolution for Unity"). Ruto sought to capitalize on Kenyatta's endorsement of Odinga by painting Odinga and Kenyatta as establishment elites: He framed his campaign message as anti-corruption, anti-greed, and anti-wealth; he labeled Kenyatta's family as one of Kenya's established "dynasties" and cast him (and by corollary, anyone politically associated with him) as motivated by power and economically entitled, amassing large amounts of wealth at the expense of ordinary citizens (Lockwood, 2023).[35]

Dissatisfaction with Kenyatta over failed promises of economic prosperity played into Ruto's hands. He won big in the Mount Kenya region (GEMA territory) by exploiting the country's economic malaise (Lockwood, 2023; Kahura, 2022). He also won over the Kikuyu community as a whole, which had become disillusioned with Kenyatta and his failed economic policies after ardently supporting him in 2013 and 2017 (Lockwood, 2023).[36] Ruto narrowly won the presidency with 50.49 percent of the vote to Odinga's 48.5 percent (KIEBC, 2023). Unsurprisingly, Odinga again challenged the election results (Anna, 2022), but the Supreme Court unanimously upheld Ruto's victory, blasting Odinga's allegations of cheating (Obulutsa & Houreld, 2022).

Post-Independence Ethnic Socioeconomic Inequalities

Ethnic inequality has been ingrained in Kenya since the British establishment of the East Africa Protectorate in 1895 (Sandbrook, 1985). The Crown's administrative system of indirect rule subjugated different ethnic groups unevenly during colonial rule; as a result, the political and socioeconomic hierarchy that emerged in post-independence Kenya centered around colonial-era perceptions and manifestations of ethnic identity that embedded Kikuyu dominance. For instance, it is widely believed in Kenyan society that the capitalist penetration and settler capitalism in the Central Province unduly benefitted the Kikuyu and gave them an unfair advantage over other ethnic groups in adapting to a modern economy, in the form of educational opportunities, land access, and farming and business ventures (Ajulu, 2002; Harbeson, 2012).[37] Upon independence, the region comprising the former Central Province and the erstwhile White Highlands—the traditional Kikuyu homelands—was already among the most developed regions of Kenya. The Kikuyu were by far the most prominent and the most prosperous among Kenya's ethnic groups after independence. By way of contrast, the Luo in the coastal region around Mombasa (the original capital of British East Africa, until 1907) contributed to the modern economy by supplying labor for the construction of the railway in Kisumu (today Kenya's third largest city) and thereby achieved some level of socioeconomic status. The Luhya in the Central Province, meanwhile, had contributed to peasant commodity production. Other ethnic groups such as the Kalenjin, Maasai, Turkana, and Samburu remained on the fringe of the settler capitalist economy until the late 1950s (Ajulu, 2002).

As discussed above, after Jomo Kenyatta became president in 1963, he consolidated his power by favoring the Kikuyu elites, appointing them to influential cabinet and civil service positions and allocating public lands to his ethnic kinsfolk, which gave them access to financial resources and allowed them to acquire property for personal gain. Kenyatta's flagrant corruption and nepotism enabled wealth accumulation among the Kikuyu elites and set the stage for subsequent governments to engage in like ethnic patronage and chauvinism through political appointments. Hence, ethnopolitical inequality became enrooted in Kenya's political system, and political ethnicity became a defining feature of Kenyan democracy (Omolo, 2002).

In post-independence Kenya, Nairobi, the capital city, and the (former) Central Province are considered the most developed regions in Kenya, while the north and the northeast are considered the most impoverished. Prior to decentralization under Uhuru Kenyatta, from 2005 to 2010, there were significant regional disparities in wage employment: Nairobi (which is majority Kikuyu, Luo, and Luhya), the Rift Valley (which is majority Kalenjin), and the Central Province (majority Kikuyu) had the highest number of wage employees, and the North Eastern Province (comprising mostly ethnic Somalis) had the fewest. Regional variations in wage employment reveal regional disparities in economic activities. Regional disparities in GDP per capita reveal a similar trend (Friedrich-Ebert-Stiftung, 2012).

The 2010 constitutional referendum that devolved fiscal and political power from the top-heavy central government to forty-seven independent county governments with elected governors and assemblies was devised a way to ameliorate the persistent ethnopolitical tensions and redress Kenya's embedded socioeconomic and political inequalities. Historically, as this chapter describes, post-independence centralization of power had enabled certain ethnic groups to engage in state capture.

Thus, the rationale for decentralization was to enable the newly created counties to participate directly in development planning and enable disenfranchised ethnic communities to participate in the political process (Cheeseman, Lynch, & Willis, 2016). It also sought to rein in rent-seeking behavior and ethnic patronage. However, some research suggests that devolution has merely brought rent-seeking and ethnic patronage to the county level, essentially localizing the pernicious behavior (D'Arcy & Cornell, 2016). After more than a decade of decentralization, the results are mixed. Northeastern Kenya, for example, has benefitted little and remains impoverished due to poor governance and corruption (Shahow, 2023). Ensuring effective delivery and management of fiscal and political responsibilities at the county level will require further political reforms.

Conclusion

Understanding the legacy of colonialism is essential to understanding the extreme socioeconomic and ethnic inequalities that persist in post-independence Kenya. Like many other sub-Saharan African countries, political dynamics in Kenya are highly ethnicized. Neopatrimonialism pervades Kenyan politics; cronyism, ethnic patronage, and rent-seeking on the part of political elites are de rigueur, rendering the state largely incapable of promoting socioeconomic development. Successive regimes attempted to centralize control, leveraging presidential powers to issue decrees and constitutional amendments to further an illicit agenda of state capture. The 2010 constitution sought to change this endemic behavior by decentralizing political power to invigorate political participation and de-ethnicize politics, with some success.

Yet ethnicity remains a fundamental aspect of Kenyan society, especially in the political sphere. Since independence, the Kikuyu have dominated Kenyan national politics and sat comfortably atop the country's socioeconomic hierarchy. Their early contact with exploitative colonial capitalism and the monetary economy imposed on their Indigenous way of life facilitated this prominence. The ethnic boundaries established by the colonial administration set the stage for fractionalized ethnopolitics in post-independence Kenya, which Jomo Kenyatta entrenched by employing the inherited colonial administrative structure as a political device. He inaugurated a neopatrimonial state in which the Kikuyu amassed significant wealth by acquiring land and key political and government appointments, creating a formidable economic and political power base. He also exacerbated colonial-era land grievances by distributing land confiscated from the Kalenjin and the Maasai by the British to his Kikuyu coethnics as post-independence spoils. The Kikuyu political elite's ensuing ethnic chauvinism and patronage displaced other ethnic groups geographically, politically, and socioeconomically, further intensifying the structural inequalities between the Kikuyu and other ethnic groups (Okello & Gitau, 2007). The synergistic effect of the Kikuyu-dominated neopatrimonial state and the ethnic disparities that buttress it has perpetuated their ascendancy in post-independence

Kenyan society. It has also fomented deep-seated ethnic tensions that endure today. Put simply, Kenya is a politically and ethnically polarized state, with empirical negative effects for the country's long-term economic growth prospects.

Before William Ruto's election in 2022, the only non-Kikuyu to serve as president was Daniel arap Moi. That political power equates to economic power is a foregone conclusion; that the pursuit of both—in a dual quest for ethnoregional supremacy and personal aggrandizement—has incentivized members of Kenya's different ethnic groups to vie for political hegemony is readily apparent in the country's post-independence political saga. To the extent that there are perceived socioeconomic benefits to be reaped by identifying or aligning with a particular ethnic group, ethnic fragmentation will remain a potent feature in Kenya's sociopolitical economy. And to the effect that the Kikuyus' privileged status in society is largely attributable to the lingering legacy of colonialism, unwinding that legacy will be key to addressing the ethnic inequalities and tensions that it created—and ultimately to promoting the country's long-term economic growth and development.

Notes

1 Makau Mutua, *Kenya's Quest for Democracy: Taming Leviathan* (Boulder, CO: Lynne Rienner, 2008), 41.
2 Dirk Berg-Schlosser and Rainer Siegler, *Political Stability and Development: A Comparative Analysis of Kenya, Tanzania, and Uganda* (Boulder, CO: Lynne Rienner, 1990), 40.
3 As described in the section on Mwai Kibaki's regime, the 2010 constitution inaugurated a weak form of federalism referred to as "devolution," establishing forty-seven independent county governments headed by elected executives known as governors. Under the new system, constituencies (of which there are 290) each elect one member of the National Assembly; 47 women elected by registered voters in the counties, 12 representatives nominated by the parliamentary political parties, and the speaker of the assembly (who is elected by the assembly and serves ex officio) round out the National Assembly's 350 members (Gathii & Otieno, 2018; Parliament of Kenya, 2025).
4 The analysis in this chapter is an inter-ethnic inquiry—that is, an analysis of how the Kikuyu, as a group, have ascended to a position of socioeconomic and political prominence nationally relative to the other major ethnic groups—not an intra-ethnic one. This chapter does not seek to interrogate the differences among the groups that constitute the Kikuyu nation.
5 Bantu is an ethnolinguistic grouping of several hundred distinct Indigenous African ethnic identities and spoken languages.
6 Martin L. Kilson Jr., "Land and the Kikuyu: A Study of the Relationship Between Land and Kikuyu Political Movements," *The Journal of Negro History* 40, no. 2 (April 1955): 106.
7 Peter Gibbon, ed., *Markets, Civil Society and Democracy in Kenya* (Uppsala, Sweden: Nordiska Afrikainstitutet, 1995), 15.
8 Davinder Pal Ahluwalia, *Post-Colonialism and the Politics of Kenya* (New York, NY: Nova Science, 1996), 19.
9 Max Siollun, *What Britain Did to Nigeria: A Short History of Conquest and Rule* (London, UK: Hurst, 2021), 284.
10 John W. Harbeson, "Political Crisis and Renewal in Kenya: Prospects for Democratic Consolidation," *Africa Today* 45, no. 2 (April–June 1998): 167–69.
11 Harbeson, "Political Crisis and Renewal in Kenya," 167–68; Daniel Branch and Nic Cheeseman, "Democratization, Sequencing, and State Failure in Africa: Lessons from

Kenya," *African Affairs* 108, no. 430 (January 2009): 3–4; David Throup and Charles Hornsby, *Multi-Party Politics in Kenya: The Kenyatta and Moi States and the Triumph of the System in the 1992 Election* (Oxford, UK: James Currey, 1998), 34–36.

12 Until the 2010 constitutional reforms, the vice presidency was largely a ceremonial position, serving at the president's discretion; the vice president also served in a secondary role as a cabinet minister. Kibaki was among the senior politicians who opposed the attempt to bar Moi from becoming president, which afforded him some loyalty despite being a Kikuyu. Kibaki was among Moi's close advisers at the beginning of his presidency. Throup and Hornsby, *Multi-Party Politics in Kenya*, 30.

13 Throup and Hornsby, *Multi-Party Politics in Kenya*, 32–34.

14 Throup and Hornsby, *Multi-Party Politics in Kenya*, 31–33.

15 Korwa G. Adar and Isaac M. Munyae, "Human Rights Abuse in Kenya Under Daniel Arap Moi, 1978–2001," *African Studies Quarterly* 5, no. 1 (Winter 2001): 1–17; Rok Ajulu, "Politicised Ethnicity, Competitive Politics and Conflict in Kenya: A Historical Perspective," *African Studies* 61, no. 2 (2002): 263; Susanne D. Mueller, "The Resilience of the Past: Government and Opposition in Kenya," *Canadian Journal of African Studies* 48, no. 2 (2014): 339; Harbeson, "Political Crisis and Renewal in Kenya," 167–68; Branch and Cheeseman, "Democratization, Sequencing, and State Failure in Africa," 3–4.

16 Ajulu, "Politicised Ethnicity, Competitive Politics and Conflict in Kenya," 263.

17 Throup and Hornsby, *Multi-Party Politics in Kenya*, 45.

18 Mueller, "Resilience of the Past," 339.

19 Shadrack Wanjala Nasong'o, "Political Transition Without Transformation: The Dialectic of Liberalization Without Democratization in Kenya and Zambia," *African Studies Review* 50, no. 1 (April 2007b): 95–96.

20 Mueller, "Resilience of the Past," 341; Throup and Hornsby, *Multi-Party Politics in Kenya*, 92–93.

21 Mueller, "Resilience of the Past," 342.

22 Shadrack Wanjala Nasong'o and Godwin R. Murunga, "Prospects for Democracy in Kenya," in *Kenya: The Struggle for Democracy*, ed. Godwin R. Murunga and Shadrack Wanjala Nasong'o (Dakar, Senegal: CODESRIA Books, 2007a), 9.

23 Bruce J. Berman, Jill Contrell, and Yash Ghai, "Patrons, Clients, and Constitutions: Ethnic Politics and Political Reform in Kenya," *Canadian Journal of African Studies* 43, no. 3 (2009): 491.

24 Nasong'o and Murunga, "Prospects for Democracy in Kenya," 9.

25 It is important to note that 2002 was by no means the beginning of the constitutional reform movement. Numerous amendments to the original 1963 constitution had rendered Kenya a highly centralized unitary state, eroding human rights and civil liberties in the process. Efforts to reinstate a multiparty state succeeded in 1991, and calls for "comprehensive" constitutional reforms began in earnest as early as 1993. Preston Chitere et al., *Kenya Constitutional Documents: A Comparative Analysis*. (Bergen, Norway: Chr. Michelsen Institute for Science and Intellectual Freedom, 2006), 3.

26 The Bomas draft was so named for the site of the NCC, Bomas of Kenya, a cultural center in Nairobi.

27 The LDP-NAK merger included a memorandum of agreement that Kibaki would select Odinga as prime minister. However, upon defeating Moi for the presidency, Kibaki did not appoint Odinga, who, along with his Luo compatriots, favored a strong prime minister. When Kibaki's 2005 referendum proposing a weak prime minister was defeated, Kibaki dismissed cabinet members who did not favor the referendum. Odinga and his supporters subsequently left NARC and formed the Orange Democratic Movement, or ODM (Berman, Contrell, & Ghai, 2009).

28 Initially, the ethnic violence was directed against the Kikuyu in the Rift Valley region and the Nyanza Province, where Kibaki was largely unpopular. The Kikuyus then retaliated against the Luos and the Kalenjins. Gabrielle Lynch, "Electing the 'Alliance of

the Accused': The Success of the Jubilee Alliance in Kenya's Rift Valley," *Journal of Eastern African Studies* 8, no. 1 (2014): 97–98; Mueller, "Resilience of the Past," 344.

29 Nic Cheeseman, Gabrielle Lynch, and Justin Willis, "Decentralisation in Kenya: The Governance of Governors," *The Journal of Modern African Studies* 54, no. 1 (March 2016): 11; Lynch, "Electing the 'Alliance of the Accused,'" 94.

30 Cheeseman, Lynch, and Willis, "Decentralisation in Kenya," 12.

31 The notorious handshake, also discussed in Chapter 1, between Kenyatta (a Kikuyu) and Odinga (a Luo) that stemmed the political impasse and restored stability in Kenya after the disputed presidential election in 2017 was a poignant example of how informal norms play a significant role in the political process. Berman et al., "Patrons, Clients, and Constitutions," 464.

32 Lynch, "Electing the 'Alliance of the Accused,'" 100.

33 Nic Cheeseman et al., "Kenya's 2017 Elections: Winner-Takes-All Politics as Usual?," *Journal of Eastern African Studies* 13, no. 2 (2019): 218.

34 See Chapter 1.

35 Peter Lockwood, "Hustler Populism, Anti-Jubilee Backlash and Economic Injustice in Kenya's 2022 Elections," *African Affairs* 122, no. 487 (April 2023): 207.

36 Lockwood, "Hustler Populism, Anti-Jubilee Backlash and Economic Injustice in Kenya's 2022 Elections," 207.

37 Ajulu, "Politicised Ethnicity, Competitive Politics and Conflict in Kenya," 254; John W. Harbeson, "Land and the Quest for a Democratic State in Kenya: Bringing Citizens Back In," *African Studies Review* 55, no. 1 (April 2012): 24.

Bibliography

Adar, Korwa G., and Isaac M. Munyae. "Human Rights Abuse in Kenya Under Daniel Arap Moi, 1978–2001." *African Studies Quarterly* 5, no. 1 (Winter 2001): 1–17, https://asq.africa.ufl.edu/wp-content/uploads/sites/168/Adar-Munyae-Vol-5-Issue-1.pdf.

Ahluwalia, Davinder Pal. *Post-Colonialism and the Politics of Kenya*. New York, NY: Nova Science, 1996.

Ajulu, Rok. "Politicised Ethnicity, Competitive Politics and Conflict in Kenya: A Historical Perspective." *African Studies* 61, no. 2 (2002): 252–68, https://doi.org/10.1080/0002018022000032947.

Anna, Cara. "After Kenya Presidential Vote Loss, Runner-Up Odinga Files Court Challenge." *PBS Newshour*, August 22, 2022, https://www.pbs.org/newshour/world/after-kenya-presidential-vote-loss-runner-up-odinga-files-court-challenge.

Bachelard, Jérôme Y. "The Anglo-Leasing Corruption Scandal in Kenya: The Politics of International and Domestic Pressures and Counter-Pressures." *Review of African Political Economy* 37, no. 124 (June 2010): 187–200, https://doi.org/10.1080/03056244.2010.483903.

Bakumenko, Stefan. "Kenya's Electoral Violence: Conditions, Challenges, and Opportunities." *Africa Up Close* (blog), The Wilson Center, June 16, 2022, https://www.wilsoncenter.org/blog-post/kenyas-electoral-violence.

Bassett, Ellen M. "The Challenge of Reforming Land Governance in Kenya Under the 2010 Constitution." *The Journal of Modern African Studies* 55, no. 4 (December 2017): 537–66, https://doi.org/10.1017/S0022278X17000441.

Berg-Schlosser, Dirk, and Rainer Siegler. *Political Stability and Development: A Comparative Analysis of Kenya, Tanzania, and Uganda*. Boulder, CO: Lynne Rienner, 1990.

Berman, Bruce J., Jill Contrell, and Yash Ghai. "Patrons, Clients, and Constitutions: Ethnic Politics and Political Reform in Kenya." *Canadian Journal of African Studies* 43, no. 3 (2009): 462–506, https://doi.org/10.1080/00083968.2010.9707567.

Branch, Daniel, and Nic Cheeseman. "Democratization, Sequencing, and State Failure in Africa: Lessons from Kenya." *African Affairs* 108, no. 430 (January 2009): 1–26, https://doi.org/10.1093/afraf/adn065.

Carter Center. "Kenya 2017 General and Presidential Elections." Election Report. Atlanta, GA: Carter Center, 2018, https://www.cartercenter.org/resources/pdfs/news/peace_publications/election_reports/kenya-2017-final-election-report.pdf.

Cheeseman, Nic, Gabrielle Lynch, and Justin Willis. "Decentralisation in Kenya: The Governance of Governors." *The Journal of Modern African Studies* 54, no. 1 (March 2016): 1–35, https://doi.org/10.1017/S0022278X1500097X.

Cheeseman, Nic, and Blessing-Miles Tendi. "Power-Sharing in Comparative Perspective: The Dynamics of 'Unity Government' in Kenya and Zimbabwe." *The Journal of Modern African Studies* 48, no. 2 (June 2010): 203–29, https://doi.org/10.1017/S0022278X10000224.

Cheeseman, Nic, et al. "Kenya's 2017 Elections: Winner-Takes-All Politics as Usual?" *Journal of Eastern African Studies* 13, no. 2 (2019): 215–34, https://doi.org/10.1080/17531055.2019.1594072.

Chitere, Preston, et al. *Kenya Constitutional Documents: A Comparative Analysis*. Bergen, Norway: Chr. Michelsen Institute for Science and Intellectual Freedom, 2006, https://www.cmi.no/publications/2367-kenya-constitutional-documents.

Cutler, David. "Timeline: Violent Path to New Kenyan Constitution." *Reuters*, August 5, 2010, https://www.reuters.com/article/world/timeline-violent-path-to-new-kenyan-constitution-idUSTRE6744ZJ.

D'Arcy, Michelle, and Agnes Cornell. "Devolution and Corruption in Kenya: Everyone's Turn to Eat?" *African Affairs* 115, no. 459 (April 2016): 246–73, https://doi.org/10.1093/afraf/adw002.

Dickovick, James Tyler, and Rachel Beatty Riedl. "Party Systems and Decentralization in Africa." *Studies in Comparative International Development* 49, no. 3 (September 2014): 321–42, https://doi.org/10.1007/s12116-013-9144-9.

Friedrich-Ebert-Stiftung. *Regional Disparities and Marginalisation in Kenya*. Nairobi, Kenya: Friedrich-Ebert-Stiftung, 2012, https://library.fes.de/pdf-files/bueros/kenia/09859.pdf.

Gathii, James Thuo, and Harrison Mbori Otieno. "Assessing Kenya's Cooperative Model of Devolution: A Situation-Specific Analysis." *Federal Law Review* 46, no. 4 (December 2018): 595–613, https://doi.org/10.1177/0067205X1804600407.

Ghai, Yash Pal. "History of Bomas Constitution: A Sad Story." *Nation*, September 9, 2020, https://nation.africa/kenya/news/politics/history-of-bomas-constitution-a-sad-story-2303406.

Ghai, Yash Pal. "Why the Bomas Draft Is the Best Constitution We Never Had." *Nation* (blog), August 25, 2020, https://nation.africa/kenya/news/politics/why-the-bomas-draft-is-the-best-constitution-we-never-had-1923846.

Gibbon, Peter, ed. *Markets, Civil Society and Democracy in Kenya*. Uppsala, Sweden: Nordiska Afrikainstitutet, 1995.

Githuku, Nicholas Kariuki. "'52 Minds on Kenya's Destiny: The View from 'the above.'" Chapter 4. In *Mau Mau Crucible of War: Statehood, National Identity, and Politics of Postcolonial* Kenya, pp. 163–218. Lanham, MD: Lexington Books, 2016.

Good, Kenneth. "Settler Colonialism: Economic Development and Class Formation." *The Journal of Modern African Studies* 14, no. 4 (December 1976): 597–620.

Harbeson, John W. "Land and the Quest for a Democratic State in Kenya: Bringing Citizens Back In." *African Studies Review* 55, no. 1 (April 2012): 15–30, https://doi.org/10.1353/arw.2012.0025.

Harbeson, John W. "Political Crisis and Renewal in Kenya: Prospects for Democratic Consolidation." *Africa Today* 45, no. 2 (April–June 1998): 161–83, https://www.jstor.org/stable/4187216.

Harneit-Sievers, Axel, and Ralph-Michael Peters. "Kenya's 2007 General Election and Its Aftershocks." *Africa Spectrum* 43, no. 1 (2008): 133–44, https://www.jstor.org/stable/40175226.

IRIN News (United Nations Office for the Coordination of Humanitarian Affairs). "Cabinet Sacked After Government Loses Constitutional Referendum." *The New Humanitarian,* November 24, 2005, https://www.thenewhumanitarian.org/news/2005/11/24/cabinet-sacked-after-govt-loses-constitutional-referendum.

IRIN News (United Nations Office for the Coordination of Humanitarian Affairs). "Government Walks Out of Constitutional Review Process." *The New Humanitarian,* March 17, 2004, https://www.thenewhumanitarian.org/report/49136/kenya-government-walks-out-constitutional-review-process.

July, Robert W. *A History of the African People*. Prospect Heights, IL: Waveland Press, 1998.

Kahura, Dauti. "Injected with 'Yellow Fever' Jab, GEMA Roots for Ruto in the Elections." *This Is Africa,* August 15, 2022, https://thisisafrica.me/politics-and-society/injected-with-yellow-fever-jab-gema-roots-for-ruto-in-the-elections.

Kameri-Mbote, Patricia. "Righting Wrongs: Confronting Land Dispossession in Post-Colonial Contexts." *East African Law Review* 35–40 (2009): 103–24, https://www.ielrc.org/content/a0909.pdf.

Karimi, Joseph, and Philip Ochieng. *The Kenyatta Succession*. Nairobi, Kenya: Transafrica, 1980.

Kenya Independent Electoral and Boundaries Commission (KIEBC), "Our Mission," accessed August 25, 2023, https://www.iebc.or.ke/iebc/?vission.

Kenya National Bureau of Statistics (KNBS). "2019 Kenya Population and Housing Census Volume IV: Distribution of Population by Socio-Economic Characteristics." February 21, 2020, https://www.knbs.or.ke/2019-kenya-population-and-housing-census-reports.

Kenyatta, Jomo. *Facing Mount Kenya: The Tribal Life of the Gikuyu*. London, UK: Mercury Books, 1965.

Kilson, Martin L., Jr. "Land and the Kikuyu: A Study of the Relationship Between Land and Kikuyu Political Movements." *The Journal of Negro History* 40, no. 2 (April 1955): 103–53, https://doi.org/10.2307/2715382.

Klopp, Jacqueline M. "Can Moral Ethnicity Trump Political Tribalism? The Struggle for Land and Nation in Kenya." *African Studies* 61, no. 2 (2002): 269–94, https://doi.org/10.1080/00020180220000032956.

Kramon, Eric, and Daniel N. Posner. "Kenya's New Constitution." *Journal of Democracy* 22, no. 2 (April 2011): 89–103, https://doi.org/10.1353/jod.2011.0026.

Lockwood, Peter. "Hustler Populism, Anti-Jubilee Backlash and Economic Injustice in Kenya's 2022 Elections." *African Affairs* 122, no. 487 (April 2023): 205–24, https://doi.org/10.1093/afraf/adad011.

Lynch, Gabrielle. "Electing the 'Alliance of the Accused': The Success of the Jubilee Alliance in Kenya's Rift Valley." *Journal of Eastern African Studies* 8, no. 1 (2014): 93–114, https://doi.org/10.1080/17531055.2013.844438.

McKinley, James C., Jr. "All Sides in Kenya Cry Fraud in Election." *The New York Times*, December 31, 1997, https://www.nytimes.com/1997/12/31/world/all-sides-in-kenya-cry-fraud-in-election.html.

Minorities at Risk Project, "Chronology for Kikuyu in Kenya," last updated July 16, 2010, https://www.mar.umd.edu/chronology.asp?groupId=50103.

Mueller, Susanne D. "The Political Economy of Kenya's Crisis." *Journal of Eastern African Studies* 2, no. 2 (2008): 185–210, https://doi.org/10.1080/17531050802058302.

Mueller, Susanne D. "The Resilience of the Past: Government and Opposition in Kenya." *Canadian Journal of African Studies* 48, no. 2 (2014): 333–52, https://doi.org/10.1080/00083968.2014.971835.

Murunga, Godwin R., Duncan Okello, and Anders Sjögren. *Kenya: The Struggle For A New Constitutional Order*, 66–78. London, UK: Zed Books, 2014.

Mutua, Makau. *Kenya's Quest for Democracy: Taming Leviathan*. Boulder, CO: Lynne Rienner, 2008.

Nasong'o, Shadrack Wanjala. "Negotiating New Rules of the Game: Social Movements, Civil Society and the Kenyan Transition." In *Kenya: The Struggle for Democracy*, edited by Godwin R. Murunga and Shadrack Wanjala Nasong'o, 19–57. Dakar, Senegal: CODESRIA Books, 2007a.

Nasong'o, Shadrack Wanjala. "Political Transition Without Transformation: The Dialectic of Liberalization Without Democratization in Kenya and Zambia." *African Studies Review* 50, no. 1 (April 2007b): 83–107, https://doi.org/10.1353/arw.2005.0126.

Nasong'o, Shadrack Wanjala, and Godwin R. Murunga. "Prospects for Democracy in Kenya." In *Kenya: The Struggle for Democracy*, edited by Godwin R. Murunga and Shadrack Wanjala Nasong'o, 3–16. Dakar, Senegal: CODESRIA Books, 2007.

Obulutsa, George, and Katharine Houreld. "Kenya Supreme Court Upholds Ruto's Presidential Victory." *Reuters*, September 5, 2022, https://www.reuters.com/world/africa/kenyas-top-court-rule-disputed-presidential-election-2022-09-04.

Okello, Duncan, and Gitau, Mburu. Introduction and Overview' in *Readings in Inequality in Kenya: Sectoral Dynamics and Perspectives*. Nairobi, Kenya: Society for International Development, 2007.

Omolo, Ken. "Political Ethnicity in the Democratisation Process in Kenya." *African Studies* 61, no. 2 (2002): 209–21, https://doi.org/10.1080/0002018022000032938.

Oucho, John O. "Undercurrents of Post-Election Violence in Kenya: Issues in the Long-Term Agenda." In *Tensions and Reversals in Democratic Transitions: The Kenya 2007 General Elections*, edited by Karuti Kanyinga and Duncan Okello, 491–31. Nairobi, Kenya: Society for International Development, 2010.

Parliament of Kenya, "Members of National Assembly," accessed March 13, 2025, https://www.parliament.go.ke/index.php/the-national-assembly/mps.

Sandbrook, Richard. *The Politics of Africa's Economic Stagnation*. Cambridge, UK: Cambridge University Press, 1985.

Shahow, Abdullahi Abdille. "Devolution Has Not Delivered for the People of North-Eastern Kenya." *The Elephant* (Nairobi, Kenya), February 24, 2023, https://www.theelephant.info/analysis/2023/02/24/devolution-has-not-delivered-for-the-people-of-north-eastern-kenya.

Siollun, Max. *What Britain Did to Nigeria: A Short History of Conquest and Rule*. London, UK: Hurst, 2021.

Throup, David, and Charles Hornsby. *Multi-Party Politics in Kenya: The Kenyatta and Moi States and the Triumph of the System in the 1992 Election*. Oxford, UK: James Currey, 1998.

Zaleza, Paul Tiyambe. "The Protracted Transition to the Second Republic in Kenya." In *Kenya: The Struggle for a New Constitutional Order*, edited by Godwin R. Murunga, Duncan Okello, and Anders Sjögren, 17–43. London, UK: Zed Books, 2014.

5

GENDERED ETHNICITY

Compounding Inequality in Resource Distribution and Decision-Making for Women in Sub-Saharan Africa

Abbyssinia Mushunje, Saul Ngarava, Simbarashe Tatsvarei, and Peter Mukarumbwa

Introduction

Globally, women have played a fundamental role in boosting economic development both indirectly through child-rearing as well as through direct participation in labor markets via entrepreneurship (Ngarava, Zhou, & Monde, 2019). Women's empowerment and gender equality are integral to the United Nations *2030 Agenda for Sustainable Development*—no fewer than fifty-four gender-specific indicators (or broad measures of average achievement in key dimensions of human development) drive the UN's Sustainable Development Goals (SDGs) (UN Women, Why Gender Equality Matters, 2018). Gender informs differences in roles and responsibilities, access to resources, and agency in decision-making (AGRA, 2018), and wide gender gaps persist in the developing world: Women are far more likely than men to be disadvantaged in terms of hunger; poverty; access to education, health care, clean water, and energy; inclusive economic participation; and overall well-being (UN Women, Fact Sheet, 2018). Most gender-related studies have focused on observed measures of gender inequality and their effects on economic growth and development. Simultaneously, ethnic diversity studies tend to concentrate on the impacts of ethnic fragmentation on public goods, economic development, technology adoption, institutional quality, and conflict. Yet *gendered ethnicity*—the ways in which ethnic heterogeneity influences gender inequality—begs further attention.

As this volume explores, ethnicity and inequality are inextricably linked in sub-Saharan Africa (UN Women, Fact Sheet, 2018). Migration has exacerbated this linkage by diminishing social capital, adaptation to labor markets, and access to services (Ireland, 2010). The resulting heterogeneous social identities hamper social cohesion, which in large part determines a society's ability to induce cooperation

DOI: 10.4324/9781003357025-7

in favor of welfare-enhancing outcomes. According to social identity theory, members of a heterogeneous society come to adopt an *us versus them* worldview—a binary between the in-group, or dominant class, and the out-group(s), or subordinate class(es), that fosters reduced cooperation (Aksoy, 2019). Ethnic fragmentation corresponds to lower levels of trust (in institutions and among actors) and social networking, leading to discrimination, intolerance, dissent, and ineffective institutional systems—and, ultimately, exclusion from the wider community. It also breeds tensions that can spill over into ethnic violence (Easterly, 2001).

Ethnic fragmentation also compounds gender inequality. Ethnic diversity's effects on trust and economic development tend to widen the gender gap by propagating poverty among women, reducing female access to education and health care, and reducing awareness and respect for women rights. Economic differentials between ethnic groups inevitably lead to social exclusion among minority ethnic groups, triggering resistance to redistributive policies (which usually favor in-groups at the expense of out-groups), thereby widening existing gender gaps. Ethnic and ethnolinguistic diversity can also expose out-groups to discrimination and impede access to public goods, including information and awareness of gender inequality issues. And ethnically driven insurgencies and civil conflicts often affect women disproportionately as well, stripping them of social protections and exposing them to physical and sexual abuse. Furthermore, ethnic diversity is associated with corruption, nepotism, and ethnic voting, all of which compromise governance and institutional quality and can deliver gender-biased outcomes. The correlations between ethnic diversity, inequality, and female discrimination thus start to become clear.

Gender inequality constrains women's participation in political and civic life across sub-Saharan Africa, resulting in the underrepresentation of their interests in both formal and informal political institutions. This underrepresentation, whether wrought by unequal access to resources, norms against gender equality, or both, disempowers women socially and politically, with negative impacts on economic opportunities and development (Gottlieb, Guy, & Robinson, 2016; Gottlieb & Robinson, 2016; Isaksson, Kotsadam, & Nerman, 2014; Kittilson, 2016; Mason et al., 2015). A 2017 study by Damilola Tobiloba Adereti and Oluwatosin Fasina cites World Bank data indicating that twenty-five of the thirty-five economies in sub-Saharan Africa had laws on the books restricting women's economic opportunities (along with other sociocultural barriers), which hampers economic advancement (Adereti & Fasina, 2017; Galiè et al., 2015). Numerous scholars have identified that restrictions on women's access to land, financial capital, social capital, and technology increase their vulnerability in multiple ways (Adereti & Fasina, 2017; Galiè et al., 2015; Namubiru-Mwaura, 2014; Raney et al., 2011; Spieldoch, Aboud, & Brody, 2014). Factors such as marital status, resource entitlements conferred through matrilineal inheritance, gender differences in community participation and access to information and labor markets, and even household dynamics also come to bear on women's ability to make decisions. Women in sub-Saharan Africa generally control and manage fewer and lower-value assets than men, who are much more likely to own land, have access to education, and command labor, machinery, and technologies. Customary patrilineal systems wherein resources are conferred through male kinship also render women more vulnerable than men: Oftentimes, wives can lose access to resources in the event of marital breakdown or a husband's death (Farnworth et al., 2016).

Denying women rights, agency, and equal access in terms of resources, decision-making, and status (including anemic or nonexistent protections against gender-based violence) has cultivated societies prone to lower labor productivity, poorer educational outcomes, lower child health and nutrition, higher child mortalities, strained social and health service systems, and, often, violent conflict (Kabeer & Natali, 2013). On the other hand, when women have equal access to income, work, and education, outcomes improve across the board: better health and lower mortality, greater economic opportunity and political participation, and heightened social stability (Hillenbrand et al., 2015; Kabeer & Natali, 2013). Expanding women's access to productive resources (i.e., the natural, human, and capital resources used to produce goods and services) bolsters their productive output, decision-making agency, and empowerment (Galiè et al., 2015; Mason et al., 2015). Alison Cook and Christy Glass have stressed that diversity among those in decision-making positions in particular tends to reduce segregation, increase pay equity and mobility for minorities and women, and advance transparency, accountability, effective communication, and implementation of innovation (Cook & Glass, 2015). In sum, heightened gender equality boosts productivity, enhances cooperation, and augments institutional functionality—all of which ultimately promote sustainable development (Wilson, 2015).

Yet the numbers are deeply disturbing, as the prominence of gender equality in the SDGs reflects. According to UN Women, in sub-Saharan Africa as of 2018:

- Women aged 25–34 were 27 percent more likely than men to be living in extreme poverty.
- More than 50 percent of the female population was food insecure at moderate or severe levels.
- Adolescent girls were 4.5 percent more likely than adolescent boys to be out of school, although educational disparities were much starker in some countries. In Nigeria, for example, 13 percent of women and girls from the wealthiest households had completed six or less years of education, while 96.5 percent in the poorest households had four years or less of primary education (defined as "education-poor").
- Only 18 percent of women had access to the internet, compared with 24.6 percent of men.
- More than one-third (37 percent) of women aged 20–24 were in a union or married before the age of 18.

- The maternal mortality rate of 556 deaths per 100,000 live births was the highest in the world, accounting for two-thirds of all maternal deaths each year.
- Of women and girls aged 15–49, 22.3 percent had experienced physical and/or sexual violence.
- Djibouti, Guinea, Mali, Sierra Leone, Somalia, and Sudan had the highest rates of female genital mutilation in the world—85 percent or greater among women aged 20–24.
- Finally, as of September 2017, women held only 23.8 percent of parliamentary seats in sub-Saharan Africa. Although World Bank data indicates that the latter figure had increased to 26 percent as of 2022, parity remains a distant goal (UN Women, Fact Sheet, 2018).[1]

As a team of researchers observed in 2015, "laws and customs that negatively affect women's access to and control over resources hamper their economic advancement, particularly in Sub-Saharan Africa." Unless specific gender equity laws are adopted, economic improvement will not be realized, and women will run the risk of being "left behind" (Galiè et al., 2015; Klugman & Tyson, 2016). However, complexities surrounding the significance and severity of the gender problem—above all, why women in some countries enjoy more access, opportunity, and overall equality than in others, and how to move the needle—remain poorly understood in sub-Saharan Africa. Focusing on economic, social, and cultural norms and institutions that structure gender roles may help explain such dynamics (Gottlieb & Robinson, 2016).

Ethnicity is a critical dimension through which gender roles influence access to and accumulation of resources and decision-making. According to a 2015 CARE USA working paper, identifying effective mechanisms for change necessitates uncovering and acknowledging differences and diversity among women as well as between women and men. Gender-transformative measures of change require questioning internalized belief systems and closely held identities, and challenging entrenched institutionalized structures, histories, and cross-ethnic power relations (Hillenbrand et al., 2015). Susan Marlow and Angela Martinez Dy assert that grappling with gender while ignoring ethnicity—and failing to consider the interrelated nature of these two key identity markers—risks a superficial understanding of social positioning and its effects (Marlow & Martinez Dy, 2018). Various conceptual and theoretical perspectives attempt to reveal the likely channels through which ethnic diversity impacts gender-related outcomes (AGRA, 2018). But only by looking at gender disparities through the lens of intersectionality does the reality that ethnicity is central to gender inequality in sub-Saharan Africa begin to emerge (Rowe, 2016).

It is important to note that not all social norms deepen inequality, even in diverse, hierarchical, or even patriarchal societies. For instance, a son brought up by a working mother is likely to show empathy and support for women, which indirectly promotes gender equality. Similarly, exposure to female leaders and role models is shown to reduce male prejudice against female leadership and inequality, thereby promoting development-enhancing opportunities for women (Churchill, Nuhu, & Lopez, 2019). However, social norms and power relations frequently restrict access to natural resources for certain social groups, and ethnicity often compounds existing gender gaps by strengthening social, cultural, and institutional norms (Cole et al., 2015). Moreover, scholars and policymakers alike suffer from a tendency to view and treat women as homogeneous, when in fact their experiences are substantially informed by differences of ethnicity (Farnworth & Colverson, 2015; Rowe, 2016).

Among other deficits, the UN's 2015 Millennium Development Goals (the precursor to the SDGs) overlooked the deep confluence of inequality, gender, and ethnicity. According to Stephen McCloskey, "Perhaps the biggest failing of the MDGs was their lack of critical analysis of the fundamental causes of global poverty and the persistently highly [*sic*] levels of regional disparity in wealth, employment, infrastructure, food security and education" (McCloskey, 2015). The 2030 SDGs seek to address that confluence by placing equity and social justice at the heart of global efforts to eradicate poverty and inequality and usher in an era of truly inclusive sustainable development (Watkins, 2014). This chapter argues that these efforts will continue to fall short unless policymakers fully understand and contend with the complex ways in which gender and ethnicity intersect with inequality. The objective of this chapter, therefore, is to identify how gender and ethnic fragmentation in sub-Saharan Africa have influenced resource distribution and decision-making.

To do so, we first examine the various approaches to development in gender studies scholarship. Our evaluation finds that conventional methodologies are insufficient to explain prevailing gender inequalities across sub-Saharan Africa in the realms of resource distribution and decision-making and that gender-related studies have largely ignored or glossed over the role of ethnic heterogeneity and established norms in preserving and perpetuating these inequalities. We then turn to the theory of intersectionality as an alternative framework to illuminate the overlapping social identity categories (and the norms and practices constructed around them) that factor into women's access to resources and opportunities for decision-making agency across the subcontinent. Three different case studies—highlighting measures to realize gender equality and financial inclusion of women in Zimbabwe, survival strategies and social capital among immigrants in South Africa, and the gender and ethnic dimensions of political representation in Burundi and Rwanda—help illustrate the how and why of sub-Saharan Africa's inclusive development conundrum. In the end, we conclude that policies seeking to advance gender equality that neglect to address ethnic inequality in tandem do so at their own peril—and that of the region and its marginalized populations.

Gender in Resource Distribution and Decision-Making

Gender studies scholarship takes various approaches with regard to development as a whole, and specifically to gendered decision-making and women's access to resources. Twentieth-century gender theories on development generally fall into three main categories: women in development (WID), which broadly addresses endeavors relating to women's inclusion in development; women and development (WAD), which focuses on unequal gender relations and demands for inclusion; and gender and development (GAD), which centers on gendered critiques of development models. The WID model tends to combine efficiency and equity arguments around stereotyping and prejudice that preclude women from participating in the productive sphere. It prioritizes improving women's productivity through education, training, access to technology, and access to labor markets. Its two underlying themes—utility maximization and economic growth—are rooted in neoclassical economics and liberal feminism, emphasizing women's capacity for rational thought and action and demanding equality with men. Thus, while WID certainly foregrounds discrimination of women in the development process, it fails to account for gendered structures of power and unequal gender relations in the context of ethnicity.

The WAD approach aims to provide an alternative to WID that illuminates the exploitation of women as essential for imperialism and capitalism, but it too overlooks ethnic-gender dynamics. In particular, WAD disregards the overarching influence of patriarchal power structures in women's marginalization and the duality between productive and reproductive demands on women. According to Eva Rathgeber, WAD gives "remarkably little specific attention to issues of gender subordination," and it tends to group all women together without duly considering how class, race, and ethnicity impact women's actual social status. The GAD methodology incorporates the social reproductive sphere to explain women's historical, systematic relegation to subordinate roles. In contrast to the neoclassical model of the household as a unit characterized by altruism and joint utility maximization, GAD concentrates on the household as an arena of conflict and inequality, highlighting the unequal distribution of resources and power within households. It argues that treating women as homogeneous with shared interests—and promoting policies with the same shortcoming—neglects gender as a dynamic and socially constructed category (Rathgeber, 1990; Wilson, 2015; Jaquette, 2017).

While WID, WAD, and GAD each fall short in their attempts to provide a holistic approach to decision-making and women's access to resources, other frameworks do explore gender's effects on resource distribution and decision-making. The Harvard analytical framework (sometimes called the gender roles framework), put forth in the 1980s, strives to fill in the gaps of the earlier models by negotiating men's and women's characteristics as distinct rather than uniform and scrutinizing the ways in which social institutions (such as ethnicity, religious institutions, and traditional/cultural institutions) work together to create and maintain disadvantages and advantages (Cole et al., 2015). The Harvard framework's starting point is the belief that development aid projects would benefit from allocating resources to women as well as men—indeed, that ignoring women in planning resource distribution is inefficient (March, Smyth, & Mukhopadhyay, 1999). The social relations framework, advanced by Naila Kabeer in the 1990s, looks at the distribution of resources, responsibilities, and power through the lens of existing gender inequalities. Its conceptual model examines how institutions (such as households, communities, markets, and states) create and perpetuate gender inequalities. Like the Harvard framework, the social relations framework aims to involve WID solutions, enabling them to be "agents of their own development" (Kabeer, 1994).

The ambivalent sexism theory, as described by Peter Glick and Susan Fiske in 1996, relies on the tension between inherent male-female interdependence and male dominance in societies to tease out two distinct manifestations of sexism: hostile and benevolent. Hostile sexism targets women who violate prescriptive gender roles by refusing to conform to traditional forms of male-female interdependence; benevolent sexism patronizes women cooperating with traditional male-female interdependence by adhering to prescriptive gender roles and remaining subordinate to men (Fiske, 2017). (Benevolent sexism is considered more acceptable than hostile sexism because it is perceived as less pernicious to women, yet this belief is extremely detrimental to women and society: Because the comparatively positive perception of benevolent sexism is a key component of ambivalent sexism, it contributes to the perpetuation and pervasiveness of gender inequalities and ultimately negatively impacts women's access to resources (Barreto & Doyle, 2023).) Finally, the social constructionist theory, which has roots going back to the mid-twentieth century (and arguably earlier), views gender differences in values, attributes, and activities—"feminine traits" versus "masculine traits"—as socially constructed, prescribed, accepted, and internalized rather than intrinsic (Trauth et al., 2016; Berger & Luckmann, 1966). Social constructivist theory does not explicitly relate to resource distribution and decision-making; rather, it asserts that gender roles are constructs of social environments and/or cultural backgrounds, and therefore tend to be fluid.

In the Global South, poor, rural women almost universally lack the access and ownership rights to resources such as water, land, livestock, and crops that men have (Galiè et al., 2015). This is supported through theories that augment the separation of roles based on gender differences (i.e., the Harvard analytical framework, the social relations framework, the ambivalent sexism theory, and the social constructionist theory). A 2016 article in the *International Journal of Agricultural Sustainability* explained that in sub-Saharan Africa, customary laws that govern access to and possession of such resources are often prejudicial to women (Farnworth et al., 2016). Furthermore, development initiatives like agricultural extension programs tend to prioritize men over women, which reduces women's participation in mainstream economies (Raney et al., 2011). Women's relative paucity of access to resources, education, technology, training, and labor markets amplifies this effect, disempowering women and relegating them to the sidelines of the mainstream economy, if not to the home (Farnworth & Colverson, 2015). Yet studies conducted in Tanzania revealed that women—given equal resources to men—boosted agricultural yields by 22 percent, and that increasing women's access to resources improved household consumption, nutrition, and welfare (Mason et al., 2015). It would seem, then, that gender parity in resource distribution has a demonstrative positive impact on development outcomes.

All the aforementioned ill effects of gender inequality in resource distribution are compounded by gender inequality in the decision-making space. Much as economic participation has historically been biased toward men, women's political participation and representation remain far below parity in sub-Saharan Africa. In a 2019 report on women's economic empowerment in Zimbabwe, the Alliance for Financial Inclusion emphasized that policymakers and regulators must focus less on one-size-fits-all, gender-neutral initiatives and interventions, which "tend to exacerbate disadvantages against women," and more on solutions and policies that address the root causes of these issues (Kittilson, 2016; Tarinda, 2019).

BOX 5.1 GENDER IN RESOURCE DISTRIBUTION AND DECISION-MAKING IN ZIMBABWE

Gender Equality and Financial Inclusion of Women

Although Zimbabwe is signatory to several regional and international conventions, protocols, and declarations that promote gender equality, the country has a long way to go. Its gender inequality index—a World Health Organization measure of gender disparities in health, empowerment, and the labor market—was 0.51 in 2022, ranking it 132nd out of 166 countries. Zimbabwe ranked 50th out of 146 countries on the World Economic Forum's 2022 Global Gender Gap index, and 8th in sub-Saharan Africa (UNDP, 2024; Moyo-Nyede & Kugarakuripi, 2023). Gender ills such as violence against girls and women are still prevalent, and rates of child marriage, youth pregnancy, and sexually transmitted infection and HIV remain high. According to the World Bank, as of 2022, 39.4 percent of women had experienced gender-based violence, 11.6 percent of women had experienced sexual assault, and 16.2 percent of women were married before the age of 18 (World Bank, 2023).

Correspondingly, women are poorly represented in decision-making and in the labor market, and women and girls are overrepresented in child labor and in the informal economy. According to the UN's Food and Agriculture Organization, women comprised 52 percent of Zimbabwe's population as of 2017, yet women's representation in parliament was only 32 percent. Only 21 percent of managerial positions in the private sector belonged to women. Although

67 percent of women lived in rural areas and depended on agriculture for their livelihoods, they owned only 10 percent of the land, and just 23 percent of women owned cattle. These figures can be attributed to the patrilineal nature of Zimbabwean society, in which sociocultural and political factors disproportionally favor men, and women traditionally have lower access to productive resources. Structural barriers such as literacy and educational levels, along with wage and income gaps, have further hindered women's empowerment and inclusion. Other barriers include a lack of participation in the political and electoral domains, stigmatization, intimidation, and others (Tarinda, 2019; UNFAO, 2024).

But there is room for optimism. In the 1990s, the newly founded Zimbabwe Women's Resource Centre and Network began work to institutionalize gender-focused budgeting in the government's economic development and poverty-reduction policymaking (Kapungu, 2008). These efforts led to the adoption of a National Gender Policy in 2004 and the creation of the Ministry of Women Affairs, Gender and Community Development in 2005 (Tarinda, 2019). In 2006, Zimbabwe introduced the Gender Budgeting and Women's Empowerment Programme, which has made great strides in placing gender on the policy agenda, reducing gender inequalities, and promoting gender-sensitive development.

These and other formal government commitments to practice gender-focused budgeting and to report on gender issues and gender mainstreaming in work plans led to more gender-sensitive recruitment processes that increased the number of women in decision-making positions. Equal employment opportunities for men and women are embedded in the public service at a ratio of 50:50. Gender equality is also an integral focus of the Ministries of Finance and Economic Development (Kapungu, 2008). Promising legislation introduced as a result of these efforts included the 2006 Domestic Violence Act, the 2001 Sexual Offences Act, and the 2008–12 National Gender Policy Implementation Strategy and Work Plan (Tarinda, 2019).In 2013, Zimbabwe's newly amended constitution took recognition of women's rights, economic empowerment, and inclusion further, paving the way for a National Gender Commission to promote gender equality that commenced operations in 2015, among other institutions and structures. The establishment of so-called *gender focal persons*—director-level staff in all line ministries, departments, and agencies responsible for "mainstreaming gender in all policies, programs and projects in their various sectors"—is another poignant indicator of Zimbabwe's commitment to gender equity and inclusion (Tarinda, 2019).

In terms of economic empowerment and financial inclusion, Zimbabwe implemented the Gender Responsive Economic Policy Management Initiative in 2013, which spawned numerous gender-focused lending institutions, along with targeted support mechanisms and training initiatives for women-operated enterprises and small and medium enterprises (SMEs). (In Zimbabwe, 57 percent of SMEs were run by women as of 2012 (RCFFT, 2012).) In 2016, the country rolled out the first phase of a National Financial Inclusion Strategy (2016–20) aimed at expanding access to financial services for women and other disadvantaged groups. This strategy worked: Women's access to bank credit increased by 39.12 percent between December 2017 and December 2018. As of 2019, nearly all Zimbabwean banks had established women's desks or units, and the country had licensed its first women-dedicated bank. Meanwhile, by December 2018, the central bank had licensed 205 microfinance institutions (MFIs), which play a central role in gender-inclusive financing, with 719 branches across the country—including in rural areas, where 70 percent of women reside. By 2018, women held 42 percent of MFI accounts (Tarinda, 2019). Phase two of the National Financial Inclusion Strategy (2022–26) is underway. According to a 2022 survey conducted by the Bank of Zimbabwe, women accounted for 54 percent of the population and 60 percent of ownership of micro, small, and medium enterprises. The overall level of financial inclusion (both formal and nonformal) increased from 68 percent in 2014 to 83 percent in 2022 (Reserve Bank of Zimbabwe, 2016, 2022).

Despite these developments, the country still has work to do to overcome its gender gap. According to the World Bank, labor force participation for women in Zimbabwe is 34 percent, compared with 53 percent for men (World Bank, 2024; Walker & Wanjiru, 2023). And, as of 2023, only six of President Emmerson Mnangagwa's cabinet ministers were women. As in much of sub-Saharan Africa, economic participation and access to resources remain biased toward men. Barriers to women's inclusion and participation include collateral issues, financial literacy, access to technology, and traditional cultural practices. Low representation of women in public- and private-sector spheres of influence also reflects Zimbabwe's gender gap (Tarinda, 2019).

Ethnicity in Resource Distribution and Decision-Making

Gender-related studies have largely neglected the role of ethnicity, concentrating instead on observable measures of gender inequality and their effects on growth and development (Churchill, Nuhu, & Lopez, 2019). In reality, ethnic heterogeneity profoundly influences economic and entrepreneurship activities in sub-Saharan Africa, with wide-ranging impacts on resource access, allocation, accumulation, and use. Ethnicity also factors centrally into development policy decision-making (Churchill, 2017).

Scholars have taken a number of approaches to unpacking ethnicity as it relates to resource distribution and decision-making. One such approach, the conflict theory, anticipates increased competition for scarce resources along group lines among individuals in diverse settings, elevating the prominence and pertinence of existing ethnic differences. Amanda Lea Robinson describes how in this model, ethnic antagonism and distrust are consequences of competition among ethnic groups for resources within ethnically heterogeneous societies, be it the rational pursuit of material or social goods or psychological responses to group inequalities resulting from such competition. (For a discussion of objective versus subjective inequalities, see Chapter 3.) On the other hand, Robinson discusses another approach, the contact theory, which holds that more contact between individuals from different (and often adversarial) ethnic backgrounds actually undermines their respective negative stereotypes and reduces mutual antipathies—potentially opening the door for cooperation and reducing ethnic strife. According to contact theory, inclusivity fosters inter-ethnic cooperation that is essential for social cohesion, trust, and nation-building (Robinson, 2020).

More broadly, the social identity theory—harkening back to the earlier in-group versus out-group discussion—explains that people inherently adopt an *us versus them* outlook in order to cope with the cognitive complexity of living in a diverse world (Aksoy, 2019). Social identity theory studies the interaction between personal and social identities, seeking to determine the circumstances in which people think of themselves as individuals or as members of a group (Harwood, 2020). In exploring the effects of heterogeneous social identities and resource inequality on cooperative behavior, Ozan Aksoy has found that cooperation significantly diminishes among those with fewer resources (in both in-group and out-group interactions) (Aksoy, 2019).

The ethnic enclave theory, as outlined by Sefa Awaworyi Churchill and Vinod Mishra in the context of ethnic diversity's impact on small business ventures, postulates that ethnic enclaves—high-concentration areas of coethnics with a common identity and interconnected economic interests—stimulate social connection. The ethnic networks thus created and the social capital that they engender encourage individuals to share information, fostering economic cooperation and growth (Churchill & Mishra, 2018). Correspondingly, the social capital theory suggests that the social relationships built and nurtured through networks such as ethnic enclaves or in-groups become resources, enabling members of those networks to share information and identify new opportunities, thereby promoting development.

The theory of middleman minorities highlights that ethnic association and prevailing cultural trends propel some ethnic groups to engage in specific trades, all to do with "market intermediation" (Churchill, 2017). According to Edna Bonacich (an original exponent of the term *middleman minority* in the 1970s), "one of the principal peculiarities of these groups is the economic role they play. In contrast to most ethnic minorities, these so-called middleman minorities occupy an intermediate rather than low-status position" within the nonhomogeneous societies in which they reside and operate, playing a niche role in economic resource distribution. For example, the involvement of Lebanese merchants in commodity trading in West Africa made them highly strategic and influential intermediaries. They traded commodities such as diamonds in Sierra Leone and cocoa in Côte d'Ivoire, through which they amassed considerable wealth and political status in society (Bonacich, 1973).

Studies like the ones discussed above (along with many others) implicate a wide range of factors in ethnic inequality—lack of access to resources, education, technology, training, and labor markets—all of which in turn perpetuate that inequality while depriving disadvantaged groups of civic participation, governmental representation, and decision-making agency. In these ways, ethnic inequality is inexorably linked to economic underdevelopment, inequitable provision of public goods and services, social unrest, democratic breakdown, and even civil wars (Churchill, 2019; Churchill, Nuhu, & Lopez, 2019; McDoom, 2019).

As Chapter 3 describes in detail, horizontal (or group-based) inequality breeds communication gaps across cultural boundaries and tension, animosity, and conflict between groups. Yet only a few empirical studies have focused on the multifarious dimensions of ethnic identity and how those facets shape resource distribution and decision-making in sub-Saharan Africa (Gershman & Rivera, 2018; Lau & Scales, 2016). Robinson has explored how ethnic diversity coincides with diminished social capital and lowered levels of trust (through Robert Putnam's constrict theory—wherein people who live in diverse areas "hunker down" and effectively stick to their own, decreasing social capital, solidarity, and trust—and contact theory, respectively) (Robinson, 2020; Putnam, 2007). Kazeem Ajide, Olorunfemi Alimi, and Simplice Asongu further identified that in sub-Saharan Africa, ethnic diversity—and ethnic fragmentation more specifically—correlates to lower levels of redistribution: When ethnic groups view one another as competitors for scarce resources, individuals belonging to one ethnic group tend to be less willing to support redistribution to assist those belonging to other ethnic groups (Ajide, Alimi, & Asongu, 2019).

On the other hand, Boris Gershman and Diego Rivera attest that, whereas "deep-rooted diversity based on cleavages formed in the distant past appears to be strongly inversely associated with regional development outcomes," ethnic diversity can be a determinant of economic growth (Gershman & Rivera, 2018). Churchill and Mishra exposit that diversity increases the talent pool and therefore the quality of local workforces while promoting cultural and social capital and bolstering institutions, which in turn nurtures entrepreneurial talent. Ethnic diversity can also affect the rate of new business development as well as financial capital—especially when ethnic preferences come into play. Some investors gravitate toward specific regions due to a preference to trade with particular ethnic or linguistic groups (Churchill, 2017; Churchill & Mishra, 2018). For instance, coastal merchants penetrated East Africa rather than other parts of Africa because of their preference to trade with Muslims (Ensminger, 1996; Fafchamps, 2000).

Above all, ethnicity studies, whether around diversity and inequality (or both), too often exhibit the same shortfall of failing to synthesize the nexus of gender. The frameworks outlined above all try to explain the intricacies of ethnic diversity and inequality, but in neglecting the intersectionality between gender and ethnicity, they fundamentally miss the inseparable role that gender plays in resource access, distribution, and use and its instrumentality in decision-making agency, policy outcomes, and ultimately development writ large. This critical bidirectional intersectionality either amplifies or reduces ethnic and gender inequalities. Its interlinked effects are unmistakable, and disregarding them risks imperiling sub-Saharan Africa's prospects for sustainable, inclusive development.

BOX 5.2 ETHNICITY IN RESOURCE DISTRIBUTION AND DECISION-MAKING IN SOUTH AFRICA

Survival Strategies and Social Capital among Immigrants in Diepsloot, South Africa

South Africa has historically been a country of choice for immigrants due to a variety of factors: historical migration streams dating back to the late nineteenth century; political, economic, and social conditions in surrounding countries that compel out-migration, and certain official interventions and amnesties for immigrants. This influx of foreign nationals has created a blended society within southern Africa, which in turn has fostered strong social networks that offer crucial survival strategies for new immigrants facing myriad challenges integrating into new societies. As Nosipho Hlatshwayo and Kambidima Wotela explain,

> Immigration has economic and social consequences in developing countries. Cities in developed countries provide access to shelter, employment, and other social facilities which is not the case in developing countries. African cities face challenges ranging from absent or ineffective provision of basic services, poor housing, few secure employment opportunities, and insufficient income. Competition for limited resources, especially employment opportunities, between locals and foreign nationals breeds conflict.

Diepsloot is a township situated northwest of Johannesburg, about 35 kilometers from the city's central business district. Its total area is approximately 5.6 square kilometers, and its estimated population as of 2017 was 350,000 people spread among about 30,000 households. Diepsloot is ethnically diverse. Most of its population comes from South Africa's Limpopo Province, which is home to the Venda, Tsonga, Shangaan, and Pedi ethnic groups. Locals account for 77 percent of the township's population; the rest consists of foreign nationals from Bangladesh, Lesotho, Malawi, Mozambique, Pakistan, Somalia, and Zimbabwe. Higher educational levels among immigrants have translated to a higher proportion of male immigrants to South African–born males in the labor force. Most of the southern African migrants in Diepsloot are relatively young (twenty to twenty-nine years old), as migration tends to decline with age. Diepsloot's population as a whole is thus quite young: 56 percent of people are under the age of 35.

The economy is a mixture of formal and informal businesses, the latter of which largely comprise subsistence businesses insufficient to elevate people above the poverty line. Roughly 47 percent of the population is employed in either the formal or informal sector—meaning that roughly half of the township's population is unemployed. Housing—which consists of privately owned homes, makeshift shacks, and state-subsidized and bank-financed houses, all comingled—is an issue. South African nationals own the majority of the houses, many of which have backyard dwelling units erected that the owners rent out to those (both immigrants and fellow South Africans) who do not qualify for state-subsidized housing. Diepsloot residents' living standards range from low (i.e., abject poverty) to moderate (i.e., hand-to-mouth). Disease and crime are prevalent as a result. Xenophobia also spiked in both 2008 and 2013 as tensions brought about by competition for employment and housing came to a head.

Although South Africa's constitution guarantees social, physical, and economic rights to those that "live in the Republic," state support for foreign nationals is inadequate. Foreign nationals in South Africa do not have access to social grants that are available to millions of South Africans at or below the poverty line, which provide social support systems such as subsidized housing and free access to education and health care. Meanwhile, the cost of living for foreign nationals is relatively higher than average, compounding the challenges they face. Needless to say, immigrants also lack representation in government and civic spaces to advocate for greater protections and assistance. The end result is a foregone conclusion: inadequate resource acquisition and decision-making agency.

All these conditions render survival strategies anchored in various dimensions of social capital vital. Survival strategies that new immigrants rely on are rooted in ethnicity, culture, nationality, and language. These shared identity categories create a particular form of social capital that assists foreign nationals in the pursuit of resources and opportunities. As Hlatshwayo and Wotela observe,

> foreign nationals utilise different forms of social capital to achieve different means—the reliance on family at the point of entry to access shelter and employment opportunities [and then on] friendships and networks within the employment circles to access other employment opportunities.

More specifically, according to Hlatshwayo and Wotela, kinship-based physical survival strategies include the means to attain adequate food, shelter, water, and sanitation. Human survival strategies include the means to attain education to improve employment prospects, as well as language skills: In Johannesburg especially, knowledge of isiZulu (the predominant language spoken by the Zulu people, with about 13.5 million native speakers) helps with social integration, while knowledge of English bolsters employment opportunities. Economic survival strategies include entrepreneurship, informal trading, and formal employment. These kinship-based networks on both ends of the immigration chain also provide coping and integration strategies, which ultimately help perpetuate immigration despite the disincentives discussed above (Hlatshwayo & Wotela, 2018).

Gender-Ethnicity Intersectionality in Resource Distribution and Decision-Making

As this chapter has described, the majority of gender studies literature substantially fails to consider the intersectionality of gender, ethnicity, and inequality. Likewise, ethnic studies largely overlook the interplay of gender as a social identity. Making matters worse, policymakers consistently treat identity as fixed and static, particularly in terms of the ways it influences resource use. As Jacqueline Lau and Ivan Scales have noted, most studies evaluate social differences such as ethnicity and gender as separate dimensions producing distinct inequalities and resource distribution patterns (Lau & Scales, 2016). There is a dearth of scholarship into how gender interacts with ethnicity, and how given that gendered experiences are not monolithic—this interaction can be subject to change (Kittilson, 2016).

This shortfall has serious practical implications. Analyses of political, social, and economic behavior should take a more holistic approach, accounting for the multiple intersecting identities within the categories of gender and ethnicity, and the multidimensional interactions between them. For example, in their study on ethnicity and gender in the Gambia, Lau and Scales find that "identities, rather than existing as pre-formed and fixed, emerge (and are constantly shaped and re-shaped) through everyday practices. . . and regulatory regimes." As a result, the different dimensions of space, place, and power all have a key role to play, "creating particular arenas for material practices and the (re)production and contestation of social exclusion based on gender, class, ethnic, and other socio-cultural differences." In this way, identity categories like gender and ethnicity intersect in determining access to and control of natural resources (Lau & Scales, 2016). Taking the interplay of gender, ethnicity, and inequality a step further, Steven Cole, Ranjitha Puskur, Surendran Rajaratnam, and Festus Zulu explore how certain groups are systematically excluded or disadvantaged based on ethnicity and gender in Zambia, especially in rural settings. This highly gendered marginalization deprives targeted groups of assets and income and also induces vulnerability to external shocks (Cole et al., 2015).

The popularized WID, WAD, and GAD methodologies described earlier in this chapter failed to challenge racialized and ethnicized power relations in the developing world, wherein ethnic minority women are identified as homogeneous (and powerless) victims of certain socioeconomic systems in need of liberation by Western feminists, in what Kalpana Wilson calls "a reiteration of missionary women's narratives of rescue and salvation" (Wilson, 2015). This framing fundamentally misses real-world differences in gender- and ethnic-related attitudes and roles—differences between ethnic groups and between men and women (Harrison, Leitch, & McAdam, 2015; Pearse & Connell, 2016). Intersectionality theory, as first enunciated by Kimberlé Crenshaw in 1989 (Crenshaw, 1989), argues that considering gender in a vacuum homogenizes and essentializes both men and women as categories, and that taking such a blunt instrument approach blurs (or even omits) diverse and individualized markers of social identities (Marlow & Martinez Dy, 2018). By contrast, intersectionality provides a means for capturing the multiplicity of social identity categories shaping the true and varied nature of identity (Carrim & Nkomo, 2016). Rita Kaur Dhamoon emphasizes that intersectionality recognizes the simultaneous interactions between "systems of domination" (e.g., racism, patriarchy, colonialism, and apartheid) and "institutionalized processes" (e.g., racialization, gendering, and culturalization) (Dhamoon, 2011). As Kabeer explains,

> Gender inequality cuts across both vertical inequalities and other horizontal inequalities including race and caste. Its intersection with these other forms of inequality means that it is women and girls from the poorest caste, ethnic, and racial groups who have poorer levels of health, nutrition, and education, and very often suffer higher levels of violence than other women, including women from similarly poor backgrounds.
>
> *(Kabeer, 2015)*

Intersectionality is essential to understanding how gendered ethnicity comes into play with regard to resource distribution and decision-making inequalities. Kabeer expounds that the hierarchical organization of labor markets (itself a manifestation of both vertical and horizontal inequalities), along with gender and ethnic asymmetries in education and other productive assets, very often relegates women from poor and socially marginalized ethnic groups to the least desirable and poorest-paid positions, which translates to meager earning potential and diminished economic opportunity. She points to South Africa as one example of women from ethnic minorities being at the bottom of these income hierarchies, in part due to lack of or usurious access to financial services. In South Africa, although policies to promote equity and facilitate broader economic participation exist (embodied in the government's overall Black economic empowerment policy), Black women's participation in the labor force and educational levels have been lower than those of white women and even Black men, with higher unemployment rates. These statistics show that despite policy measures seeking to improve conditions for marginalized women in the formal workspace, their access to resources and their decision-making agency remain suppressed (Klasen & Minasyan, 2020; Kabeer, 2015, 2014).

In a study of Indigenous San women in Namibia, Renee Sylvain identifies that not only do these ethnic minority women face "simultaneous and mutually-reinforcing racial, ethnic, class and gender inequalities," but their intersectional discrimination limits their ability to benefit from international and national gender-progressive laws and policy initiatives—all while diminishing their access to resources and their decision-making agency (Sylvain, 2011). And in Tanzania, Juliet Elu and Linda Loubert examine the manufacturing sector to illustrate the extent to which gender inequality is influenced by gender-ethnic intersectionality. They conclude that in the presence of this linkage, effective labor market policies aimed at eradicating gender-based inequality must also target ethnic inequality (Elu & Loubert, 2013).

According to Marlow and Martinez Dy, intersectionality is difficult to operationalize because it describes a confluence of social forces. This confluence identifies particular forms of positionality, which is "the space at the intersection of structure (social position/social effects) and agency (social positioning/meaning/practice)." Thus, positionality shifts away from isolated and static positions of gender and ethnicity to the conceptual space generated by their intersections. Central to this framing is how such positioning situates actors within social hierarchies (Marlow & Martinez Dy, 2018; Anthias, 2001), which has implications for the resource distribution and decision-making spaces alike. Kabeer contends that intersectionality tends to intensify the disadvantages associated with gender and ethnic inequality (Kabeer, 2015).

Figure 5.1 depicts the conceptual linkages between ethnic diversity, inequality, and institutional framework in an economy, highlighting the manifold factors that affect inequality in varying degrees: demographic factors such as gender, urbanization, education level and disparity, and share of children and the elderly in the population; macroeconomic factors such as inflation, unemployment, financial development, and foreign investments; environmental factors such as natural resources; cultural and political factors such as ethnic, religious, and linguistic diversity; and other factors beyond the ones outlined above. The solid and broken lines demonstrate a dual-feedback mechanism: While demographic factors, macroeconomic factors, environmental factors, cultural and political factors, and other omnibus factors directly influence inequality, the same factors can also work indirectly through institutions to affect inequality. Regarding ethnic diversity's effect on inequality specifically, it can influence income distribution among racial, ethnic, language, and other religious groups. However, the basis of the distribution is mainly dependent on the institutional framework: Institutions may exacerbate inequality if they comprise individuals who favor group loyalty, hence the bidirectional arrows (Ajide, Alimi, & Asongu, 2019).

Miki Caul Kittilson also identifies a confluence of several interrelated factors—including resources, economy, socialization, and political context—that work together to compound differences in gender and ethnicity (Kittilson, 2016). In further findings that echo and reinforce this chapter's earlier discussion, Jessica Gottlieb maintains that members of marginalized groups (namely, women and ethnic minorities) in Mali face barriers to civic engagement (Gottlieb, 2016). Cole et al. reveal how institutionalized norms in Zambia exacerbate gender inequalities in resource distribution: Access to resources like land has an ethnic basis for Zambian women, disproportionately excluding them from participating in the mainstream economy (Cole et al., 2015). Cathy Rozel Farnworth and Kathleen Colverson refocus the macroeconomic lens to the household, identifying that women in sub-Saharan Africa experience weaker access to productive resources and decision-making power within the household, which amounts to lower and less effective participation in community-level decision-making bodies, local markets, value chain networks, and innovation platforms (Farnworth & Colverson, 2015).

BOX 5.3 GENDER-ETHNICITY INTERSECTIONALITY IN DECISION-MAKING IN RWANDA AND BURUNDI

Political Representation and the Gender and Ethnic Divide in Rwanda and Burundi

As of 2018, twenty-seven countries in sub-Saharan Africa have enacted legislated quotas or reserved seats for female parliamentarians, representing 35 percent of the countries worldwide that have done so. Motivating this trend is a recognition in many of these countries, plagued by war and civil conflict for years, that postwar transitional periods present an opportunity for inclusion of previously excluded groups. Interestingly, Melanie Hughes has found that every additional year of internal conflict improves the rate of women's participation in politics by 1.2 percent in sub-Saharan Africa (Hughes, 2009). However, a 2018 case study by Andrea Guariso, Bert Ingelaere, and Marijke Verpoorten identified skepticism on the impact of gender quotas in sub-Saharan Africa for several reasons. For one, gender quotas have generally been introduced as de facto authoritarian, implemented by regimes with dominant ruling parties. Furthermore, there has been a failure to change the underlying social structures that render women subordinate; in patriarchal societies, ethnic decision-making crowds out gendered decision-making and ethnic identity crowds out gender identity (Guariso, Ingelaere, & Verpoorten, 2018).

Burundi and Rwanda both suffered from large-scale post-independence inter-ethnic violence, a legacy of Belgian colonialist institutionalization of favoritism of the Tutsi ethnic minority (roughly 14 percent of the overall population) over the Hutu majority (about 85 percent). After independence in 1962, Burundi was under a Tutsi-led military dictatorship, while Rwanda was a Hutu-dominated republic. The decades that followed saw marked discrimination of the respective ethnic groups deprived of power, punctuated by waves of ethnic violence. After a 2003 ceasefire in Burundi, a new constitution ensured a more equitable division of national assembly and ministerial positions among Hutus (60 percent) and Tutsis (40 percent)—reversing the status quo of minority Tutsi dominance. The new constitution also instituted a 30 percent gender quota. The Rwandan ceasefire came about in 1994, but the country's new constitution (adopted in 2003) remained silent on ethnicity. It did introduce gender quotas, also guaranteeing 30 percent of all decision-making body posts to women. By 2013, 64 percent of parliamentarians in Rwanda were women, and as of 2018, minority Tutsis held 60 percent of ministerial positions (Guariso, Ingelaere, & Verpoorten, 2018). In Burundi, as of 2023, women held 38.2 percent of seats in the national parliament—up from 18.4 percent in 2003.[2] Thus, it is evident that after both Rwanda and Burundi introduced gender quotas, and to some positive effect, both effectively reversed ethnic power relations.

The historical changes in the power dynamics in these two countries have meant that Hutu women in Rwanda and Tutsi women in Burundi have no increase in political decision-making agency: Ethnicized decision-making has overrun gendered decision-making. For both countries, Guariso, Ingelaere, and Verpoorten find a higher correlation between ethnicity and gender within ethnicities than within gender, demonstrating that decision-making tends to be driven by ethnic representation rather than gender. In other words, both Hutus and Tutsis value their representatives' ethnic identities more than their gender. The authors further observed that Tutsi women feel more comfortable and represented by Tutsi men than by Hutu women, with the converse also holding true for Hutu women. These allegiances—deriving from long-standing, heavily loaded asymmetric power relations that structure meanings and inter relations of ethnicity in post-colonial sub-Saharan Africa—indicate that ethnic identification continues to overshadow gender association in decision-making in Burundi and Rwanda (Guariso, Ingelaere, & Verpoorten, 2018).

Conclusion

Despite limited progress in addressing class and gender differences in resource distribution and decision-making in sub-Saharan Africa, gender inequalities persist. This chapter has explored the myriad ways in which ethnicity, as reflected in cultural, social, and institutional norms, can preserve, amplify, and perpetuate gender disparities due to the embedded cultural norms in societies that subjugate women.

But it is important to recognize that ethnic diversity can also bridge gender gaps (Churchill, Nuhu, & Lopez, 2019). In sub-Saharan Africa, Gottlieb and Robinson emphasize that gender gaps in decision-making arenas such as politics and civic participation are significantly smaller among matrilineal ethnic groups (in which wives maintain strong ties with their kinship networks of origin) compared with patrilineal and mixed-descent groups. They also observe that resource entitlements conferred through matrilineal inheritance tend to be the most significant source of female empowerment, greater than any single positive economic shock (Gottlieb & Robinson, 2016).

Looking at the bigger picture, gender and ethnic inequality are inherently detrimental to human capital formation and economic development (Churchill, Nuhu, & Lopez, 2019). Throughout sub-Saharan Africa, women and members of marginalized ethnic groups remain disadvantaged in their access to all the determining factors of economic empowerment, civic engagement, and political agency—namely, access to resources, education and training, technology, labor markets, and credit—and this effect is compounded for women who are also members of marginalized ethnic groups. Prevalent ethnic heterogeneity across the subcontinent serves to strengthen cultural, social, and institutional norms that preserve existing gender gaps—particularly those stereotyping men as protectors and breadwinners and implicitly condoning violence against women. Ethnic heterogeneity is associated with cultural drift and isolation, depressing social cooperation and hindering cross-cultural learning. It can further impede gender equality by buttressing socioeconomic conditions that normalize traditional gender roles, labor market inequalities, discrimination, and marginalization, promoting prejudice and reinforcing the exclusion of women. Eroded trust and animosity among contesting ethnic groups only exacerbate the problem.

As this chapter has laid out, intersectionality theory is central to understanding the nuanced relationship between gender and ethnicity. Intersectionality explains how ethnicity as a social institution shapes gender inequality, and thus how ethnic diversity and inequality affect the degree of gender inequality in society.

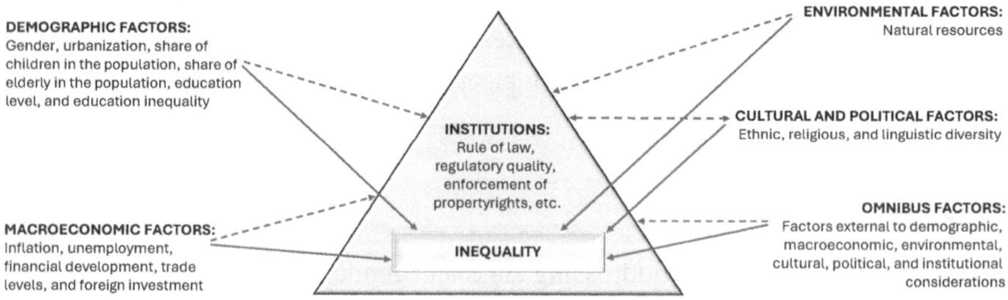

FIGURE 5.1 Conceptual Linkages between Institutions, Ethnic Diversity, and Inequality

Source: Ajide, Alimi, and Asongu (2019).

Note: The solid and broken lines indicate direct and indirect effects, respectively.

In sub-Saharan Africa, women have demonstrably less access to resources and less decision-making agency—conditions that worsen if they belong to ethnic minority groups. The need for further study of gendered ethnicity in this context is therefore self-evident. Even more importantly, policies targeting gender inequality cannot afford to neglect the eradication of ethnic inequality. Both of these focus areas are paramount to achieving sustainable, inclusive development in sub-Saharan Africa.

Notes

1 See also World Bank Open Data, "Proportion of Seats Held by Women in National Parliaments (%)—Sub-Saharan Africa," accessed February 27, 2024, https://data.worldbank.org/indicator/SG.GEN.PARL.ZS?locations=ZG.
2 See World Bank, "Burundi Gender Landscape," *Gender Data Portal*, accessed October 13, 2024, https://genderdata.worldbank.org/en/economies/burundi.

Bibliography

Adereti, Damilola Tobiloba, and Oluwatosin O. Fasina. "Gender Analysis of Food Security Status of Rural Households in Ondo State, Nigeria." *Russian Agricultural Sciences* 43, no. 4 (July 2017): 353–60, https://doi.org/10.3103/S1068367417040024.

Ajide, Kazeem B., Olorunfemi Y. Alimi, and Simplice A. Asongu. "Ethnic Diversity and Inequality in Sub-Saharan Africa: Do Institutions Reduce the Noise?" *Social Indicators Research* 145 (April 2019): 1033–62, https://doi.org/10.1007/s11205-019-02122-y.

Aksoy, Ozan. "Crosscutting Circles in a Social Dilemma: Effects of Social Identity and Inequality on Cooperation." *Social Science Research* 82 (August 2019): 148–63, https://doi.org/10.1016/j.ssresearch.2019.04.009.

Alliance for a Green Revolution in Africa (AGRA). *Africa Agriculture Status Report 2018: Catalyzing Government Capacity to Drive Agricultural Transformation*. Nairobi, Kenya: Alliance for a Green Revolution in Africa, 2018, https://agra.org/wp-content/uploads/2018/09/AASR-2018.pdf.

Anthias, Floya. "New Hybridities, Old Concepts: The Limits of 'Culture.'" *Ethnic and Racial Studies* 24, no. 4 (July 2001): 619–41, https://doi.org/10.1080/01419870120049815.

Barreto, Manuela, and David Matthew Doyle. "Benevolent and Hostile Sexism in a Shifting Global Context." *Nature Reviews Psychology* 2 (February 2023): 98–111, https://doi.org/10.1038/s44159-022-00136-x.

Berger, Peter L., and Thomas Luckmann. *The Social Construction of Reality: A Treatise in the Sociology of Knowledge*. Garden City, NY: Anchor Books, 1966.

Bonacich, Edna. "A Theory of Middleman Minorities." *American Sociological Review* 38 (October 1973): 583–94, https://doi.org/10.2307/2094409.

Carrim, Nasima Mohamed Hoosen, and Stella M. Nkomo. "Wedding Intersectionality Theory and Identity Work in Organizations: South African Indian Women Negotiating Managerial Identity." *Gender, Work and Organization* 23, no. 3 (May 2016): 261–77, https://doi.org/10.1111/gwao.12121.

Churchill, Sefa Awaworyi. "Income and Ethnic Fractionalisation: Evidence from British Microdata." *Economic Issues* 24, no. 1 (2019): 21–34, https://www.economicissues.org.uk/Files/2019/EI_March2019_churchill.pdf.

Churchill, Sefa Awaworyi. "Microfinance and Ethnic Diversity." *Economic Record* 93, no. 300 (March 2017): 112–41, https://doi.org/10.1111/1475-4932.12310.

Churchill, Sefa Awaworyi, and Vinod Mishra. "The Impact of Ethnic Diversity on Microenterprise Start-Ups." *Applied Economics* 50, no. 40 (2018): 4328–42, https://doi.org/10.1080/00036846.2018.1444264.

Churchill, Sefa Awaworyi, Ahmed Salim Nuhu, and Karely Lopez. "Persistence of Gender Inequality: The Role of Ethnic Divisions." *Applied Economics* 51, no. 8 (2019): 781–96, https://doi.org/10.1080/00036846.2018.1513635.

Cole, Steven M., et al. "Exploring the Intricate Relationship Between Poverty, Gender Inequality and Rural Masculinity: A Case Study from an Aquatic Agricultural System in Zambia." *Culture, Society and Masculinities* 7, no. 2 (2015): 154–70, https://hdl.handle.net/20.500.12348/235.

Cook, Alison, and Christy Glass. "Diversity Begets Diversity? The Effects of Board Composition on the Appointment and Success of Women CEOs." *Social Science Research* 53 (September 2015): 137–47, https://doi.org/10.1016/j.ssresearch.2015.05.009.

Crenshaw, Kimberlé. "Demarginalizing the Intersection of Race and Sex: A Black Feminist Critique of Antidiscrimination Doctrine, Feminist Theory and Antiracist Politics." *The University of Chicago Legal Forum* 1989, no. 1 (1989): 139–167, https://scholarship.law.columbia.edu/faculty_scholarship/3007.

Dhamoon, Rita Kaur. "Considerations on Mainstreaming Intersectionality." *Political Research Quarterly* 64, no. 1 (March 2011): 230–43, https://doi.org/10.1177/1065912910379227.

Easterly, William. "Can Institutions Resolve Ethnic Conflict?" *Economic Development and Cultural Change* 49, no. 4 (July 2001): 687–706, https://doi.org/10.1086/452521.

Elu, Juliet U., and Linda Loubert. "Earnings Inequality and the Intersectionality of Gender and Ethnicity in Sub-Saharan Africa: The Case of Tanzanian Manufacturing." *American Economic Review* 103, no. 3 (May 2013): 289–92, https://doi.org/10.1257/aer.103.3.289.

Ensminger, Jean. *Making a Market: The Institutional Transformation of an African Society*. New York, NY: Cambridge University Press, 1996.

Fafchamps, Marcel. "Ethnicity and Credit in African Manufacturing." *Journal of Development Economics* 61, no. 1 (2000): 205–35, https://doi.org/10.1016/S0304-3878(99)00068-1.

Farnworth, Cathy Rozel, and Kathleen E. Colverson. "Building a Gender-Transformative Extension and Advisory Facilitation System in Sub-Saharan Africa." *Journal of Gender, Agriculture and Food Security* 1, no. 1 (2015): 20–39, https://hdl.handle.net/10568/68323.

Farnworth, Cathy Rozel, et al. "Gender and Conservation Agriculture in East and Southern Africa: Towards a Research Agenda." *International Journal of Agricultural Sustainability* 14, no. 2 (2016): 142–65, https://doi.org/10.1080/14735903.2015.1065602.

Fiske, Susan T. "Prejudices in Cultural Contexts: Shared Stereotypes (Gender, Age) Versus Variable Stereotypes (Race, Ethnicity, Religion)." *Perspectives on Psychological Science* 12, no. 5 (September 2017): 791–99, https://doi.org/10.1177/1745691617708204.

Galiè, Alessandra, et al. "Exploring Gender Perceptions of Resource Ownership and Their Implications for Food Security Among Rural Livestock Owners in Tanzania, Ethiopia, and Nicaragua." *Agriculture and Food Security* 4, no. 1 (2015): 1–14, https://doi.org/10.1186/s40066-015-0021-9.

Gershman, Boris, and Diego Rivera. "Subnational Diversity in Sub-Saharan Africa: Insights from a New Dataset." *Journal of Development Economics* 133 (July 2018): 231–63, https://doi.org/10.1016/j.jdeveco.2018.01.003.

Gottlieb, Jessica. "Why Might Information Exacerbate the Gender Gap in Civic Participation? Evidence from Mali." *World Development* 86 (October 2016): 95–110, https://doi.org/10.1016/j.worlddev.2016.05.010.

Gottlieb, Jessica, Guy Grossman, and Amanda Lea Robinson. "Do Men and Women Have Different Policy Preferences in Africa? Determinants and Implications of Gender Gaps in Policy Prioritization." *British Journal of Political Science* 48, no. 3 (July 2016): 611–36, https://doi.org/10.1017/S0007123416000053.

Gottlieb, Jessica, and Amanda Lea Robinson. "The Effects of Matrilineality on Gender Differences in Political Behavior Across Africa." Working Paper. Berkeley: University of California, April 20, 2016.

Guariso, Andrea, Bert Ingelaere, and Marijke Verpoorten. "When Ethnicity Beats Gender: Quotas and Political Representation in Rwanda and Burundi." *Development and Change* 49, no. 6 (November 2018): 1361–91, https://doi.org/10.1111/dech.12451.

Harrison, Richard, Claire Leitch, and Maura McAdam. "Breaking Glass: Toward a Gendered Analysis of Entrepreneurial Leadership." *Journal of Small Business Management* 53, no. 3 (2015): 693–713, https://doi.org/10.1111/jsbm.12180.

Harwood, Jake. "Social Identity Theory." *International Encyclopedia of Media Psychology*, June 13, 2020, https://doi.org/10.1002/9781119011071.iemp0153.

Hillenbrand, Emily, et al. "Measuring Gender-Transformative Change: A Review of Literature and Promising Practices." Working Paper. Atlanta, GA: CARE USA, October 2015, https://prevention-collaborative.org/wp-content/uploads/2021/08/CARE_2015_Measuring-Gender-Transformative-Change.pdf.

Hitlin, Steven, Hye Won Kwon, and Rengin Firat. "In- and Out-Groups Across Cultures: Identities and Perceived Group Values." *Social Science Research* 97 (July 2021). Article no. 102569

Hlatshwayo, Nosipho, and Kambidima Wotela. "Social Capital as Survival Strategy for Immigrants in South Africa: A Conceptual Framework." In *Immigration and Development*, edited by Tiago Sequeira, 137–44. London, UK: IntechOpen, 2018.

Hughes, Melanie M. "Armed Conflict, International Linkages, and Women's Parliamentary Representation in Developing Nations." *Social Problems* 56, no. 1 (2009): 174–204, https://doi.org/10.1525/sp.2009.56.1.174.

Ireland, Patrick Richard. "Ethnicity, Nationalism and Migration in Sub-Saharan Africa." In *The International Studies Encyclopedia*, Vol. 3, edited by Robert A. Denemark and Renée Marlin-Bennett, 1796–816. Oxford, UK: Wiley-Blackwell, 2010.

Isaksson, Ann-Sofie, Andreas Kotsadam, and Måns Nerman. "The Gender Gap in African Political Participation: Testing Theories of Individual and Contextual Determinants." *Journal of Development Studies* 50, no. 2 (2014): 302–18, https://doi.org/10.1080/00220388.2013.833321.

Jaquette, Jane S. "Women/Gender and Development: The Growing Gap Between Theory and Practice." *Studies in Comparative International Development* 52, no. 2 (June 2017): 242–60, https://doi.org/10.1007/s12116-017-9248-8.

Kabeer, Naila. "The Challenges of Intersecting Inequality." *Maitreyee: E-Bulletin of the Human Development and Capability Association* 24 (July 2014): 5–10, https://en.unesco.org/inclusivepolicylab/sites/default/files/publication/document/2017/2/Group%20inequality%20intersectionality.pdf.

Kabeer, Naila. "Gender, Poverty, and Inequality: A Brief History of Feminist Contributions in the Field of International Development." *Gender and Development* 23, no. 2 (2015): 189–205, https://doi.org/10.1080/13552074.2015.1062300.

Kabeer, Naila. *Reversed Realities: Gender Hierarchies in Development Thought*. London, UK: Verso, 1994.

Kabeer, Naila, and Luisa Natali. "Gender Equality and Economic Growth: Is There a Win-Win?" IDS Working Paper No. 417. Brighton, UK: Institute of Development Studies, February 2013, https://doi.org/10.1111/j.2040-0209.2013.00417.x.

Kapungu, Roselyn. "The Zimbabwe Gender Budgeting and Women's Empowerment Programme." *Agenda: Empowering Women for Gender Equity* 78 (January 2008): 68–78, https://www.jstor.org/stable/27739462.

Kittilson, Miki Caul. "Gender and Political Behavior." In *Oxford Research Encyclopedia of Politics*, edited by William R. Thompson. Oxford, UK: Oxford University Press, 2016, https://doi.org/10.1093/acrefore/9780190228637.013.71. https://futures.issafrica.org/geographic/regions/sub-saharan-africa/#forecast

Klasen, Stephen, and Anna Minasyan. "Affirmative Action and Intersectionality at the Top: Evidence from South Africa." GLO Discussion Paper No. 467. Essen, Germany: Global Labor Organization, 2020, https://hdl.handle.net/10419/213568.

Klugman, Jeni, and Laura Tyson. *Leave No One Behind: A Call to Action for Gender Equality and Women's Economic Empowerment*. Report of the UN Secretary-General's High-Level Panel on Women's Economic Empowerment. New York, NY: United Nations, 2016, https://www.unwomen.org/sites/default/files/2023-01/hlp-wee-report-2016-09-call-to-action-en.pdf.

Lau, Jacqueline D., and Ivan R. Scales. "Identity, Subjectivity and Natural Resource Use: How Ethnicity, Gender and Class Intersect to Influence Mangrove Oyster Harvesting in the Gambia." *Geoforum* 69 (February 2016): 136–46, https://doi.org/10.1016/j.geoforum.2016.01.002.

March, Candida, Ines Smyth, and Maitrayee Mukhopadhyay. *A Guide to Gender-Analysis Frameworks*. Oxford, UK: Oxfam Great Britain, 1999, https://hdl.handle.net/10546/115397.

Marlow, Susan, and Angela Martinez Dy. "Is It Time to Rethink the Gender Agenda in Entrepreneurship Research?" *International Small Business Journal* 36, no. 1 (February 2018): 3–22, https://doi.org/10.1177/0266242617738321.

Mason, Ryan, et al. "Determinants of Food Security in Tanzania: Gendered Dimensions of Household Headship and Control of Resources." *Agriculture and Human Values* 32, no. 3 (September 2015): 539–49, https://doi.org/10.1007/s10460-014-9568-5.

McCloskey, Stephen. "From MDGs to SDGs: We Need a Critical Awakening to Succeed." *Policy and Practice: A Development Education Review* 20 (Spring 2015): 186–94, https://www.developmenteducationreview.com/issue/issue-20/mdgs-sdgs-we-need-critical-awakening-succeed.

McDoom, Omar Shahabudin. "Inequality, Ethnicity, and Status in a Ranked Society: Intermarriage in Mindanao, the Philippines." *Research in Social Stratification and Mobility* 59 (February 2019): 71–80, https://doi.org/10.1016/j.rssm.2018.11.007.

Moyo-Nyede, Simangele, and Jonathan Kugarakuripi. "In Zimbabwe, Majority Support Gender Equality, Think Greater Efforts Are Needed." Afrobarometer Dispatch No. 610, February 28, 2023, https://www.afrobarometer.org/publication/ad610-in-zimbabwe-majority-support-gender-equality-think-greater-efforts-are-needed.

Namubiru-Mwaura, Evelyn. "Land Tenure and Gender: Approaches and Challenges for Strengthening Rural Women's Land Rights." Women's Voice, Agency, and Participation Research Series, Working Paper No. 6. Washington, DC: World Bank Group, 2014, https://hdl.handle.net/10986/21033.

Ngarava, Saul, Leocadia Zhou, and Nomakhaya Monde. "Gendered Water Insecurity: A Structural Equation Approach for Female Headed Households in South Africa." *Water* 11, no. 2491 (2019): 1–19, https://doi.org/10.3390/w11122491.

Pearse, Rebecca, and Raewyn Connell. "Gender Norms and the Economy: Insights from Social Research." *Feminist Economics* 22, no. 1 (2016): 30–53, https://doi.org/10.1080/13545701.2015.1078485.

Putnam, Robert D. "*E Pluribus Unum*: Diversity and Community in the Twenty-First Century." *Scandinavian Political Science* 30, no. 2 (June 2007): 137–74, https://doi.org/10.1111/j.1467-9477.2007.00176.x.

Raney, Terri, et al. "Gender Differences in Assets." ESA Working Paper No. 11–12. Rome, Italy: Agricultural Development Economics Division, United Nations Food and Agricultural Organization, March 2011, https://www.fao.org/agrifood-economics/publications/detail/en/c/120333.

Rathgeber, Eva M. "WID, WAD, GAD: Trends in Research and Practice." *The Journal of Developing Areas* 24, no. 4 (July 1990): 489–502, https://www.jstor.org/stable/4191904.

Research Continental-Fonkom and FinMark Trust (RCFFT). *FinScope MSME Survey Zimbabwe 2012.* Washington, DC: World Bank Group, 2012, https://documents.worldbank.org/curated/en/780081468137402417.

Reserve Bank of Zimbabwe. *National Financial Inclusion Strategy (2016–2020).* Harare, Zimbabwe: Reserve Bank of Zimbabwe, 2016, https://www.rbz.co.zw/documents/BLSS/FinancialInclusion/National-Financial-Inclusion-Strategy.pdf.

Reserve Bank of Zimbabwe. *National Financial Inclusion Strategy II (2022–2026).* Harare, Zimbabwe: Reserve Bank of Zimbabwe, 2022, https://www.rbz.co.zw/documents/BLSS/FinancialInclusion/Zimbabwe_National_Financial_Inclusion_Strategy_II_2022-2026.pdf.

Robinson, Amanda Lea. "Ethnic Diversity, Segregation and Ethnocentric Trust in Africa." *British Journal of Political Science* 50, no. 1 (January 2020): 217–39, https://doi.org/10.1017/S0007123417000540.

Rowe, Andrea M. "Designing Equality of Opportunity in National Innovation Systems." PhD diss., McMaster University, 2016, https://macsphere.mcmaster.ca/bitstream/11375/20657/2/Rowe_Andrea_M_2016September_PhDPoliticalScience.pdf.

Spieldoch, Alexandra, Georgina Aboud, and Alyson Brody. *Gender and Food Security: Towards Gender—Just Food and Nutrition Security.* Bridge 2014 Overview Report. Brighton, UK: Institute of Development Studies, 2014, https://www.genderequalityinnovations.org/wp-content/uploads/2020/01/IDS_Bridge_Food_Security_Report_Online.pdf.

Sylvain, Renee. "At the Intersections: San Women and the Rights of Indigenous Peoples in Africa." *The International Journal of Human Rights* 15, no. 1 (2011): 89–110, https://doi.org/10.1080/13642987.2011.529690.

Tarinda, Samuel. *Gender, Women's Economic Empowerment and Financial Inclusion in Zimbabwe.* Kuala Lumpur, Malaysia: Alliance for Financial Inclusion, August 2019, https://www.afi-global.org/publication/gender-womens-economic-empowerment-and-financial-inclusion-in-zimbabwe.

Trauth, Eileen M., et al. "The Influence of Gender Ethnic Intersectionality on Gender Stereotypes About IT Skills and Knowledge." *Database for Advances in Information Systems* 47, no. 3 (August 2016): 9–39, https://doi.org/10.1145/2980783.2980785.

UN Food and Agricultural Organization (UNFAO), "Women in the Changing World of Work: Planet 50-50 by 2030," *Family Farming Knowledge Platform*, 2017, accessed November 18, 2024, https://www.fao.org/family-farming/detail/en/c/522478

UN Women. "Fact Sheet—Sub-Saharan Africa." In *Turning Promises into Action: Gender Equality in the 2030 Agenda for Sustainable Development*, pp. 2–5. New York, NY: UN Women, 2018, https://www.unwomen.org/sites/default/files/Headquarters/Attachments/Sections/Library/Publications/2018/SDG-report-Fact-sheet-Sub-Saharan-Africa-en.pdf.

UN Women. *Why Gender Equality Matters Across All SGDs: An Excerpt of Turning Promises into Action—Gender Equality in the 2030 Agenda for Sustainable Development.* New York, NY: UN Women, 2018, https://www.unwomen.org/sites/default/files/Headquarters/Attachments/Sections/Library/Publications/2018/SDG-report-Chapter-3-Why-gender-equality-matters-across-all-SDGs-2018-en.pdf.

United Nations Development Programme (UNDP), "Gender Inequality Index," accessed December 7, 2024, https://hdr.undp.org/data-center/thematic-composite-indices/gender-inequality-index#/indicies/GII.

Walker, Keith, and Eunice Wanjiru. "Zimbabwe's Women Decry Political Underrepresentation." *Deutsche Welle*, September 15, 2023, https://www.dw.com/en/zimbabwes-women-decry-political-underrepresentation/a-66820954.

Watkins, Kevin. "Leaving No One Behind: An Equity Agenda for the Post-2015 Goals." *Maitreyee: E-Bulletin of the Human Development and Capability Association* 24 (July 2014): 18–22, https://en.unesco.org/inclusivepolicylab/sites/default/files/publication/document/2017/2/Group%20inequality%20intersectionality.pdf.

Wilson, Kalpana. "Towards a Radical Re-Appropriation: Gender, Development and Neoliberal Feminism." *Development and Change* 46, no. 4 (July 2015): 803–32, https://doi.org/10.1111/dech.12176.

World Bank. "Persistent Gender Disparities Hinder Women's Safety and Productivity in Zimbabwe." April 29, 2024, https://www.worldbank.org/en/news/feature/2024/04/29/persistent-gender-disparities-hinder-women-s-safety-and-productivity-in-afe-zimbabwe.

World Bank. *Zimbabwe Gender-Based Violence Assessment: Scope, Programming Gaps, and Entry Points*. Washington, DC: World Bank Group, 2023, https://documents.worldbank.org/curated/en/099062823005529216.

6

ETHNIC INEQUALITY AND AGRICULTURAL RESOURCE ALLOCATION AND DISTRIBUTION IN NIGERIA

The Need for Inclusive Growth

Victor Olusegun Okoruwa, Tolulope Rachael Jerumeh, and Aderonke Mary Omotola

Introduction

The agricultural sector in Nigeria has the potential to generate employment for more than 70 percent of the population, account for about 60 percent of non-oil exports, contribute to 60 percent of the gross domestic product (GDP), and provide for more than 80 percent of the country's food needs (Central Bank of Nigeria, 2009; Onwuemenyi, 2008). However, these potentials have remained largely unexploited, resulting in a downward trend in the sector's performance both domestically and globally. This decline explains the growing gap between the country's food demand and supply, which in turn cultivates an insatiable appetite for food imports and declining levels of national food self-sufficiency. The value of food imports in Nigeria has been fluctuating over the years, reaching an all-time high of 30.1 percent in 2011; in 2017, it was pegged at 16.3 percent (CEIC Data, 2024). However, the country's food exports have been meager, averaging about 3.78 percent between 2000 and 2023 (World Bank, 2025).

The dismal performance of the country's agricultural sector is primarily linked to low productivity (Aye, 2011). To grapple with the situation, successive governments in Nigeria have initiated programs, policies, and institutions and increased budgetary allocation to the sector. These budgetary allocations are often spent either on physical structures, grants, or other inputs distributed to farmers or on funding to agencies that perform agriculture-related services (Agene et al., 2017). Despite these interventions, agricultural production hovers at a subsistence level. A possible explanation for this stagnation is that most of these interventions did not reach the intended targets, thus minimizing their impacts. For example, federal

DOI: 10.4324/9781003357025-8

government programs like Operation Feed the Nation, the Green Revolution, and the river basin development authorities (among others) favored capital-intensive agriculture and large-scale commercial farmers who corruptly enriched themselves at the expense of poor peasant farmers (Otaha, 2013). The federal government also introduced the rice value chain through backward integration; however, the program resulted in more difficult production conditions for millers and farmers, because import quotas set for investors with rice-milling capacity were instead diverted to cronies who then sold to large traders and corporations. Additionally, evidence suggests that under the 1999–2010 Fertilizer Market Stabilization Program (FMSP), only 11 percent of the subsidized fertilizer reached the smallholder farmers for whom it was intended (FMARD, 2012).

Moreover, disproportionate allocation and distribution of investment funds is a major contributing factor to the Nigerian agricultural sector's low performance. Favoritism and ethnic inclination serve as the basis for allocating and distributing development funds in the country, with no consideration for regional needs or disparities, or the effects of social and economic investments and infrastructural facilities on the space economy (Raheem, 2014). Evidence abounds of ethnic inequality in terms of agricultural input subsidy allocation and distribution to farmers. Analysis of the federal government's Agricultural Credit Guarantee Scheme Fund (ACGSF) by the Central Bank of Nigeria reveals that in 2015, the northwest zone received the highest number of loans (5,142, valued at ₦439,600,000), followed by the southwest zone (2,514 loans, valued ₦449,927,000); by contrast, the north-central zone had the fewest loans guaranteed (only 686, valued at ₦103,000,000) (CBNDFD, 2015). Furthermore, an evaluation of public spending on fertilizer subsidy (PSFS) and agriculture public expenditure reviews (AgPER) undertaken by the African Union's Comprehensive African Agricultural Development Programme shows that subsidy program participation rates are consistently higher in the north than in the south. Interestingly, although northern farmers are better represented, targeting has been better in the southern zones—that is, the benefits of PSFS and AgPER in absolute terms are progressive (inequality-reducing) in the southern zones and regressive (inequality-increasing) in the northern zones (Olomola et al., 2014).

In essence, as this chapter will explore, the convergence of political influence and economic power breeds inequality in the distribution of income, input supply (i.e., the external resources required to support crop production such as pesticides, fertilizers, machinery, seeds, feeds, and tools), and other opportunities, all of which results in suboptimal allocation and distribution of intended national resources. More specifically, as William Easterly and Ross Levine have observed, ethnically fragmented societies may give rise to uncoordinated government ministries, each pursuing its own rent-seeking strategy without considering the corollary or ancillary effects of its actions, or formulating preferential public policies aimed at benefitting the political leader's ethnic group (Easterly & Levine, 1997). By implication, the ethnic bias observed in agricultural input allocation and distribution in Nigeria may well be connected to the interference of the prevailing political leadership—a conclusion supported by the aforementioned incongruities in agricultural input subsidy allocation.

As indicated above, under the ACGSF program, the highest numbers of loans were guaranteed in the northwest and the southwest (though the northwest was more than double that of the southwest) under the leadership duo of President Muhammadu Buhari (from Katsina in the northwest) and Vice President Yemi Osinbajo (from Ogun in the southwest). Figure 6.1 offers further evidence: It shows that farmers in the southeast have the least representation in terms of credit access in virtually all time periods considered (from 1981 to 2016)—a timeframe during which the country had no presidents from the region. More recently, the proposition of rural grazing area (RUGA) settlements for Fulani herders in all states of the federation is widely believed to be born out of ethnic bias and favoritism on the part of President Buhari (an ethnic Fulani) despite the disquieting implications for the rest of the country (Ademola, 2020). (The RUGA policy, which was ultimately suspended amid widespread public outcry, had aimed to resolve ongoing disputes over cattle grazing between nomadic Fulani herders and sedentary farmers, who were mostly from other ethnic groups (Apikins, 2020). See Chapter 10 for a detailed examination of Nigeria's protracted herder-farmer conflict.)

Nigeria's persistent ethnic inequality problem is all the more dire given ethnic fragmentation's grave ramifications for economic development (which Chapter 1 explores in detail). Easterly and Levine have shown that GDP per capita growth rate is inversely related to the degree of ethnic fragmentation in a country, and that poor economic performance in most African states is due in no small part to the large number of different ethnic groups living within a given country (Easterly &

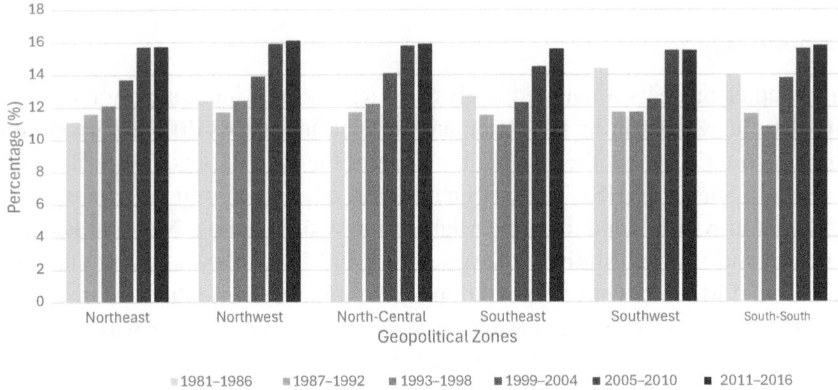

FIGURE 6.1 Value of Loans Guaranteed by Region

Source: Oyeronke Abosede Adejumo and Bolarinwa Titus Omonona, "Analysis of the Performance of the Agricultural Credit Guarantee Scheme Fund in Nigeria (1981 to 2016)," *IOSR Journal of Agriculture and Veterinary Science* 10, no. 10 (October 2017): 24–30.

Levine, 1997). On the other hand, ensuring just and fair inclusion for all members of society produces substantive and sustained economic growth. Ensuring that growth is more equitable and inclusive is thus a primary focal point of development policy: Fostering inclusive and sustainable growth is critical to the United Nations *2030 Agenda for Sustainable Development* and the Sustainable Development Goals, and the United Nations Development Programme (UNDP) has well established that a great many households globally are not participating in or benefitting equally from the growth process (UNDP, 2017; UN, 2015).

Inclusive growth refers to economic growth that results in wider access to sustainable socioeconomic opportunities—while protecting society's most vulnerable members—in an environment of fairness and equality (Agene et al., 2017). According to the African Development Bank, seven broad and mutually reinforcing pillars underpin the concept of inclusive growth: improved agricultural productivity; better regional integration; job creation, with an emphasis on enhancing skills for competitiveness and productivity; broader access to basic social services and infrastructures; increased access to business opportunities; unfettered access to productive knowledge and skills; and social protection and inclusion (Kanu, Salami, & Numasawa, 2014). In other words, growth is considered inclusive if the benefits that result from the proposed intervention(s) are all-encompassing, reaching the poor, the vulnerable, and the marginalized. Rapid growth is unquestionably necessary for consequential poverty reduction, but for this growth to be sustainable in the long run, it must be broad-based across sectors and must include a majority of a country's labor force (World Bank, 2009). Promoting inclusive growth should be a top policy priority, especially in a resource-rich country like Nigeria that has grown reasonably over the years—and particularly over the last decade—but has not achieved a substantial reduction in poverty rates.

Methodology

This chapter presents a detailed analysis of agricultural input supply and the extent of inclusiveness in its allocation and distribution across different geopolitical zones in Nigeria,[1] using the panel component of the World Bank's Nigeria General Household Survey (GHS). The GHS panel, part of a larger, regional project across sub-Saharan Africa, conducted in collaboration with Nigeria's National Bureau of Statistics and Federal Ministry of Agriculture and Rural Development along with the Bill and Melinda Gates Foundation, ~~ to improve agricultural statistics, is a nationwide survey of five thousand households collected in four waves between 2010 and 2019 (World Bank Microdata Library, 2023). We chose this dataset because it is the only nationally representative survey in Nigeria with a central focus on agricultural households. Our study extracted agricultural input supply data from the GHS panel's four waves (2010–11, 2012–13, 2015–16, and 2018–19) (World Bank Microdata Library, Panel 2010–2011, 2020; World Bank Microdata Library, Panel 2012–2013, 2020; World Bank Microdata Library, Panel 2015–2016, 2020;

World Bank Microdata Library, Panel 2018–2019, 2021), including demographic distribution characteristics. To grasp the actuality and extent of ethnic inequality in agricultural input allocation and distribution in Nigeria, we analyzed the four waves separately based on the political leadership during these periods. Accordingly, 2010–11 (wave 1) and 2012–13 (wave 2), which fell during the leadership of President Goodluck Jonathan (who hailed from the south-south zone), were studied jointly, while 2015–16 (wave 3) and 2018–19 (wave 4), periods during which President Buhari (from the country's northwest) was either president or president-elect, were also considered together. Our data analysis method included estimating a random-effects Tobit model to identify the factors influencing farmers' access to inputs in Nigeria, including seed, fertilizer, credit, and land, and applying a social opportunity function (SOF).

Social Opportunity Function

If n individuals in a society are arranged in ascending order of their incomes (that is, $x_1, x_2, x_3, \ldots\ldots, x_n$), with the first individual being the poorest and the nth individual the richest, and if the n individuals are associated with opportunity, $y_1, y_2, y_3, \ldots\ldots, y_n$, then Izfal Ali and Hyun Hwa Son defined SOF as

$$O = O\left(y_i \ldots\ldots\ldots y_n\right) = O(\bar{y}, E) \tag{6.1}$$

$$Y_i \ \ldots\ldots\ldots Y_n (i = 1, 2, 3 \ldots\ldots\ldots n)$$

where O is SOF and y_i is the opportunity enjoyed by the ith person in the population with income x_i; y_i can take binary values of 0 and 100, indicating, respectively, that the ith person is deprived or enjoys a certain opportunity (Ali & Son, 2007). Then, the average opportunity available for the whole population is defined as

$$\bar{y} = \frac{1}{n}\sum_{i=1}^{n} y_i \tag{6.2}$$

The SOF O is required to satisfy the property of an increasing function of its argument's opportunity. That is, if the average opportunity ($\bar{y}$) available to society is increased, the SOF must increase. Another requirement of O is the transfer principle: Any transfer of opportunity from a poorer person to a richer person must decrease the SOF, and any transfer of opportunity from a richer person to a poorer person must increase the SOF. For example, suppose that t amount of opportunity is transferred from a poorer person with income x_1 to a richer person with income x_2; after the transfer, the poorer person will have $y_1 - t$ opportunities and the richer person will enjoy $y_2 + t$ opportunities. Thus,

$$O\left(y_1 - t, y_2 + t, y_3, \ldots\ldots y_n\right) \leq O\left(y_1, y_2, y_3, \ldots\ldots\ldots y_n\right) \tag{6.3}$$

(for all non-negative values of t).

Given that opportunity distribution vectors approximate opportunity function,

$$Q(O) \approx \left(y_1, y_2, y_3, \ldots\ldots\ldots y_n\right) \tag{6.4}$$

$$Q(t) \approx \left(y_1 - t, y_2 + t, y_3, \ldots\ldots\ldots, y_n\right) \tag{6.5}$$

and the cumulative distribution constructed as:

$$Q^c(O) \approx \left(y_1, \frac{y_1 + y_2}{2}, \frac{y_1 + y_2 + y_3}{3}, \ldots\ldots\ldots, \frac{y_1 + y_2 + \ldots\ldots + y_n}{n} \right) \tag{6.6}$$

$$Q^c(t) \approx \left(y_1 - t, \frac{y_1 + y_2}{2}, \frac{y_1 + y_2 + y_3}{3}, \ldots\ldots\ldots, \frac{y_1 + y_2 + \ldots\ldots + y_n}{n} \right) \tag{6.7}$$

where $Q^c(t)$ and $Q^c(O)$ may be called the generalized concentration curves of the distributions $Q(t)$ and $Q(O)$. Hyun Hwa Son shows that the concentration curve has a one-to-one relationship with the SOF. A generalized concentration curve satisfies the properties of (i) increasing the function of its arguments and (ii) it being quasi-concave (Son, 2011). Suppose the population is ordered in ascending order of individuals' incomes and associated with the opportunity vector, and suppose further that $\overline{y}_p$ is the average opportunity enjoyed by the bottom p percent of the population, where p varies from 0 to 1 and $\overline{y}$ is the mean opportunity available to the whole population. Then $\overline{y}_p$ will be equal to $\overline{y}$ when $p = 100$ (which covers the whole population). As $\overline{y}_p$ varies with p, a curve $\overline{y}_p$ is sketched for different values of p. Given the two distributions, if the generalized concentration curve of one is higher than that for another at all points, then the SOF implied by the former distribution is higher than the SOF implied by latter distribution. To avoid ambiguity in the distribution comparison, the social opportunity index is calculated from the area under the generalized concentration curve, expressed as

$$\phi = 2\int_0^1 \overline{y}C(p)dp = \overline{y}E \tag{6.8}$$

where E is the relative equity opportunity index (EOI), defined as $1 - C$, where C is the concentration of opportunity. Opportunity is relatively equitable if E is greater than 1, and relatively inequitable if E is less than 1. The absolute index of opportunity is derived from the following equation:

$$\phi = \overline{y} + E^* \tag{6.9}$$

where $E^* = \bar{y}(E-1)$ is the absolute EOI: Opportunity is absolutely equitable if E^* is greater than 0, and opportunity is absolutely inequitable if E^* is less than 0. The greater the SOF captured by φ, the greater will be $\bar{y}$, the average opportunity that is available to the whole population. If everyone in the population enjoys the same opportunity, then it can be shown that φ will be equal to $\bar{y}$. As such, the deviation of φ from $\bar{y}$ indicates how opportunities are distributed across the population: If φ is greater than $\bar{y}$, then opportunities are equitably distributed (i.e., pro-poor); if φ is less than $\bar{y}$, then opportunities are inequitably distributed (i.e., anti-poor).

Random-Effects Tobit Model

The random-effects Tobit model involves the estimation of limited dependent variable panel data using an objective function where the integrals appear not to have a closed-form solution (Calzolari, Magazzini, & Mealli, 2001). The model allows for censoring effects as well as temporal or spatial correlation across observations, along with unobserved heterogeneity (Chen, XiaoXiang, & Chen, 2014). Following Wei Wang and Michael Griswold (Wang & Griswold, 2016), the random-effects Tobit regression is modeled as follows:

$$Y_{it} = \left(Y_{i1}, \ldots, Y_{iN}\right)$$

and

$$Y_{it}^* = X_{it}'\beta^* + Q_{it}'\gamma_i + \sigma_\mu \mu_{it} \tag{6.10}$$

$$\mu_{it} \sim N\left(0, \sigma_\mu^2\right) \text{ and } \gamma_i \sim N\left(0, \sigma_\mu^2\right)$$

where Y_{it} is the truncated normally distributed response at time point i (for $i = 1, 2, 3, \ldots, n$) for subject t ($t = 1, 2, \ldots, N$ sample size); Y_{it}^* represents the uncensored latent variable; β^* and γ_i' are the vectors of fixed-effects and random-effects parameters for covariates X_{it}' and Q_{it}, respectively, independent of the error term μ_{it}. For a given left and right censoring at 1 and l, respectively, the relationship between the latent variable Y_{it}^* and uncensored latent variable Y_{it} is given as:

$$Y_{it} = \begin{cases} 1 & \text{for } Y_{it}^* \le 1 \\ Y_{it}^* \quad \text{for} & 1 < Y_{it}^* < l \\ l & \text{for } Y_{it}^* \ge l \end{cases} \tag{6.11}$$

If the censoring of Y_{it} is at one side, then only a lower (or upper) limit is needed: $1 = -\infty$ or $l = +\infty$. As a result of the individual effect of $Q_{it}'\gamma_i$, the observations on the outcome for each individual $\left(Y_{it} = Y_{i1}, \ldots, Y_{iN}\right)$ are correlated (Calzolari,

Magazzini, & Mealli, 2001). However, according to Christian Gourieroux and Alain Monfort, the conditional joint density function based on the individual effect γ_i can be expressed as

$$f\left(Y_i \mid X_i, \gamma_i; \varphi\right) = \prod_{t:Y_{it}>0} \frac{1}{\sigma_\mu} \theta\left(\frac{Y_{it} - X'_{it}\beta^* - Q'_{it}\gamma_i}{\sigma_\mu}\right) x \prod_{t:Y_{it}=0} \delta\left(\frac{-X'_{it}\beta^* - Q'_{it}\gamma_i}{\sigma_\mu}\right) \tag{6.12}$$

where θ and δ are the cumulative and density functions following $N(0, 1)$ distribution. Because γ_i is not observable, hence unsuitable for inference, the solution is to integrate out its effect (Gourieroux & Monfort, 1993):

$$f\left(Y_i \mid X_i; \varphi\right) = \int f\left(Y_i \mid X_i, \gamma_i; \varphi\right) P^\gamma(\gamma) \tag{6.13}$$

Giorgio Calzolari, Laura Magazzini, and Fabrizia Mealli point out that due to censoring of observations, the estimated regression coefficients obtained from the Tobit model do not show actual changes in the explained variable when there is a unit change in the independent variables. They suggest, however, that the effects of the independent variables in the random-effects Tobit model can be evaluated using the marginal effects of a unit change in the *i*th variable of *X* on *Y*:

$$\frac{\delta E(Y)}{\delta X_i} = \beta_i \phi(U) \tag{6.14}$$

where

$$U \frac{\beta X}{\sigma_\mu} = \frac{\beta X}{\sqrt{\sigma_\mu^2 + \sigma_\varepsilon^2}} \tag{6.15}$$

and $\phi(U)$ is the cumulative normal distribution function, and σ_μ and σ_ε are the standard deviations of the error term and random-effects, respectively (Calzolari, Magazzini, & Mealli, 2001).

Our study considered three specifications of the random-effects Tobit model, differentiated based on the inclusion of interaction variables and one main effect variable (zone) in addition to the main effects' variables. The first model (Equation 6.16) was specified to include the government dummy variable and the zone dummy variables, while the second model (Equation 6.17) captured the effect of the government dummy variable and the interaction variables (sector * expenditure and zone * government) on the dependent variable. The final model (Equation 6.18) is a combination of all the variables in models one and two. The random-effects Tobit models are thus specified as follows:

$$PCA_{ij} = \beta_{0ij} + \beta_1 AGE_{ij} + \beta_2 AGE2_{ij} + \beta_3 SEX_{ij} + \beta_4 HSIZ_{ij} + \beta_5 MAR_{ij} \\ + \beta_6 EDU_{ij} + \beta_7 EXTS_{ij} + \beta_8 MOBP_{ij} + \beta_9 SOCG_{ij} + \beta_{10} LOC_{ij} \\ + \beta_{11} TEXP_{ij} + \beta_{12} GOVT_{ij} + \beta_{13} ZONE_{ij} + \mu_{ij} \tag{6.16}$$

$$PCA_{ij} = \beta_{0ij} + \beta_1 AGE_{ij} + \beta_2 AGE2_{ij} + \beta_3 SEX_{ij} + \beta_4 HSIZ_{ij} + \beta_5 MAR_{ij} \\ + \beta_6 EDU_{ij} + \beta_7 EXTS_{ij} + \beta_8 MOBP_{ij} + \beta_9 SOCG_{ij} + \beta_{10} LOC_{ij} \\ + \beta_{11} TEXP_{ij} + \beta_{12} LOCEXP_{ij} + \beta_{13} GOVT_{ij} + \beta_{14} GOVZONE_{ij} + \mu_{ij} \tag{6.17}$$

$$PCA_{ij} = \beta_{0ij} + \beta_1 AGE_{ij} + \beta_2 AGE2_{ij} + \beta_3 SEX_{ij} + \beta_4 HSIZ_{ij} + \beta_5 MAR_{ij} \\ + \beta_6 EDU_{ij} + \beta_7 EXTS_{ij} + \beta_8 MOBP_{ij} + \beta_9 SOCG_{ij} + \beta_{10} LOC_{ij} \\ + \beta_{11} TEXP_{ij} + \beta_{12} LOCEXP_{ij} + \beta_{13} GOVT_{ij} + \beta_{14} ZONE_{ij} \\ + \beta_{14} GOVZONE_{ij} + \mu_{ij} \tag{6.18}$$

where β_{ij} are the parameters to be estimated, $i = 1, 2, \ldots n, j$ is equal to 1, 2, 3, or 4 (representing the four waves of panel data considered in the study), and μ is error *d* term. Principal component analysis is the index representing the level of inclusive growth, censored at 0.0225 (Calzolari, Magazzini, & Mealli, 2001).

We selected fourteen explanatory variables for our analysis. The variables' specifications with respect to the household head are given as follows:

- SEX = sex of farmer respondent (*D* = 1 if male, 0 otherwise)
- AGE = age (in years)
- AGE2 = age-squared
- MAR = marital status (*D* = 1 if married, 0 otherwise)
- EDUC = education (*D* = 1 if educated, 0 otherwise)
- HSIZ = household size (i.e., number of household members)
- EXTS = access to extension service (*D* = 1 if yes, 0 otherwise)
- MOBP = mobile phone ownership (*D* = 1 if yes, 0 otherwise)
- SOCG = social group (*D* = 1 if a member, 0 otherwise)
- LOC = location of respondent (1 if rural area, 0 otherwise)
- TEXP = log total expenditure in naira
- LOCEXP = interaction term between location and expenditure in naira
- GOVT = government dummy (*D* = 1 if under Jonathan's administration, 0 for Buhari's)
- ZONE = zone: north-central = 1 (base category); northwest = 2; northeast = 3; southwest = 4; southeast = 5; south-south = 6

- GOVZONE = interaction term between government and zone: north-central + government = 1 (if Jonathan—base category); northwest + government = 2; northeast + government = 3; southwest + government = 4; southeast + government = 5; south-south + government = 6

Resource Allocation and Distribution Theories

Resource allocation and distribution theories differ widely based on the size of the units examined, ranging from intrahousehold theories to larger organizational theories (covering public entities and universities, for example) to macro-level nationwide and global economic theories (Ledford & Lynch, 2019). In most cases, the factors affecting the different units vary considerably. This chapter focuses on three main theories to investigate the possible causes of disproportionate resource allocation and distribution in a country like Nigeria: public choice theory, social identity theory, and core-periphery theory.

Public choice theory, developed by James Buchanan and Gordon Tullock, applies economics principles to public policy decision-making and political behavior. It suggests that states act in their own self-interest, requiring corrective action in the distribution of goods to support constituency groups and prevent market failure (Buchanan & Tullock, 1962; Olson, 1971). The theory posits that the personal interests of government officials, politicians, and bureaucrats supersede those of the public, and that government policies and practices should be as efficient and effective as possible (Udama, 2013). Most of Nigeria's post-independence governments would seem to confirm public choice theory, having demonstrably placed either personal or ethnic group interests (or both) over those of the public. The confluence of political influence and economic power in Nigeria engenders inequality in the distribution of income, input supply, and other opportunities, all of which amount to suboptimal allocation of national resources. The concept of self-interest in governance helps to explain inequitable resource allocation and distribution and the resulting ethnic fragmentation in Nigeria, where little regard is given to region-specific needs or disparities.

Social identity theory, devised by Dominic Abrams and Michael A. Hogg, explains the influence of social groups on inter-group relations in terms of people's innate desire for group associations and the positive social and emotional by-products of said associations (Abrams & Hogg, 1988). Social identity refers to the ways that people base self-concepts on their membership in social groups; these groups can be as prosaic as football clubs or knitting circles, or they can encompass broad-scale identity categories like ethnicity, nationality, race, religious or political affiliation, gender, or sexual orientation (Leaper, 2011). Every individual belongs to one or more categories of social group, and membership in a given group greatly influences several life outcomes.

Thomas Ball and Nyla Branscombe have shown that due to the distinctiveness of each group, losses experienced in a particular group can create anxiety, as members may grow concerned about the future viability of the group as a separate entity. They further explain that this dynamic is particularly important for members of a minority group whose individualities are dominated by the cultural values of the majority group (Ball & Branscombe, 2019). This scenario is evident in Nigeria's southern zones, where feelings of marginalization around resource allocation and representation in key leadership positions are prevalent. This tendency is explained by symbolic motives that underlie inter-group attitudes and behaviors and account for the inclination toward favoring one's own group as a means of serving and securing members' sense of identity (Sanchez-Mazas & Licata, 2015).

Core-periphery theory, espoused by Paul Krugman, describes how countries can "endogenously become differentiated into an industrialized 'core' and an agricultural 'periphery,'" which helps to elucidate development lag in Nigeria (Krugman, 1991, 1998; Ottaviano & Puga, 1998). This "new economic geography" attempts to determine whether a country's population and industrial activity are in a core (spatially clustered) or deconcentrated (Klimczuk & Klimczuk-Kochańska, 2019). It also seeks to explain how labor mobility can concentrate economic activity in a single core region (or regions)—namely, because transportation costs are low enough, and the products' desire for products and the share of the manufacturing expenditure are large enough—and to unravel the causes of unequal distribution of economic activity and their progression through time (Mossay, 2006; Krugman, 1998). The core-periphery model explains why some people in the world exist within the cores (where there is abundance) and others in the peripheries (which are almost invariably regions with higher poverty rates). As with public choice theory, the state's self-interest supersedes that of those in the periphery (Ledford & Lynch, 2019).

In essence, according to Yuko Aoyama, James Murphy, and Susan Hanson, the core-periphery concept helps to demystify why some regions and countries are unable to grow their economies and remain chronically poor, while others become wealthy and powerful. Aoyama, Murphy, and Hanson further argue that the core-periphery model provides a framework for understanding how regional or national economics (generally) and development (specifically) depend to a degree on distance between regions or places (Aoyama, Murphy, & Hanson, 2011). Consistent with this perspective, Hossein Mirshojaeian Hosseini and Shinji Kaneko have found that spatial distance significantly influences local or provincial budgets. In other words, the distance of a given state or province from the capital (or "core") has a negative relationship with its budget (Hosseini & Kaneko, 2012).

Agricultural Resource Allocation and Distribution in Nigeria

Table 6.1 presents the distribution of inputs across geopolitical zones in Nigeria from 2010 to 2018. The table shows that the amount of credit spent by farmers in the northern region was between ₦15,432 and ₦18,430 in 2010, while the amount spent by farmers in the south was between ₦15,203 and ₦38,382.[2] On the average, farmers in the north accessed less credit than those in the southern region until

2018, when the pattern reversed and northern farmers accessed more credit than those in the southern zones. The table also indicates that farmers in the northern zones had favorable fertilizer access and distribution relative to their counterparts in south for all the years considered, although the average quantity of fertilizer received by farmers in the northwest and northeast zones dropped off dramatically in 2015, probably because of the Boko Haram insurgency's continued escalation in these two zones in 2013 and 2014 (Allen, Lewis, & Matfess, 2014).

The table further documents that seed distribution was extremely large in 2010 compared with the years that followed across all six zones, though the northern zones had more access (between 187.88 and 860.3 kilograms) than the southern zones (between 101.32 and 494.64 kilograms). That year, among the southern zones, farmers in the south-south zone received the highest quantity of seeds (494.64 kilograms), while farmers in the north-central zone received the most among the northern zones (860.3 kilograms). In 2012, the average seed quantities accessed reversed, with southern farmers receiving more (59.14 kilograms) than their northern counterparts (35.77 kilograms). The trend flipped again for 2015 and 2018, when farmers in the northern zones accessed marginally more seeds (averages of 67.82 and 64.37 kilograms, respectively) than those in the southern zones (averages of 61.3 and 38.57, respectively). For the years 2015 and 2018, farmers in the southeast zone had more seed access than farmers in the other southern zones. As in 2010, farmers in the north-central zone accessed more seeds than farmers in the other northern zones in 2012 and 2015; farmers in the northeast zone received more seeds than their northern neighbors in 2018.

Table 6.1 indicates that the quantity of land accessed by farmers in all six zones declined over the years considered. The land area accessed by farmers in the north-central zone was the largest on average for the period between 2010 and 2015, while the lowest land acquisition within the same period (except for 2015) was among farmers of the southwest zone. The year 2018 saw a steep decline in the land area accessed by farmers across the board—unsurprising given the ongoing Boko Haram insurgency in the north and the sharp increase in herder-farmer skirmishes in the south, both of which displaced a great many rural residents and made it impossible for those farmers to cultivate their land.

TABLE 6.1 Average Quantity of Agricultural Resources Accessed by Farmers Across Geopolitical Zones

	2010	*2012*	*2015*	*2018*	*2010*	*2012*	*2015*	*2018*
Zone	*Fertilizer (in kilograms)*				*Seeds (in kilograms)*			
North-central	118.14	37.50	204.00	112.44	860.30	59.10	66.53	60.11
	(11.60)	(17.67)	(23.11)	(40.87)	(20.72)	(13.27)	(20.33)	(24.11)
Northeast	135.52	50.01	20.00	100.67	187.88	34.07	54.40	67.23
	(14.10)	(8.96)	(15.73)	(25.50)	(11.32)	(15.67)	(11.98)	(11.65)

(Continued)

TABLE 6.1 (Continued)

	2010	*2012*	*2015*	*2018*	*2010*	*2012*	*2015*	*2018*
Zone	*Fertilizer (in kilograms)*				*Seeds (in kilograms)*			
Northwest	136.00	106.87	18.00	102.01	272.52	14.16	82.55	65.78
	(15.91)	(33.53)	(9.25)	(13.45)	(14.70)	(16.55)	(15.63)	(17.29)
Southeast	41.05	13.66	69.00	96.88	138.85	57.68	66.47	44.15
	(12.02)	(10.01)	(16.22)	(50.11)	(17.40)	(21.32)	(23.11)	(14.1)
South-south	68.12	25.07	60.00	87.07	494.64	58.65	60.55	33.90
	(17.02)	(7.56)	(13.32)	(36.99)	(46.53)	(15.82)	(18.55)	(8.31)
Southwest	70.00	15.45	62.00	88.00	101.32	61.10	56.87	37.66
	(18.53)	(10.22)	(24.19)	(23.44)	(21.95)	(20.10)	(13.41)	(18.28)
	Land (in hectares)				*Credit (in naira)*			
North-central	21.00	16.50	10.67	3.73	15,432	11,239	11,487	20,004
	(6.34)	(6.29)	(6.23)	(7.38)	(28.01)	(15.35)	(21.05)	(14.90)
Northeast	18.57	11.33	10.23	2.45	15,001	10,401	10,851	16,876
	(4.28)	(13.58)	(9.56)	(2.51)	(27.40)	(27.23)	(7.86)	(56.01)
Northwest	10.44	8.40	15.51	2.80	18,430	9,218	11,158	15,455
	(2.42)	(6.89)	(7.99)	(3.56)	(20.72)	(10.76)	(12.51)	(10.76)
Southeast	19.07	10.55	13.33	5.66	15,203	12,821	11,848	10,066
	(7.49)	(11.43)	(6.76)	(8.67)	(12.26)	(11.63)	(14.57)	(12.44)
South-south	19.34	11.25	9.80	4.43	38,382	11,772	11,715	12,320
	(4.25)	(12.11)	(5.91)	(12.11)	(15.18)	(20.58)	(13.41)	(15.03)
South-south	11.02	9.87	8.88	7.11	17,182	10,921	11,175	10,356
	(7.49)	(6.58)	(7.02)	(6.77)	(10.55)	(19.62)	(15.07)	(15.78)

Source: Constructed from World Bank GHS panels (2010 15 dataset).

Note: Values in parentheses are standard deviations.

Looking at the big picture, the table reveals that the years during which Jonathan was president (i.e., 2010, 2012, and the early part of 2015) showed somewhat more equitable resource allocation and distribution. Nevertheless, the southern zones had better access to credit during Jonathan's administration (which spanned the period between early 2010 and early 2015), with farmers from Jonathan's native south-south zone benefitting to different degrees over their counterparts in the other southern zones and the northern zones. Interestingly, the northern zones had better access to seeds than the southern zones in 2010, and to fertilizer in all four of the years considered. In 2015 and 2018 (during Buhari's administration), the northern zones continued to enjoy the agricultural input supply access they received during Jonathan's administration, and they found themselves benefitting from preferential access to credit relative to their southern counterparts—a reversal from the Jonathan years (Buhari, again, hailing from the northwest zone). This distribution offers a glimpse at how the ethnicity of the country's leadership can influence resource allocation and distribution. Tables 6.2–6.5 present a more granular view of equity in resource distribution from 2010 to 2018 under the two administrations.

Fertilizer Allocation and Distribution

The decile distribution of fertilizer access presented in Table 6.2 was higher in the fourth decile for all but the southwest zone within the period between 2010 and 2012, which shows that the rich at the bottom end of the income distribution are favored in accessing fertilizer. Similarly, the opportunity index (OI) for fertilizer access for the period between 2010 and 2012 reveals that there was more opportunity in the northern zones than the southern ones (except for the southwest). For example, in the north-central zone, the OI increased from 23.32 to 28.90; in the northeast, it rose from 28.85 to 42.80, while in the northwest, it went from 33.93 to 48.21. The southwest zone seems to be the only zone with more opportunity in the southern region.

Access to fertilizer has been improving nationally since 2011, but the opportunities are uneven across ethnic group/zone lines, which implies a strong overlap between political elites and those who hold economic power. Furthermore, most of the agricultural policies described in this chapter favored the north regardless of who was in power between 2010 and 2018 for two reasons: Northerners had been in power for more than fifteen years, and more of the agricultural produce comes from the northern region owing to its larger arable land area. In addition, the EOI shows that the northwest, northeast, and southwest zones had equitable distribution values of 1 in 2010 and 2015, while the other zones remained inequitable. This finding reflects both resource allocation priorities—fertilizer access overall and equitable distribution—during the period from 2012 to 2015.

The inequitable distribution of fertilizer opportunity in 2012 may owe, at least in part, to the contest for power in the 2015 general election, during which the majority of agricultural policies were neglected as the incumbent, Jonathan, endeavored to win at all costs. But disparate (and depressed) access to fertilizer dates back to the 1999–2010 FMSP. As mentioned in the introduction, evidence suggests that only 11 percent of the FMSP's subsidized fertilizer reached the smallholder farmers it was allocated to (FMARD, 2012). In 2011, the federal government, under Jonathan, introduced the Growth Enhancement Support Scheme (GESS) as part of the broader Agricultural Transformation Agenda (ATA). GESS sought to remedy the FMSP's shortcomings (which reportedly included rampant favoritism and corruption) by introducing a mobile phone–based electronic wallet system that farmers could use to gain access to subsidized agricultural inputs through accredited private-sector vendors using special vouchers. The e-wallet also afforded access to vital agricultural information through an agricultural extension service, as well as micro lending and insurance assistance (FMARD, 2012; Akin-Olagunju & Omonona, 2013).

Unfortunately, the e-wallet system proved to be little better than the FMSP; a 2014 report issued under the auspices of the World Bank and the African Union's Comprehensive African Agricultural Development Programme found that regional distribution of fertilizer subsidies and fertilizer vouchers during the e-wallet fertilizer project favored the northeast and northwest zones. The report further stated that the northeast and northwest zones' respective shares of fertilizer vouchers were 30.6 percent and 38.1 percent, and 30.9 percent and 46.9 percent during the e-wallet subsidy scheme, and that more farmers in the northeast and northwest zones received subsidized fertilizer using the GESS e-wallet than any other zones. Needless to say, farmers in Nigeria's north extolled the e-wallet fertilizer subsidy scheme (Olomola et al., 2014; FMARD, 2014).

All the same, in the 2015 presidential race, the majority of Buhari's votes came from the northern part of the country, while Jonathan got hefty support from the south. Jonathan's support (in relative terms) decreased along a northward path, and Buhari's seemed to decline from north to south. This pattern demonstrates that the northerners expected to benefit from policies favorable to the north once Buhari was elected. In Table 6.2, the fertilizer EOI over the entire period under consideration (2010–18) shows inequitable distribution for the south-south (Jonathan's region), southeast, and north-central zones, thus suggesting the possibility of regional favoritism in access to fertilizer and implying the existence of ethnic inequalities in the allocation and distribution of agricultural input resources.

Seed Allocation and Distribution

Opportunity in access to seeds seems to have been gradually declining in the southern region (except in the southeast zone) and rising in the northern region of the country between 2010 and 2015. Disaggregated by zone, Table 6.4 shows increasing inequality in access to seeds, with OIs ranging from 36.54 to 28.08 for the southwest and south-south zones, respectively, and from 23.47 to 21.38 for northeast zone in the period from 2010 to 2015. On the other hand, OIs range from 15.95 to 34.05 for the north-central, northwest, and south-south zones, respectively, indicating declining inequality in seed access. Generally, inequality in seed access appears to be lowest and declining in the southern zones when compared with their northern counterparts from 2010 to 2018. However, the EOI values indicate a lack of equity in seed distribution in all six geopolitical zones. The implication is that bounded access to high-quality seeds certified by the National Agricultural Seed Council remains a sizable problem in the country; while access opportunity seems to increase in the southern region, it is waning in the northern region (Chibuzo et al., 2023). Although data from Table 6.3 does not suggest that either the Jonathan or Buhari administrations attempted to influence distribution in favor of any ethnic group or region, overall equity in and opportunity access to seed input seems much improved between 2010 and early 2015 (during Jonathan's administration) than the period after 2015 (during Buhari's administration).

TABLE 6.2 Opportunity and Equity in Fertilizer Distribution by Zone

Zone	*Population Share (%)*	*2010*	*2012*	*2015*	*2018*	*Zone*	*Population Share (%)*	*2010*	*2012*	*2015*	*2018*
North-central	GHS panel wave					Southeast	GHS panel wave				
	1	11.81	16.12	8.54	16.01		1	12.08	11.03	13.86	22.45
	2	14.22	16.11	12.32	18.95		2	15.18	14.71	15.30	24.67
	3	17.65	44.21	14.67	10.57		3	16.77	15.09	16.11	25.90
	4	18.67	45.92	19.90	13.07		4	20.47	19.77	21.77	31.78
	OI ($\overline{y}$)	23.32	28.90	21.11	15.95		OI ($\overline{y}$)	17.56	19.61	22.99	28.95
	EOI (φ)	0.88	0.92	0.99	0.87		EOI (φ)	0.90	0.93	0.97	0.97
Northeast	GHS panel wave					South-south	GHS panel wave				
	1	13.15	10.21	09.15	26.84		1	10.11	13.69	15.76	30.06
	2	15.04	12.52	12.00	28.77		2	11.25	14.68	16.88	32.71
	3	16.11	15.53	15.98	32.55		3	16.11	15.67	18.29	35.43
	4	18.23	18.19	10.32	34.72		4	19.07	16.67	19.00	38.99
	OI ($\overline{y}$)	28.85	42.80	39.71	23.47		OI ($\overline{y}$)	32.33	22.24	31.13	31.21
	EOI (φ)	1.00	0.93	0.99	0.98		EOI (φ)	0.98	0.95	0.98	0.99
Northwest	GHS panel wave					Southwest	GHS panel wave				
	1	12.51	08.87	11.88	18.99		1	26.11	22.24	12.20	38.45
	2	13.32	11.88	14.56	23.46		2	09.00	12.89	13.00	41.52
	3	13.56	11.08	14.76	25.04		3	13.91	13.00	23.28	44.30
	4	15.11	14.89	14.00	32.09		4	14.53	14.13	14.19	46.31
	OI ($\overline{y}$)	33.93	48.21	41.16	26.20		OI ($\overline{y}$)	40.23	48.00	31.13	36.54
	EOI (φ)	1.00	0.72	1.00	0.99		EOI (φ)	1.00	0.86	0.71	0.78

Source: Constructed from World Bank GHS panels (2010–15 dataset).

Notes: OI refers to opportunity index; EOI refers to equity opportunity index.

TABLE 6.3 Opportunity and Equity in Seed Distribution by Zone

Zone	*Population Share (%)*	*2010*	*2012*	*2015*	*2018*	*Zone*	*Population Share (%)*	*2010*	*2012*	*2015*	*2018*
North-central	GHS panel wave					Southeast	GHS panel wave				
	1	16.01	16.23	10.98	17.68		1	22.45	21.73	37.23	17.27
	2	18.95	17.43	11.45	16.00		2	24.67	22.50	37.96	20.60
	3	10.57	11.00	12.72	16.32		3	25.90	22.79	39.72	21.27
	4	13.07	22.50	13.05	19.44		4	31.78	33.78	40.05	23.22
	OI ($\bar{y}$)	15.95	18.04	34.05	19.56		OI ($\bar{y}$)	15.95	18.04	34.05	20.33
	EOI (φ)	0.87	0.98	0.91	0.88		EOI (φ)	0.97	0.99	0.98	0.99
Northeast	GHS panel wave					South-south	GHS panel wave				
	1	26.84	33.02	20.11	12.83		1	30.06	26.77	28.71	28.96
	2	28.77	35.07	23.41	13.95		2	32.71	29.03	30.67	30.00
	3	32.55	37.56	25.33	16.60		3	35.43	31.73	32.67	21.00
	4	34.72	38.91	33.67	17.07		4	38.99	33.11	33.61	19.44
	OI ($\bar{y}$)	23.47	27.21	21.38	30.19		OI ($\bar{y}$)	31.21	25.95	28.08	35.11
	EOI (φ)	0.98	0.99	0.86	0.89		EOI (φ)	0.99	0.78	0.96	0.88
Northwest	GHS panel wave					Southwest	GHS panel wave				
	1	18.99	8.77	33.52	16.32		1	38.45	35.20	28.31	15.25
	2	23.46	40.23	35.20	17.12		2	41.52	36.54	30.89	19.33
	3	25.04	41.89	39.56	18.97		3	44.30	39.32	32.77	17.07
	4	32.09	43.23	39.98	19.92		4	46.31	45.01	40.16	16.19
	OI ($\bar{y}$)	26.20	30.08	30.57	17.67		OI ($\bar{y}$)	36.54	31.40	29.69	31.22
	EOI (φ)	0.99	0.98	0.99	0.93		EOI (φ)	0.78	0.97	0.99	0.95

Source: Constructed from World Bank GHS panels (2010–15 dataset)

Notes: OI refers to opportunity index; EOI refers to equity opportunity index.

Land Allocation and Distribution

It has been well established that access to land is instrumental to poverty reduction, socioeconomic empowerment, and sustainable economic growth and development (Cotula, Toulmin, & Quan, 2006; de Janvry & Sadoulet, 2008). The importance of land access and property rights is perhaps why territorial disputes are so prevalent and why they are more difficult to solve than other conflict issues. In Nigeria, as elsewhere in sub-Saharan Africa, land issues are a leading cause of conflict. As other chapters in this volume chronicle, conflicts over farmland can undermine food security, cause community discord, erode trust, and snowball into prolonged, sometimes violent conflagrations with lasting socioeconomic consequences for individuals and communities, as well as for economic growth and development on the national level (Okeaya-Inneh, 2023; Mbazor & Ojo, 2019; Omotara, 2016).

For the south-south and north-west zones from 2010 to the earlier part of 2015 under Jonathan's administration, Table 6.3 shows EOI values at or close to 1.00 in some geopolitical zones, indicating inclusiveness in that period. In 2010, the EOI was 1.00 for the south-south zone, while in the northwest, it was 1.00 in 2015 (the year that Buhari took office). These findings indicate strong ethnic loyalties founded on assumptions that when a coethnic is voted into power, they will most likely share and support their compatriots' basic political views and hence respond to their needs.

Credit Allocation and Distribution

Table 6.5 shows the distribution of credit across the six geopolitical zones. Unsurprisingly, the decile distribution figures appear to suggest that rich farmers were more favored in accessing credit than poor farmers. Similarly, the OI seems to indicate inequality in credit access across all zones. However, here again, these disparities were less pronounced during the 2010–15 period (during Jonathan's administration) compared with 2018 (during Buhari's administration). Furthermore, the OI values appear to indicate that cross-access to credit was similar across all geopolitical zones, although relative to the southern zones, the north fared better in credit access opportunity. Similarly, the EOI values illustrate that credit distribution was neither inclusive nor equitable: The value for most of the zones was less than 1. Only two zones in the southern region demonstrated an equitability uptrend in credit access distribution: the southeast zone, which had an EOI of 1 and 1.02 in 2012 and 2015, respectively, and the south-south zone, which had an EOI of 1 in 2010.

The leadership in question during the 2010–15 period (President Jonathan) may have favored distribution of credit access to these zones, the southern region being his homeland. The northern zones show consistently inequitable distribution of credit opportunity among farmers, though the northwest evidenced equitable distribution in 2012. In sum, Jonathan's administration seems to have worked to

TABLE 6.4 Opportunity and Equity in Land Distribution by Zone

Zone	*Population Share (%)*	*2010*	*2012*	*2015*	*2018*	*Zone*	*Population Share (%)*	*2010*	*2012*	*2015*	*2018*
North-central	GHS panel wave					Southeast	GHS panel wave				
	1	11.88	12.99	14.71	19.84		1	11.41	16.73	19.05	14.16
	2	12.05	13.34	15.00	20.46		2	12.07	15.01	21.00	15.17
	3	12.22	14.78	15.55	18.49		3	13.04	13.43	21.06	16.55
	4	13.64	15.54	16.10	13.44		4	15.00	15.90	22.09	18.88
	OI ($\bar{y}$)	*33.11*	34.67	37.51	29.98		OI ($\bar{y}$)	25.03	22.64	33.55	23.44
	EOI (φ)	0.99	0.97	0.99	0.99		EOI (φ)	0.95	0.98	0.99	0.98
Northeast	GHS panel wave					South-south	GHS panel wave				
	1	18.00	16.06	18.09	18.91		1	13.78	11.42	10.15	22.41
	2	17.02	18.08	17.07	21.96		2	13.00	12.89	13.29	29.85
	3	17.56	20.19	17.56	27.49		3	15.05	11.99	16.12	20.00
	4	19.00	21.82	18.01	30.76		4	15.76	10.13	17.92	18.23
	OI ($\bar{y}$)	41.07	33.58	43.22	40.40		OI ($\bar{y}$)	44.32	46.89	50.11	30.91
	EOI (φ)	0.89	0.88	0.97	0.93		EOI (φ)	1.00	0.96	0.87	0.78
Northwest	GHS panel wave					Southwest	GHS panel wave				
	1	07.38	08.95	15.90	13.01		1	09.78	17.89	12.54	28.24
	2	11.42	12.66	8.34	19.71		2	10.65	19.32	12.10	36.03
	3	14.77	18.21	11.55	18.16		3	13.43	03.11	13.76	36.77
	4	18.61	18.80	14.65	16.77		4	14.21	14.67	14.20	39.58
	OI ($\bar{y}$)	33.96	40.11	41.15	37.60		OI ($\bar{y}$)	26.98	28.71	33.59	42.67
	EOI (φ)	0.99	0.98	1.00	0.75		EOI (φ)	0.98	0.87	0.99	0.88

Source: Constructed from World Bank GHS panels (2010–15 dataset)

Notes: OI refers to opportunity index; EOI refers to equity opportunity index.

ensure equity in credit distribution during his administration, but he does appear to have shown favor to the southern region over the north. The aforementioned GESS, which brought about the e-wallet program, aimed to ensure equitability and opportunity in agricultural input resource allocation and distribution.

It is important to note that in 2018, the insecurity of the Boko Haram incursion, along with regional and ethnoreligious conflicts (particularly with Fulani herders, as mentioned above), displaced farmers from their land in the north, thus limiting their agricultural input access and exacerbating resource distribution inequality. Yet the credit OI values adduce that the northern region still fared better in terms of available opportunity than the southern zones (though the north-central zone appears to have had low opportunity relative to the other northern zones). For example, in Plateau state—one of the most ethnically diverse states in Nigeria, in the north-central region—disputes between indigenes and settlers over resources and representation that exploded into deadly conflicts during this period fueled resource inequality, although this has been a reoccurring issue for over a decade. In any case, credit distribution was inequitable across all zones in 2018, with EOI values less than 1 seeming to indicate ethnic favoritism. Considering the leadership during this period (President Buhari's administration), favoritism and inequality were also evident (and prevalent) because political appointments favored northerners. At the same time, Buhari's time in power saw herder versus farmer conflicts escalating to violence more frequently as battles for scarce resources stirred tensions over ethnicity. Although sub-Saharan Africa has a long history of contentions over resources between farmers and herders, this issue has been particularly polarizing in Nigeria. Hence, credit allocation and distribution have been impacted by conflict over access to resources—particularly in areas that have exacerbated ethnoregional inequalities.

Factors Influencing Inclusive Access to Agricultural Inputs in Nigeria

Our study estimated a random-effects Tobit model to identify the factors influencing inclusive access in terms of pooled agricultural inputs supply in Nigeria. We specified three models differentiated based on the inclusion of the main effect (zone) and the interaction variables defined in the methodology section above. Using the inclusive access index generated by principal component analysis, censored at 0.0025, we observed that only 34 percent of farmers in any given zone in a given year had access to agricultural inputs (see Table A6.1). Evaluating these data points in model one indicates that 20.5 percent of the change in the level of inclusive input access resulting from the explanatory variables is produced by marginal changes in the value of positive inclusive access. The remaining 79.5 percent is due to changes in the probability of having marginal or no inclusion at all in terms of access to agricultural inputs. This result is consistent with those observed for models two and three.

Residuals of Tobit regressions are often heteroscedastic and/or non-normally distributed in panel data settings (Amore & Murtinu, 2021), which means that any incorrect assumption of homoscedasticity in the model's estimation will produce misleading

TABLE 6.5 Opportunity and Equity in Credit Distribution by Zone

Zone	*Population Share (%)*	*2010*	*2012*	*2015*	*2018*	*Zone*	*Population Share (%)*	*2010*	*2012*	*2015*	*2018*
North-central	Wave					Southeast	Wave				
	1	23.17	20.66	34.48	15.04		1	19.66	18.76	20.59	05.99
	2	27.27	21.36	35.53	15.23		2	21.77	19.53	21.00	07.47
	3	28.03	21.90	35.84	15.99		3	24.99	19.72	23.49	08.79
	4	30.92	23.90	37.08	15.66		4	25.90	20.73	23.91	10.30
	OI ($\bar{y}$)	31.64	26.86	41.80	15.45		OI ($\bar{y}$)	31.15	25.44	29.55	16.00
	EOI (φ)	0.99	0.98	0.78	0.95		EOI (φ)	0.99	1.00	1.02	0.88
Northeast	Wave					South-south	Wave				
	1	25.78	30.57	20.50	15.34		1	17.56	29.06	33.11	06.66
	2	34.53	33.02	22.11	14.05		2	23.55	30.17	38.72	10.15
	3	36.18	35.78	23.67	14.53		3	29.67	32.67	38.91	09.84
	4	37.92	42.77	26.39	13.33		4	35.61	33.09	40.45	10.47
	OI ($\bar{y}$)	25.30	33.05	29.88	23.98		OI ($\bar{y}$)	21.71	24.78	31.94	19.05
	EOI (φ)	0.86	0.87	0.99	0.75		EOI (φ)	1.00	0.99	0.78	0.93
Northwest	Wave					Southwest	Wave				
	1	39.83	18.49	27.28	15.88		1	26.76	27.88	26.71	05.65
	2	40.62	19.99	29.56	16.31		2	30.56	32.83	28.38	11.36
	3	44.71	23.45	31.32	15.45		3	33.11	35.62	29.33	08.52
	4	45.32	27.71	33.87	16.04		4	39.50	40.23	32.56	07.26
	OI ($\bar{y}$)	33.79	19.03	26.66	28.77		OI ($\bar{y}$)	29.70	30.37	25.10	19.80
	EOI (φ)	0.97	1.00	0.99	0.98		EOI (φ)	0.76	0.96	0.99	0.99

Source: Constructed from World Bank GHS panels (2010–15 dataset).

Notes: OI refers to opportunity index; EOI refers to equity opportunity index.

results. As such, it is standard practice to test for the presence of heteroscedasticity after estimating the model. Accordingly, we employed the likelihood ratio test, which—when significant—implies the presence of heteroscedasticity. The outputs of the likelihood ratio test for the three models specified were significant, indicating that the residuals are indeed heteroscedastic (see Table A6.2). It was therefore important to run a robust random-effects panel analysis to correct for heteroscedasticity. Table 6.6 shows the results of that analysis. Significant Wald chi-squared (chi^2) test ($p < 0.001$), ranging from 1,194 to 1,202, indicate a good fit of the models to the data.

For model one, only two out of the seventeen explanatory variables are not significant and thus do not influence inclusive access to inputs: The positive effect of age and the negative effect of age-squared imply that as people get older, the impact of age on inclusive access lessens. Implicatively, younger people have a higher tendency to influence inclusiveness, as they are more likely to take on risks than older people. This reasoning is in lockstep with the life-cycle hypothesis, which assumes that individuals incur debt when younger with an expectation that future income will enable them to pay it off. Household size, marital status, and education have demonstrative positive impacts on inclusiveness, while access to extension service and possession of a mobile phone have negative but weak effects. A point increase in rural area residency raises inclusiveness by 3.27 points—a plausible result given that more than 70 percent of Nigerians reside and subsist in rural areas: Because farmers are the intended recipients of agricultural input subsidies, it is only logical that rural farmers will benefit more. Additional naira spent by households also increases the likelihood of inclusive input access by 8.5 percent.

Results from Table 6.6 further reveal that government also has an influence on improving inclusive input access. From the definition of the variable, a positive sign denotes that at any point in time, the government plays a key role in ensuring that access is more equitable and inclusive in Nigeria. This is perhaps one of the most important takeaways from our study: *Public governance* (defined as the formal and informal rules, values, practices, procedures, and interactions within state-owned institutions and between nonstate organizations, state-owned institutions, and citizens, with the aim of ensuring that public interests are addressed [Dzingirai, Karonga, & Mazenge, 2023]) matters in achieving economic growth and narrowing inequality, as it can leverage or undermine the impact of economic policies on inclusive access by influencing spending, investment, and efficiency of service delivery (OECD, 2015).

Government plays a central role in delivering inclusive (or non-inclusive) access to agricultural inputs, and model one reveals that the ethnoregional origin of those in power factors into how decisions are made to provide that access. The statistical significance of the interaction terms in model two ($p < 0.001$), representing the interplay between government and zones, denotes that the interaction terms are indeed an important part of the model. Additionally, Table 6.6 shows the interplay between farmers' locations and total expenditure. Although the relationship between total expenditure and inclusive access was positive in model one, the inclusion of the sectoral expenditure in model two changed the positive sign to negative. The positive sign of location and expenditure interaction implies that expenditures made by rural dwellers account for the positive relationship previously observed.

From the results presented for model one, we can deduce that farmers in the north-central zone, compared with farmers in the southwest, southeast, and south-south zones, were less likely to have access to inclusive and sustainable inputs between 2010 and 2018. However, farmers in the northwest were more likely to benefit from inclusive input access than those in the north-central zone. We can also infer that, relative to being from the north-central zone during Buhari's administration, inclusiveness increased by 49.7 percent for farmers from the northwest during Jonathan's administration. Farmers from the southwest and southeast were less likely to benefit from inclusive access to inputs than those in the northwest under Buhari's administration. Counterintuitively, farmers from the south-south zone were also 48.1 percent less likely to benefit from inclusive input supply policy—a rather shocking result given that President Jonathan is from the south-south zone; one would expect that he would formulate policies that benefit his home region and ethnic group. It also suggests that Jonathan's administration was focused on improving farmers' livelihoods and productivity regardless of their region or ethnicity.

The results for the periods under Buhari are a stark contrast to those under Jonathan. That Buhari's administration was prone to favoritism and ethnic inclination in the allocation and distribution of resources owned and controlled by the state is evident. Higher participation rates recorded for northern farmers in programs like the federal government's fertilizer subsidy scheme, the ACGSF, and others reinforce this point. Another clear illustration is the fact that contestations for key appointments to government positions during Buhari's administration were demonstrably skewed in favor of the north—a highly divisive matter.

Overall, we can conclude from the results in Table 6.6 that President Jonathan was less concerned with accumulating wealth for his compatriots and coethnics and more aligned with the ministerial responsibility of ensuring equitable allocation and distribution of agricultural inputs—an indispensable prerequisite for bolstering economic growth. National accounts data obtained from the World Bank and the Organisation for Economic Co-operation and Development underscore the connectedness of inclusive input access and economic growth. Although Nigeria's GDP growth rate decreased between 2010 and 2012, it averaged 5.65 percent and increased from 4.3 percent in 2012 to 6.3 percent in 2014, all years representing periods under Jonathan's leadership. In 2015, however, when Buhari assumed power, GDP growth plummeted to a two-decade low of 2.65 percent; 2016 saw an economic contraction of −1.62 percent, followed by marginally revived but minimal growth in 2017 (World Bank Open Data, 2024). The observed GDP growth trajectory during these periods is a clear indication that inclusive resource access is central to economic development.

Model three represents an unrestricted model, and its results are consistent with those of models one and two. However, we notice a slight deviation: The south-south and government interaction variable changed from negative to positive following the inclusion of zone dummies in model three. Hence, by implication, parts of the south-south did benefit from more inclusive access to inputs during the Jonathan administration. However, nationally, the extent of inclusiveness was higher in the northern zones than in the southern zones.

TABLE 6.6 Empirical Estimates of Factors Influencing Inclusive Access to Agricultural Inputs in Nigeria

Variables	*Model One*				*Model Two*				*Model Three*			
	Coeff.	*S.E.*	*P > Z*	*dy/dx*	*Coeff.*	*S.E.*	*P > Z*	*dy/dx*	*Coeff.*	*S.E.*	*P > Z*	*dy/dx*
Age	0.010**	0.005	2.11	0.023***	0.009**	0.005	2.01	0.021***	0.010**	0.005	2.04	0.021***
Age-squared	−1E−4***	5E−5	−2.67	−2E−4***	−1E−4***	5E−5	−2.62	0.000***	−1E−4***	5E−5	−2.63	−2E−4***
Sex	−0.220**	0.098	−2.23	−0.519***	−0.239**	0.101	−2.37	−0.564***	−0.228**	0.101	−2.25	−0.537***
Household size	0.021***	0.005	4.63	0.006	0.021***	0.005	4.61	0.006	0.022***	0.005	4.74	0.009
Marital status	0.262***	0.093	2.81	0.565***	0.282***	0.095	2.98	0.606***	0.280***	0.095	2.93	0.599***
Education	0.095***	0.027	3.5	0.225***	0.089***	0.027	3.33	0.200***	0.087***	0.027	3.25	0.172***
Extension service	−0.065*	0.033	−1.95	−0.039	−0.041	0.033	−1.24	0.005	−0.035	0.033	−1.07	0.040
Mobile phone	−0.065**	0.028	−2.34	−0.078	−0.050*	0.028	−1.83	−0.025	−0.048*	0.028	−1.75	−0.017
Social group	0.012	0.071	0.18	−0.069	0.035	0.074	0.48	−0.026	0.054	0.072	0.75	0.008
Location	3.268***	0.893	8.79	2.198***	−1.166	0.741	−1.57	−0.941	−1.013	0.782	−1.29	−0.633
Total expenditure	0.085***	0.355	4.51	0.183***	−1.699***	0.313	−5.43	−1.083***	−1.539***	0.325	−4.73	−0.929***
Government	1.285***	0.096	13.42	2.699***	1.276***	0.102	12.53	2.462***	0.611***	0.157	3.9	1.919***
Northwest	0.426***	0.042	10.08	0.527***					−1.056***	0.263	−4.01	−0.943***
Northeast	−0.032	0.046	−0.7	0.110					−0.736***	0.242	−3.04	−0.365
Southwest	−1.128***	0.131	−8.13	−0.466***					−0.922***	0.339	−2.72	−0.399
Southeast	−0.190***	0.055	−3.47	−0.135					−0.381	0.253	−1.51	−0.347
South-south	−0.500***	0.062	−8.03	−0.225**					−1.060***	0.266	−3.98	−0.725
Location + expenditure (LOCEXP)					1.770***	0.313	5.65	1.228***	1.609***	0.326	4.94	1.076***
Northwest + government					0.497***	0.047	10.68	0.889***	1.554***	0.268	5.81	1.828***
Northeast + government					0.005	0.052	0.09	0.149	0.741***	0.247	3	0.511
Southwest + government					−1.371***	0.446	−3.07	−0.762	−0.463	0.564	−0.82	−0.373
Southeast + government					−0.162***	0.062	−2.63	−0.022	0.221	0.261	0.85	0.337
South-south + government					−0.481***	0.077	−6.23	−0.150	0.579**	0.277	2.09	0.582**
Constant	−5.007***	0.384	−13.06		−0.561	0.742	−0.76		−0.068	0.788	−0.09	
Diagnostics log likelihood		−6813.560			−6790.337				−6759.412			
Wald Chi² (23)		1194.35			1202.45				1201.84			
Probability > Chi²		0.0000			0.0000				0.000			
No. of observations		8,089			8,089				8,089			

Source: Constructed from World Bank GHS panels (2010–15 dataset).

Notes: Coeff. denotes coefficient; S.E. denotes standard error. $P > Z$ indicates the probability that the Z-statistic is greater than the Z-score/value; dy/dx is the derivative of variable y with respect to x (i.e., the rate of change of y relative to x). The asterisks (*, **, and ***) indicate significance at 1 percent, 5 percent, and 10 percent, respectively. The base category for zone is north-central. For the interaction terms, the base category is north-central + government.

Conclusion

This chapter has presented a detailed analysis of agricultural input supply and the extent of equity and inclusiveness in input access, allocation, and distribution across Nigeria's six geopolitical zones. Results from the regional analysis show that farmers from the northeast, northwest, and north-central zones are more likely to access subsidized inputs than those in southern zones. Similarly, the OIs for virtually all the agricultural input resources considered illustrate that the northern zones benefitted from more opportunity than the southern zones.

The regression results from our study demonstrate that government plays a pivotal role in ensuring and expanding equitable and inclusive access to agricultural inputs in Nigeria. The data indicates that President Jonathan's administration was more equitable and inclusive in terms of agricultural input supply, suggesting that his primary strategy was to improve the livelihoods and productivity of farmers regardless of their locus or ethnicity. The data also uncovers a reversal during the Buhari years, when northerners tended to enjoy more inclusive access to agricultural inputs than their counterparts in the south. This north-south divide provides clear evidence that favoritism and ethnic inclination can play a significant role in the allocation and distribution of nationally owned and controlled resources.

Two interesting (and concerning) inferences arise from this study: The structural and institutional arrangement in Nigeria seems to be such that northerners reap economic benefits at greater rates than southerners irrespective of who is in power, and this observed ethnic fragmentation and bias only become more pronounced when a northerner is at the helm. For these reasons, we posit that although allocation and distribution of resources should be all-inclusive, it should primarily be on a regional distributive system—one that recognizes individual states' capacities and resource efficiency in proportion to their contribution to the agricultural share of the economy. This model will serve as an incentive to states that are already contributing their fair share while motivating others who may be operating at a suboptimal level.

Appendix

TABLE A6.1 Decomposition of Tobit Effects of the Specified Models

Model	*Fraction of the Censored Sample*	*Fraction of Mean Total Response of the Uncensored Sample*
One	0.341	0.205
Two	0.341	0.201
Three	0.341	0.201

Source: Constructed from World Bank GHS panels (2010–15 dataset).

TABLE A6.2 Tobit Model Regression Results

Variables	*Model One*			*Model Two*			*Model Three*		
	Coefficient	*S.E.*	*Z*	*Coefficient*	*S.E.*	*P > Z*	*Coefficient*	*S.E.*	*P > Z*
Age	0.012	0.008	1.54	0.011	0.008	1.33	0.011	0.008	1.4
Age-squared	−2E−04	8E−05	−1.92	−1E−04	8E−05	−1.56	−1E−04	8E−05	−1.64
Sex	0.534***	0.105	5.07	0.549***	0.105	5.24	0.540***	0.105	5.16
Household size	0.030***	0.008	3.75	0.039***	0.008	4.95	0.037***	0.008	4.61
Marital status	−0.580***	0.091	−6.37	−0.599***	0.090	−6.64	−0.597***	0.090	−6.61
Education	−0.045	0.053	−0.85	−0.027	0.053	−0.51	−0.025	0.053	−0.46
Extension service	−0.523***	0.062	−8.43	−0.437***	0.062	−7.02	−0.433***	0.062	−6.96
Mobile phone	−0.264***	0.064	−4.12	−0.165**	0.065	−2.54	−0.167**	0.065	−2.58
Social group	0.195***	0.066	2.96	0.203***	0.066	3.09	0.221***	0.066	3.36
Sector	1.005***	0.080	12.56	0.131	0.255	0.51	0.079	0.254	0.31
Total expenditure	−0.052	0.032	−1.65	−0.466***	0.084	−5.56	−0.436***	0.084	−5.21
Government	0.028	0.068	0.41	0.153	0.105	1.45	0.388***	0.090	4.33
Northwest	0.324***	0.079	4.12				−0.116	0.123	−0.95
Northeast	−0.263***	0.083	−3.16				−0.208*	0.108	−1.92
Southwest	−1.097***	0.112	−9.78				−0.534***	0.119	−4.5
Southeast	−0.211**	0.089	−2.38				−0.794***	0.126	−6.29
South-south	−0.670***	0.091	−7.34				0.014	0.117	0.12
Sector + expenditure (2011)				0.417***	0.090	4.64	−0.510***	0.113	−4.5
Northwest + government				0.778***	0.113	6.91	0.976***	0.154	6.36
Northeast + government				−0.043	0.116	−0.37		0.163	2.95
							.480***		
SW + government				−2.625***	0.313	−8.38	−1.841***	0.333	−5.53
SE + government				−0.390***	0.127	−3.06	−0.406**	0.168	−2.42
SS + government				−0.952***	0.145	−6.56	−0.452**	0.180	−2.52
Constant	−1.280	0.241	−5.32***	−0.754**	0.325	−2.32	−0.413	0.330	−1.25
Likelihood ratio test									
LR Chi (17)	2496.21			2429.86			2423.11		
Probability > Chi²	0.0000			0.0000			0.0000		
Diagnostics log likelihood		−8060.02		−8002.66			−7968.18		
Wald Chi² (23)		695.87		766.24			807.97		
Probability > Chi²		0.0000		0.0000			0.000		
No. of observations		8,089		8,089			8,089		

Source: Constructed from World Bank GHS panels (2010–15 dataset).

Notes: S.E. stands for standard error. *Z* stands for *Z*-statistic. *P* > *Z* indicates the probability that the *Z*-statistic is greater than the *Z*-score/value. The asterisks (*, **, and ***) indicate significance at 1 percent, 5 percent, and 10 percent, respectively. Base category for zone is north-central. For the interaction terms, the base category is north-central + government.

Notes

1 Shortly after assuming the role of military head of state, Sani Abacha orchestrated Nigeria's reorganization into the six geopolitical zones described in this chapter—north-central, northeast, northwest, southeast, south-south, and southwest—to better reflect the country's economic, political, and cultural realities (Nwala, 1997).
2 The 2010 naira/U.S. dollar exchange rate was N150.30 (Central Bank of Nigeria, 2024).

Bibliography

Abrams, Dominic, and Michael A. Hogg. "Comments on the Motivational Status of Self-Esteem in Social Identity and Intergroup Discrimination." *European Journal of Social Psychology* 18, no. 4 (August/September 1988): 317–34, https://doi.org/10.1002/ejsp.2420180403.

Adejumo, Oyeronke Abosede, and Bolarinwa Titus Omonona. "Analysis of the Performance of the Agricultural Credit Guarantee Scheme Fund in Nigeria (1981 to 2016)." *IOSR Journal of Agriculture and Veterinary Science* 10, no. 10 (October 2017): 24–30.

Ademola, Emmanuel Oluniyi. "Herder-Farmer Conflicts and RUGA Policy: Why Nigerian Stakeholder Are at Loggerheads over Rural Grazing Settlements." *Ethnic Studies Review* 43, no. 3 (2020): 103–21, https://doi.org/10.1525/esr.2020.43.3.103.

Agene, Deborah, et al. "Is There Any Relationship Between Agricultural Performance and Inclusive Growth in Nigeria?" *Journal of Internet Banking and Commerce* 22, no. 8 (May 2017): 1–26, https://www.icommercecentral.com/open-access/is-there-any-relationship-between-agricultural-performance-and-inclusive-growth-iin-nigeria.pdf.

Akin-Olagunju, Olaide Asimiyu, and Bolarin T. Omonona. "Fertilizer Subsidy Administration in Nigeria: Challenges and Prospects." *Nigerian Journal of Rural Extension and Development* 7 (January 2013): 1–8, https://journals.ui.edu.ng/index.php/njred/article/view/925/773.

Ali, Ifzal, and Hyun Hwa Son. "Measuring Inclusive Growth." *Asian Development Review* 24, no. 1 (2007): 11–31, https://doi.org/10.1142/S0116110507000024.

Allen, Nathaniel, Peter M. Lewis, and Hilary Matfess. "The Boko Haram Insurgency, by the Numbers." *The Washington Post*, October 6, 2014, https://www.washingtonpost.com/news/monkey-cage/wp/2014/10/06/the-boko-haram-insurgency-by-the-numbers.

Amore, Mario Daniele, and Samuele Murtinu. "Tobit Models in Strategy Research: Critical Issues and Applications." *Global Strategy Journal* 11, no. 3 (August 2021): 1–25, https://doi.org/10.1002/gsj.1363.

Aoyama, Yuko, James T. Murphy, and Susan Hanson. *Key Concepts in Economic Geography*. London, UK: Sage, 2011.

Apikins, Maina Williams. "The Federal Government of Nigeria's Rural Grazing Area (RUGA) Policy: The Demystification of the Elite's Theory?" *International Journal of Advanced Studies in Economics and Public Sector Management* 8, no. 1 (February 2020): 229–43, https://internationalpolicybrief.org/wp-content/uploads/2023/10/ARTICLE19-17.pdf.

Aye, Goodness Chioma. "Sensitivity and Integration of Efficiency Estimates from Input Distance Functions and Stochastic Production Frontiers: Application to Maize Production in Benue State Nigeria." PhD diss., University of Pretoria, South Africa, 2011, https://hdl.handle.net/2263/28829.

Ball, Thomas C., and Nyla R. Branscombe. "When Do Groups with a Victimized Past Feel Solidarity with Other Victimized Groups?" In *Confronting Prejudice and Discrimination:*

The Science of Changing Minds and Behaviors, edited by Robyn K. Mallet and Margo J. Monteith, 73–92. London, UK: Elsevier Academic Press, 2019.

Buchanan, James M., and Gordon Tullock. *The Calculus of Consent: Logical Foundations of Constitutional Democracy*. Ann Arbor: University of Michigan Press, 1962.

Calzolari, Giorgio, Laura Magazzini, and Fabrizia Mealli. "Simulations-Based Estimations of Tobit Model with Random Effects." In *Econometric Studies: A Festschrift in Honour Joachim Frohn*, edited by Helmut Lütkepohl, Lothar Knüppel, and Ralph Friedmann, 349–69. Münster, Germany: LIT Verlag, 2001.

CEIC Data, "Nigeria NG: Imports: % of Goods Imports: Food, 1962–2017," accessed December 7, 2024, https://www.ceicdata.com/en/nigeria/imports/ng-imports--of-goods-imports-food.

Central Bank of Nigeria. *Annual Report and Financial Statements for the Year Ended 31st December, 2008*. Abuja, Nigeria: Central Bank of Nigeria, 2009, https://www.cbn.gov.ng/out/2010/publications/reports/gov/annual%20report%202008final.pdf.

Central Bank of Nigeria, "Statistical Bulletin 2010, Part D: External Sectors Statistics," Table D.3.1: Monthly Average Official Exchange Rate of the Naira (naira/US$1.00 in 2010), accessed March 19, 2024, https://www.cbn.gov.ng/out/2011/publications/statistics/2010/PartD/PartD.html.

Central Bank of Nigeria Development Finance Department (CBNDFD). "Report of the Activities of the Business Unit for the Month of October, 2015." Abuja, Nigeria, October 2015.

Chen, Feng, Ma XiaoXiang, and Suren Chen. "Refined-Scale Panel Data Crash Rate Analysis Using Random-Effects Tobit Model." *Accident Analysis and Prevention* 73 (December 2014): 323–32, https://doi.org/10.1016/j.aap.2014.09.025.

Chibuzo, Uzoma Izuogu, et al. "A Review of the Nigerian Seed System." *Selekcija i Semenarstvo* 29, no. 2 (2023): 39–49, https://scindeks-clanci.ceon.rs/data/pdf/0354-5881/2023/0354-58812302039U.pdf.

Cotula, Lorenzo, Camilla Toulmin, and Julian Quan. "Better Land Access for the Rural Poor: Lessons from Experience and Challenges Ahead." London, UK: International Institute for Environment and Development, October 2006, https://www.iied.org/12532iied.

de Janvry, Alain, and Elisabeth Sadoulet. "Access to Land and Development." In *The New Palgrave Dictionary of Economics*, edited by Matias Vernengo, Esteban Perez Caldentey, and Barkley J. Rosser Jr., 1–5. London, UK: Palgrave Macmillan, 2008, https://doi.org/10.1057/978-1-349-95121-5_2126-1.

Dzingirai, Mufaro, Billy F. Karonga, and Talent Mazenge. "Demystifying Governance of Zimbabwean Public Sector Enterprises in Attainment of the Sustainable Development Goals." In *Governance as a Catalyst for Public Sector Sustainability*, edited by Neeta Baporikar, 50–70. Hershey, PA: IGI Global, 2023.

Easterly, William, and Ross Levine. "Africa's Growth Tragedy: Policies and Ethnic Divisions." *The Quarterly Journal of Economics* 112, no. 4 (November 1997): 1203–50, https://doi.org/10.1162/003355300555466.

Federal Ministry of Agriculture and Rural Development (FMARD). *The Growth Enhancement Support Scheme (GESS), Under Agricultural Transformation Agenda (ATA)*. Abuja, Nigeria: Federal Ministry of Agriculture and Rural Development, 2012.

FMARD. *Ten Million Farmers Captured in Agric e-Wallet Scheme*. Abuja, Nigeria: Federal Ministry of Agriculture and Rural Development, 2014, https://hdl.handle.net/10986/22345.

Gourieroux, Christian, and Alain Monfort. "Simulation-Based Inference: A Survey with Special Reference to Panel Data Models." *Journal of Econometrics* 59, nos. 1–2 (September 1993): 5–33, https://doi.org/10.1016/0304-4076(93)90037-6.

Hosseini, Hossein Mirshojaeian, and Shinji Kaneko. "Pattern and Determinants of Public Budget Allocation to Border Regions in Iran." IDEC Development Policy Discussion Paper. Hiroshima, Japan: Hiroshima University Graduate School for International Development and Cooperation, January 2012, https://ir.lib.hiroshima-u.ac.jp/00032034.

Kanu, Benedict S., Adeleke Oluwole Salami, and Kazuhiro Numasawa. *Inclusive Growth: An Imperative for African Agriculture*. Tunis-Belvedere, Tunisia: African Development Bank Group, April 2014, https://www.afdb.org/fr/documents/document/inclusive-growth-an-imperative-for-african-agriculture-47448.

Klimczuk, Andrzej, and Magdalena Klimczuk-Kochańska. "Core-Periphery Model." In *The Palgrave Encyclopedia of Global Security Studies*, edited by Scott N. Romaniuk, Manish Thapa, and Péter Marton, 1–8. Cham, Switzerland: Palgrave Macmillan, 2019, https://doi.org/10.1007/978-3-319-74319-6_320.

Krugman, Paul. "Increasing Returns and Economic Geography." *Journal of Political Economy* 99, no. 3 (1991): 483–99, https://www.jstor.org/stable/2937739.

Krugman, Paul. "What's New About the New Economic Geography?" *Oxford Review of Economic Policy* 14, no. 2 (Summer 1998): 7–17, https://www.jstor.org/stable/23606492.

Leaper, Campbell. "More Similarities than Differences in Contemporary Theories of Social Development? A Plea for Theory Bridging." In *Advances in Child Development and Behavior*, Vol. 40, edited by Janette B. Benson, 337–78. London, UK: Elsevier Academic Press, 2011.

Ledford, Andrew K., and Scott M. Lynch. "Comparing Theories of Resource Distribution: The Case of Iran." *Socius: Sociological Research for a Dynamic World* 5 (January–December 2019): 1–15, https://doi.org/10.1177/2378023119886406.

Mbazor, David Ngwoke, and Babajide Ojo. "Impacts of Land Disputes on Community Development." *TeMA Journal of Land Use, Mobility and Environment* 12, no. 1 (2019): 83–96, https://doi.org/10.6092/1970-9870/5888.

Mossay, Pascal. "The Core-Periphery Model: A Note on the Existence and Uniqueness of Short-Run Equilibrium." *Journal of Urban Economics* 59, no. 3 (May 2006): 389–93, https://doi.org/10.1016/j.jue.2005.10.007.

Nwala, T. Uzodinma. *Nigeria, Path to Unity and Stability: Abuja National Constitutional Conference (1994–95)—Background, Issues and Personal Reminiscences*. Nsukka, Nigeria: Niger Books and Publishing Co., 1997.

Okeaya-Inneh, Adaze. "Land-Use Conflicts Undermine Food Security in Nigeria." D+C (Development and Cooperation), November 15, 2023, https://www.dandc.eu/en/article/climate-crisis-and-population-growth-increase-pressure-arable-land-west-africa.

Olomola, Aderibigbe, et al. *Agricultural Public Expenditure Review at the Federal and Subnational Levels in Nigeria (2008–12)*. Washington, DC: World Bank Group, August 2014.

Olson, Mancur. *The Logic of Collective Action: Public Goods and the Theory of Groups*. Cambridge, MA: Harvard University Press, 1971.

Omotara, Opeyemi A. "Conflicts over Farmland and Its Socioeconomic Effects on Rural Residents of Southwestern Nigeria." *Nigerian Journal of Rural Sociology* 16, no. 3 (2016): 29–34, https://doi.org/10.22004/ag.econ.287473.

Onwuemenyi, O. "Taking Agriculture to Commercial Status in Nigeria." *The Punch* (Lagos, Nigeria), September 21, 2008.

Organisation for Economic Co-operation and Development (OECD). *Policy Shaping and Policy Making: The Governance of Inclusive Growth*. Paris: OECD Publishing, 2015.

Otaha, Imo Jacob. "Food Insecurity in Nigeria: Way Forward." *African Research Review* 7, no. 4 (September 2013): 26–35, https://doi.org/10.4314/afrrev.v7i4.2.

Ottaviano, Gianmarco I. P., and Diego Puga. "Agglomeration in the Global Economy: A Survey of the 'New Economic Geography.'" *World Economy* 21, no. 6 (August 1998): 707–31, https://doi.org/10.1111/1467-9701.00160.

Raheem, Wasiu M., et al. "Regional Imbalances and Inequalities in Nigeria: Causes, Consequences and Remedies." *Research on Humanities and Social Sciences* 4, no. 18 (2014): 163–74, https://www.iiste.org/Journals/index.php/RHSS/article/view/14898.

Sanchez-Mazas, Margarita, and Laurent Licata. "Xenophobia: Social Psychological Aspects." In *International Encyclopedia of the Social and Behavioral Sciences*, 2nd ed., Vol. 25, edited by James D. Wright, 802–7. Oxford, UK: Elsevier, 2015.

Son, Hyun Hwa. "On the Concept of Equity in Opportunity." Chapter 3. In *Equity and Well-Being: Measurement and Policy Practice*, edited by Son, Hyun Hwa, 32–48. Manila, Philippines: Asian Development Bank, 2011, https://www.adb.org/sites/default/files/publication/29288/equity-well-being.pdf.

Udama, Rawlings Akonbede. "Understanding Corruption in Nigeria and Its Implications to National Security and Sustainable Development." *IOSR Journal of Humanities and Social Science* 10, no. 1 (March–April 2013): 60–73.

United Nations (UN). *Transforming Our World: The 2030 Agenda for Sustainable Development*. New York, NY: United Nations, 2015, https://sdgs.un.org/2030agenda.

United Nations Development Programme (UNDP). *UNDP's Strategy for Inclusive and Sustainable Growth.* New York, NY: United Nations Development Programme, 2017, https://www.undp.org/publications/undps-strategy-inclusive-and-sustainable-growth.

Wang, Wei, and Michael E. Griswold. "Estimating Overall Exposure Effects for the Clustered and Censored Outcome Using Random Effect Tobit Regression Models." *Statistics in Medicine* 35, no. 27 (2016): 4948–60, https://doi.org/10.1016/j.aap.2014.09.025.

World Bank, "Food Exports (% of Merchandise Exports)—Nigeria," *World Bank Open Data*, accessed March 28, 2025, https://data.worldbank.org/indicator/TX.VAL.FOOD.ZS.UN?locations=NG.

World Bank. "What Is Inclusive Growth?" *Economic Policy and Debt Department (PRMED) Knowledge Brief*, February 10, 2009.

World Bank Microdata Library, "General Household Survey 2010–2019: Uniform Panel Data: Nigeria, 2010–2019," last modified May 18, 2023, https://microdata.worldbank.org/index.php/catalog/5835.

World Bank Microdata Library, "General Household Survey, Panel 2010–2011, Wave 1: Nigeria, 2010–11," last modified April 20, 2020, https://doi.org/10.48529/y9e2-b753.

World Bank Microdata Library, "General Household Survey, Panel 2012–2013, Wave 2: Nigeria, 2012–13," last modified April 20, 2020, https://doi.org/10.48529/kxpy-aa72.

World Bank Microdata Library, "General Household Survey, Panel 2015–2016, Wave 3: Nigeria, 2015–16," last modified January 30, 2020, https://doi.org/10.48529/7xmj-q133.

World Bank Microdata Library, "General Household Survey, Panel 2018–2019, Wave 4: Nigeria 2018–19," last modified October 5, 2021, https://doi.org/10.48529/1hgw-dq47.

World Bank Open Data, "GDP Growth (annual %)—Nigeria," accessed March 20, 2024, https://data.worldbank.org/indicator/NY.GDP.MKTP.KD.ZG?locations=NG.

7

REGIONAL TRADE PERFORMANCE AND POVERTY

An Assessment of the Economic Growth Linkage in Nigeria

Emmanuel Olawale Ogunkola and Olugboyega A. Oyeranti

Introduction

Trade liberalization has led to increased regionalization and globalization. Simultaneously, regional economies in sub-Saharan Africa have become integrated, and trade is increasingly recognized as an engine for inclusive economic growth and poverty reduction globally. Trade has played a critical role in reducing poverty; further integration of developing countries into an open global economy will be essential for achieving the goal of ending extreme poverty by 2030, the very first of the United Nations Sustainable Development Goals, as outlined in the *2030 Agenda for Sustainable Development* (World Bank Group & WTO, 2015; UN, 2015). The Washington Consensus—which emerged in the early 1980s in response to the debt crisis in the developing world—also signaled widespread support for liberalization to foster economic growth and poverty reduction, and recognition of the beneficial effects thereof (Williamson, 2009).

From 1990 to 2010, the global economy witnessed 32 percent growth in gross domestic product (GDP) per capita, which has translated into a 40 percent reduction in the global extreme poverty rate and the elevation of more than one billion people out of poverty (Lakner, Negre, & Prydz, 2014).[1] In 2000, 28 percent of the world's population was estimated to be living in extreme poverty; that figure was 16 percent in 2010 and 8.6 percent in 2018 (UNDESA, 2019). This declining trend in extreme poverty (which unfortunately has stagnated amid low growth, setbacks due to COVID-19, and increased fragility, according to the World Bank (World Bank, 2024)[2]) was due to the remarkable economic growth experienced in China and India. Reading between the lines, countries that have made trade a key part of their development strategies have grown at a faster rate than those that have not (Higgins & Prowse, 2010). Accordingly, we view economic growth as being

DOI: 10.4324/9781003357025-9

dependent on openness to trade, which in turn provides the necessary ingredients for alleviating poverty. We describe this type of growth as "pro-poor growth"—growth that helps the poor to escape from poverty and thereby increase (in relative terms) their average living standard at a faster rate than the rate for the rest of the world's population.

However, according to the UN, global progress to eliminate poverty has been uneven. As of 2024, more than 37 percent of sub-Saharan Africa's population was still living below the new poverty line of $2.15 per person per day (Aguilar et al., 2024), and the pace of progress in eradicating poverty has notably slowed in recent years. The number of people living in extreme poverty has risen in several African countries, including the Democratic Republic of Congo, Madagascar, Mozambique, and Nigeria (Jobarteh, 2023).[3] Based on findings from the global Multidimensional Poverty Index, the United Nations Development Programme (UNDP) reported in 2017 that more Nigerians were multidimensionally poor than in the previous decade. More specifically, the report showed that the number of multidimensionally poor people in Nigeria increased from eighty-six million to ninety-eight million between 2007 and 2017 (UNDP, 2019). According to Nigeria's National Bureau of Statistics, by 2022, that number had risen to 133 million—63 percent of the country's population (National Bureau of Statistics, 2022).

In the same time frame, Africa's export merchandise trade with the rest of the world—which had risen from US$3.4 billion in 1948 to US$601 billion in 2013—steadily declined to US$552 billion and US$396 billion in 2014 and 2015, respectively (although it had recovered to $665.4 billion by 2022).[4] Moreover, trade performance in Nigeria and other raw material– and oil-exporting countries in Africa experienced large declines in current account balances owing to a sharp decline in commodity prices between 2013 and 2016 (Klitgaard, 2016). During that period, commodity prices collapsed, leading to lower export earnings, with imports reducing at a slower pace. While all regions of Africa saw a decline in external balances since 2014, Central Africa and North Africa were the most severely hit—unsurprisingly, given the role of oil and other commodities in West Africa, political turmoil, and increasing security challenges posed by terror threats in both regions. At the same time, intra-African trade performance was unimpressive. In 2018, the African Export-Import Bank reported that only 15 percent of international trade by African countries took place within the African continent. This percentage was much lower than in Europe (67 percent), Asia (58 percent), and North America (48 percent). The relatively low trade performance in African continents was due to two distinct sets of barriers—tariff barriers and non-tariff barriers (AEIB, 2018; UNCTAD, 2019).

The 2018 African Continental Free Trade Area (AfCFTA) agreement aimed to address the phenomenon of low intra-African trade by creating a single market for the free movement of goods and services within the African continent. The agreement came into force on May 30, 2019, after the required ratification by twenty-two African Union member states. Nigeria became a signatory to the agreement on July

7, 2019 (Adebiyi & Isiadinso, 2019). According to the African Development Bank, “a borderless Africa is the foundation for a competitive continental market that could serve as a global business center.” The expectation was that this continental market would allow agricultural and industrial production across national boundaries and therefore offer economies of scale to investors, while creating bigger markets and providing new opportunities for small and large firms. It also aimed to eliminate monopoly positions while enhancing cross-border spillovers between coastal and landlocked countries (ADBG, 2019). A 2024 report by the African Export-Import Bank documented some notable progress in terms of GDP increases as well as expanded intra-industry and intra-African trade (Afreximbank, 2024). According to the Brookings Institution, “in the evolving context of intra-African trade, significant progress has been made in creating a more integrated and sustainable economic environment across the continent” since 2021 (Mene, 2025).

The motivation for this study stemmed from the need to ascertain whether Nigeria’s trade performance can be an engine for poverty reduction by empirically testing the growth channel accompanying increased trade performance. Against that backdrop, this chapter examines the linkages between trade performance, growth, and poverty level with a view to evaluating and improving the implementation of the AfCFTA’s protocols. To investigate this interconnectedness between trade in Africa and its impact on growth and poverty in Nigeria, we investigated the impact of growth in twenty-five sectors of the Nigerian economy on the country’s poverty level. To do so, we employed a fully modified ordinary least squares (FM-OLS) methodology to analyze the variables highlighted in the next section. This approach helps prevent problems of serial correlation and endogeneity, which often arise with models that attempt to capture the cyclical dependencies between trade and poverty through the economic growth link.[5] Ordinary least squares (OLS) may provide inconsistent estimators for the behavioral parameters in an equation that predicts endogenous variables (especially when the series are persistent), which FM-OLS can overcome by incorporating stationarity testing in its analysis and including the first difference of the variables’ leads and lags.

The use of FM-OLS derives from a theory by Yoosoon Chang and Peter Phillips that addresses the issue of time series estimation and inferences in the presence of uncertainty. Their theory proposed that time series regressions with an unknown mixture of I(0), I(1), and I(2) regressors that include vector autoregression with unknown cointegrating ranks can apply FM-OLS (Chang & Phillips, 1995). Similarly, excluding trade policy variables addresses potential problems of measurement error—a major issue found in earlier studies. For the purposes of this study, it is important to note that data that could represent policy variables, such as index of export penetration, export/import documents, and time, were only available from 2015 to 2019 from all the sources considered for this study and are therefore limited in scope. Thus, we decompose the value of regional imports and exports as distinct trade variables in the model presented below. Our data derives from the UNESCO Institute of Statistics, the World Bank Development Index, and the

Central Bank of Nigeria (CBN) annual statistical bulletins. The scope of the study is from 1981 to 2019.

Survey and Review of the Literature

Theoretical Literature Review

Adam Smith was the first to attempt to explain the reasons for growth differentials among countries. He argued that the division of labor and specialization were responsible for organizational efficiency (or lack thereof), and that output differences among countries arise as a result (Smith, 1776). Several growth theories have been developed since then. Although most of their proponents agreed on the role of factors of production and technology as drivers of growth, there has been no agreement on the definition of the factors, their relative importance, or the degree of their impact on growth. For instance, economics literature has identified the following factors as pertinent to economic growth for most countries: trade (Pomeranz, 2000), human capital (Lucas Jr., 1993; Barro, 1996), technology (Kuznets, 1966), foreign direct investment (Lyroudi, Papanastasiou, & Athanasios, 2004), and natural resources (Shaban, 1987).[6]

Theoretically, the trade-growth-poverty nexus revolves around the neoclassical approach, the endogenous growth approach, and the institutional approach.[7] The choices of rational individuals acting solely through markets are the premise of the neoclassical approach. Comparative advantage in the form of technology differences (as in the Ricardian model) or resource endowment (as in the Heckscher-Ohlin model) determines trade patterns among countries. In general, neoclassical models of international trade theory predict that a country will have a static gain from lowering its trade barriers: Lowering trade barriers will lead to a reallocation of resources, and as resources are used more efficiently, the welfare of the country as a whole will improve. In other words, efficient allocation results in capital accumulation, and once capital is accumulated, it will flow from low-productivity to higher-productivity areas and foster growth convergence among countries (Berg & Krueger, 2003). This theory focuses on accumulating capital and eliminating barriers to trade as prerequisites for development (Saad-Filho, 2010).

Moreover, lowering trade barriers increases foreign competition. As a result, managers and workers boost their efforts to survive amid fierce foreign competition, which produces X-efficiency gains.[8] These gains, as stated in the neoclassical models of Robert Solow and Trevor Winchester Swan (Solow, 1956; Swan, 1956), are assumed to possess only a level effect and not a growth effect. However, the dynamic gains of trade liberalization are tied to the so-called new growth theories that emerged as an alternative to neoclassical growth theory (Aghion, Caroli, & García-Peñalosa, 1999). The endogenous growth theory that was developed and proliferated in the mid-1980s was one such example. Endogenous growth theory tries to explain economic growth from within the system. Its main postulate is that trade openness can accelerate growth over the long term only if it leads to technological advancement that is transferred and dispersed to other locations. That is to say, trade can affect long-run growth through its impact on technological change by enabling activities that may not have been possible before—for instance, by reducing costs and enhancing profitability due to economies of scale (Majeed, 2010; Nursini, 2017).

The endogenous growth model, therefore, shows that as trade provides access to imported products, the effective size of markets increases, which correspondingly raises returns owing to innovation and affects a country's specialization in research-intensive technologies and production systems. The model's emphasis is on the fact that trade allows a poor country to remove domestic shortages, to overcome the diseconomies of a small domestic market, and to accelerate the learning rate of the economy. Because knowledge is a non-rival good (that is, a good that can be consumed or possessed by multiple people with no effect on its supply), opening the economy can reduce unnecessary wasting of resources devoted to research and development from a global point of view: Increased foreign competition in research and development resulting from trade liberalization can eliminate redundancy in research across countries. According to Gene Grossman and Elhanan Helpman, the resulting larger global stock of knowledge provides an extra boost to growth (Grossman & Helpman, 1991).

In the 1990s, institutional factors emerged as a new mode of interpreting economic outcomes. The institutional approach considers the relationship between trade, growth, and poverty as conditional on the existence of efficient institutions. Economists began to highlight factors such as government policies and reform programs as gauges of institutional quality (North, 1990) and control of corruption (Aidt, Dutta, & Sena, 2008), and to underscore some human development indicators (including life expectancy, literacy, and fertility) as central to achieving inclusive growth. Accordingly, policymakers and aid donors have recently turned their attention to the role of institutional factors in the interplay between trade, economic performance, and poverty. Trade reform, changes in tariffs, and quotas are all institutional reforms in that they set new rules and expectations and establish new constraints and opportunities for economic policy (Cicowiez & Conconi, 2008). In these ways, institutional reforms are paramount to stimulating economic growth (Dava, 2012).

Methodological Literature Review

Broadly, empirical studies have employed time series, cross-country, or panel data in examining the links between trade, economic growth, and poverty. A review of earlier studies reveals six main categories of methodologies adopted in empirical investigations of the trade-growth-poverty correlation. The most common approaches rely on OLS regression, cointegration and error correction, dynamic panel estimation, the generalized method of moments (GMM) technique, computable general equilibrium (CGE) modeling, and a series of mixed and multidimensional techniques.[9]

OLS is the most widely used approach for estimating linear models. It allows for the estimation of unknown parameters in a linear regression by minimizing the sum of squared vertical differences between the observed responses in the dataset and responses forecasted by the linear approximation. Studies that employ this technique argue that OLS provides accurate estimates of trade effects on output and poverty. However, least squares estimators yield poor estimates for nonlinear processes due to inadequate extrapolation properties, and they are also sensitive to the presence of outliers, which can badly skew the results of a least squares analysis. Similarly, OLS is inconsistent whenever a model does not correspond to conditional expectations, which occurs when the error term and a lagged dependent variable correlate or when an explanatory variable is subject to measurement errors.

Cointegration models also gained the attention of scholars for capacity to separate short- from long-term dynamics without the need to assume, as with linear models, that one variable is exogenous. The premise with cointegration is that while series with nonstationary properties may drift apart in the short term, they will converge toward equilibrium in the long run. The error correction model, which is a restricted vector autoregression, complements cointegration models by focusing on how shocks in a system can speedily affect a variable or series, making this technique appealing to researchers who investigate the interaction between trade and poverty. A downside of these methods is that while cointegration does not show the speed of adjustment and the path of causality, error correction models require that one of the variables be exogenous, which may reduce the number of possible observations in the analysis.

Dynamic panel analysis involves the inclusion of a lag of the dependent variable on the right-hand side of the regression equation, such that the history of the model is contained within the lagged dependent variable. This approach enables researchers to find long-run coefficients for explanatory variables as well as contemporaneous ones. It also allows them to determine the influence of the past, which the lagged dependent variable captures, and it can model the direction of causal relationships. However, the major weaknesses of dynamic panel estimation are that the models themselves are too complex, their estimations are computationally intensive, and they restrict the estimation of very large samples.

GMM is a technique for constructing estimators similar to maximum likelihood (ML) estimation. It uses assumptions about specific moments of the random variables (i.e., moment conditions) instead of assumptions about the entire distribution, which makes GMM more robust than ML at estimating the cost of efficiency (because it uses extra moment conditions). GMM generalizes the method of moments by permitting the number of moment conditions to be greater than the number of parameters. When there are more moment conditions than parameters, the estimator is overidentified. This procedure can efficiently combine the moment conditions when the estimator is overidentified. Three major drawbacks of the GMM approach are that the estimates are usually less statistically significant, the parameters are usually measured with more errors, and the approach itself has poor sample properties, such as large bias and inefficiency in small samples.

CGE models allow for the calibration of several parameters with the values of a social accounting matrix and then using experiments to observe a new equilibrium by shocking the initial equilibrium and introducing distortions. The resulting distortions and shocks generate wide-ranging implications beyond the sector in which those disturbances occur. Among the major features that make this technique such a powerful analysis tool are that it lets researchers investigate the effects of trade, and it enables a multisectoral analysis of output on poverty. However, this approach assumes constant elasticity of substitution, which undermines both efficiency gains and the productivity factor in international competition for trade.

Numerous scholars have employed the above-noted methods to probe the trade-growth-poverty nexus. Talah Arabiyat, Metri Mdanat, and Ghazi Samawi applied different econometric techniques, including GMM, FM-OLS, and the dynamic OLS method, for both aggregate and province-level panel data for Jordan (Arabiyat, Mdanat, & Samawi, 2020).[10] J. Humberto Lopez used a macroeconomic dataset to estimate dynamic panel models to study the short- and long-term impacts of policies on growth, inequality, and poverty. His findings indicated that pro-growth policies ultimately lead to lower poverty levels, though some of these policies may lead to higher inequality and poverty levels in the short run (Lopez, 2004). Matthias Busse and Jens Koeniger used dynamic panel estimation and found that trade openness has a positive, highly significant impact on economic growth, especially for developing countries (Busse & Koeniger, 2015). Likewise, Ahmed Ezzat employed a dynamic panel model for twenty-three Middle East and North Africa countries from 1995 to 2015 to examine the effects of trade openness on multidimensional poverty and its severity. That study concluded that trade openness hampers poverty alleviation efforts and in fact increases poverty's intensity in these countries (Ezzat, 2018).

Enobong Udoh and Ndeh Anyara estimated and ranked state performance in Nigeria using the arc elasticity approach—a parametric analysis that involves using percentage point changes to capture the responsiveness of one variable to another between two given points—to determine the presence of inclusive growth across the country. The study reported that at the subnational level, growth led to poverty reduction in seventeen states, but the results were non-inclusive when considered based on national aggregates (Udoh & Anyara, 2017). Cyn-Young Park and Racquel Claveria constructed a multidimensional approach to measure the effect of regional integration on growth, inequality, and poverty. Their multidimensional regional integration index depends on six-dimensional indexes, which capture twenty-six indicators. Park and Claveria concluded that while regional integration, trade, and regional value chains are significant drivers of economic growth, social and institutional integration, infrastructure, connectivity, investment, and finance drastically reduce poverty (Park & Claveria, 2018).

Empirical Literature Review

Three major positions have emerged from the empirical literature. The first argues that trade-led growth results in poverty reduction (a belief widely accepted by economists),[11] while the second maintains that trade does not support growth but rather results in increased poverty. The third view suggests that the relationship between trade and growth as related to poverty is ambiguous. Proponents of the trade-led growth position, which assumes that the benefits of trade-led growth trickle down and close the poverty gap, include T. N. Srinivasan and Jagdish Bhagwati; Stephan Klasen; David Dollar and Aart Kraay; Njoroge Lucas Kamau; Miet Maertens, Liesbeth Colen, and Johan Swinnen; Katja Mann; Alisa DiCaprio, Amelia Santos-Paulino, and Maria Sokolova; and Angkeara Bong and Gamini Premaratne (Srinivasan & Bhagwati, 2002; Klasen, 2010; Dollar & Kraay, 2004; Kamau, 2010; Maertens, Colen, & Swinnen, 2011; Mann, 2015; DiCaprio, Santos-Paulino, & Sokolova, 2017; Bong & Premaratne, 2018). They all perceive growth as the engine that raises the average income of the poor—what we call the income effect of growth (and what the traditional literature refers to as the trickle-down effect of growth),[12] wherein the benefits of growth initially reaped by the wealthy progressively convey to the poor as the rich expend their wealth. Two studies in particular—one by James Thornton, Richard J. Agnello, and Charles R. Link in 1978, the other by Bashir Olayinka Kolawole and Olufunsho Abayomi Omobitan in 2014 (the latter focusing specifically on Nigeria)—found that growth has a demonstrated negative effect on poverty. What that means is, as growth increases due to trade, poverty declines (Thornton, Agnello, & Link, 1978; Kolawole & Omobitan, 2014). Park and Claveria also established that regional integration (largely in the form of institutional and social integration), regional value chains, and enhanced movement of people all strongly propel economic growth as more connectivity improves wealth redistribution. Furthermore, they found that increased investment as a result of integration measurably reduced poverty across the 156 economies they examined (Park & Claveria, 2018).

The empirical literature suggests a variety of transmission mechanisms. For example, Neil McCulloch, L. Alan Winters, and Xavier Cirera illustrated how changes in trade transmit to households by way of three distinct channels: distribution, enterprise, and government (McCulloch, Winters, & Cirera, 2001). Hala Sakr also highlighted the market, enterprise, government, and investment climate as conduits through which trade-induced growth affects poverty (Sakr, 2012), and Ahmed Ezzat identified economic growth, the labor market, households, markets for goods and services, and government revenues as mechanisms that transmit trade signals to the various segments in the economy (Ezzat, 2018).[13] Of all these channels, this study focuses primarily on economic growth because it is most frequently advocated as a key driver of poverty reduction. Put simply, most policymakers and institutions see economic growth as a vital engine for alleviating poverty—meaning that the current thinking on how best to reduce poverty revolves around placing economic growth at the center of development strategies (Udoh & Anyara, 2017).

Notwithstanding the growth-poverty reduction link that some studies report, the empirical literature is also replete with studies that have found trade openness to stymie growth.[14] For instance, Philip Omoke noted that trade liberalization in Nigeria reduced rural wages and rural income by 0.4 and 0.6 percent, respectively, resulting in a 0.2 percent reduction in rural unemployment (Omoke, 2006). In the same vein, Gafar Ijaiya, Mukaila Ijaiya, Raji Bello, and Michael Ajayi—arguing that economic growth in Nigeria has not reduced poverty—recommended policy shifts to ensure stability and promote inclusive growth by minimizing distortions, promoting infrastructural development, and encouraging massive investment in the agricultural sector (Ijaiya et al., 2011). And Taofeek Olusola Ayinde contended that trade liberalization policy in Nigeria has not been beneficial, identifying capital expenditure as the only variable that has an impact on growth *and* trickles down to the populace. Given that trade liberalization increases the frequency of macroeconomic distortions, he concluded that for Nigeria to benefit from regional trade, sound economic policies are necessary to mitigate the negative trade-offs associated with regionalization (Ayinde, 2013). Alfredo Saad-Filho, Mohammed Ali Trabelsi, and Naoufel Liouane further demonstrated that the poor do not benefit from globalization in most developing countries because of corruption, inefficiency, and misprioritized public policies (Saad-Filho, 2010; Trabelsi & Liouane, 2013). According to Kang-Kook Lee, trade openness actually raises the intensity of poverty by increasing inequality in developing countries (Lee, 2014).

Empirical findings by Adewale Stephen Bakare reveal that Nigeria's impressive economic growth between 1980 and 2008 has not reduced poverty in the country, indicating that—at least in the case of Nigeria—the data does not support the so-called trickle-down phenomenon underpinning the view that growth improves poverty (Bakare & Simoen, 2013). Stephanie Gangas suggested that the level of growth witnessed in Nigeria between 1980 and 2013 has in fact increased the level of poverty, mainly through unemployment (Gangas, 2017). Evidence from outside sub-Saharan Africa points in a similar direction: Taleb Awad-Warrad and Buthaina Muhtaseb examined the correlation between trade and poverty reduction through the channels of economic growth and employment. They found that trade has been a major source of growth in the Jordanian economy, largely driven by increased wages and the attendant foreign direct investment inflows. However, they illustrate that growth has yet to translate into poverty alleviation, owing to the country's high level of inflation, rapid population growth, and an influx of foreign labor and refugees (Awad-Warrad & Muhtaseb, 2017). In his aforementioned study of trade openness and multidimensional poverty, Ahmed Ezzat observed that although theoretical models predict and emphasize a positive relationship between trade openness and poverty alleviation,[15] in reality, regionalization restricts efforts to reduce the existence and intensity of multidimensional poverty. Ezzat also noted that the capacity of trade to reduce headcount poverty (i.e., the number of people living below the national poverty line) is fragile due to a multifaceted set of economic and institutional factors.

The last group of empirical studies found the trade-growth-poverty nexus to be equivocal, which is consistent with the view put forward by Simon Kuznets in the mid-twentieth century that the impact of regional trade on poverty depends on the stage of economic growth prevailing in a country. Kuznets further explained that in the first stages of economic growth, structural changes lead to a massive shift of labor from agriculture to other sectors, thereby increasing both poverty and inequality. Then, as economic growth continues, productivity increases in all sectors cause poverty rates to reduce as incomes converge (Kuznets, 1957; Aghion, Caroli, & García-Peñalosa, 1999). Michael Bruno, Martin Ravallion, and Lyn Squire compiled data from forty-five countries, each with at least four distributional surveys over at least two decades, and found the effect of growth on poverty and inequality to be indeterminate (Bruno, Ravallion, & Squire, 1998). Perhaps unsurprisingly, Marilyne Huchet-Bourdon, Chantal Le Mouël, and Mariana Vijil observed that trade openness facilitated more rapid growth in countries with higher-quality products available for export, but that countries with lower-quality products suffered from a decline in growth accompanied by an increase in the severity of poverty as a result of trade openness (Bourdon, Mouël, & Vijil, 2011). Likewise, Emílio Dava determined that poor countries do not benefit from trade openness because they produce goods less intensive in research and development, while only rich countries enjoy substantial gains from trade (Dava, 2012). Athanasios Vamvakidis, Dirk Willem te Velde, Henry Tumwebaze, and Alex Thomas Ijjo all noted that the pattern of influence between trade and poverty is inconclusive (Vamvakidis, 1998; te Velde, 2011; Tumwebaze & Ijjo, 2015). Ramo Mabugu and Margaret Chitiga Mabugu found that trade openness has no demonstrable impact on poverty in the short run and that, conversely, poverty decreases in the long run even in the absence of the trade-induced total factor productivity that comes with liberalization, with poor households benefitting the most (Mabugu & Mabugu, 2014). Lastly, in their study, Arabiyat, Mdanat, and Samawi confirmed that while trade openness had a notable positive effect on inclusive growth, it came with high-level inequality, which in turn weakened the growth experienced in various provinces of Jordan (Arabiyat, Mdanat, & Samawi, 2020).

Gaps in the Literature

Most studies that interrogate the interplay of trade, growth, and poverty share the common finding that regional trade (as reflected in the quality of trade policies) is associated with rapid economic growth through technological advancement and income redistribution effects that lift people out of poverty. The income redistribution mechanism—as sustained by the growth channel—is indeed a major way in which trade alleviates poverty. In other words, growth that is associated with freer trade is an essential vehicle for sustained poverty alleviation, as the price effects of a reduction in labor, goods, and services stemming from technological innovations *increase* the real income of the poor in purchasing power terms. As this shift occurs, the expenditure of the poor also fuels growth (Winters, 2002; McCulloch, Winters, & Cirera, 2001; Winters, McCulloch, & McKay, 2004; World Bank Group & WTO, 2018).[16]

Yet these studies remain subject to debate and criticism. Some of them fail to provide a direct link between trade liberalization and poverty through any specific transmission mechanism, be it growth, labor markets, households, markets for goods and services, and government revenues.[17] In examining indicators to measure trade openness, some studies tend to capture more than just trade policy variables. Other sources of poor economic performance (such as low government expenditure, corruption, infrastructural gaps, rule of law, and others) can be highly correlated among themselves. As such, when all these policy indicators are included in regression analyses, it can be difficult to ascertain the distinct effects of different policies. Certain cross-country studies insufficiently address the causality between trade and growth, and some evince serious endogeneity problems and measurement errors. Francisco Rodriguez and Dani Rodrik argued that because policy-based measures may be correlated with factors that independently boost growth independent of trade, the use of such measures could undermine empirical analysis results (Rodríguez & Rodrik, 2001). Some studies also present methodologies that ignore or overlook assumptions that explain the dynamics of the economy in question.[18] And—significantly—most analyze growth impact holistically at the macro level by country or at the state or province level. To the best of our knowledge, this study is one of the few that disaggregates and examines the growth link's impact on poverty at the sectoral level.[19]

Theoretical Framework and Model Specification

This study hinges on the neoclassical framework. Drawing from Fahad Israr and Miguel Rocha de Sousa, the neoclassical theory of international trade predicts that, in general, a country will ultimately achieve long-term GDP gains from lowering its trade barriers (Israr & de Sousa, 2018). Gene Grossman and Elhanan Helpman, Paul Romer, Robert Barro, and Xavier Sala-i-Martin have all similarly contended that trade openness improves economic growth over the long term (Grossman & Helpman, 1991; Romer, 1990; Barro & Sala-i-Martin, 1997). These positive outcomes promote a more efficient reallocation of resources and corollary improvements to citizen welfare overall. Elevated competition also induces greater productivity of output (although some studies have shown that it can also cause countries that fail to adapt to lose out from trade) (Duong et al., 2022; Barone & Cingano, 2011; IMF Staff, 2001). Moreover, economic openness increases domestic imports of goods and services due to new technological knowledge; this spillover effect eliminates redundancy in research, leading to more foreign direct investment inflows.

The standard neoclassical model derives from aggregating various models that express the choices of rational individuals acting solely through markets.[20] It begins from the premise of a fixed technological coefficient and elasticities of labor and capital that can be enhanced depending on the combination of the two factors. In this model, the state of technological evolution alters the value of the constant coefficient at any point in time. For our analysis, we assume a Cobb-Douglas production function in which output (*Y*) depends on capital, labor, and technology. The coefficients in this general specification need not sum to one; no constant returns to scale technology is assumed. The general form of the production function in the neoclassical model expressed at time (*t*) is as follows:

$$Y(t) = A(t)K(t)^{\alpha} L(t)^{1-\alpha} \tag{7.1}$$

where *Y* is domestic production, *A* is technological advancement, *K* is capital stock, *L* is labor, and (*t*) denotes time.

We extend the model and further assume that savings, human capital accumulation, and international trade can determine technological progress. This extension is necessary because in developing countries, domestic saving fuels innovation as banks, in turn, utilize savings in the form of loans to finance innovative projects, thereby attracting foreign inflow of capital. In this case, the presence of savings in financial institutions is assumed to ensure a steady flow of funds for investments in innovative information and communication technology products by banks and other private investors (Aghion et al., 2016). In this way, domestic saving improves economic growth by increasing investment through the adoption of new technology. Likewise, human capital accumulation through schooling—which affects employment levels—is an engine of economic growth. Thus, our model becomes

$$A(t) = \gamma \cdot T(t)^{\alpha} S(t)^{\delta} \tag{7.2}$$

where γ is constant, *T* represents trade openness measures, and *S* denotes the level of saving. By putting Equation (7.2) in Equation (7.1), we get:

$$Y(t) = \gamma \cdot T(t)^{\delta 1} S(t)^{\delta 2} K(t)^{\alpha} L(t)^{1-\alpha} \tag{7.3}$$

Taking the log of Equation (7.3) yields the following Nigerian growth model:

$$\ln Y_t = \beta_1 + \beta_2 \ln I_t + \beta_3 \ln E_t + \beta_4 \ln S_t + \beta_5 \ln K_t + \beta_6 \ln L_t + \mu_t \tag{7.4}$$

In Equation (7.4), all variables are transformed into a different log of the original variable; the β_s are the partial unknown growth coefficients, where β_1 is the constant term, $\ln Y_t$ is the log of real GDP, $\ln Y_t$ is the log of import within the region (IMP), $\ln E_t$ is exports within the region (EXP), $\ln S_t$ is real saving (SAV), $\ln K_t$ is real capital stock (CST), $\ln L_t$ is a skilled worker (SWK), and μ_t is white noise. (Equation (7.3) is the mathematical specification, while Equation (7.4) is the econometric specification, which must always include a stochastic error term.)

We measure GDP by the real GDP (i.e., real GDP at market prices less indirect taxes net of subsidies) obtained from the CBN's 2020 statistical bulletin (Central Bank of Nigeria, 2020).[21] IMP and EXP are the real merchandise imports and exports.[22] The trade statistics utilized represent trade within low- and middle-income economies in sub-Saharan Africa, obtained from the World Bank's World Development Indicators (WDIs) for 2020.[23] Savings is captured by accumulated savings data for Nigeria from the CBN's 2020 statistical bulletin (Central Bank of Nigeria, 2020).[24] Capital stock represents inventories and stocks of goods held by firms to meet temporary or unexpected fluctuations in production or sales and work in progress. Data on skilled workers comes from the WDIs as estimated by the UN's International Labour Organization for Nigeria. Random disturbances (μ_t) attempt to capture unobserved shocks like sudden changes in resource availability and other unexplained changes.

Thus, we also estimate the following models:

$$\text{LNRGDP} = \text{LNCST} + \text{LNSAV} + \text{LNSWK} + \text{LNTRA} \tag{7.5}$$

$$\text{LNPOV} = \text{LNSGDP} \tag{7.6}$$

where LNPOV = poverty and LNSGDP = sectoral GDP composition for Nigeria. When we specify the twenty-five sectors in Equation (7.6), our model becomes

$$\begin{aligned}\text{LNPOV} &= \beta_1 + \beta_2 \text{ LNAGC} + \beta_3 \text{ LNCRP} + \beta_4 \text{ LNLIS} + \beta_5 \text{ LNFOR} + \\ &\beta_6 \text{ LNFIS} + \beta_7 \text{ LNIND} + \beta_8 \text{ LNCPN} + \beta_9 \text{ LNSOM} + \beta_{10} \text{ LNMAN} + \\ &\beta_{11} \text{ LNCON} + \beta_{12} \text{ LNTRA} + \beta_{13} \text{ LNSER} + \beta_{14} \text{ LNTRT} + \beta_{15} \text{ LNINC} + \\ &\beta_{16}\text{LNUTI} + \beta_{17}\text{LNACF} + \beta_{18}\text{LNFIN} + \beta_{19}\text{LNREE} + \beta_{20}\text{LNPST} + \\ &\beta_{21}\text{LNASB} + \beta_{22}\text{LNPUA} + \beta_{23}\text{LNEDU} + \beta_{24}\text{LNHHS} + \beta_{25}\text{LNAER} + \\ &\beta_{26}\text{LNOTS}\end{aligned} \tag{7.7}$$

where the twenty-five sectors are as follows: agriculture (AGC); crop production (CPR); livestock (LIS); forestry (FOR); fishing (FIS); industry (IND); crude oil, petroleum, and natural gas (CPN); solid minerals (SOM); manufacturing (MAN); construction (CON); trade (TRA); services (SER); transport (TRT); information and communication (INC); utilities (UTI); accommodation and food services (ACF); finance and insurance (FIN); real estate (REE); professional, scientific, and technical (PST) services; administration and supply and business (ASB) services;

public administration (PUA); education (EDU); human health and social services (HHS); arts, entertainment, and recreation (AER); and other services (OTS).

We collected data from 1981 to 2019. As part of the pre-estimation procedure for the study, we first applied the augmented Dickey-Fuller (ADF) test to determine whether the variables outlined in Equations (7.5) and (7.7) are stationary or not. Nonstationary series were transformed to stationary series through differencing to obtain meaningful statistics and to avoid the unit root problem. See Equation (7.8), which explains how the inclusion of a constant can obtain the difference stationary series of Y through a random walk process; this is part of the theoretical background of the basic unit root testing. (Most economic time series are usually far from stationary when expressed in their original units of measurement.)

We present the unit root model as follows:

$$d\left(Y_t\right) = v(1)Y_{t-1} + v(2) + \mu_t \tag{7.8}$$

and

$$d\left(Y_t\right) = v(1)Y_{t-1} + v(2) + v(3)@\text{Trend} + \mu_t \tag{7.9}$$

The model in Equation (7.8) includes an intercept indicated by the parameter $v(2)$, which represents a random walk with drift. The model in Equation (7.9), with a trend and an intercept, represents a random walk with drift around a stochastic trend.

Having completed the tests of stationarity indicated in Equations (7.8) and (7.9), the question arises as to whether these variables could be combined to make a prediction. Therefore, we utilized the Johansen cointegration approach to test whether the determined variables have common trends. (This test was necessary to identify scenarios wherein two or more nonstationary series are integrated such that they cannot drift from equilibrium over the long term; it also reveals the degree of sensitivity of two variables—namely, trade and poverty—to the same average GDP over a specified period.) The preliminary time series analysis tests also included a test of long-run convergence among variables. We based our economic framework on the unrestricted trace rank test to determine the existence of cointegration and the number of cointegrating vectors in the model.

The proposed model for the Granger causality test[25] is given as

$$\begin{aligned} \Delta\text{GRW}_t = C_o + \sum\nolimits_{i=1}^{q} \varphi_i \Delta\text{RGDP}_{t-i} + \sum\nolimits_{i=0}^{r} \delta_i + \Delta\text{CST}_{t-i} + \\ \sum\nolimits_{i=0}^{s} \beta_i \Delta\text{SAV}_{t-i} + \sum\nolimits_{i=0}^{t} \sigma_i \Delta\text{SWK}_{t-i} + \sum\nolimits_{i=0}^{u} \varepsilon_i \Delta\text{IMP}_{t-i} + \\ \sum\nolimits_{i=0}^{v} \pi_i \Delta\text{EXP}_{t-i} + \varnothing_i \text{ECM}_{t-i} + \mu_{2t} \end{aligned} \tag{7.10}$$

where Δ is the first difference operator; φ, δ, β, σ, ε, and π are the coefficients on GRW (growth), CST, SAV, SWK, IMP, and EXP; μ is the error term; q, r, s, t, u, and v are the optimal lag lengths selected based on Akaike information criterion and Schwarz Bayesian criterion; $ECMt-1$ is the error correction mechanism, which was taken from the long-run relationship; and $\varnothing$ stands for the speed of adjustment to the long-run equilibrium.

Estimation Results and Analysis

As a prerequisite to time series analysis—and one of the conditions for using the FM-OLS methodology adopted for the study—the variables' stationarity properties have to be verified. This verification is important because regressing nonstationary variables often leads to spurious regressions, which at best yield inconsistent inferences. This stationarity condition of most economic data also underscores the desirability of the FM-OLS methodology. For instance, FM-OLS incorporates stationarity testing in its analysis by including the first difference of the variables' leads and lags, which thus provides a double check on the variables' stationarity properties. As mentioned above, a test of long-run convergence among variables is a part of the preliminary tests for a time series analysis. This long-run convergence testing is often performed on the basis of a cointegration test (for which we employed the Johansen approach). For brevity, the results of these two tests, as carried out on the variables used for this analysis, are reported in the appendix; this section presents the results of the analysis performed as described at the beginning of this chapter.

Ascertaining the unit root status of our series to determine the unit root's order of integration reveals the differencing operations required to make the series stationary. Because standard inference procedures do not apply to regressions (as they contain integrated dependent or integrated repressors'), determining whether a series is stationary or not before using it in a regression analysis is essential. (See the appendix for the full results.) The ADF test for model one indicates that all variables are nonstationary at level. However, after finding the first difference between our variables, all the variables are stationary. The estimates for model two in the appendix show a mixed pattern of integrated processes, thus making the application of FM-OLS appropriate for the model's estimation. The ADF test results show that only one variable was found to be stationary at level—sixteen at the first difference and seven after the second difference.

A summary of the Johansen cointegration test results, which included thirty-nine observations from 1981 to 2019, appears below. Detailed results are presented in the appendix.

Tables 7.1 and 7.2 show that there are two cointegrating equations for the unrestricted cointegration rank test (trace) and one cointegration equation for the unrestricted cointegration rank test (maximum eigenvalue). Therefore, because

TABLE 7.1 Unrestricted Cointegration Rank Test (Trace)

Hypothesized		*Trace*	*0.05 Critical*	
No. of Coefficients	*Eigenvalue*	*Statistic*	*Value*	*Probability***
None*	0.654777	62.24536	47.85613	0.0013
At most 1*	0.456148	32.46557	29.79707	0.0241
At most 2	0.405250	15.41139	15.49471	0.0515
At most 3	0.030323	0.862193	3.841466	0.3531

Source: Authors' data and computations.

Notes: Trace test indicates two cointegrating equations at the 0.05 level. An * denotes rejection of the hypothesis at the 0.05 level; ** *p*-values derive from MacKinnon, Haug, & Michelis, 1999.

TABLE 7.2 Unrestricted Cointegration Rank Test (Maximum Eigenvalue)

Hypothesized		*Max-Eigen*	*0.05 Critical*	
No. of Coefficients	*Eigenvalue*	*Statistic*	*Value*	*Probability***
None*	0.654777	29.77979	27.58434	0.0257
At most 1	0.456148	17.05418	21.13162	0.1695
At most 2*	0.405250	14.54920	14.26460	0.0451
At most 3	0.030323	0.862193	3.841466	0.3531

Source: Authors' data and computations.

Notes: Max-eigenvalue test indicates one cointegrating equation at the 0.05 level. An * denotes rejection of the hypothesis at the 0.05 level; ** *p*-values derive from MacKinnon, Haug, & Michelis, 1999.

the trace statistics and the maximum eigenvalue are higher than the critical values, the null hypothesis of no cointegration is rejected at the 5 percent level. The *p*-values of less than 0.05 corroborate this result. This finding has two implications: that variables in both models have at most two cointegrating equations (as indicated by the 0.0451 probability value in Table 7.2), which implies that an equilibrium is attainable as the variables can move together in the long run in the presence of transitory shocks; and that these variables can attain equilibrium in the long run—even in the face of temporary shocks, which may bring about distortion.

Tables 7.3 and 7.4 present the results of our regression analysis for models one and two, which is the estimated aggregated model in Equation (7.4).

Table 7.3 indicates that all the variables included in the model, except merchandise imports, are positively related to growth in Nigeria. In other words, our measures for capital stock, national savings, human capital proxied by skilled labor/work, and merchandise exports within the region all stimulate economic growth; the only one that does not is merchandise imports. This outcome may be owed to the negative impact of rising imports relative to exports on Nigeria's exchange rate and the attendant distortion of the country's balance of payment position. Table 7.3 also indicates that capital stock, national savings, and merchandise exports are found to be statistically significant below the 5 percent probability value threshold in the model.

TABLE 7.3 Estimates of Regression Analysis (Model One)

Regressor	*Coefficients*	*P-Value*
Constant	−20.300 (3.443)	0.0000
LNCST	0.978 (0.137)	0.0000
LNSAV	0.167 (0.056)	0.0054
LNSWK	0.047 (0.064)	0.4755
LNIMP	−0.127 (0.127)	0.1323
LNEXP	0.185 (0.064)	0.0066
Summary statistics		
Adj. R^2	0.994	

Source: Authors' data and computations.

Notes: Model one considers the interaction between growth and trade. Figures in parentheses denote standard errors.

TABLE 7.4 Estimates of Regression Analysis (Model Two)

Regressor	*Coefficients*	*P-Value*
Constant	−0.659 (0.206)	0.0108
LNACF	−0.187 (0.447)	0.0386
LNAER	−3.880 (1.097)	0.0063
LNAGC	−31.426 (21.453)	0.1770
LNASB	−17.997 (4.842)	0.0048
LNCON	0.458 (0.841)	0.5988

(*Continued*)

TABLE 7.4 (Continued)

Regressor	*Coefficients*	*P-Value*
LNCPN	9.338 (2.850)	0.0096
LNCPR	23.165 (18.094)	0.2325
LNEDU	5.376 (2.591)	0.0678
LNFIN	2.119 (0.547)	0.0038
LNFIS	−0.029 (0.342)	0.9328
LNFOR	−0.113 (0.411)	0.7893
LNHHS	−11.394 (4.659)	0.0370
LNINC	0.295 (0.907)	0.7522
LNLIS	6.546 (4.118)	0.1464
LNMAN	2.788 (0.917)	0.0140
LNOTS	1.043 (1.382)	0.4698
LNPST	23.280 (4.587)	0.0007
LNPUA	6.584 (2.179)	0.0144
LNREE	1.491 (2.256)	0.5252
LNSER	−2.009 (3.223)	0.5486
LNSOM	0.251 (0.182)	0.2022
LNTRA	−2.387 (1.221)	0.0823
LNTRT	−1.235 (0.746)	0.1322
LNUTI	0.235 (0.200)	0.2700
LNIND	−13.513 (3.903)	0.0071
Summary Statistics		
Adj. R^2	0.764	

Source: Authors' data and computations.

Notes: Figures in parentheses denote standard errors.

Table 7.4 illustrates the effects of growth in the various sectors on poverty. As we outlined in the introduction, one of this chapter's primary aims is to trace the impact of trade on poverty through the growth link. By splitting the Nigerian economy into sectors, we were able to examine the impact of growth in each of the twenty-five sectors on the country's poverty level. The table shows that of these twenty-five sectors, ten are statistically significant: accommodation and food services; AER; ASB services; crude petroleum and natural gas; finance and insurance; HHS; manufacturing; PST services; public administration; and industry.[26] The sectors in which growth has helped to reduce the poverty level are accommodation and food services; crude petroleum and natural gas; finance and insurance; manufacturing; PST services; and public administration. On the other hand, we found that growth in four sectors has actually exacerbated poverty: AER; ASB services; HHS; and industry. The actual output of the FM-OLS estimates applied is presented in the appendix.

The bivariate Granger causality test analyzed how useful certain variables are in forecasting other variables. In this regard, we can say that if variable x is not useful in forecasting y, then x does not Granger-cause y. The test thus determines the direction of causation between trade, growth, and poverty in Nigeria. The pairwise Granger causality test results show that there is causation from growth to poverty, from export to growth, and from import to growth. These results imply that we can predict poverty level from the degree of growth, and that trade can determine the volume of growth in Nigeria. This outcome is consistent with the neoclassical trade model's theoretical expectation that causality will run one way from trade to growth, thereby further confirming the validity of both models one and two. The appendix presents the full Granger causality test results.

Conclusion

This chapter has offered an appraisal of Nigeria's regional trade experience and potential along its sectoral growth path. Its insights are particularly salient in light of the country's becoming a signatory to the AfCFTA agreement—which seeks to create a single continental market for the free movement of goods and services within the African continent—on July 7, 2019. We sought to hinge the study on realistic theoretical and empirical foundations. Beyond the discussion of the potential effects of trade on the level of poverty (as is discussed widely in the literature), we estimated a modified neoclassical model linking selected trade variables to growth, and another model that connects poverty to twenty-five sectors in the Nigerian economy. The results clearly demonstrate the effects of regional trade in Africa on economic growth and poverty in Nigeria: While regional trade has had a positive impact on economic growth in Nigeria overall, only six sectors of the Nigerian economy (namely, accommodation and food services; crude petroleum and natural gas; finance and insurance; manufacturing; PST services; and public administration) have experienced poverty reduction effects from trade-resultant growth, and growth in four sectors (AER; ASB services; HHS; and industry) has actually aggravated the poverty situation in the country. The remaining fifteen sectors produced statistically insignificant coefficients, which suggests limited or inconclusive evidence as to whether these sectors exhibit some level of influence on poverty.

Poverty can hinder development by eroding the environmental and socioeconomic cornerstones of human development in what becomes a vicious cycle, one with the potential to entrench a poor community deeper into poverty in the absence of well-targeted interventions. A productive economy transforms land, labor, capital, and other inputs into goods and services, while low productivity hinders economic growth, job creation, and living standards. The need for action on poverty reduction in Nigeria is urgent: As Chapter 2 details, more than eighty-seven million Nigerians were living below the poverty line as of 2019, with an average of six people falling into poverty every minute. The Nigerian Bureau of Statistics reported that 133 million Nigerians (or 63 percent of the population) were multidimensionally poor as of 2022, and the World Bank projected the following year that thirteen million more would fall below the poverty line by 2025 (Onu et al., 2019; Ichedi, 2022; Sulaimon, 2023).

Nigeria's rampant inequality, widespread poverty, and chronic underdevelopment call for drastic action on the part of government and policymakers to reverse course and prevent the poverty crisis from compromising the country's development aspirations. While this chapter reveals that trade has had a positive impact on overall growth, the nuanced picture is more of a sticky wicket. Our research suggests that Nigeria could leverage trade integration to harness the benefits of the AfCFTA through the development of flexible protocols, such as regulatory processes to facilitate integration and ensuring transparent rules. Liberalizing the trade regime and enhancing trade and transport facilitation could also help develop value chains and facilitate the efficient reallocation of factors of production, making Nigeria more cost-competitive in Africa.[27]

It is not surprising that the vital accommodation and food services sector (both components of which are necessities of life) contributes to poverty reduction. Crude petroleum and natural gas—another of the six sectors whose growth contributes to poverty reduction—has been the main foreign exchange earner in Nigeria over the years, and both finance and insurance have played central roles as well, inasmuch as businesses depend on finance to start up or expand. The manufacturing sector has also been resilient, even in the face of inadequate power (a major challenge in the country). Although the study results presented in this chapter suggest that regional imports have not supported growth, the AfCFTA's implementation could help Nigeria secure a more balanced and sustainable export base by diversifying away from extractive commodities and toward manufacturing. This shift could effectuate economies of scale, increased access to cheaper raw materials, and improvements in the quality of goods and services due to the elimination of barriers and competition. In addition, as small and medium enterprises become integrated, expanded value chains could lead to a reduction in poverty.

The Nigerian government must develop and implement policies and programs to foster higher productivity in the six sectors found to be helping reduce poverty. Such initiatives should ensure transparency in order to reduce investment risk. Furthermore, policymakers should provide access to microfinancing to enable new firms to compete with incumbents and allow productive firms to scale up their operations. Access to microfinance in particular, especially when augmented with grants and other social safety nets, can reduce poverty (World Bank, 2015). However, without proper financial inclusion, governments would have limited success at best in ameliorating conditions for the poorest of the poor.

Policymakers must also prioritize reversing the negative effects of the sectors whose growth has been found to exacerbate poverty. For example, investing in sustainable infrastructure and improving education through basic educational financing would improve human capital outcomes. Well-funded technical and vocational education and training programs facilitated by nongovernmental bodies and civil society could boost entrepreneurial ecosystems, offering a system of mentorship and apprenticeships for millions of Nigerians outside the formal school system, or for those who possess only primary education. Such education initiatives are imperative, as human capital development is essential for sustained growth and poverty reduction in the country.

Ending poverty in Nigeria will entail improving the country's economic productivity and expanding opportunities for its citizens—and particularly for those in rural communities—by advancing agricultural and industrial technological innovation. Increased investment in health care is also linked to economic growth, and consequently to reducing poverty. Reforms and sector-specific policies such as these would strengthen macroeconomic resilience, promote private-sector development, and improve the efficiency of public service delivery. In these ways, government and other stakeholders can help to spur growth that will reduce poverty across all the sectors of the Nigerian economy, thereby fostering sustainable and inclusive development.

Appendix

TABLE A7.1 ADF Test Results (Model One)

Series	*Level*	*First Difference*	*Order*
LNRGDP			I(1)
Intercept	**−0.792280** (−2.945842)	**−3.157565*** (−2.948404)	
Intercept and trend	**−0.310750** (−3.540328)	**−3.233500** (−3.544284)	

(Continued)

TABLE A7.1 (Continued)

Series	*Level*	*First Difference*	*Order*
LNCST			I(1)
Intercept	**−0.358693**	**−3.798620***	
	(−2.945842)	(−2.948404)	
Intercept and trend	**1.107891**	**−3.753726***	
	(−3.540328)	(−3.544284)	
LNSAV			I(1)
Intercept	**−0.493346**	**−4.345603***	
	(−2.945842)	(−2.948404)	
Intercept and trend	**−1.396385**	**−4.303254***	
	(−3.540328)	(−3.544284)	
LNSWK			I(1)
Intercept	**−1.991344**	**−7.560769***	
	(−2.957110)	(−2.948404)	
Intercept and trend	**−3.540328**	**−5.645937***	
	(−3.540328)	(−3.557759)	
LNIMP			I(1)
Intercept	**−6.626683**	**−11.32210***	
	(0.168393)	(0.149318)	
Intercept and trend	**−6.556273**	**−6.704165***	
	(0.170579)	(0.324483)	
LNEXP			I(1)
Intercept	**−6.749382**	**−8.338970***	
	(0.167532)	(0.279508)	
Intercept and trend	**−7.701815**	**−6.530410***	
	(0.164067)	(0.47499)	

Source: Authors' data and computations.

Notes: Bold figures are test statistics; only the absolute values are considered. Figures in parentheses are the critical values at the 5 percent level. Asterisks (*) indicate significance at the 5 percent level.

TABLE A7.2 ADF Test Results (Model Two)

Series	*Level*	*First Difference*	*Second Difference*	*Order*
LNPOV			N/A	I(1)
Intercept	**−2.624917**	**−6.967387***		
	(−2.971853)	(−2.976263)		
Intercept and trend	**−4.102907**	**−6.949185***		
	(−3.580623)	(−3.587527)		
LNACF			N/A	I(1)
Intercept	**0.234137**	**−4.474753***		
	(−2.971853)	(−2976263)		
Intercept and trend	**0.149609**	**−4.227680***		
	(−2.971853)	(−3.5875227)		

(*Continued*)

TABLE A7.2 (Continued)

Series	*Level*	*First Difference*	*Second Difference*	*Order*
LNAER			N/A	I(1)
Intercept	**0.149609**	**−4.332711***		
	(−2.971853)	(−2.976263)		
Intercept and trend	**−1.977613**	**−4.227680***		
	(−3.580623)	(−3.587527)		
LNAGC			N/A	I(1)
Intercept	**−0.404695**	**−4.848075***		
	(−2.971853)	(2.976263)		
Intercept and trend	**−1.655582**	**−4.746144***		
	(−3.580633)	(−3,587527)		
LNASB				I(2)
Intercept	**−1.635420**	**−2.768835**	**−7.709120***	
	(−2.976263)	(−2.976263)	(−2.981038)	
Intercept and trend	**0.583540**	**−3.136359**	**−7.81629***	
	(−3.580633)	(−3.587527)	(−3.595026)	
LNCON			N/A	I(1)
Intercept	**0.523870**	**−3.32864***		
	(−2.971853)	(−2.976263)		
Intercept and trend	**−1.993487**	**−3.265004**		
	(−3.587527)	(−3.587527)		
LNCPN			N/A	I(1)
Intercept	**−1.060607**	**−5.022317***		
	(−2.971853)	(−2.976263)		
Intercept and trend	**−0.809464**	**−5.449820***		
	(−3.580623)	(−3587527)		
LNCPR			N/A	I(1)
Intercept	**0.520445**	**4.911799***		
	(−2.971853)	(−2.976263)		
Intercept and trend	**−1.614648**	**−4.821422***		
	(−3.580623)	(−3.587527)		
LNEDU				I(2)
Intercept	**−0.984234**	**−1.505884**	**−10.97026***	
	(−2.981038)	(−2.981038)	(−2981038)	
Intercept and trend	**−2.265027**	**−1.009389**	**−11.08051***	
	(−3.595026)	(−3.595026)	(−3.595026)	
LNFIN			N/A	I(1)
Intercept	**−1.156346**	**−7.026134***		
	(−2.971853)	(−2.976263)		
Intercept and trend	**−3.223444**	**−6.959896***		
	(−3.580623)	(−3.587527)		
LNFIS			N/A	I(1)
Intercept	**0.269482**	**−4.235555***		
	(−2.971853)	(−2.991878)		
Intercept and trend	**−2.876605**	**−5.508513***		
	(−3.580623)	(−3.612199)		

(*Continued*)

TABLE A7.2 (Continued)

Series	*Level*	*First Difference*	*Second Difference*	*Order*
LNFOR				I(2)
Intercept	**0.340749**	**−1.874874**	**−5.773683***	
	(−2.976263)	(−2.976263)	(−2.981038)	
Intercept and trend	**−2.876605**	**−2.098160**	**−5.672836***	
	(−3.580623)	(−3.587527)	(−3.595026)	
LNHHS				I(2)
Intercept	**−0.830087**	**−1.879515**	**−5.780473***	
	(−2.976263)	(−2.976263)	(2.981038)	
Intercept and trend	**−2.086151**	**−1.610577**	**−5.821852***	
	(3.587527)	(−3.587527)	(−3.595026)	
LNINC			N/A	I(1)
Intercept	**−0.312842**	**−3.645323***		
	(−2.971853)	(2.976263)		
Intercept and trend	**−1.075097**	**−3.587439**		
	(−3.580623)	(−3.587527)		
LNIND			N/A	I(1)
Intercept	**−0.690609**	**−4.991221***		
	(−2.971853)	(−2.976263)		
Intercept and trend	**−2.192557**	**−4.900323***		
	(−3.580623)	(−3.587527)		
LNLIS			N/A	I(1)
Intercept	**−0.491719**	**−3.012338***		
	(−2.976263)	(−2.976263)		
Intercept and trend	**−2.020970**	**−2.653186**		
	(−3.587527	(−3.587527)		
LNMAN				I(2)
Intercept	**0.041767**	**−2.554037**	**−6.589445***	
	(−2.976263)	(−2.976263)	(−2.981038)	
Intercept and trend	**−2.987796**	**−2.883926**	**−3.747775***	
	(−3.587527)	(−3.587527)	(−3.622033)	
LNOTS			N/A	I(1)
Intercept	**−0.225617**	**−5.015270***		
	(−2.971853)	(−2.976263)		
Intercept and trend	**−2.309972**	**−4.888054***		
	(−3.580623)	(−3.587527)		
LNPST			N/A	I(1)
Intercept	**−0.463005**	**−3.090207***		
	(−2.976263)	(−2.976263)		
Intercept and trend	**−1.941061**	**−2.911099**		
	(−3.587527)	(−3.587527)		

(*Continued*)

TABLE A7.2 (Continued)

Series	*Level*	*First Difference*	*Second Difference*	*Order*
LNPUA			N/A	I(1)
Intercept	**−1.446120**	**−5.400162***		
	(−2.971853)	(−2.976263)		
Intercept and trend	**−0.447240**	**−5.799059***		
	(−3.580623)	(−3.587527)		
LNREE				I(2)
Intercept	**−1.328075**	**−1.651426**	**−5.616850***	
	(−2.976263)	(−2.976263)	(−2.981038)	
Intercept and trend	**−1.700425**	**−1.692961**	**−5.739494***	
	(−3.587527)	(−3.587527)	(−3.595026)	
LNSER				I(2)
Intercept	**−0.444085**	**−2.912976**	**−7.524514***	
	(−2.976263)	(−2.976263)	(−2.981038)	
Intercept and trend	**−3.303236**	**−2.794632**	**−4.627668***	
	(−3.632896)	(−3.587527)	(−3.612199)	
LNSOM			N/A	I(0)
Intercept	**−0.113243**	**−3.616177***		
	(−2.976263)	(−2.976263)		
Intercept and trend	**−7.638873**	**−4.620301***		
	(−3.587527)	(−3.587527)		
LNTRA				I(1)
Intercept	**−0.514588**	**−2.627103**	**−8.042476***	
	(−2.976263)	(−2.976263)	(−2.981038)	
Intercept and trend	**−2.437052**	**−2.519625**	**−8.029878***	
	(−3.595026)	(−3.587527)	(−3.595026)	
LNTRT			N/A	I(1)
Intercept	**0.011947**	**−5.227402***		
	(−2.971853)	(−2.976263)		
Intercept and trend	**−1.750755**	**−5.138887**		
	(−3.580623)	(−3.587527)		
LNUTI			N/A	I(1)
Intercept	**−0.767510**	**−4.946854**		
	(−2.971853)	(−2.976263)		
Intercept and trend	**−1.767755**	**−4.866867**		
	(−3.58062)	(−3.587507)		

Source: Authors' data and computations.

Notes: Bold figures are test statistics; only the absolute values are considered. Figures in parentheses are the critical values at the 5 percent level. Asterisks (*) indicate significance at the 5 percent level. N/A denotes not applicable.

TABLE A7.3 FM-OLS Results (Model One)

Dependent variable: LNRGDP

Method: Fully modified ordinary least squares (FM-OLS)

Date: July 23, 2021

Sample (adjusted): 1982–2019

Included observations: 38 after adjustments

Cointegrating equation deterministics: C

Long-run covariance estimate (Bartlett kernel, Newey-West fixed bandwidth) = 4.0000

Variable	*Coefficient*	*Standard Error*	*t-Statistic*	*Probability*
LNCST	0.978525	0.137043	7.140270	0.0000
LNSAV	0.167384	0.056128	2.982186	0.0054
LNSWK	0.046709	0.064682	0.722137	0.4755
LNIMP	−0.127320	0.082425	−1.544679	0.1323
LNEXP	0.184963	0.063701	2.903627	0.0066
C	−20.30084	3.443938	−5.894660	0.0000

R-squared	0.994172	Mean dependent variable	8.716065
Adjusted *R*-squared	0.993261	Standard deviation dependent variable	2.320506
Standard error of regression	0.190489	Residual sum of squares	1.161155
Long-run variance	0.049788		

Source: Authors' data and computations.

TABLE A7.4 FM-OLS Results (Model Two)

Dependent variable: LNPOV

Method: Fully modified ordinary least squares (FM-OLS)

Date: July 23, 2021

Sample (adjusted): 1983–2019

Included observations: 37 after adjustments

Cointegrating equation deterministics: C @TREND @TREND^2

Long-run covariance estimate (Bartlett kernel, Newey-West fixed bandwidth) = 4.0000

Regressor equations estimated using differences

Variable	*Coefficient*	*Standard Error*	*t-Statistic*	*Probability*
LNACF	1.082943	0.447448	2.420268	0.0386
LNAER	−3.880236	1.097109	−3.536782	0.0063

(Continued)

TABLE A7.4 (Continued)

Variable	*Coefficient*	*Standard Error*	*t-Statistic*	*Probability*
LNAGC	−31.42639	21.45377	−1.464842	0.1770
LNASB	−17.99709	4.842125	−3.716775	0.0048
LNCON	0.458474	0.840889	0.545225	0.5988
LNCPN	9.338267	2.850494	3.276017	0.0096
LNCPR	23.16542	18.09392	1.280287	0.2325
LNEDU	5.376022	2.590639	2.075172	0.0678
LNFIN	2.119698	0.546998	3.875146	0.0038
LNFIS	−0.029689	0.342200	−0.086758	0.9328
LNFOR	−0.113235	0.411248	−0.275345	0.7893
LNHHS	−11.39372	4.658600	−2.445740	0.0370
LNINC	0.295331	0.907008	0.325610	0.7522
LNLIS	6.546072	4.118472	1.589442	0.1464
LNMAN	2.788131	0.916939	3.040695	0.0140
LNOTS	1.042914	1.382316	0.754469	0.4698
LNPST	23.28022	4.587656	5.074536	0.0007
LNPUA	6.584565	2.178962	3.021882	0.0144
LNREE	1.491105	2.255890	0.660983	0.5252
LNSER	−2.009090	3.223561	−0.623252	0.5486
LNSOM	0.250933	0.182419	1.375588	0.2022
LNTRA	−2.387169	1.220841	−1.955348	0.0823
LNTRT	−1.235389	0.746301	−1.655349	0.1322
LNUTI	−0.235280	0.200179	−1.175348	0.2700
LNIND	−13.51387	3.903498	−3.461990	0.0071
C	−0.659767	0.205912	−3.204119	0.0108
@TREND	0.084410	0.029154	2.895380	0.0177
@TREND^2	−0.001541	0.000724	−2.126883	0.0623
R-squared	0.763768	Mean dependent variable		0.034068
Adjusted *R*-squared	0.055072	Standard deviation dependent variable		0.178700
Standard error of regression	0.173710	Residual sum of squares		0.271577
Long-run variance	0.003590			

Source: Authors' data and computations.

TABLE A7.5 Pairwise Granger Causality Tests

Date: July 19, 2021
Sample: 1981–2019
Lags: 1

Null hypothesis	Observations	F-Statistic	Probability
LNGRW does not Granger-cause LNPOV	38	21.6008	5.E−05
LNPOV does not Granger-cause LNGRW		0.97656	0.3302
LNIMP does not Granger-cause LNPOV	38	2.71810	0.1082
LNPOV does not Granger-cause LNIMP		2.79421	0.1035
LNEXP does not Granger-cause LNPOV	38	0.11858	0.7326
LNPOV does not Granger-cause LNEXP		0.32175	0.5742
LNIMP does not Granger-cause LNGRW	38	10.6179	0.0026
LNGRW does not Granger-cause LNIMP		3.36374	0.0757
LNEXP does not Granger-cause LNGRW	38	5.73806	0.0224
LNGRW does not Granger-cause LNEXP		0.03487	0.8530
LNEXP does not Granger-cause LNIMP	38	0.22610	0.6374
LNIMP does not Granger-cause LNEXP		0.13692	0.7136

Source: Authors' data and computations.

Notes

1 Until 2022, extreme poverty was defined as living on US$1.90 per person per day (i.e., the monetary value of a person's consumption), using 2011 prices. In September 2022, the World Bank updated the international poverty line to $2.15 per person per day, based on 2017 purchasing power parities (World Bank, 2022).
2 World Bank, *Poverty, Prosperity, and Planet Report: Pathways Out of the Polycrisis* (Washington, DC: World Bank Group, 2024), 49.
3 Mustapha Jobarteh, "Poverty: Current Path," in *Sub-Saharan Africa Geographic Futures*, edited by Jobarteh, Mustapha (Pretoria, South Africa: Institute for Security Studies African Futures and Innovation Program, December 2023), 18–19.
4 This downtrend represented a decline in the share of global merchandise exports from 7.3 percent in 1948 to 2.4 percent in 2015 in terms of trade volume, and −28.4 percent when considered in dollars (Statista, 2024, 2025; UNCTAD, 2019).
5 Data with serial correlation can be detected with a Breusch-Godfrey (or Lagrange multiplier) test. FM-OLS modeling, instrumental variables estimation, and maximum likelihood techniques can all address endogeneity.
6 Shaban compared factor intensities of input and output from land under various tenure statuses in India. This methodology applies to the aggregate production function, which is used to model growth in economics (Shaban, 1987).
7 Although neoclassical thought is similar to endogenous growth theory—in that both emphasize the role of technical change and scientific innovation in the growth process—they differ in terms of one major assumption: Endogenous growth theory discards the neoclassical foundation of capital's diminishing marginal productivity and assumes the possibility of a production scale effect throughout the economy. The institutional

approach appears to be inconsistent with the neoclassical model, but it agrees with the endogenous framework on the role of government in creating an environment attractive to investment and ensuring the protection of intellectual property rights to sustain competition.

8 X-efficiency refers to the degree of efficiency gained by firms in an imperfect market structure (Leibenstein, 1966).

9 Recent empirical studies have resorted to more creative strategies, including constructing myriad measures of openness. See, e.g., Udoh & Ayara, 2017; Park & Claveria, 2018.

10 Devised by Peter Phillips and Bruce Hansen in 1990, FM-OLS modifies least squares to account for serial correlation and endogeneity in the regressors, thereby providing optimal estimates (Phillips & Hansen, 1990).

11 See, e.g., Dollar, 1992; Sachs & Warner, 1995; Srinivasan & Bhagwati, 2002.

12 Recent literature has moved away from the trickle-down effect of growth idea to the concept of pro-poor growth. See, e.g., Cicowiez & Conconi, 2008.

13 Two other studies also discuss these four channels. See Cicowiez & Conconi, 2008; Winters & Martuscelli, 2014.

14 See, e.g., Harrison, 1996; McCombie & Thirlwall, 1999; Yanikkaya, 2003; Son & Kakwani, 2008.

15 According to Ezzat, this positive relationship can occur through several channels: By accelerating economic growth, trade openness provides jobs and income for low-skilled labor in developing countries; and by providing incomes for households, it increases the market size. Additionally, through government revenues, restrictions on tariffs can affect expenditures for poverty alleviation (Ezzat, 2018).

16 Several cross-country studies also support this claim. See, e.g., Berg & Krueger, 2003; Dollar & Kraay, 2004; Duran, Mulder, & Onodera, 2018.

17 See, e.g., Ogujiuba, Oji, & Adenuga, 2004; Ogoh & Orbunde, 2012; Gangas, 2017; Arabiyat, Mdanat, & Samawi, 2020.

18 See, e.g., Okoh, 2004; Bamidele, 2005; Manson, Ogujiuba, & Adeola, 2007; World Bank Group & WTO, 2015; Ezzat, 2018. Okoh employed stationarity tests, cointegration tests, and a vector error correction model without providing necessary background or a review of relevant literature on the peculiarities of the situation in Nigeria. Bamidele's analysis included the period when Nigeria was yet to embrace a full market economy, during which total trade as a percentage of GDP was insignificant. Manson, Ogujiuba, and Adeola's empirical model considered only cross-country studies conducted by foreign authors, which failed to account for the dynamics and realities of the Nigerian economy. The previously cited 2015 report by the World Bank Group and the WTO presented an aggregated analysis for sub-Saharan Africa and the entire developing world, with conclusions too general to be applied to any single country. Lastly, Ezzat's study was based on a panel of twenty-three countries in the MENA region for the period 1995–2015.

19 Udoh and Ayara came the closest, but they considered only the impact of state-level inclusive growth in Nigeria, using the arc elasticity measure (Udoh & Anyara, 2017).

20 While they may not model individual behavior directly, these models are usually based on or derived directly from aggregated models of individual choices.

21 The use of real GDP is to account for real growth exclusively and not nominal growth, as defined in the explanatory notes of the 2015 statistical bulletin. See Central Bank of Nigeria, 2015.

22 The use of IMP and EXP as the real merchandise imports and exports was informed by data availability, as all other policy variables that could be considered had very limited coverage. In addition, policy-based variables can be correlated with effects not related to trade. See Rodríguez & Rodrik, 2001.

23 See World Bank, World Development Indicators database, accessed April 1, 2024, https://datacatalog.worldbank.org.

24 For the purposes of this study, the term *savings* comprises savings and time deposits with money deposit banks, national provident funds, federal savings banks, and federal mortgage banks; time deposits with merchant banks and other deposit institutions; premium bonds, savings certificates, and stamps; and life insurance funds. Data availability issues precluded consideration of informal savings.

25 We used the Granger causality test to investigate patterns of causation among our empirical datasets. In other words, as a statistical hypothesis, this method helps to determine whether time series analysis is useful in forecasting another time series—for instance, whether trade can be used to forecast poverty or growth.

26 Although the nonsignificant variables are also part of our results and are included in table 7.4, we do not focus on the implications of their estimated coefficients.

27 Recently, the country has in fact implemented policies to eliminate impediments around trade, such as designating the Nigeria Customs Service as the authority for the administration of rules of origin; leveraging alternative financing options to rehabilitate major trade corridors (e.g., the Lagos-Lakaji and Port-Harcourt-Ngala trunk roads); modernizing railways; and increasing investments in transport and storage facilities, marine fleets, transport education (e.g., seafarers, aviators, and engineers), freight forwarding, and supply chain management services (Awoyemi, 2023).

Bibliography

Adebiyi, Olaleye, and Ogochukwu Isiadinso. "An Overview of the African Continental Free Trade Agreement: Implications for Nigeria." *Andersen Tax LLC Newsletter*, July 2019, https://drive.google.com/file/d/1DHPcaTPWm26SF44wKMgAzYj0csTLhqTI/view.

Afreximbank. *African Trade Report 2024: Climate Implications of the AfCFTA Implementation.* Cairo: Egypt: African Export-Import Bank, 2024, https://media.afreximbank.com/afrexim/African-Trade-Report_2024.pdf.

African Development Bank Group (ADBG). *African Economic Outlook 2019.* Abidjan, Côte d'Ivoire: African Development Bank, 2019, https://www.afdb.org/en/documents/document/african-economic-outlook-aeo-2019-107319.

African Export-Import Bank (AEIB). *African Trade Report 2018: Boosting Intra-African Trade—Implications of the African Continental Free Trade Area Agreement.* Cairo, Egypt: Afreximbank, 2018, https://www.tralac.org/documents/news/2042-african-trade-report-2018-afreximbank/file.html.

Aghion, Philippe, Eve Caroli, and Cecelia García-Peñalosa. "Inequality and Economic Growth: The Perspective of the New Growth Theories." *Journal of Economic Literature* 37, no. 4 (December 1999): 1615–60, https://doi.org/10.1257/jel.37.4.1615.

Aghion, Phillipe, et al. "When Does Domestic Savings Matter for Economic Growth?" *IMF Economic Review* 64, no. 3 (2016): 381–407, https://doi.org/10.1057/imfer.2015.41.

Aguilar, Raul Andres Castaneda, et al. "September 2024 Global Poverty Update from the World Bank: Revised Estimates up to 2024." *Data Blog* (World Bank), September 20, 2024, https://blogs.worldbank.org/en/opendata/september-2024-global-poverty-update-from-the-world-bank--revise.

Aidt, Toke, Jayasri Dutta, and Vania Sena. "Governance Regimes, Corruption and Growth: Theory and Evidence." *Journal of Comparative Economics* 36, no. 2 (2008): 195–220, https://doi.org/10.1016/j.jce.2007.11.004.

Alkire, Sabina, and Selim Jahan. "Assessing Multidimensional Poverty—One Index at the Global Level: Poverty Is Multidimensional and Goes Beyond Income Deprivations." *Human Development Reports*, February 17, 2018, https://hdr.undp.org/content/assessing-multidimensional-poverty-one-index-global-level.

Arabiyat, Talah S., Metri Mdanat, and Ghazi Samawi. "Trade Openness, Inclusive Growth, and Inequality: Evidence from Jordan." *The Journal of Developing Areas* 54, no. 1 (2020): 121–33, https://www.jstor.org/stable/26643873.

Awad-Warrad, Taleb Moh'd, and Buthaina M. A. Muhtaseb. "Trade Openness and Inclusive Economic Growth: Poverty Reduction Through the Growth-Unemployment Linkage." *International Journal of Economics and Financial Issues* 7, no. 2 (2017): 348–54, https://www.econjournals.com/index.php/ijefi/article/view/3813.

Awoyemi, Olufemi. "The African Continental Free Trade Area (AfCFTA) and Industrial Development in Nigeria: Challenges and Prospects." *Proshare*, June 21, 2023, https://www.proshare.co/articles/the-african-continental-free-trade-area-afcfta-and-industrial-development-in-nigeria-challenges-and-prospects?menu=Business&classification=Read&category=Trade%20Investment.

Ayinde, Taofeek Olusola. "Trade Liberalisation, Growth and Poverty Reduction in Nigeria." *Journal of Economics and Sustainable Development* 4, no. 18 (2013): 93–106, https://iiste.org/Journals/index.php/JEDS/article/view/8844/9297.

Bakare, Adewale Stephen, and Ilemobayo Akinwumi Simoen. "Does Economic Growth Reduce Poverty in Nigeria?" *Developing Country Studies* 3, no. 9 (2013): 62–68, https://www.iiste.org/Journals/index.php/DCS/article/view/7604.

Bamidele, Reuben. "Globalization and Manufacturing." *The Nigerian Journal of Economic and Social Studies* 47, no. 2 (July 2005): 281–300.

Barone, Guglielmo, and Federico Cingano. "Service Regulation and Growth: Evidence from OECD Countries." *The Economic Journal* 121, no. 555 (September 2011): 931–57, https://doi.org/10.1111/j.1468-0297.2011.02433.x.

Barro, Robert J. "Determinants of Economic Growth: A Cross-Country Empirical Study." NBER Working Paper No. 5698. Cambridge, MA: National Bureau of Economic Research, August 1996, https://www.nber.org/system/files/working_papers/w5698/w5698.pdf.

Barro, Robert J., and Xavier Sala-i-Martin. "Technological Diffusion, Convergence, and Growth." *Journal of Economic Growth* 2, no. 1 (March 1997): 1–26, https://doi.org/10.1023/A:1009746629269.

Berg, Andrew, and Anne Krueger. "Trade, Growth, and Poverty: A Selective Survey." IMF Working Paper No. 03/30. Washington, DC: International Monetary Fund, February 2003, https://www.imf.org/external/pubs/ft/wp/2003/wp0330.pdf.

Bong, Angkeara, and Gamini Premaratne. "Regional Integration and Economic Growth in Southeast Asia." *Global Business Review* 19, no. 6 (December 2018): 1403–15, https://doi.org/10.1177/0972150918794568.

Bruno, Michael, Martin Ravallion, and Lyn Squire. "Equity and Growth in Developing Countries: Old and New Perspectives on Policy Issues." In *Income Distribution and High-Quality Growth*, edited by Vito Tanzi and Ke-young Chu, 117–44. Cambridge: MIT Press, 1998.

Busse, Matthias, and Jens Koeniger. "Trade and Economic Growth: A Re-Examination of the Empirical Evidence." *Economics Bulletin* 35, no. 4 (2015): 2862–76, https://doi.org/10.2139/ssrn.2009939.

Central Bank of Nigeria. "Statistical Bulletin." Vol. 26, December 2015, https://www.cbn.gov.ng/out/2016/sd/2015%20statistical%20bulletin%20contents%20and%20narratives.pdf.

Central Bank of Nigeria. "Statistical Bulletin." Vol. 31, December 2020, https://www.cbn.gov.ng/Out/2021/STD/2020%20Statistical%20Bulletin_Explanatory%20Notes_Final_Modified.pdf.

Chang, Yoosoon, and Peter C. B. Phillips. "Time Series Regression with Mixtures of Integrated Processes." *Econometric Theory* 11, no. 5 (December 1995): 1033–94, https://doi.org/10.1017/S0266466600009968.

Cicowiez, Martin, and Adriana Conconi. "Linking Trade and Pro-Poor Growth: A Survey." In *Trade and Poverty in the Developing World*, edited by John Cockburn and Paolo Giordano, 7–29. Nairobi, Kenya: Poverty and Economic Policy Network, 2008, https://www.pep-net.org/sites/pep-net.org/files/typo3doc/pdf/promotionnal_material/Proceedings_TradePoverty.pdf.

Dava, Emílio. "Trade Liberalization and Economic Growth in the SADC: A Difference-in-Difference Analysis." IESE Conference Paper No. 8. Presented at the Third International Instituto de Estudos Sociais e Económicos [Institute of Social and Economic Studies] Conference, Abidjan, Côte d'Ivoire, September 4–5, 2012, https://www.iese.ac.mz/lib/publication/III_Conf2012/IESE_IIIConf_Paper8.pdf.

DiCaprio, Alisa, Amelia U. Santos-Paulino, and Maria V. Sokolova. "Regional Trade Agreements, Integration, and Development." UNCTAD Research Paper No. 1. Geneva, Switzerland: United Nations Conference on Trade and Development, July 2017, https://unctad.org/system/files/official-document/ser_rp2017d1_en.pdf.

Dollar, David. "Outward-Oriented Developing Economies Really Do Grow More Rapidly: Evidence from 95 LDCs, 1976–1985." *Economic Development and Cultural Change* 40, no. 3 (April 1992): 523–44, https://doi.org/10.1086/451959.

Dollar, David, and Aart Kraay. "Trade, Growth, and Poverty." *The Economic Journal* 114, no. 493 (February 2004): F22–F49, https://doi.org/10.1111/j.0013-0133.2004.00186.x.

Duong, Khoa Dang, et al. "How Foreign Direct Investment, Trade Openness, and Productivity Affect Economic Growth: Evidence from 90 Middle-Income Countries." *SciPap (Scientific Papers of the University of Pardubice, Series D, Faculty of Economics and Administration)* 30, no. 3 (2022): 1–12, https://doi.org/10.46585/sp30031615.

Duran, Jose, Nanno Mulder, and Osamu Onodera. "Trade Liberalisation and Economic Performance: Latin America Versus East Asia, 1970–2006." OECD Trade Policy Paper No. 70. Paris, France: Organization for Economic Co-operation and Development, 2018, https://doi.org/10.1787/244284387510.

Ezzat, Ahmed M. "Trade Openness: An Effective Tool for Poverty Alleviation or an Instrument for Increasing Poverty Severity?" Working Paper No. 1248. Giza, Egypt: Economic Research Forum, November 2018, https://erf.org.eg/app/uploads/2018/11/1248.pdf.

Gangas, Stephanie. "Relationship Between Economic Growth and Poverty Reduction in Nigeria." *Pyrex Journal of Business and Finance Management Research* 3, no. 2 (2017): 34–56.

Grossman, Gene M., and Elhanan Helpman. *Innovation and Growth in the Global Economy*. Cambridge: MIT Press, 1991.

Harrison, Ann. "Openness and Growth: A Time-Series, Cross-Country Analysis for Developing Countries." *Journal of Development Economics* 48, no. 2 (March 1996): 419–47, https://doi.org/10.1016/0304-3878(95)00042-9.

Higgins, Kate, and Susan Prowse. "Trade, Growth, and Poverty: Making Aid for Trade Work for Inclusive Growth and Poverty Reduction." ODI Working Paper No. 313. London, UK: Overseas Development Institute, February 2010, https://assets.publishing.service.gov.uk/media/57a08b2c40f0b652dd000b46/ODI-WP313.pdf.

Huchet-Bourdon, Marilyne, Chantal Le Mouël, and Mariana Vijil. "The Relationship Between Trade Openness and Economic Growth: Some New Insights on the Openness Measurement Issue." Presented at the Thirteenth International Congress of the European

Association of Agricultural Economists, Zurich, Switzerland, August 30–September 2, 2011, https://hal.science/hal-01987393v1/document.

Ichedi, Sunday Joel "Nigeria Launches Its Most Extensive National Measure of Multidimensional Poverty." *National Bureau of Statistics News Release, Federal Government of Nigeria*, November 17, 2022, https://ophi.org.uk/sites/default/files/2023-07/Nigeria_MPI_2022_press_release.pdf.

Ijaiya, Gafar T., et al. "Economic Growth and Poverty Reduction in Nigeria." *International Journal of Business and Social Science* 2, no. 15 (August 2011): 147–54, https://www.ijbssnet.com/journals/Vol_2_No_15_August_2011/17.pdf.

IMF Staff. "Global Trade Liberalization and the Developing Countries." *International Monetary Fund Issue Brief*, November 2001, https://www.imf.org/external/np/exr/ib/2001/110801.htm.

Israr, Fahad, and Miguel Rocha de Sousa. "Long-Run Analysis of Trade Openness on Economic Growth for Pakistan: Evidence from Standard and Optimal Time Series Tests." CEFAGE Working Paper No. 2018/01. Évora, Portugal: Center for Advanced Studies in Management and Economics, University of Évora, 2018, https://api.cefage.uevora.pt/assets/9d96e0d8-91f3-41f1-b213-761df698d912.

Jobarteh, Mustapha. "Poverty: Current Path." In *Sub-Saharan Africa Geographic Futures*, edited by Jobarteh, Mustapha. Pretoria, South Africa: Institute for Security Studies African Futures and Innovation Program, December 2023, https://futures.issafrica.org/geographic/regions/sub-saharan-africa/#poverty.

Kamau, Njoroge Lucas. "The Impact of Regional Integration on Economic Growth: Empirical Evidence from COMESA, EAC and SADC Trade Blocs." *American Journal of Social and Management Sciences* 1, no. 2 (2010): 150–63, https://scihub.org/AJSMS/PDF/2010/2/AJSMS-1-2-150-163.pdf.

Klasen, Stephan. "Measuring and Monitoring Inclusive Growth: Multiple Definitions, Open Questions, and Some Constructive Proposals." ADB Sustainable Development Working Paper No. 12. Manila, Philippines: Asian Development Bank, June 2010, https://www.adb.org/sites/default/files/publication/28492/adb-wp12-measuring-inclusive-growth.pdf.

Klitgaard, Thomas. "What Caused Last Year's Commodity Price Crash?" *World Economic Forum*, March 24, 2016, https://www.weforum.org/stories/2016/03/what-caused-last-years-commodity-price-crash.

Kolawole, Bashir Olayinka, and Olufunsho Abayomi Omobitan. "Raging Poverty and Agricultural Output in Nigeria: An Empirical Investigation." *Journal of Economics and Sustainable Development* 5, no. 6 (2014): 63–72, https://www.iiste.org/Journals/index.php/JEDS/article/view/11934.

Kuznets, Simon. *Modern Economic Growth: Rate, Structure and Spread*. New Haven, CT: Yale University Press, 1966.

Kuznets, Simon. "Quantitative Aspects of the Economic Growth of Nations: II, Industrial Distribution of National Product and Labor Force." *Economic Development and Cultural Change* 5, no. S4 (July 1957): 1–111, https://doi.org/10.1086/449740.

Lakner, Christoph, Mario Negre, and Espen Beer Prydz. "Twinning the Goals: How Can Promoting Shared Prosperity Help to Reduce Global Poverty?" Policy Research Working Paper No. 7106. Washington, DC: World Bank Development Research Group, November 2014, https://hdl.handle.net/10986/20611.

Lee, Kang-Kook. "Globalization, Income Inequality and Poverty: Theory and Empirics." *Social System Studies* 28 (March 2014): 109–34, https://www.ritsumei.ac.jp/acd/re/ssrc/result/memoirs/kiyou28/28-05.pdf.

Leibenstein, Harvey. "Allocative Efficiency vs. 'X- Efficiency.'" *American Economic Review* 56, no. 3 (June 1966): 392–415, https://www.jstor.org/stable/1823775.

Lopez, Jorge Humberto. "Pro-Growth, Pro-Poor: Is There a Trade-Off?" World Bank Policy Research Working Paper No. 3378. Washington, DC: World Bank Development Research Group, August 2004, https://hdl.handle.net/10986/14124.

Lucas, Robert E., Jr. "Making a Miracle." *Econometrica* 61, no. 2 (1993): 251–72, https://doi.org/10.2307/2951551.

Lyroudi, Katerina, John Papanastasiou, and Vamvakidis Athanasios. "Foreign Direct Investment and Economic Growth in Transition Economies." *South-Eastern Europe Journal of Economics* 2, no. 1 (2004): 97–110, https://asecu.gr/old_files/Seeje/issue02/lyroudi.pdf.

Mabugu, Ramos, and Margaret Chitiga Mabugu. "Can Trade Liberalization in South Africa Reduce Poverty and Inequality While Boosting Economic Growth? Macro-Micro Reflections." *Development Southern Africa* 31, no. 2 (2014): 257–74, https://doi.org/10.1080/0376835X.2013.871197.

MacKinnon, James G., Alfred A. Haug, and Leo Michelis. "Numerical Distribution Functions of Likelihood Ratio Tests for Cointegration." *Journal of Applied Econometrics* 14, no. 5 (September/October 1999): 563–77.

Maertens, Miet, Liesbeth Colen, and Johan Swinnen. "Globalisation and Poverty in Senegal: A Worst-Case Scenario?" *European Review of Agricultural Economics* 38, no. 1 (March 2011): 31–54, https://doi.org/10.1093/erae/jbq053.

Majeed, Muhammad Tariq. "Inequality, Trade Openness and Economic Growth in Asia." *Applied Econometrics and International Development* 10, no. 2 (2010): 201–10, https://www.usc.es/economet/reviews/aeid10216.pdf.

Mann, Katja. "The EU, a Growth Engine? The Impact of European Integration on Economic Growth in Central Eastern Europe." FIW Working Paper No. 136. Vienna, Austria: Research Focus on International Economics (Forschungsschwerpunkt Internationale Wirtschaft), January 2015, https://www.econstor.eu/bitstream/10419/121136/1/N_136.pdf.

Manson, Nwafor, Kanayo Ogujiuba, and Adenikinju Adeola. "The Impacts of Trade Liberalization on Poverty in Nigeria: Dynamic Simulations in a CGE Model." Presented at the Centre for the Study of African Economies (CSAE) Economic Development in Africa Conference, Oxford University, Oxford, UK, March 18–20, 2007, https://doi.org/10.2139/ssrn.3173110.

McCombie, John S. L., and Anthony Philip Thirlwall. "Growth in the International Context: A Post-Keynesian View." In *Foundations of International Economics: Post-Keynesian Perspectives*, edited by Johan Deprez and John T. Harvey, 35–90. London, UK: Routledge, 1999.

McCulloch, Neil, Leonard Alan Winters, and Xavier Cirera. *Trade Liberalization and Poverty: A Handbook*. London, UK: Centre for Economic Policy Research, 2001, https://cdi.mecon.gob.ar/bases/docelec/kr1123.pdf.

Mene, Wamkele. "Intra-African Trade and Its Potential to Accelerate Progress Toward the SDGs." *Brookings Institution*, January 29, 2025, https://www.brookings.edu/articles/intra-african-trade-and-its-potential-to-accelerate-progress-toward-the-sdgs.

National Bureau of Statistics. *Nigeria Multidimensional Poverty Index (2022)*. Abuja, Nigeria: Federal Government of Nigeria, November 2022, https://www.nigerianstat.gov.ng/elibrary/read/1241254.

North, Douglass C. *Institutions, Institutional Change and Economic Performance*. Cambridge, UK: Cambridge University Press, 1990.

Nursini, Nursini. "Effect of Fiscal Policy and Trade Openness on Economic Growth in Indonesia: 1990–2015." *International Journal of Economics and Financial Issues* 7, no. 1 (2017): 358–64, https://www.econjournals.com/index.php/ijefi/article/view/3363/pdf.

Ogoh, Augustine O., and Emmanuel Orbunde. "Globalization and the Challenges for Poverty Eradication and Development in Africa: The Nigerian Experience." *Journal of Humanities and Social Science* 5, no. 2 (2012): 40–47, https://doi.org/10.9790/0837-0524047.

Ogujiuba, Kanayo Kingsley, George Okechukwu Oji, and Adeniyi Adenuga. "Is 'Trade' Openness Valid for Nigeria's Long-Run Growth: A Cointegration Approach?" AIAE Working Paper. Enugu, Nigeria: African Institute for Applied Economics, December 2004 (published through the University Library of Munich), https://econwpa.ub.uni-muenchen.de/econ-wp/it/papers/0412/0412009.pdf.

Okoh, Rosemary N. "The Global Market Place: How Far Can Nigeria Go with the Present Non-Oil Product Mix?" Presented at the "African Development and Poverty Reduction: The Micro-Macro Link" Conference, Somerset West, South Africa, October 13–15, 2004, https://www.tips.org.za/files/The_global_market_place_Okoh.pdf.

Omoke, Philip C. "Trade Policy Reforms and Rural Poverty in Nigeria." Presented at the Ninth Annual Purdue University Global Trade Analysis Project (GTAP) Conference on Global Economic Analysis, Addis Ababa, Ethiopia, June 15–17, 2006, https://gtap.agecon.purdue.edu/uploads/resources/download/2456.pdf.

Onu, Emele, et al. "Six People Fall into Extreme Poverty in This Nation Every Minute." *Bloomberg*, February 22, 2019, https://www.bloomberg.com/news/articles/2019-02-22/six-people-fall-into-extreme-poverty-in-this-nation-every-minute.

Park, Cyn-Young, and Racquel Claveria. "Does Regional Trade Integration Matter for Inclusive Growth? Evidence from the Multidimensional Regional Integration Index." ADB Economics Working Paper Series, No. 559. Manila, Philippines: Asian Development Bank, October 2018, https://www.adb.org/sites/default/files/publication/460681/ewp-559-regional-integration-inclusive-growth.pdf.

Phillips, Peter C. B., and Bruce E. Hansen. "Statistical Inference in Instrumental Variables Regression with I(1) Processes." *Review of Economic Studies* 57, no. 1 (January 1990): 99–125, https://doi.org/10.2307/2297545.

Pomeranz, Kenneth. *The Great Divergence: China, Europe, and the Making of the Modern World Economy*. Princeton, NJ: Princeton University Press, 2000.

Rodríguez, Francisco, and Dani Rodrik. "Trade Policy and Economic Growth: A Skeptic's Guide to the Cross-National Evidence." In *NBER Macroeconomics Annual 2000*, Vol. 15, edited by Ben S. Bernanke and Kenneth Rogoff, 261–338. Cambridge: MIT Press, 2001, https://www.nber.org/system/files/chapters/c11058/c11058.pdf.

Romer, Paul M. "Endogenous Technological Change." *Journal of Political Economy* 98, no. 5, pt. 2 (October 1990): S71–S102, https://doi.org/10.1086/261725.

Saad-Filho, Alfredo. "Growth, Poverty and Inequality: From Washington Consensus to Inclusive Growth." DESA Working Paper No. 100. New York, NY: United Nations Department of Economic and Social Affairs, November 2010, https://digitallibrary.un.org/record/3859080?v=pdf.

Sachs, Jeffrey D., and Andrew Warner. "Economic Reform and the Process of Global Integration." In *Brookings Papers on Economic Activity, 1: 1995—Macroeconomics*, edited by William Brainard and George L. Perry, 1–118. Washington, DC: Brookings Institution, 1995, https://www.brookings.edu/wp-content/uploads/1995/01/1995a_bpea_sachs_warner_aslund_fischer.pdf.

Sakr, Hala M. "Trade Policy and Poverty Eradication (with Special Reference to the Egyptian Case)." Presented at the First Joint Research Workshop, University Paris 1 (Panthéon-Sorbonne) and Cairo University, Cairo, Egypt, May 2012.

Shaban, Radwan Ali. "Testing Between Competing Models of Sharecropping." *Journal of Political Economy* 95, no. 5 (October 1987): 893–920, https://www.jstor.org/stable/1833122.

Smith, Adam. *An Inquiry into the Nature and Causes of the Wealth of Nations*. Vol. 2. London, UK: Strahan and Cadell, 1776.

Solow, Robert M. "A Contribution to the Theory of Economic Growth." *The Quarterly Journal of Economics* 70, no. 1 (February 1956): 65–94, https://doi.org/10.2307/1884513.

Son, Hyun H., and Nanak Kakwani. "Global Estimates of Pro-Poor Growth." *World Development* 36, no. 6 (June 2008): 1048–66, https://doi.org/10.1016/j.worlddev.2007.10.002.

Srinivasan, Thirukodikaval Nilakanta, and Jagdish Bhagwati. "Outward-Orientation and Development: Are Revisionists Right?" In *Trade, Development and Political Economy: Essays in Honour of Anne O. Krueger*, edited by Deepak Lal and Richard H. Snape, 3–26. London, UK: Palgrave, 2002, https://doi.org/10.1057/9780230523685_1.

Statista, "Trade Balance of Merchandise in Africa from 2005 to 2019 (in Million U.S. Dollars)," accessed November 20, 2024, https://www.statista.com/statistics/1181807/trade-balance-of-merchandise-in-africa.

Statista, "Value of Merchandise Exports from Africa Between 2005 and 2022 (in Million U.S. Dollars)," accessed March 30, 2025, https://www.statista.com/statistics/1181447/value-of-merchandise-exports-in-africa.

Sulaimon, Olanrewaju. "World Bank Projects 13mln More Nigerians Will Fall Below Poverty Line by 2025." *Nigerian Tribune*, April 24, 2023, https://www.zawya.com/en/economy/africa/world-bank-projects-13mln-more-nigerians-will-fall-below-poverty-line-by-2025-luwq683k.

Swan, Trevor Winchester "Economic Growth and Capital Accumulation." *Economic Record* 32, no. 2 (November 1956): 334–61, https://doi.org/10.1111/j.1475-4932.1956.tb00434.x.

te Velde, Dirk Willem. "Regional Integration, Growth and Convergence." *Journal of Economic Integration* 26, no. 1 (March 2011): 1–28, https://doi.org/10.11130/jei.2011.26.1.1.

Thornton, James R., Richard J. Agnello, and Charles R. Link. "Poverty and Economic Growth: Trickle Down Peters Out." *Economic Inquiry* 16, no. 3 (July 1978): 385–94, https://doi.org/10.1111/j.1465-7295.1978.tb00509.x.

Trabelsi, Mohammed Ali, and Naoufel Liouane. "Trade Liberalization and Fight Against Poverty." *International Journal of Economics and Financial Issues* 3, no. 2 (2013): 370–75, https://www.econjournals.com/index.php/ijefi/article/view/399/pdf.

Tumwebaze, Henry Karamuriro, and Alex Thomas Ijjo. "Regional Economic Integration and Economic Growth in the COMESA Region, 1980–2010." *African Development Review* 27, no. 1 (March 2015): 67–77, https://doi.org/10.1111/1467-8268.12123.

Udoh, Enobong, and Ndem Anyara. "An Investigation of (Non-) Inclusive Growth in Nigeria's Sub-Nationals: Evidence from Elasticity Approach." *Economies* 5, no. 4 (December 2017): 1–17, https://doi.org/10.3390/economies5040043.

United Nations (UN). *Transforming Our World: The 2030 Agenda for Sustainable Development*. New York, NY: United Nations, 2015, https://sdgs.un.org/2030agenda.

United Nations Conference on Trade and Development (UNCTAD). "Economic Development in Africa Report 2019: Made in Africa—Rules of Origin for Enhanced Intra-African Trade." *UNCTAD News Release*, June 26, 2019, https://unctad.org/press-material/facts-figures-0.

United Nations Department of Economic and Social Affairs (UNDESA). *Monthly Briefing on the World Economic Situation and Prospects*, no. 131, October 2019, https://www.un.org/development/desa/dpad/wp-content/uploads/sites/45/publication/Monthly_Briefing_131.pdf.

United Nations Development Programme (UNDP). "MPI—More Nigerians Are Multidimensionally Poor than a Decade Before 2017." *UNDP News Release*, July 10, 2019, https://www.undp.org/nigeria/press-releases/mpi-more-nigerians-are-multidimensionally-poor-decade-2017.

UNDP. *The Real Wealth of Nations: Pathways to Human Development.* UNDP Human Development Report 2010, 20th Anniversary Edition. New York, NY: United Nations Development Programme, 2010, https://hdr.undp.org/content/human-development-report-2010.

UNDP and Oxford Poverty and Human Development Initiative. *Global Multidimensional Poverty Index 2019: Illuminating Inequalities*. New York, NY: United Nations Development Programme, 2019, https://hdr.undp.org/system/files/documents/mpi2019publication.pdf.

Vamvakidis, Athanasios. "Regional Integration and Economic Growth." *The World Bank Economic Review* 12, no. 2 (May 1998): 251–70, https://doi.org/10.1093/wber/12.2.251.

Williamson, John. "A Short History of the Washington Consensus." *Law and Business Review of the Americas* 15, no. 1 (2009): 7–23, https://doi.org/10.1093/acprof:oso/9780199534081.003.0002.

Winters, Leonard Alan. "Trade Liberalisation and Poverty: What Are the Links?" *The World Economy* 25, no. 9 (September 2002): 1339–67, https://doi.org/10.1111/1467-9701.00495.

Winters, Leonard Alan, and Antonio Martuscelli. "Trade Liberalization and Poverty: What Have We Learned in a Decade?" *Annual Review of Resource Economics* 6, no. 1 (2014): 493–512, https://doi.org/10.1146/annurev-resource-110713-105054.

Winters, Leonard Alan, Neil McCulloch, and Andrew McKay. "Trade Liberalization and Poverty: The Evidence So Far." *Journal of Economic Literature* 42, no. 1 (March 2004): 72–115, https://doi.org/10.1257/002205104773558056.

World Bank, "Does Microfinance Still Hold Promise for Reaching the Poor?" March 30, 2015, https://www.worldbank.org/en/news/feature/2015/03/30/does-microfinance-still-hold-promise-for-reaching-the-poor.

World Bank, "Fact Sheet: An Adjustment to Global Poverty Lines," last updated September 14, 2022, https://www.worldbank.org/en/news/factsheet/2022/05/02/fact-sheet-an-adjustment-to-global-poverty-lines.

World Bank. *Poverty, Prosperity, and Planet Report: Pathways Out of the Polycrisis*. Washington, DC: World Bank Group, 2024, https://hdl.handle.net/10986/42211.

World Bank Group and World Trade Organization (WTO). *The Role of Trade in Ending Poverty*. Geneva, Switzerland: World Trade Organization, 2015, https://hdl.handle.net/10986/22081.

World Bank Group and WTO. *Trade and Poverty Reduction: New Evidence of Impacts in Developing Countries*. Geneva, Switzerland: World Trade Organization, 2018, https://documents.worldbank.org/curated/en/968461544478747599.

Yanikkaya, Halit. "Trade Openness and Economic Growth: A Cross-Country Empirical Investigation." *Journal of Development Economics* 72, no. 1 (October 2003): 57–89, https://doi.org/10.1016/S0304-3878(03)00068-3.

PART 3

Governance and Ethnic Identity in Sub-Saharan Africa

8

NOT EVERYTHING IS ABOUT ETHNICITY

Conflict and the Politics of Belonging in Africa

James Siguru Wahutu

Introduction

Social science literature is replete with discussions—and (mis)perceptions and faulty conclusions—about how ethnicity impedes Africa's development. Ethnicity is frequently posited as an African predicament and a reason for the continent's lack of economic transformation. Bookshelves around the world are thick with works about what I call the *problematics* of ethnicity and how and why ethnicity has stunted African progress. A challenge in understanding ethnicity in Africa is that many scholars engaging with it are not ethnicity scholars; often, they study questions such as development, conflict, and politics and include ethnicity in their empirical models as an explanatory variable. To wit, whereas the Global North has gender, race, and ethnic studies scholars, there are no equivalent ethnicity scholars in Africa. Further complicating matters is the fact that ethnicity inquiries often start from colonial Africa, almost as if these groups did not exist before Europeans landed on the continent's shores. Framing why African people identify in specific ways through this lens strips their agency from them and places it with colonial authorities. Scholars in the Global North and in Africa fall into this trap (Berman, 1998).[1] Categories manufactured during the colonial tribalization process continue to form the academic underpinnings of ethnicity even when the reality is quite different.

This obsession with regurgitating non-reality-based narratives is partly born out of what Julian Go calls an "imperialistic unconscious," which he defines as the process through which scholarship has continued to reproduce and mirror "the wider culture of northern dominance" in explaining what identity is, what diversity means, and what constitutes good versus bad diversity (Go, 2013).[2] In the Global North, diversity is considered praiseworthy and central to societal improvement;

DOI: 10.4324/9781003357025-11

in Africa, ethnicity is often measured by ethnolinguistic diversity and portrayed as predisposing societies to conflict. In this view, to accomplish any development goal in Africa, diversity must be flat. This scholarship is mired in antiquated Lugardian and Hegelian fantasies about Africa and its inhabitants (Lugard, 1965; Hegel, 1956).

An added wrinkle in the discourse on ethnicity is that scholars in the Global North have tended to conflate tribalism and ethnicity in their rush to blame one or the other for whatever shortcoming they are studying—a penchant that persists despite work by Global South scholars showing that what we refer to as *tribes* are nothing more than political entities created by colonial administrations (Mafeje, 1971; Mamdani, 2012). This continued conflation is underpinned by early scholarship that reduces the continent—and its peoples—to mere parts of the imperial project. As such, those early scholars for a long time acted not just as the "ruling material force" but also as part of the "intellectual force" in defining identity on the continent (Mafeje, 1971; Marx & Engels, 1965).[3] Their preoccupation with identity in Africa was not just an intellectual exercise but was geared toward allowing the invading and occupying forces to govern the occupied. Many of them took a leaf from Henry Maine and focused on using "kinship as a basis for social order," thus imposing group identities on individuals through surveillance tools such as the census (Mamdani, 2012).

As Carola Lentz reminds us, early scholars "were well aware of the multi-ethnicity of the political entities they investigated, even if they tended to concentrate on the one dominant group" (Lentz, 1995).[4] Nevertheless, scholars have continued to pay lip service to the challenge of "delimiting and naming the unit under investigation, only to spend the rest of the text using terms like [the Hutu, the Luo, the Igbo]," implying homogeneous sociocultural entities "for the purposes of cultural comparison" (Lentz, 1995).[5] This homogenization has further complicated narratives about identity in Africa, inasmuch as it bred the perception that ethnic groups have origin stories that are pure, quantifiable, and distinct. The quest to quantify ethnicity in the Global North has led to measures such as the ethnolinguistic fractionalization index, Charles Lewis Taylor and Michael C. Hudson's subsequent index, and categories like "ethnic cores" and the amorphous "politically relevant ethnic group" (Taylor & Hudson, 1972; Green, 2020; Posner, 2004; Wucherpfennig et al., 2011). These measures focus on *naming* groups and flattening identities to make it easier to run models rather than seeking to understand how these identities are *claimed.* They treat ethnic identity as akin to racial identity, implicitly arguing that if one is born Hutu, they could never become Tutsi, or that if one is Ijesha, they could not be simultaneously Yoruba. These scholars are engaged in counting exercises that tell us little about how identity operates on the continent and have more to do with backfitting people and ideas into convenient models.

This willful oversimplification has prompted many scholars in the Global North to define failures and successes in Africa myopically in terms of tribes as political entities. Identity becomes the starting premise of any scholarly work interested in explaining any phenomenon on the continent. Consequently, Global North scholars present poor governance or policy failures or development deficiencies in Africa as a consequence of ethnicity. This myopia is ever-present in scholarship on politics and conflict, which fixates on ethnicity's role in exacerbating tensions. In Kenya, for example, the 1980s and 1990s saw a flood of scholarship that sought to explain pre- and post-electoral violence through the lens of ethnolinguistic differentiation. This generalization caused scholars and policymakers alike to gloss over the political machinations of then-president Daniel arap Moi and thus provide inaccurate solutions to problems that were not as prevalent as everyone insisted, giving short shrift to the real and dire issues of brazen corruption, gross misgovernance, and dismal growth (Kagwanja, 2003). The insistence on conflating tribes with ethnicity obfuscates intra-ethnic economic, cultural, and power relations in favor of inter-ethnic relations.

It is essential to remember the roots of the term *ethnicity* in its modern sense. In 1935, Julian Huxley and Alfred C. Haddon proposed using the terms *ethnic group* or *people* rather than *race* in reference to Europeans as a way to reject *race*'s biological meaning (Huxley & Haddon, 1935; Dubow, 1994). They were part of a group of scholars that had begun eschewing assumptions about race and attendant notions of heredity as a constitutive of human behavior. When it came to Africans, however, this disjuncture between heredity and human behavior only went so far. Writing about West Africa, Immanuel Wallerstein clung to the primordial notion of *tribe* by arguing that those in the rural "Gemeinschaft-like community" belonged to "tribes," whereas those in urban areas belonged to "ethnic groups." Wallerstein viewed membership in these urban ethnic groups as "a matter of social definition," unlike rural tribal affiliations and membership in such groups (Wallerstein, 1960).[6]

Scholars such as Mahmood Mamdani have pushed back on the notion of tribal affiliation and reminded us that it was indirect rule by the British in Africa that originated the concept of the tribe as we understand it today: "The colonized majority was effectively fragmented into so many administratively driven political minorities," such that "the political minority was called 'the tribe.'" In other words, the central claim of the indirect rule state—and indeed the whole colonial enterprise in Africa—was that "that the native identity [was] by nature tribal." To be clear: The cultural identities that underpinned the colonialist construct of the ethnic group certainly predated the African colonial project. Ethnicity always existed in African societies, but prior to colonialism, it existed as a *cultural* identity. Crucially, as Mamdani explained, "every ethnic group had ways of absorbing strangers. You could become a Muganda or a Yoruba." By creating tribes, the colonial administration reified identity by ensuring that the amorphous grouping referred to as an ethnic group flattened into a singular ethnolinguistic/regional/religious group; in this framework, identity was not just totalizing but politically driven (Mamdani, 2001, 2012).

The erasure of *Kwihutura* (a loss of "Hutuness") and *Gucupira* (a loss of "Tutsiness") by Belgian colonialists in Rwanda by sealing off Tutsi from Hutu identities exemplifies this flattening (Mamdani, 2001, 2012). The Tutsi migrated to modern-day Rwanda in the fifteenth century and established a feudal system that persisted until colonization. As minority rulers, they distributed land and political power through Tutsi chiefs whose power derived from the ownership of cattle and land. The serfdom they imposed referred to subjugated ethnic identities as "Hutu," which was more a class distinction than an ethnic identity. However, there was social mobility between Hutu and Tutsi. *Kwihutura* could be attained through the accumulation of wealth. Conversely, a Tutsi lacking property could face *Gucupira*. In essence, Hutu and Tutsi were perceived as economic distinctions rather than ethnic ones (Rennie, 1972).

This chapter proposes a different approach to thinking about and engaging with ethnicity as a category for analysis. I argue that scholars need to consider ethnicity as an act of *claiming* rather than *naming*. I look to Saul Dubow, who discusses the act of claiming ethnicity as "a strand of thought that conceives of ethnicity in a situational, contextual, and subjective sense." In this sense, ethnicity becomes a form of identity "that acquires content and meaning through a process of conscious assertion" (Dubow, 1994).[7] This conception contrasts with naming, wherein identity is primordial, static, and essentialist, imposed by external actors (Hutchinson & Smith, 1996; Schraml, 2014). Claiming captures why and how individuals would be willing to claim a common origin, one that is a "selective representation of a complex situation." It pays little attention to the heterogeneity of cultural origins and treats ethnicity as a lived experience. Claiming embodies the fluid nature of origin and identity as a selective process, situating African agency at the center of knowledge and leveraging different parts of this heterogeneity of origins depending on context (Sharp, 1980).[8]

Ethnicity, framed thusly, operates as a matrix of identities. Such an approach straddles a middle ground by anchoring the definition of ethnicity in how a group, through its members and others, distinguishes itself on several bases, one of which may be "cultural-regional criteria" (Gulliver, 1969).[9] This would mean that scholars have to acknowledge that Africans, just like Westerners, objectivate their shared experiences, which form "both the basis and the instrument of the collective stock of knowledge" about identity (Berger & Luckmann, 1966).[10] Sociologists will recognize this framework as one influenced by scholars of knowledge such as Peter Berger and Thomas Luckmann and borrowing from Patricia Hill Collins and Kimberlé Crenshaw (Berger & Luckmann, 1966; Collins, 1990; Crenshaw, 1989, 1991). Contrary to the naming approach, which flattens the complexity of identity, claiming encompasses the fact that identities are intersectional and can be selectively leveraged in ways that compound how marginalization, perpetration, and victimization may unfold.

Naming Versus Claiming

Wallerstein and his contemporaries popularized a methodology that continues to affect the way that African identities are treated today—namely, as flat and one-dimensional (Wallerstein, 1960). This flattening is ubiquitous in scholarship on politics and conflict on the continent. The discourse around it is almost always explicitly connected to a unidimensional account of ethnicity that focuses on naming groups over claiming identities (Amodio & Chiovelli, 2018; Bhavnani, 2006; Ndegwa, 1997). Scholars and observers discuss conflict in Africa with zeal, rotely attributing perpetrators' motivations to some hazy version of ethnicity. This articulation perceives perpetrators and victims as embodying already prescribed identities. Complexity is reduced to a morality tale in which identity is static and primordial and belongs to the "Gemeinschaft-like community" (Wallerstein, 1960).[11] We see this proliferation of naming by scholars because ethnicity is "a dazzling, ambiguous category, at once descriptive and evaluative-normative" (Lentz, 1995).[12] Scholars view ethnic diversity, in whichever form they choose to define it, as detrimental to Africa's success. When studying atrocity, for example, ethnic fractionalization is an easier sell to Global North audiences than political machinations of the state or even the effects of climate change or rising inequality. The prevailing notion among Global North scholars is that poor economic policies and underdevelopment in multiethnic societies in the Global South are unequivocally the result of ethnic heterogeneity and fractionalization. This argument centers on a perceived inability to agree on macroeconomic stabilization policies. Not enough attention is paid to the indirect mechanisms (political, religious, and social) through which ethnicity affects economic development. (Addressing this oversight is partly the aim of this book.) Naming allows scholars to imply chaos in Africa without explicitly saying so.

The effects of this tendency to name extend beyond scholarship on ethnic identity. In discourse about the war in Sudan's Darfur region, scholars have generally defined the perpetrators as coming from "Arab" communities and the victims as "Black African," "Christian," or "Animist" communities. This bifurcation persists despite the reality that the victims of the conflict's violence and the targets of its genocide were not always ethnically distinct from the militias attacking them (Mamdani, 2007; Brehm, O'Brien, & Wahutu, 2021; Wahutu, 2018). Mamdani explained the politicization of the conflict in Darfur—which originated long before rebel groups rose up against the government in Khartoum for oppressing Darfur's non-Arab population—as a grave example of ethnicity's weaponization but also of its multidimensional nature:

> One of the campaign's constant refrains has been that the ongoing genocide is racial: "Arabs" are trying to eliminate "Africans." But both "Arab" and "African" have several meanings in Sudan. There have been at least three meanings of "Arab." Locally, "Arab" was a pejorative reference to the lifestyle of the nomad as uncouth; regionally, it referred to someone whose primary language was Arabic. In this sense, a group could become "Arab" over time. This process, known as Arabisation, was not an anomaly in the region: [T]here was Amharisation in Ethiopia and Swahilisation on the East African coast. The

> third meaning of "Arab" was "privileged and exclusive"; it was the claim of the riverine political aristocracy who had ruled Sudan since independence, and who equated Arabisation with the spread of civilisation and being Arab with descent.
>
> *(Mamdani, 2007)*

Nor is the naming pitfall exclusive to academia: Some scholarship in the discipline of journalism, too, tends to conflate African journalists' use (and concept) of ethnicity as parallel to how Western journalists use (and understand) the term. By taking a naming approach to analysis, scholars and journalists alike have assumed a global convergence of media narratives about conflict in Africa. Such work ignores scholarship, such as that by Emmanuel Alozie, demonstrating how African journalists have sought to contextualize the historical roots of ethnic identity and the effect of colonization on identity in Africa. Alozie reflects on a 1994 article in Nigeria's *The Guardian* newspaper, titled "The Horror of Rwanda," to explain ethnicity like this:

> The story follows the same refrain. Ethnic nationalities lumped together, join hands together to win independence from colonial masters so that they can handle their own affairs and hold their destinies in their own hands. [. . .] As colonialists depart, the union welded together, usually by force, begins groaning over the strains of diversity.
>
> *(Alozie, 2010; The Horror of Rwanda, 1994)*[13]

In my work on African coverage of Darfur, I provide three explanations for African journalists' focus on ethnicity when covering conflicts on the continent, two of which center on the claiming of ethnicity, while one focuses on naming. I state that ethnicity was understood by both journalists and the sources they quoted as a social fact, used as a maker of affinity and othering, and used as an overarching identity within which other equally important identities were nestled (Wahutu, Representations of Africa in African Media, 2018). Here, I focus on the two explanations anchored in claiming.

From an African standpoint, the term *ethnicity* conveys a nuanced understanding of identity in Africa. It is a way to domesticate the news to audiences that understand ethnicity as a connotative rather than denotative form of identity. My conversations with newspeople across the continent saw them espousing both explanations simultaneously. These journalists' perspectives on the Darfur conflict primarily consolidate around political marginalization due to a dereliction of duty by Khartoum rather than a pitting of primarily Gemeinschaft-like communities against each other. Consider the following responses to the question of whether ethnic identity had played a role in the atrocities: One editor from Kenya said, "If you mean ethnicity as in all types of ethnicity, religious, tribal, Arab, African[,] whatever. . . [then] I would say it has played a role." As another from South Africa explained,

> [There are] other overlaying factors which accentuate the differences—you know, the religious factor, the fundamentalist kind of religious versus whatever, you know, Christian animist. I mean, I know that in Darfur those lines—the ethnic, religious lines—are not as clear as they are. . . in South Sudan and North Sudan, but still I think they are there in some form.[14]

These responses reveal that even when editors and journalists discussed some version of ethnic identity, the desire to highlight the malleability of ethnic identity—not just in Darfur but across the continent—was always there. When conceptualized this way, *ethnic identity* encapsulates the true intersectional and polyvalent nature of ethnicity as an identity category, while also "reproducing already present structures of knowledge about identity in African societies" (Wahutu, Social, Field and Regional Conditions of Knowledge, 2018).[15] This notion of malleability captures my argument that ethnicity needs to be viewed as having multiple constituent roles in society, that it needs to be viewed through a multidimensional lens. For the African journalists I interviewed—and I believe that their views are representative of African journalists as a whole—ethnicity is not the same everywhere, nor is there one way to define it. Much like Tade Okediji contends that accurate and robust measures of ethnic diversity and fragmentation must recognize the overlapping characteristics of ethnicity (including ethnolinguistic, racial, religious, and other cultural factors) (Okediji, 2005), for journalists and editors, ethnicity constitutes a matrix of identities from which actors can tap into one facet or another depending on political expediency and cultural reorganization, such as through marriage. They view ethnicity through a constructionist lens, noting that boundaries are devised through which the espousal of a particular ethnic identity allows individuals to pass through.

These journalists—and Africans generally—discuss ethnicity as a marker of what Francis Nyamnjoh maintains is the reality of Africans who find themselves straddling multiple "forms of identity and belonging, and who are willing or are forced to be both 'citizens' and 'subjects,'" depending on which strand of their identity they accentuate (Nyamnjoh, 2005).[16] This straddling, he explains, has strategic political, economic, and cultural purposes. In this calculus, Nyamnjoh urges us to acknowledge that in actuality, Africans are active agents in deciding which strand of their identity to accentuate at any given time or for any given reason, and that they do "not accept sacrificing" any strand permanently. Sometimes they are more civic than ethnic citizens, and sometimes the reverse, but I do not think this adaptability is reducible. Yet, as David William Cohen and Atieno Odhiambo argue, the vast majority of scholars who include ethnicity in their analyses continue to struggle with how to analyze the "joint, concurrent construction of layered ethnic and 'state-national' cultures, both of which [. . .] to a large extent construct each other in their deliberate contrasts" (Cohen & Odhiambo, 1992).[17]

Polydimensionality, African Ethnicity, and Conflict

One of the lasting legacies of the colonial experience in Africa was the colonialist logic that because every European belonged to some sort of nation, every African had to belong to a tribe (Iliffe, 1979; Lynch, 2018). A lasting effect of this sophism is epitomized in how early scholars of the continent took this European logic as self-evident in their work. Even when nuanced, as in Wallerstein's case, there was still the sense that the category of the tribe was unimpeachable and had to be reified. A consequence of Wallenstein's approach is that being ethnic was conflated with being urbanized, modern, and potentially capitalist. In a perverse sense, being ethnic meant that Africans had imbibed the message of civilization, but only to the extent that it allowed them to move away from their primordial state into something more recognizable. Of course, the problem here is that most Africans still lived in rural areas, and as such (in the colonialist worldview), most of Africa was still "tribal," stuck in a "pre-modern" state. The notion of tribe thus ensured that colonialists viewed large swaths of the continent as in need of civilization and modernization—which was a convenient (if specious) rationale for the African colonial project writ large. Examinations by scholars such as Wallerstein (that is to say, Western scholars) need to be understood as being part of colonialism's "ruling material force" that sought to provide colonial fantasies a patina of intellectual legitimacy (Wallerstein, 1960, 1979; Mafeje, 1971).

Six-plus decades after the independence wave, we are in a moment that asks us to focus not just on the origins but also on the multiple crosscutting particularities of ethnic identities. Borrowing from Okediji, I argue that scholars need to recognize that ethnic identities have a nesting quality: Within each group are "subsidiary identifications that also form distinct identities on cultural *and* linguistic terms." Consequently, there has to be an appreciation of the fact that sources of ethnic differentiation "may act independently of each other and, at times, in cooperation with each other" (Okediji, 2005).[18] From this vantage point, ethnic identity is polydimensional and thus more open and fungible in ways that many scholars fail to recognize. This multifariousness in and of itself is not a new concept. Indeed, Ronald Cohen and John Middleton argued in 1970 that the absorption of groups into larger groups and the "process by which groups merge, amalgamate, and develop into new collectivities with new and/or emerging identities" is as old as "man himself" (Cohen & Middleton, 1970).[19]

Viewing ethnicity in this way—as a multifaceted, fluid identity construct rather than a flat, immutable monolith—forces us to reckon with the reality that ethnic identity operates within regimes that "have a close communication with culture, knowledge, history" (Barthes, 1977). That reckoning necessitates an appreciation that ethnic identity in Africa is intersectional and, at times, may result in interlocking systems of marginalization (Collins, 1990; Crenshaw, 1989). It is an identity constructed by groups of people through social processes as a response to and through a process of struggle (Anderson, 1983; Lynch, 2018). Instead of transposing a simplistic, Global North understanding of race onto African identities, this approach problematizes the practice of presenting ethnic groups and ethnic identity in Africa as unidimensional and static, thereby yielding a more apt and refined understanding of the true nature of ethnicity in Africa. An intersectional approach takes seriously this polyvalence and allows for nuances akin to those seen in Abner Cohen's study of Hausa immigrants in Ibadan, Nigeria (Cohen, 1969); Enid Schildkrout's work on Mossi immigrants in Kumasi, Ghana (Schildkrout, 1978); John David Yeadon Peel's exposition of the Ijesha's relationship to the larger Yoruba identity (Peel, 1989, 1983); David Cohen and Atieno Odhiambo's examination of the Luo in Kenya (Cohen & Odhiambo, 1989, 1992); and Gabrielle Lynch's exploration of the Sengwer-Pokot in Kenya (Lynch, 2006). A more recent example of the utility of polyvalence in identity is Miray Philips's work on religion and cultural trauma theory (Philips, 2023).

Polydimensionalizing African ethnicity studies challenges the tendency in the literature to consider amalgamated groups' marginalization without differentiating the multiple subgroups within the larger whole. That problematic tendency effectively erases those subgroups, whose "claims cannot be understood as resulting from discrete sources of discrimination" (Crenshaw, 1989).[20] For example, a Yoruba Muslim who is Ijesha and resides outside of Ilesha can be disenfranchised due to any or multiple aspects that form part of their identity; lumping them as Yoruba fails to capture this nuance. Polydimensionality also yields a better understanding of the atrocities in Darfur, which we can think of as a conflict between communities with "homelands (*dar*) and those without." In a north-south context, Darfur was a conflict between northern, landless ("Arab") communities and southern, land-rich ("non-Arab" or "Black") communities, while in a south-south context, it was between "land-poor and land-rich" communities, both being "southern and 'Arab'" (Mamdani, 2010).[21] In addition, polydimensionality explains instances wherein the Gimmer from Darfur (a pro-government African community) was defined as an "Arabised" community by other African communities (Mamdani, 2007). Ethnicity, understood this way, exists at the level of connotation, where its "contextual reference and positioning" operate at the intersection of "coded signs" and "deep semantic codes" (Hall, 1993),[22] allowing it to be more malleable than scholars from the Global North tend to imagine.

As I have argued elsewhere, discourse on ethnic identity by Africans is often accompanied by a recognition of ethnicity as a placeholder for multiple intersecting identities and as a marker for who belongs and who does not (Wahutu, Representations of Africa in African Media, 2018; Wahutu, Social, Field and Regional Conditions of Knowledge, 2018; Wahutu, 2019). Ethnicity is shorthand for various strands of identity, and a marker for what Collins has called a "matrix of domination" (Collins, 1990). This matrix views race, class, and gender as interlocking systems of oppression and contextualizes social relations of domination as they relate to the experience of Black women. (Specifically, race, class, and gender constitute axes of oppression that characterize Black women's experience.) As such, taking an intersectional approach to studying ethnicity allows scholars to understand processes like *Kwihutura* better, or how the Giriama in Kenya, while emphasizing their group distinction, do not necessarily stop being part of the Mijikenda. This approach also nudges us toward acknowledging that ethnic identities are "simultaneously rooted in linguistic, cultural, and socioeconomic similarities, and communal experiences of marginalization, neglect, injustice, and achievement" (Lynch, 2018). Finally, as David William Cohen and Atieno Odhiambo remind us about the Luo in Kenya, a connotative understanding of ethnicity allows us to think of identity as a process of "the constitution and reconstitution" at different levels of heightened consciousness regarding its internal authenticity and "its rhetorical affirmation. . . through the resonating of custom and the valorization of culture" (Cohen & Odhiambo, 1992).[23]

Conclusion

Broadly speaking, this chapter has focused on presumptions about identity in Africa. Specifically, I argue that scholarship in the Global North fails to comprehend the polydimensional nature of ethnicity on the continent and how it operates. Furthermore, I contend that this denotative focus of naming groups and flattening complex identities in place of a connotative focus on how identities are claimed and negotiated hampers the discourse on ethnicity in Africa. The latter methodology requires scholars to apply an intersectional framework, wherein ethnicity is just one strand among many along which marginalization can occur. A sociology of knowledge approach that fully considers ethnicity *as defined by Africans*—that is, one that understands and acknowledges membership in any particular ethnic group as an act of claiming an identity—would also allow for an appreciation of ethnicity as "situational, contextual, and subjective." Viewed in this way, ethnicity is a form of identity "that acquires content and meaning through a process of conscious assertion," unlike naming, which views identity as a primordial, static, and essentialist construct imposed by external forces (Hutchinson & Smith, 1996; Schraml, 2014). The former is dynamic and contextual, whereas the latter treats ethnicity the same way that the Global North treats race—simplistically, one-dimensionally, and statically (Dubow, 1994).[24]

Crucially, these myopic presumptions have also affected policy prescriptions around underdevelopment, inequality, and conflict in post-independence Africa. For policies around conflict mitigation and resolution, this faulty premise undergirds the shortsighted tendency to model ethnic identity as either-or, which fails to impart the multitudinal ways that identity is assumed and instrumentalized in

African countries. Meanwhile, even for scholars who zero in on elite capture, the constant focus on ethnicity often misses the ubiquitous role of class in widening economic inequality. Tade Okediji and I have demonstrated that during the early years of the Moi regime in Kenya, class considerations seem to have been the president's foremost concern as he worked to cement his political position (Okediji & Wahutu, 2017).

Michael Bratton, Ravi Bhavnani, and Tse-Hsin Chen have suggested that voters across Africa tend to focus on economic interests—and specifically "government performance in macroeconomic policy management"—over ethnic allegiances (Bratton, Bhavnani, & Chen, 2011).[25] And Bratton and Mwangi Kimenyi have found evidence that, in the Kenyan electorate at least, geographical and economic mobility seem to have fostered "the abandonment" of ethnic identity as a voting priority and "the emergence of policy voting" (Bratton & Kimenyi, 2008).[26] Ghana is another country in which economic reforms and public policy, under the auspices of structural adjustment, have intensified ethnic tensions by producing geographically diverse outcomes, essentially undermining the state's ability to balance ethnic interests by centralizing economic policymaking rather than taking a decentralized/market-based approach (Oelbaum, 2004). All of this points to the conclusion that focusing on ethnic identity as an intractable problem is likely to lead to misguided policy prescriptions that do little to mitigate inequality and conflict in Africa.

Notes

1 Bruce J. Berman, "Ethnicity, Patronage and the African State: The Politics of Uncivil Nationalism," *African Affairs* 97, no. 388 (July 1998): 306.
2 Julian Go, "For a Postcolonial Sociology," *Theory and Society* 42, no. 1 (January 2013): 49.
3 See Mafeje, "Ideology of 'Tribalism,'" 254; and Karl Marx and Frederick Engels, *The German Ideology* (London, UK: Lawrence & Wishart, 1965), 61.
4 Carola Lentz, "'Tribalism' and Ethnicity in Africa: A Review of Four Decades of Anglophone Research," *Cahiers des sciences humaines* 31, no. 2 (1995): 315.
5 Lentz, "'Tribalism' and Ethnicity in Africa," 315–16.
6 Immanuel Wallerstein, "Ethnicity and National Integration in West Africa," *Cahiers d'études Africaines* 1, no. 3 (1960): 130–31.
7 Saul Dubow, "Ethnic Euphemisms and Racial Echoes," *Journal of Southern African Studies* 20, no. 3 (September 1994): 368.
8 John Sharp, "Can We Study Ethnicity? A Critique of Fields of Study in South African Anthropology," *Social Dynamics* 6, no. 1 (1980): 14.
9 Philip Hugh Gulliver, ed., *Tradition and Transition in East Africa: Studies of the Tribal Element in the Modern Era* (Berkeley: University of California Press, 1969), 24.
10 Peter L. Berger and Thomas Luckmann, *The Social Construction of Reality: A Treatise in the Sociology of Knowledge* (New York, NY: Anchor, 1966), 68.
11 Wallerstein, "Ethnicity and National Integration in West Africa," 130.
12 Lentz, "'Tribalism' and Ethnicity in Africa," 304.
13 Emmanuel C. Alozie, "Voices in the Hills of Rwanda: African Press Accountability of the 1994 Pogrom," *International Communication Gazette* 72, no. 7 (November 2010): 608; "The Horror of Rwanda," *The Guardian* (Lagos, Nigeria), May 12, 1994, 17.
14 Author interviews, cited in Wahutu, Representations of Africa in African Media, 2018.

15 Wahutu, "Social, Field and Regional Conditions of Knowledge," 193.
16 Francis B. Nyamnjoh, *Africa's Media: Democracy and the Politics of Belonging* (London, UK: Zed Books, 2005), 26.
17 David William Cohen and Eisha Stephen Atieno Odhiambo, *Burying SM: The Politics of Knowledge and the Sociology of Power in Africa* (Portsmouth, NH: Heinemann, 1992), 110.
18 Tade O. Okediji, "The Dynamics of Ethnic Fragmentation: A Proposal for an Expanded Measurement Index," *The American Journal of Economics and Sociology* 64, no. 2 (April 2005): 651–52.
19 Ronald Cohen and John Middleton, eds., *From Tribe to Nation in Africa: Studies in Incorporation Processes* (Ann Arbor: University of Michigan Press, 1970), 10.
20 Kimberlé Crenshaw, "Demarginalizing the Intersection of Race and Sex: A Black Feminist Critique of Antidiscrimination Doctrine, Feminist Theory and Antiracist Politics," *The University of Chicago Legal Forum* 1989, no. 1 (1989): 140.
21 Mahmood Mamdani, *Saviors and Survivors: Darfur, Politics, and the War on Terror* (New York, NY: Three Rivers Press, 2010), 71.
22 Stuart Hall, "Encoding, Decoding," in *The Cultural Studies Reader*, ed. Simon During (London, UK: Routledge, 1993), 512–13.
23 Cohen and Odhiambo, *Burying SM*, 92.
24 Dubow, "Ethnic Euphemisms and Racial Echoes," 368.
25 Michael Bratton, Ravi Bhavnani, and Tse-Hsin Chen, "Voting Intentions in Africa: Ethnic, Economic or Partisan?," Afrobarometer Working Paper No. 127, ed. Michael Bratton (Accra, Ghana: Afrobarometer, January 2011), 14.
26 Michael Bratton and Mwangi S. Kimenyi, "Voting in Kenya: Putting Ethnicity in Perspective," *Journal of Eastern African Studies* 2, no. 2 (2008): 287.

Bibliography

Alozie, Emmanuel C. "Voices in the Hills of Rwanda: African Press Accountability of the 1994 Pogrom." *International Communication Gazette* 72, no. 7 (November 2010): 589–617, https://doi.org/10.1177/1748048510378148.

Amodio, Francesco, and Giorgio Chiovelli. "Ethnicity and Violence During Democratic Transitions: Evidence from South Africa." *Journal of the European Economic Association* 16, no. 4 (August 2018): 1234–80, https://doi.org/10.1093/jeea/jvx034.

Anderson, Benedict. *Imagined Communities: Reflections on the Origin and Spread of Nationalism*. London, UK: Verso, 1983.

Barthes, Roland. *Elements of Semiology*. Translated by Annette Lavers and Colin Smith. New York, NY: Hill and Wang, 1977.

Berger, Peter L., and Thomas Luckmann. *The Social Construction of Reality: A Treatise in the Sociology of Knowledge*. New York, NY: Anchor, 1966.

Berman, Bruce J. "Ethnicity, Patronage and the African State: The Politics of Uncivil Nationalism." *African Affairs* 97, no. 388 (July 1998): 305–41, https://doi.org/10.1093/oxfordjournals.afraf.a007947.

Bhavnani, Ravi. "Ethnic Norms and Interethnic Violence: Accounting for Mass Participation in the Rwandan Genocide." *Journal of Peace Research* 43, no. 6 (November 2006): 651–69, https://doi.org/10.1177/0022343306069290.

Bratton, Michael, Ravi Bhavnani, and Tse-Hsin Chen. "Voting Intentions in Africa: Ethnic, Economic or Partisan?" Afrobarometer Working Paper No. 127. edited by Michael Bratton. Accra, Ghana: Afrobarometer, January 2011, https://www.afrobarometer.org/wp-content/uploads/2022/02/AfropaperNo127.pdf.

Bratton, Michael, and Mwangi S. Kimenyi. "Voting in Kenya: Putting Ethnicity in Perspective." *Journal of Eastern African Studies* 2, no. 2 (2008): 272–89, https://doi.org/10.1080/17531050802058401.

Cohen, Abner. *Custom and Politics in Urban Africa: A Study of Hausa Migrants in Yoruba Towns*. New York, NY: Routledge, 1969.

Cohen, David William, and Eisha Stephen Atieno Odhiambo. *Burying SM: The Politics of Knowledge and the Sociology of Power in Africa*. Portsmouth, NH: Heinemann, 1992.

Cohen, David William, and Eisha Stephen Atieno Odhiambo. *Siaya: The Historical Anthropology of an African Landscape*. Nairobi, Kenya: Heinemann Kenya, 1989.

Cohen, Ronald, and John Middleton, eds. *From Tribe to Nation in Africa: Studies in Incorporation Processes*. Ann Arbor: University of Michigan Press, 1970.

Collins, Patricia Hill. *Black Feminist Thought: Knowledge, Consciousness, and the Politics of Empowerment*. Boston, MA: Unwin Hyman, 1990.

Crenshaw, Kimberlé. "Demarginalizing the Intersection of Race and Sex: A Black Feminist Critique of Antidiscrimination Doctrine, Feminist Theory and Antiracist Politics." *The University of Chicago Legal Forum* 1989, no. 1 (1989): 139–67, https://scholarship.law.columbia.edu/faculty_scholarship/3007.

Crenshaw, Kimberlé. "Mapping the Margins: Intersectionality, Identity Politics, and Violence Against Women of Color." *Stanford Law Review* 43, no. 6 (July 1991): 1241–99, https://doi.org/10.2307/1229039.

Dubow, Saul. "Ethnic Euphemisms and Racial Echoes." *Journal of Southern African Studies* 20, no. 3 (September 1994): 355–70, https://doi.org/10.1080/03057079408708407.

Go, Julian. "For a Postcolonial Sociology." *Theory and Society* 42, no. 1 (January 2013): 25–55, https://doi.org/10.1007/s11186-012-9184-6.

Green, Elliott. "Ethnicity, National Identity and the State: Evidence from Sub-Saharan Africa." *British Journal of Political Science* 50, no. 2 (April 2020): 757–79, https://doi.org/10.1017/S0007123417000783.

Gulliver, Philip Hugh, ed. *Tradition and Transition in East Africa: Studies of the Tribal Element in the Modern Era*. Berkeley: University of California Press, 1969.

Hall, Stuart. "Encoding, Decoding." In *The Cultural Studies Reader*, edited by Simon During, 508–17. London, UK: Routledge, 1993.

Hegel, Georg Wilhelm Friedrich. *The Philosophy of History*. New York, NY: Dover, 1956.

"The Horror of Rwanda." *The Guardian*. Lagos, Nigeria, May 12, 1994.

Hutchinson, John, and Anthony D. Smith, eds. *Ethnicity*. Oxford, UK: Oxford University Press, 1996.

Huxley, Julian, and Alfred C. Haddon. *We Europeans: A Survey of "Racial" Problems*. 1st ed. London, UK: Jonathan Cape, 1935.

Iliffe, John. *A Modern History of Tanganyika*. Cambridge, UK: Cambridge University Press, 1979.

Kagwanja, Peter Mwangi. "Facing Mount Kenya or Facing Mecca? The *Mungiki*, Ethnic Violence and the Politics of the Moi Succession in Kenya, 1987–2002." *African Affairs* 102, no. 406 (January 2003): 25–49, https://doi.org/10.1093/oxfordjournals.afraf.a138810.

Lentz, Carola. "'Tribalism' and Ethnicity in Africa: A Review of Four Decades of Anglophone Research." *Cahiers des sciences humaines* 31, no. 2 (1995): 303–28, https://horizon.documentation.ird.fr/exl-doc/pleins_textes/pleins_textes_4/sci_hum/42875.pdf.

Lugard, Frederick. *The Dual Mandate in British Tropical Africa*. 5th ed. London, UK: Frank Cass & Co., 1965.

Lynch, Gabrielle. "Ethnicity in Africa." In *Oxford Research Encyclopedia of African History*, edited by Thomas Spear. Oxford, UK: Oxford University Press, 2018, https://doi.org/10.1093/acrefore/9780190277734.013.32.

Lynch, Gabrielle. "Negotiating Ethnicity: Identity Politics in Contemporary Kenya." *Review of African Political Economy* 33, no. 107 (March 2006): 49–65, https://doi.org/10.1080/03056240600671282.

Mafeje, Archie. "The Ideology of 'Tribalism.'" *The Journal of Modern African Studies* 9, no. 2 (August 1971): 253–61, https://doi.org/10.1017/S0022278X00024927.

Mamdani, Mahmood. "Making Sense of Non-Revolutionary Violence: Some Lessons from the Rwandan Genocide." Lecture delivered at the University of Durban, Westville, South Africa, August 8, 2001, https://ccs.ukzn.ac.za/files/Mahmood%20Mamdani's%20Frantz%20Fanon%20lecture.pdf.

Mamdani, Mahmood. "The Politics of Naming: Genocide, Civil War, Insurgency." *London Review of Books* 29, no. 5 (March 2007): 5–8, https://www.lrb.co.uk/the-paper/v29/n05/mahmood-mamdani/the-politics-of-naming-genocide-civil-war-insurgency.

Mamdani, Mahmood. *Saviors and Survivors: Darfur, Politics, and the War on Terror*. New York, NY: Three Rivers Press, 2010.

Mamdani, Mahmood. "What Is a Tribe?" *London Review of Books* 34, no. 17 (September 2012): 1–7, https://www.lrb.co.uk/the-paper/v34/n17/mahmood-mamdani/what-is-a-tribe.

Marx, Karl, and Frederick Engels. *The German Ideology*. London, UK: Lawrence & Wishart, 1965.

Ndegwa, Stephen N. "Citizenship and Ethnicity: An Examination of Two Transition Moments in Kenyan Politics." *American Political Science Review* 91, no. 3 (September 1997): 599–616, https://doi.org/10.2307/2952077.

Nyamnjoh, Francis B. *Africa's Media: Democracy and the Politics of Belonging*. London, UK: Zed Books, 2005.

Nyseth Brehm, Hollie, Michelle L. O'Brien, and j. Siguru Wahutu. "Problems with Oversimplified Categories in the Study of Collective Violence." *Sociology of Development* 7, no. 4 (Winter 2021): 394–415, https://doi.org/10.1525/sod.2020.0006.

Oelbaum, Jay. "Ethnicity Adjusted? Economic Reform, Elections, and Tribalism in Ghana's Fourth Republic." *Commonwealth and Comparative Politics* 42, no. 2 (July 2004): 242–73, https://doi.org/10.1080/1466204042000299281.

Okediji, Tade O. "The Dynamics of Ethnic Fragmentation: A Proposal for an Expanded Measurement Index." *The American Journal of Economics and Sociology* 64, no. 2 (April 2005): 637–62, https://doi.org/10.1111/j.1536-7150.2005.00382.x.

Okediji, Tade O., and j. Siguru Wahutu. "The Role of Ethnicity in Political Formation in Kenya: 1963–2007." In *Dissent, Protest and Dispute in Africa*, edited by Emmanuel Mbah and Toyin Falola, 133–51. New York, NY: Routledge, 2017.

Peel, John David Yeadon. "The Cultural Work of Yoruba Ethnogenesis." In *History and Ethnicity*, edited by Elizabeth Tonkin, Maryon McDonald, and Malcolm Chapman, 198–215. London, UK: Routledge, 1989.

Peel, John David Yeadon. *Ijeshas and Nigerians: The Incorporation of a Yoruba Kingdom, 1890s–1970s*. Cambridge, UK: Cambridge University Press, 1983.

Philips, Miray. "'We Love Martyrdom, but We Also Love Life': Coptic Cultural Trauma Between Martyrdom and Rights." *American Journal of Cultural Sociology* 11, no. 2 (June 2023): 220–47, https://doi.org/10.1057/s41290-022-00162-5.

Posner, Daniel N. "Measuring Ethnic Fractionalization in Africa." *American Journal of Political Science* 48, no. 4 (2004): 849–63, https://doi.org/10.1111/j.0092-5853.2004.00105.x.

Rennie, John Keith "The Precolonial Kingdom of Rwanda: A Reinterpretation." *Transafrican Journal of History* 2, no. 2 (1972): 11–54, https://www.jstor.org/stable/24520214.

Schildkrout, Enid. *People of the Zongo: The Transformation of Ethnic Identities in Ghana*. Cambridge, UK: Cambridge University Press, 1978.

Schraml, Carla. "How Is Ethnicity Experienced? Essentialist and Constructivist Notions of Ethnicity in Rwanda and Burundi." *Ethnicities* 14, no. 5 (2014): 615–33, https://doi.org/10.1177/1468796813519781.

Sharp, John. "Can We Study Ethnicity? A Critique of Fields of Study in South African Anthropology." *Social Dynamics* 6, no. 1 (1980): 1–16, https://doi.org/10.1080/02533958008458265.

Taylor, Charles Lewis, and Michael C. Hudson. *World Handbook of Political and Social Indicators*. 2nd ed. New Haven, CT: Yale University Press, 1972.

Wahutu, j. Siguru. "Representations of Africa in African Media: The Case of the Darfur Violence." *African Affairs* 117, no. 466 (January 2018): 44–61, https://doi.org/10.1093/afraf/adx039.

Wahutu, j Siguru. "Social, Field and Regional Conditions of Knowledge: News on Darfur in African Media." PhD diss., University of Minnesota, 2018, https://conservancy.umn.edu/server/api/core/bitstreams/6a18e9ef-48a2-4f62-afe6-5b4bbe9f3183/content.

Wahutu, j. Siguru. "'We Have Failed as a Continent': Covering an African Atrocity for an African Audience." In *Media and Mass Atrocity: The Rwanda Genocide and Beyond*, edited by Allan Thompson, 237–52. Ottawa, Canada: Centre for International Governance Innovation, 2019.

Wallerstein, Immanuel. *The Capitalist World-Economy*. Cambridge, UK: Cambridge University Press, 1979.

Wallerstein, Immanuel. "Ethnicity and National Integration in West Africa." *Cahiers d'études Africaines* 1, no. 3 (1960): 129–39, https://doi.org/10.3406/cea.1960.2951.

Wucherpfennig, Julian, et al. "Politically Relevant Ethnic Groups Across Space and Time: Introducing the GeoEPR Dataset." *Conflict Management and Peace Science* 28, no. 5 (2011): 423–37, https://doi.org/10.1177/0738894210393217.

9

SOCIOECONOMIC INEQUALITY IN SUB-SAHARAN AFRICA AND ITS LINKS TO GOVERNANCE SYSTEMS

Promise M. Hlungwani, Abbyssinia Mushunje, Simbarashe Tatsvarei, Peter Mukarumbwa, and Saul Ngarava

Introduction

It is widely accepted that inequality, poverty, and social exclusion go hand in hand in Africa and around the world. The United Nations Development Programme (UNDP) notes that although poverty and inequality are distinct concepts, they are intimately related, and the World Bank considers inequality a major factor in poverty trends. Moreover, their linkage is bidirectional: While inequality intrinsically prevents the benefits of economic growth from reaching the poor, it also serves to stymie growth and development on a national level (UNDP, 2005). Considerable contemporary policy attention has been devoted to inequality, poverty, and social exclusion in Africa, as reflected in the United Nations Sustainable Development Goals (UN, 2015). Yet, notable gaps exist in the empirical literature regarding how horizontal inequality (that is, inequality across different groups) manifests within and across countries over time.

A central question when it comes to considering Africa's long-standing development dilemma is how to address the persistent and worsening problem of inequality in terms of access to resources, opportunities, and, ultimately, development outcomes. A number of studies postulate that the majority of inequality in Africa stems from the governance systems that prevail among African countries (Crocker, 2019), which are neither uniform nor systematic. The literature has shown that different countries experience disparate challenges in implementing institutions that are equitable, responsive, accountable, and progressive. This chapter explores the extent to which governance systems—and inherent flaws found in them—can explain observed inequalities in Africa.

To understand the current state of governance in sub-Saharan Africa, one must first define the concept of governance itself. Per the World Bank, governance,

DOI: 10.4324/9781003357025-12

broadly defined, encompasses "the set of traditions and institutions by which authority in a country is exercised," including the process by which governments are chosen, monitored, and replaced; the government's capacity to effectively formulate and implement sound policies; and the respect, on the part of citizens and the state, for the institutions that govern economic and social interactions among the various members of society. The World Bank uses six broad categories, called Worldwide Governance Indicators (also referred to as global governance indicators), to measure the following dimensions of governance: *Voice and accountability* measures how freely citizens of a country participate in choosing a government to lead them, the extent of freedom of expression and association in society, and the existence and functioning of a free media. *Political stability and absence of violence* are defined as the likelihood that a government can be destabilized unconstitutionally (i.e., through violent means). *Government effectiveness* refers to the quality of public services and policy formulation and implementation, as well as the quality of the civil service—including its independence from political pressures. *Regulatory quality* gages the government's provision of sound policies and regulations that permit and promote private-sector development. *Rule of law* covers adherence to and confidence in the rules of society, particularly the quality of contract enforcement, property rights, policing, the court system, and the likelihood of crime and violence. And finally, *control of corruption* entails the extent to which public institutions and political power are exercised for private gain, including state capture by elites and private interests (World Bank, 2025). Figure 9.1 depicts the global governance indicators for sub-Saharan Africa between 2009 and 2019.

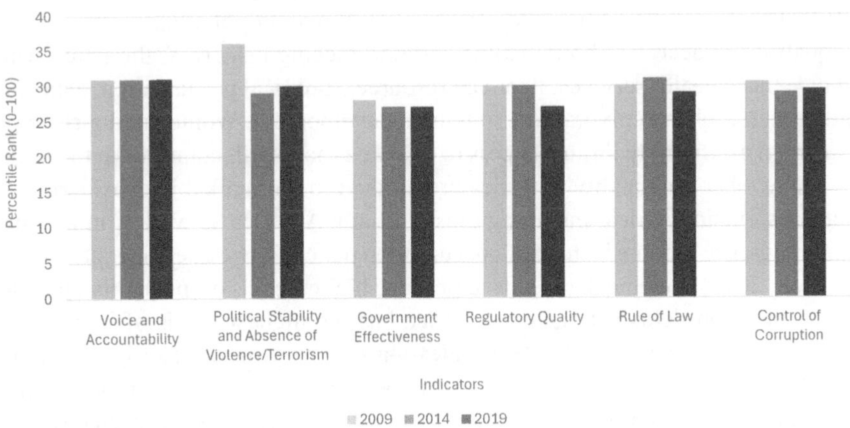

FIGURE 9.1 Global Governance Indicators for Sub-Saharan Africa, 2009–19

Source: World Bank, Worldwide Governance Indicators for 2020, https://databank.worldbank.org/source/worldwide-governance-indicators, accessed March 21, 2025.

Figure 9.1 illustrates that, collectively, sub-Saharan Africa has not fared well in any of the six indicators over the past decade, and that no single indicator shows signs of overall improvement. The subcontinent performed worst in government effectiveness, followed by regulatory quality and rule of law, while voice and accountability, political stability, and control of corruption all hovered around 30 percent—indicative of substandard governance systems (World Bank, 2020). To attempt to unpack the conditions underlying this poor performance, this chapter first looks at patterns that emerge in dimensions of inequality in sub-Saharan Africa at the national and regional levels, which are disaggregated into economic, social, and political factors that manifest through ethnicity, income, gender, age, migratory status, disability, geographic, and location. This chapter then seeks to identify the mechanisms and dynamics through which governance, institutional quality, and policy influence inequality. Finally, it recommends specific shifts in those policy dynamics and governance mechanisms to reduce inequality, improve economic growth, and foster sustainable long-term development in Africa.

Dimensions and Patterns of Inequality in Africa

The challenge of achieving consistent economic growth in sub-Saharan Africa amid widespread inequality in access to social services, decent employment, income, and wealth is a matter of grave concern. The subcontinent continues to be one of the most unequal regions in the world (Odusola et al., 2017).[1] In fact, the whole continent of Africa exhibits the second-highest level of inequality in the world; out of the ten most unequal countries globally, seven are in Africa (Beegle et al., 2016; Seery, Okanda, & Lawson, 2019). This striking inequality manifests in wealth, race, class, and ethnicity in countries across the continent (de Waal, 2015). In sub-Saharan Africa, realization of full human potential is hampered by inequalities in access to both income and non-income resources; the latter, which include basic health services, financial resources, political participation, education, and property, plays a pivotal role in human development. Women and girls in particular have extremely limited access to resources across all countries in the region.

The levels of inequality in Africa are all the more remarkable considering that countries outside Africa, including those in Latin America as well as in advanced economies, use income instead of consumption per capita to assess inequality (Beegle et al., 2016). Income data tends to produce higher levels of inequality compared to consumption data. Yet, southern Africa has the highest levels of inequality in the world, as measured by the Gini index—a summary measure of inequality that measures "the extent to which the distribution of income or consumption among individuals or households within an economy deviates from a perfectly equal distribution," per the World Bank. A Gini index of 0 represents perfect equality, while an index of 100 reflects total inequality (Odusola et al., 2017; World Bank DataBank, 2024). According to a 2017 UNDP report, ten of the world's nineteen most unequal countries are in sub-Saharan Africa. As Figure 9.2 shows, Botswana,

FIGURE 9.2 Map of Income Inequality in Africa

Source: Odusola et al. (2017).

Note: Calculations based on the World Bank's World Development Indicators as of 2016.

Central African Republic, Comoros, Lesotho, Namibia, South Africa, Swaziland (Eswatini), and Zambia all have Gini indexes above 50 (Odusola et al., 2017; Beegle et al., 2016).

Patterns of inequality in Africa have historical roots. This is particularly true in southern Africa: Racially discriminatory policies and colonial-era legacies of land dispossession during the colonial period bred high levels of inequality in countries in this region. Remarkable differences are evident between central and western Africa, whose post-independence histories are characterized by a system of communal land tenure, and eastern and southern Africa, where white settler economies characterized by large plantations, estates, and privately owned small family plots dominated (Cornia, 2017). Other interesting patterns of inequality in Africa emerge in terms of country traits: Research has shown that there are no statistical differences in inequality levels between fragile and non-fragile states,[2] landlocked and coastal nations, or resource-poor and resource-rich countries (controlling for the four subregions—namely, northern, southern, western, and eastern Africa). In fact, a 2016 UNDP working paper noted that resource-rich countries such as Nigeria, the Democratic Republic of the Congo (DRC), and South Africa have high levels of inequality (Beegle et al., 2016; Bhorat, Naidoo, & Pillay, 2016).

African countries exhibit a clear pattern in which regional income disparities, a high urban-rural divide, and unequal levels of education dominate in countries with high levels of horizontal inequality (Beegle et al., 2016). Moreover, conditions at birth are a major determinant of one's poverty status in adulthood, greatly exacerbating inequality of opportunity in Africa (World Bank, 2012). And, according to a 2019 Oxfam International briefing paper, although the continent has seen significant growth in gross domestic product since 2000, "entrenched poverty and alarmingly high and rising inequality" persist. These trends, coupled with the worsening income gap in Africa, make the challenge of achieving sustainable development in Africa in the foreseeable future that much more daunting (Seery, Okanda, & Lawson, 2019).[3]

Along with Namibia, inequality in South Africa is the highest in Africa, owing to the political and economic systems inherited from the respective colonial regimes in those countries. According to the International Monetary Fund (IMF), as of 2020, South Africa had one of the highest levels of inequality of any country in the world, with wealth concentrated in the upper levels of society: The top 20 percent of the population held more than 68 percent of the nation's income, compared with 7 percent possessed by the poorest 40 percent. Unequal access to opportunities (in terms of education, health, and jobs), along with low growth and rising unemployment, has perpetuated inequality (IMF, 2020).

Broadly speaking, inequality is anchored in colonial legacies of racial exclusion and repression, political and socioeconomic segregation, and military conquest (Gelb, 2004). In South Africa, the government's strict racial segregation system known as apartheid (1948–94) and the political, social, and economic exclusions that it engendered institutionalized deep disparities between Blacks' and whites' access to resources (income and non-income alike). Although codified systems of racial discrimination were instituted during the British colonial period between 1806 and 1910, those disparities became entrenched after the discovery of minerals in South Africa in the 1920s, when forced labor in the burgeoning national mining industry became the foundation of systematized racial discrimination. The pattern thus established for the country's racialized economic growth and development moved from secondary to tertiary sectors. The government subsequently adopted an import substitution strategy aimed at building domestic political support among urban whites at the expense of the marginalized Black population, which was relegated to the poor regions of the country that lacked the necessary infrastructural support required for growth and development. Needless to say, this strategy widened South Africa's racial inequality gap and sent unemployment among the Black population soaring due to increased capital intensity (Gelb, 2004). Even after the end of apartheid in 1994, according to a 2020 IMF report, South Africa has one of the highest levels of income inequality in the world, with a Gini index of more than

60 (IMF, Six Charts Explain South Africa's Inequality, 2020). As of 2023, Statista ranked South Africa as having the highest level of income inequality in Africa, with a Gini index of 63 (Statista, 2025).

Understanding the Governance-Inequality Conundrum

The ways in which governance influences or causes inequality across Africa are rarely the same from country to country, but they can generally be understood in terms of several broad categories: inherited colonial governance structures, democratization versus authoritarianism, levels of corruption, natural resource abundance and wealth distribution, and the ethnoregional dimension. The administrative institutions and hierarchical socioeconomic structures that colonial authorities instituted in resource-rich sub-Saharan Africa created ideal conditions for higher levels of inequality. Prior to independence, resources, income, and wealth in colonized states were concentrated among small populations of white settlers; upon independence, this same affluence shifted to a small cluster of Indigenous elites—a class that directly resulted from the *indirect rule* system, which (as earlier chapters in this volume describe) amalgamated diverse ethnic groups into politically expedient units and selectively co-opted members of certain groups to serve as proxies of colonial authority (World Bank, 2016; Siollun, 2021). Although contemporary sub-Saharan African governments recognize the existence of these inherited and reinforced inequalities, and most have made varying degrees of efforts to reduce them, such efforts are almost invariably marked by resistance from incumbent elites (Odusola et al., 2017). Elite reticence to disrupt the status quo (and its attendant advantages)—and the concomitant marginalization of non-elite ethnic, regional, political, religious, and social groups—has not only exacerbated inequalities but in some cases also resulted in unrest and even armed conflict (Harsch, 2018).

The literature on development roundly acknowledges that socioeconomic inequality is antithetical to sustainable long-term development. As the UN's *2030 Agenda for Sustainable Development* plainly put it, "Inclusive and sustainable economic growth. . . will only be possible if wealth is shared and income inequality is addressed" (UN, 2015). Yet, understanding specifically how governance affects the interplay between the inequality and underdevelopment—with a mind to realigning Africa's governance systems to address persistent and worsening income inequality continent-wide—requires taking a closer look at the dimensions of governance captured by the global governance indicators outlined in this chapter's introduction: voice and accountability, political stability and absence of violence, government effectiveness, regulatory quality, rule of law, and control of corruption.

Voice and Accountability

Accountability as a tenet of good governance demands that African countries implement reforms that will make public officials answerable to the general populace. Building effective, accountable, and inclusive institutions requires that civil society, the private sector, and government work together to establish and respect parameters such as inclusiveness and equal participation in the governance process. Yet, some critics contend that such progressive frameworks are incompatible with the challenges inherent to Africa's immense ethnic diversity. A burgeoning literature is finding that ethnic diversity (and more specifically ethnic fragmentation, as earlier chapters delve into) is a major factor in skewed equity in African countries. Augustin Kwasi Fosu has maintained that the existence of ethnically based interest groups is likely to result in suboptimal provision of public goods, which in turn promotes inter-country and inter-regional inequalities (Fosu, 2017). Paolo Mauro has concluded that ethnolinguistic fractionalization leads to a greater probability of political instability and economic underdevelopment (Mauro, 1995). William Easterly and Ross Levine have attributed Africa's poor economic performance to its high level of ethnic diversity, which they maintain works indirectly through public policies, political instability, and other economic factors (Easterly & Levine, 1997).

Ethnic conflicts in Liberia (1989–2003), Sierra Leone (1991–2002), Rwanda (1994), the DRC (1998–2003), Côte d'Ivoire (2002–7), and Kenya (2007) are clear examples of such disparities resulting in dramatic social strife. Most of those countries are categorized as having medium income inequality levels (see Figure 9.2). Many such conflicts arise because certain regions or groups lack a voice and a means to engage in income-earning activities as a result of resource diversion by the ethnic elites in power. Often, this resource diversion goes toward the purchase of weapons for the sole purpose of strengthening the military against attempts to challenge elite power and rule (La Porta et al., 1999; Easterly, 2001; Acemoglu & Robinson, 2010).

Ethnic diversity becomes problematic when people try to advance their ethnic self-interests at the expense of the other groups in their country. The best hope for alleviating the resulting income and other resource distribution inequalities—and the inevitable ethnic conflicts that they catalyze—is to foster governance and institutional quality that gives the public a voice and holds government accountable to the citizenry. Post-apartheid South Africa offers compelling evidence that achieving broader consultation, accountability, and transparency in governance helps to ameliorate civil conflicts and long-standing inequalities. Rupert Taylor has illustrated how the democratic reforms instituted by F. W. de Klerk in South Africa inaugurated a newly inclusive political era wherein Blacks and other minorities could participate in governance (Taylor, 2002). Negotiations between the country's interest groups prevented violence during the transition to independence. The new constitution advocated social justice, human rights, and the rule of law. It guaranteed freedom of association, language, and religion. It also incorporated mechanisms for power-sharing to prevent domination by any ethnic or racial group. To address the roots of persistent poverty and inequality that had plagued Black South Africans and other minorities for decades, the new democratic government created affirmative action programs and launched the Reconstruction and Development

Programme to promote business ventures for disenfranchised and marginalized groups. It also established the Truth and Reconciliation Commission to acknowledge the atrocities of the past and begin to heal the wounds and injustices of the apartheid system (Irobi, 2005).

Access to information, too—and especially the promotion of free and independent news media—is paramount to ensuring that citizens are informed about government policies, projects, and programs. The fact that most Africans remain disconnected from the internet makes it all that much more difficult for people to know what government is doing and how it affects them, their families, their communities, and their livelihoods. Mauritania and the Central African Republic, for instance, face huge challenges in terms of access to information, especially in rural areas: Poor internet access, low mobile phone penetration, and bandwidth limitations due to outdated technology make connectivity a challenge. In Uganda, for example, the internet is regulated to the extent that citizens cannot use social media platforms. Even where online networks and services are available, large numbers of people are unable to access them affordably or use them optimally to enhance their social and economic well-being; this lack of access stands in stark contrast to that in more mature economies, where levels of human development and equality are higher (Gillwald, 2017). When communities are uninformed or misinformed, lack access to and even awareness of developmental initiatives, and have no way to make their voices heard, inequalities persist.

A lack of accountability also perpetuates the kind of bad governance that reproduces social ills (Crocker, 2019). Time and again in Africa, political elites centralize power and authority by disenfranchizing their competitors (often of rival ethnic groups), whom they label as traitors, saboteurs, or enemies of progress. Evidence from Uganda, Rwanda, and Burundi's Great Lakes region indicates rampant politics of exclusion on ethnic, regional, or other solipsistic grounds to ensure that the incumbent president remains unchallenged. Another case in point is the shrinking democratic space in Zimbabwe after President Emmerson Mnangagwa assumed power in 2017. In August 2018, the regime went so far as to shoot at pro-democracy demonstrators protesting deteriorating economic and political conditions under Mnangagwa, who had won his first full term in the general election that July in an election not considered free or fair. The government never prosecuted the soldiers who perpetrated these crimes against the civilians, and in January 2019 it shut down the internet in response to such demonstrations. Zimbabwe's high court days later ordered the "immediate and full restoration" of internet access, saying that the government had no right to deny citizens internet access. However, according to Amnesty International, Zimbabwe's 2023 general election—in which Mnangagwa was reelected—was marred by internet shutdowns, citizen arrests, and voter intimidation (Banerjee, 2018; Amnesty International, 2019; Mavhinga, 2021; Associated Press/Agence France Presse/Reuters, 2019; Amnesty International UK, 2023; Gavin, 2023).

Although the 2010–11 Arab Spring pro-democracy uprisings, when excluded citizens in countries including Egypt, Libya, Morocco, and Tunisia took to the streets to demand governance reforms, arguably received more global attention, social, economic, and political exclusion have fueled conflict in sub-Saharan African countries as well, including Burkina Faso, Chad, Mali, Mauritania, and Niger, among others. A 2024 study published by the IMF found that,

> while various factors can fuel conflict,. . . discontent with state institutions among marginalized groups is a key driver of unrest in the region. Such distrust reflects perceptions that governments fail to address equity issues and inclusive growth—including the fair allocation of natural resources and human capital development.
>
> *(Afzal & Harun, 2020; Khan & Mezran, 2016; Latif & El Gamal, 2024)*

Oftentimes, when faced with such popular uprisings, those in power use national resources to reward loyalists (whether revenues from strategic natural resources or funds from government coffers), and their opponents are marginalized and denied access to basic services and public goods. This epitomic bad governance entrenches inequality by sidelining certain groups while co-opting others into the elite power and influence matrix.

Electoral violence is another tool that government elites too often turn to in order to suppress political resistance and stay in power. Known and suspected members of a ruling regime's opposition are routinely subjected to intimidation and even physical violence, especially in rural areas. Members of opposing groups and parties in the DRC, Malawi, Mozambique, and Uganda attest to high levels of intolerance, voter intimidation, persecution, and exclusion. Reports of government agents coercing people to vote for certain candidates (sometimes by force) are not at all uncommon—anecdotes that can be read as leadership having little legitimacy even among its supposed supporters. Many incumbent leaders, consumed with preserving single-party rule, enlist the army as kingmakers of sorts in suppressing or ensuring votes (Human Rights Watch, 2019; Mavhinga, 2017; UNOHCHR, 2024). And political leaders need the full support of the military to gain and maintain power: Robert Mugabe's 2017 ouster from the presidency in Zimbabwe demonstrated just how influential military support can be in determining the course of governance on the continent (Zimbabwe Democracy Institute, 2018). Such an environment, wherein political leaders need the might and full support of the military to gain and maintain power, naturally makes it acutely challenging to imbue a culture of good governance. When the people's voice is suppressed and the government's only accountability lies in the hands of a mercurial military establishment, national cohesion is subject to fracture, collective decision-making is dampened, and the elite powers that be hold immense power—all of which serves to stoke socioeconomic inequalities.

Nor do men and women share the burden of misgovernance equally. Although many African nations exhibit some degree of women's political participation, most of the data indicates that women are underrepresented in governance across the continent, despite the fact that they often constitute the majority of the population. According to the Brookings Institution, as of 2022, 24 percent of national parliamentarians and 21 percent of local government leaders in Africa were women. The continent also ranked well below the global average of 20 percent for female ministers in national cabinet positions (Nwankwor, 2022). There is, however, evidence of progress in Rwanda and South Africa, which use an electoral system based on pure proportional representation. South Africa broke new ground in its 2019 national elections, when the party lists resulted in 46 percent of parliamentary members being women (Ramakhula, 2019).

An increase in the number of women in politics and positions of power may be seen as progress, but the numbers are only half the battle: Culture and religion both affect women's ability to participate in politics and governance, in sub-Saharan Africa especially. It is common practice that women in Muslim-dominated countries are excluded from the public space; women's rights to property and access to income and any form of political participation are severely limited in Nigeria and much of North Africa's Muslim societies (Siapno, 2002). The influence of religion on governance practices qualifies the axiom that religion is the opium of the people, inasmuch as those in positions of political leadership can use religion as a means to subjugate women and influence public policy decisions. Deeply engrained beliefs promulgated by patriarchal religious and cultural institutions dramatically curtail women's political participation by virtue of their inherent emphasis on male supremacy in social and economic affairs (Ramakhula, 2019). Such proscriptions not only cement gender inequalities but also inculcate women's invisibility in political engagement and representation. More broadly, religion can be employed to mobilize groups (adherents) in a manner that can be pernicious to the interests of society.

Political Stability and the Absence of Violence

According to Augustin Fosu, political governance is measured by electoral competitiveness, constraint on the government executive, and the inclusiveness of the polity (Fosu, 2017), but the importance of political stability cannot be discounted: Governance that is disrupted by coups d'état and civil wars can hardly thrive. The prevailing hypothesis on the link between political stability and inequality is that a more democratic distribution of political rights is associated with more equal income distribution (Cornia, 2017; Gradstein, Milanovic, & Ying, 2001; Posner, 1997). And, over the last twenty years, Africa has transitioned toward more democratic leadership: According to the UNDP, only four democratic nations existed in Africa in 1990, and that number had increased to twenty by 2019 (Cornia, 2017). However, these ostensibly democratic governments often end up being little more than a smokescreen for one-party, elite-driven, quasi- (or full) authoritarian regimes. In other words, through processes of elite capture, governments that arise out of electoral processes turn out not to be accountable as representative governments (Ndulu & O'Connell, 1999; Canen & Wantchekon, 2022; Hassan, 2022).

Unfortunately, few studies have been done with respect to Africa specifically that point to the nature of the relationship between constitutional democracy and inequality; most such studies were carried out in Asia. According to Frances Stewart, there is no evidence that the general shift toward democratic governance in Africa since the mid-1990s has measurably diminished inequality (Cornia, 2017).[4] Yet, David Brady, Agnes Blome, and Hanna Kleider have argued that, in Eastern Europe and Asia, income distribution is egalitarian despite these two regions' restrictive political rights. They contend that other factors, such as ideology, must be considered when examining the relationship between inequality and democracy (Brady, Blome, & Kleider, 2017). For example, whereas strong democracies in Christian societies tend to result in reduced inequality, the same is not always true in Communist, Confucian, Buddhist, or Hindu societies, whose ideologies are all based on promoting equality in societies (for reasons that are beyond the scope of this chapter) (Gelb, 2004).

Although some critics believe that economic growth is not directly correlated to democracy, stronger and more inclusive political institutions are generally believed to improve economic outcomes at both the macro and micro levels in Africa (as elsewhere). Fisayo Fagbemi and Adeyemi Fajingbesi have argued that citizens who are poor and economically disenfranchised often resort to conflict as a means to express their frustration over inequality, poverty, unemployment, deprivation, and injustices. Thus, they maintain, good governance and political stability go a long way toward promoting the sense of stability and inclusiveness that sustainable development requires (Fagbemi & Fajingbesi, 2022). At a March 2023 meeting of the UN Security Council, Cristina Duarte, the special adviser on Africa to the secretary general, highlighted the success of Mozambique's 2019 Maputo Accord at promoting peace and security by fostering inclusion and reconciliation—which, Duarte noted, is also an effective way to promote income distribution. After years of inequality and political strife, the accord signaled a shift by the government of Mozambique to focus on national ownership, building trust in society and ensuring a human-centered process. At the same meeting, the Ghanaian representative emphasized the need for "development policies that support African efforts to address the root causes of conflict, including the socioeconomic inequalities that have destabilized [many] countries." The underlying message is that promoting inclusive development as a mechanism to alleviate conflict is the way forward for Africa (UN, 2023).

Government Effectiveness

Derek Luyt has observed that Africa has historically lagged behind the rest of the world in forming strong institutions (Luyt, 2008). Patrimonialist states in which the ruler has absolute power and there is no distinction between the private and public domains are still rife in Africa, and the UNDP's 2017 report found that this trend was actually increasing among sub-Saharan African states (Harsch, 2018; Odusola et al., 2017; Cammack, 2007; Bøås, 2001). Patrimonialist systems were embedded in pre-colonial/Indigenous cultural systems of governance, and the colonial powers exploited them to institute hierarchical ruling structures in the form of indirect rule. The end result was countries that were all but ungovernable and extremely vulnerable to ethnic conflicts in the post-independence period.

Regional distribution of resources and opportunities for economic growth, along with economic structure, are important factors in accounting for income disparities in a given country's economy. A 2017 study by Abebe Shimeles and Tiguene Nabassaga found that government failure to address inequality resulting from differential opportunity (whether due to gender, ethnicity, region, or other factors) can result in social tensions and, ultimately, conflict. That study also found statistically significant differences in access to education between majority ethnic group (i.e., politically dominant) areas and minority ethnic group areas—with the former, unsurprisingly, having increased access to educational opportunities (Shimeles & Nabassaga, 2017). Evidence from Kenya supports this observation: In provinces where the elites come from, access to and quality of higher education tend to be better (Murunga & Nasong'o, 2006; D'Arcy & Cornell, 2016). In Nigeria too, national politics is all about ethnic empowerment, clientelism, and resource redistribution (Adegbami & Uche, 2015). (Earlier chapters in this volume cover these issues in Kenya and Nigeria in some detail.)

In most instances, conflicts arise when ethnic groups seek to dominate one another, especially in terms of access to and control over certain strategic resources (such as land, water, or minerals) (Nygård et al., 2017). Before colonial rule, there were Indigenous systems in place to mitigate conflict over natural resources. However, the institution of indirect rule created a hegemonic structure among extrinsically manufactured amalgamations of ethnic groups that has persisted through independence. This context makes it all the more imperative for national governments to effectively manage and equitably allocate natural resources to ensure access for all groups in society; inequitable access signals governmental ineffectiveness.

To be sure, different ethnic groups challenging each other for access to land, water, and other natural resources is a story as old as time, and certainly not one unique to the African continent. That being said, many such conflicts between herders and farmers persist today in countries such as Kenya, Nigeria, and South Sudan. Ethnic tensions and severe socioeconomic inequality almost invariably underly such conflicts. In Nigeria, for example, nomadic Fulani herders from the north (a region that suffers from dramatic economic disparities compared to the country's south) have engaged in fierce communal clashes with sedentary farmers of other Indigenous ethnic groups, many of whom are also Christians. (See Chapter 10 for a detailed discussion of those conflicts.) (Hillesund, 2019). Similar conflicts have arisen in Chad between predominantly Muslim Arab herders and Black African farmers (Campbell, 2019). In some extreme cases, marginalized or oppressed groups have attempted secession, seeking independence and autonomous self-governance. Such scenarios have been met with varied success: South Sudan successfully separated from Sudan in 2011, albeit after a decades-long and bloody civil war that claimed the lives of more than two million Sudanese; Nigeria's Biafra region unsuccessfully attempted to secede in 1967, spurring a short (two and a half years) but devastating civil war during which at least one million Nigerians perished. The two conflicts both stemmed from strikingly north-south ethnoregional divides. Regardless of the political outcomes, however, the consequences of such conflicts include tragic loss of human life along with destruction of infrastructure, human capital, and institutions. Political instability and economic uncertainty wrought by such conflicts in turn impede investment and economic growth—not just during the fighting but also afterward, making it difficult for a country to escape what the IMF labels the "conflict trap" (IMF, 2019).

Weak governance structures are seen as the cause as well as the consequence of ethnic and regional cleavages. According to the greed and grievance theory advanced by Paul Collier and Anke Hoeffler, ethnic and religious hatreds are widely perceived as a cause of civil conflict, which implies that diversity is a fertile ground for the existence and escalation of inequality-based grievances and conflicts. While they acknowledge that inter-group conflicts are more prevalent in fractionalized communities than in homogenous societies, Collier and Hoeffler argue that the source of inter-group tension is not diversity per se, but polarization. It is in this context that governance plays a critical role in shaping the political outcomes of rebellion and civil conflict, because polarization is necessarily an outcome of governance. Reminiscent of Amartya Sen's pivotal 1973 text *On Economic Inequality*, Collier and Hoeffler contend that poor regions or groups may rebel to induce redistribution, and rich regions or groups may mount secessionist rebellions to preempt redistribution (Collier & Hoeffler, 2004).[5] Nevertheless, both aspects of rebellion reflect the need to strengthen government institutions to reduce levels of inequality and to ensure that all citizens enjoy similar benefits.

Regulatory Quality

Regulatory quality assesses whether a government provides sound policies and regulations that permit and promote private-sector development. According to Kwabena Gyimah-Brempong, regulatory deficiencies can promote tax exemptions and defective tax administration, in the process eroding the tax base and undermining income redistribution possibilities from the rich to the poor. Reduced tax revenues resulting from defective tax regimes can also lead to diminished human capital investment as a result of reduced funding. Reduced funding lowers human capital development for the poor, but the elites can fund development through non-public resources, which in turn perpetuates inequality. This distortion can lead to the siphoning of public resources by the well-connected, which then hampers efficient provision of social programs for those in need (Gyimah-Brempong, 2002). However, Juzhong Zhuang, Emmanuel de Dios, and Anneli Lagman-Martin have argued that interventions to ameliorate these challenges are merely theoretical, with no empirical evidence to support their efficacy. For example, the presence of effective tax regimes might only improve growth prospects and not necessarily reduce inequality (Zhuang, de Dios, & Lagman-Martin, 2010). Moreover, no sub-Saharan African governments have as yet implemented meaningful policies or regulations to permit and promote private-sector development.[6]

The boom in commodity prices between 2010 and 2018—which has not translated to better quality of life in Africa—has put into perspective the capacity of governments to provide sound policies to improve societal income inequalities. This disconnect is particularly evident in Angola, Nigeria, and South Africa, where economic growth has failed to transform levels of inequality (Tsikata, 2015). While revenues were high, institutional and governance failures have dampened hopes for an equal growth distribution path. A key component of these failures has been a dearth of controls to curb revenue outflows and manage available resources to increase access to education and health care. High levels of income growth and the disproportionately allocated societal benefits associated with them enrich the very few elites and therefore perpetuate existing income gaps. This inequity causes widespread failure to meet development targets, affecting even middle-income countries such as South Africa.

A 2013 UNDP study conducted from 1970 to 1995 illustrated that African states that tend to be more authoritarian and suffer from poor governance were the ones with higher levels of resource dependence (UNDP, Humanity Divided, 2013). Evidence also suggests that after an initial wave of democratization on the continent during the 1960s and 1970s, the discovery of natural resources in many of those countries (including Nigeria, Democratic Republic of Congo, Angola, and Equatorial Guinea) has reversed their courses back toward authoritarianism. The 2017 UNDP study on sub-Saharan Africa showed that out of fifty-five countries, resource-dependent nations have very low performance scores on political pluralism, functional governance, and electoral processes—all of which serve to perpetuate income inequality (Odusola et al., 2017).

According to the 2017 UNDP report, though a linear relationship could not be established between political rights and resource dependence, evidence suggests that governments with high resource dependence tend to be less effective and less transparent and have lower levels of civil society participation (Odusola et al., 2017; Cornia, 2017). However, robust empirical work is lacking, and the resource-causality link remains poorly understood. One paradigm suggests that natural resource discoveries lead to weak institutions as politicians fall into rent-seeking behavior, regardless of the initial strength of the institutions. A rise in corruption after the discovery of oil in Uganda's Rift Valley offers a prime example, as does the discovery of natural gas in Tanzania, where a strong separatist debate between Zanzibar and mainland Tanzania emerged at the time due to perceived inequitable distribution of gas revenues (Odusola et al., 2017; Brophy & Wandera, 2018; Neureiter, 2012). The discovery of natural resources and subsequent resource abundance pose a bigger challenge in countries where institutions were already weak prior to the discovery. However, in countries whose institutions were already strong in terms of transparency and accountability, the discovery of natural resources tends to foster efforts to maximize resource-driven growth, thereby enhancing institutions. In Ghana, for example, the discovery of offshore oil in 2007 has been a major growth driver, and the country's socioeconomic indicators—which were already reasonably strong—have continued to perform well.

Even for those countries that have fared well on the democratic front, institutional weaknesses have the potential to diminish resource-driven growth, hamper socioeconomic progress, and forestall any inequality diminution. Institutional weaknesses include rampant corruption in government, lack of property rights, ineffective rule of law, and poor governance that fails to diversify the economy and promote growth-enhancing policies to alleviate poverty and inequality, such as investment in public infrastructure like schools, hospitals, roads, and public works. Good governance must promote accountability and transparency mechanisms for political leaders. One weakness in that area is in the licensing of natural resources contracts: Oftentimes, personnel responsible for these processes use their positions for personal gain (Odusola et al., 2017; Şit et al., 2024). For example, José Eduardo dos Santos, the former authoritarian leader of Angola, presided over a predatory regime that was notorious for corruption, human rights abuses, and political persecution. His family infamously looted the revenues from the country's rich resources, which included oil, diamonds, and gold (Dolan, 2022; Alfa, 2017).

Regulatory quality is captured in the paradigm of good governance (which, broadly, includes political stability, the rule of law, the regulation of quality services, and freedom of press). Ahmet Şit et al. show that institutions and good governance significantly affect economic growth in sub-Saharan African countries. They recommend promoting good governance that prioritizes high-quality institutions, advancing the rule of law, and improving public services and infrastructure, along with a regulatory environment that encourages investment, innovation, and entrepreneurship to create a framework for sustainable development (Şit et al., 2024). The IMF suggested in 2014 that developing countries can use progressive taxation as a redistributive tool (Ostry, Berg, & Tsangarides, 2014). State institutions could then intervene to reduce potential inequalities emerging from dependence on natural resources. Other policies that governments can adopt to reduce inequality in resource-dependent economies include flexible ownership structures for extractive industries, achievable human capital upgrading strategies, and appropriate social welfare programs. Failure to implement such policies contributes to poor governance and a lack of transparency into the fiscal policies of the state.

Rule of Law

Maintaining the rule of law—which, broadly defined, refers to the government's adherence to and the public's confidence in the social contract—is a cornerstone of political stability and economic growth. In countries that rank highly in terms of the rule of law, government policies—particularly with regard to contract enforcement, property rights, policing, and the court system—encourage both local and international investment, resulting in economic growth and higher standards of living. Conversely, countries with weak rule of law demonstrate poor governmental accountability and transparency, and hence cultivate an unattractive investment climate and, ultimately, poor economic growth. This positive correlation between rule of law and economic growth and development is widely affirmed in the literature (Xu, 2011).

Unfortunately, as scholars like Charles Manga Fombad have attested, Africa suffers from a rule of law crisis. The last two decades in particular have witnessed a steady weakening in the rule of law in most African countries (Fombad, 2018). Despite some promising gains in the early 1990s, a number of sub-Saharan African countries—including Burundi, the Central African Republic, Chad, the DRC, Somalia, and South Sudan—have been embroiled in ongoing turmoil stemming from weak rule of law since the 2010s. Fombad and others have also argued that crises around the rule of law are at the epicenter of many of Africa's current developmental dilemmas—namely, economic decline, high levels of inequality, political instability, unemployment, poverty, and endemic corruption (Fombad, 2018). According to a 2016 report by the World Justice Project (WJP), the status of the rule of law in Africa is deteriorating at an alarming rate. The WJP's Rule of Law Index ranks nations around the world based on eight factors: constraints on government powers, absence of corruption, open government, fundamental rights, order and security, regulatory enforcement, civil justice, and criminal justice. The 2016 index ranked South Africa 43rd globally (a drop of seven positions from 2015); the country dropped even further to 52nd in 2021; Ghana, which ranked 44th in 2016 (a drop of ten positions from the previous year), dropped to 58th in 2021; and Botswana dropped fourteen points to rank 55th in 2016 (although it did improve slightly to rank 51st in 2021). Several other sub-Saharan African countries performed far worse, showing dramatic declines in adherence to the rule of law: Zimbabwe, at 108th in 2016 (a drop of eight positions from 2015), fell to 127th in 2021; and Cameroon, ranked 109th in 2016 (a drop of twelve positions from 2015), fell to 135th in 2021 (World Justice Project, 2016, 2021).

Africa's acute rule of law crisis has remained a major development challenge, derailing the continent's progress. Weak rule of law begets an unattractive investment environment, exacerbating already substantial socioeconomic inequalities and depressing opportunities for sustainable economic growth. Numerous studies have consistently and definitively linked higher levels of socioeconomic inequality with weak rule of law. Poor rule of law creates a class of individuals who are materially disadvantaged and whose rights tend either to be violated or ignored. These marginalized groups exhibit poor political participation and less robust integration into the legal framework and the social and economic life of a country. Weak rule of law is also demonstrably associated with high levels of corruption, creating fertile ground for criminal networks and fragile states—a major problem in the East African bloc in particular. Criminal networks plunder natural resources and engage in trafficking, drugs, and firearms throughout the region, malefactions that not only threaten human security but also breed socioeconomic inequality both in the region and beyond. The literature is awash with evidence on how poor rule of law has reduced social cohesion in many African countries and too often triggered violent conflict, which in turn perpetuates existing socioeconomic inequalities. Significant inequalities resulting from fragile state institutions, weak regulatory frameworks, feeble criminal justice systems, and inadequate border control policies are also consequences of poor rule of law (Barro, 2000; Brinks, 2008; UNDP, 2013; Waldorf, 2019).

Control of Corruption

Two perspectives exist on the relationship between corruption and inequality. One is that corruption preserves or widens existing inequalities (Johnston, 1989; You & Khagram, 2005). The other is that corruption and inequality have an inverted, U-shaped relationship, implying that both low and high levels of corruption correspond to low inequality, whereas intermediate levels of corruption cause high inequality (Chong & Calderón, 2000; Fakir et al., 2017; Li, Xu, & Zou, 2000; Bulut & Çavuşoğlu, 2023). In Africa, there is ample evidence that corruption has negatively impacted the distribution of resources. Elites in the bureaucracy often abuse their positions by manipulating resources to build personal wealth and networks of power at the expense of the citizenry. In Zimbabwe, for instance, public hospitals (among other institutions) frequently lack basic equipment and provisions while individuals in government are implicated in grand corruption schemes. One such example is the Drax scandal, which saw the country's minister of health charged with criminal abuse of power over a US$60 million contract for personal protective equipment during the COVID-19 pandemic (Mutsaka, 2020). (He was later acquitted after the prosecutor admitted that the charges "were imprecise and badly drafted.") (Kukurigo, 2021).

Scholars contend that corruption increases income inequality through several channels. Sanjeev Gupta, Hamid Davoodi, and Rosa Alonso-Terme have argued that corruption decreases economic growth, which is more likely to decrease the income share of the poor than the rich, in the process perpetuating income inequality and poverty (Gupta, Davoodi, & Alonso-Terme, 1998). Jean Hindriks, Michael Keen, and Abhinay Muthoo have demonstrated that corruption leads to a tax system biased in favor of the rich and powerful, thus rendering the tax system regressive—which implies that the poor bear a disproportionate share of the tax burden (Hindriks, Keen, & Muthoo, 1999). This situation occurred in Ghana (as was discovered after the 1981 coup d'état by Jerry Rawlings), South Africa (during the Jacob Zuma administration from 2009 to 2018), and in Zimbabwe, where Emmerson Mnangagwa's government implicated predecessor Robert Mugabe in shoddy dealings that saw ministers accumulating vast amounts of properties and land (World Bank, 2016). According to Zhuang, de Dios, and Lagman-Martin, corruption's effect on inequality manifests through imperfections in the capital market by way of asset distribution and expenditure by the state (Zhuang, de Dios, & Lagman-Martin, 2010). The World Bank concluded in 2016 that lower corruption levels are statistically associated with lower inequality levels, and that inequality is exacerbated when the poor suffer through regressive taxes, lower economic growth, ineffective social spending, and unequal distribution of assets (World Bank, 2016).

Conclusion

According to the World Bank, more than half of the world's population expresses distrust in government institutions. People's trust in public institutions continues to erode, and "there is an urgency for renewing the current social contract in countries around the world."[7] Perhaps nowhere is this discontent more evident than in Africa. As this chapter demonstrates—as do years of dismal global governance indicator rankings—sub-Saharan Africa in particular performs quite poorly in terms of adherence to the norms and tenets of good governance.

Income inequalities are varied across Africa as a whole. They are most prevalent and pronounced in southern Africa, explained in part by South Africa's legacy of apartheid; inequality is medium to low in East and Central Africa, and relatively lower in North and West Africa. Numerous scholars have found that historical factors, including lackluster institutional development and complex post-colonial political economies, account for high income inequality in Africa (Cornia, 2019; Heldring & Robinson, 2018). Additionally, Lucas Chancel et al. show that settler colonization—which resulted in high land and capital accumulation and concentration among whites, along with colonial and apartheid policies that restricted access to education and economic opportunities—also explains southern Africa's high levels of income inequality (Chancel et al., 2023). These results support an earlier finding by Facundo Alvaredo, Denis Cogneau, and Thomas Piketty that high levels of income inequality are common among countries that experienced European settler colonization, wherein European settlers controlled large swaths of land and capital and the Indigenous people were excluded from access to education (human capital) and employment opportunities (Alvaredo, Cogneau, & Piketty, 2021). Chancel et al. also suggest that religion accounts for differences in inequality across countries in Africa—and specifically that the spread of Islam may account for lower levels of inequality in West African and northeastern regions of sub-Saharan Africa and North Africa (Chancel et al., 2023).

In general, poor governance perpetuates income inequality. But as this chapter highlighted, factors like political instability and corruption—both outcomes of poor governance—further intensify inequality. When citizens are not active and voluntary participants in choosing their governments have limited access to information, and lack freedom of expression, inequality perdures. Ethnic diversity (i.e., fragmentation) and women's exclusion from decision-making and lack of equitable access to resources all exacerbate broader socioeconomic inequality as well.

Good governance plays an essential role in reducing inequalities. The provision of most government services is fraught with political influence, pressure, and rent-seeking in both public- and private-sector policies such that any redistributive efforts are alternately minimal or minimized, ultimately having the opposite effect of amplifying existing inequalities. This dynamic takes on an ethnic dimension in sub-Saharan Africa, and it becomes especially pronounced in resource-rich nations. Further compounding the problem, rampant corruption in sub-Saharan African countries unequivocally increases inequality, which in turn sustains corruption. Corruption also often manifests in regressive tax regimes and tax evasion, lower social spending, disincentivized investment in human capital, unequal resource distribution, and siphoning of poverty alleviation funds—all of which strengthen the mechanisms through which inequality prevails.

Notwithstanding any given nation's specific circumstances or history, strong evidence indicates that shifting policy directives to focus on reducing inequalities is central to ameliorating Africa's lackluster economic growth and cultivating long-term, sustainable development across the continent. Policies likely to improve the inequality quandary include ensuring transparency in availing economic opportunities, ensuring women's access to land, setting minimum wages and equalizing workers' pay, encouraging labor-intensive industries, plugging loopholes in tax evasion by the rich, and fostering social protection programs (Şit et al., 2024; Seery, Okanda, & Lawson, 2019; Leibbrandt & Shipp, 2019). The African Development Bank has also suggested that government policies and donor interventions that promote a strong middle class will go a long way toward lowering both income inequalities and poverty levels (ADB, 2024). At the end of the day, the international development community can ill afford to neglect the impact of inequality on Africa's economic future. In the words of former UN Undersecretary-General for Economic and Social Affairs José Antonio Ocampo, "Ignoring inequality in the pursuit of development is perilous" (Harsch, 2006).

Notes

1 Ayodele Odusola et al., eds. *Income Inequality Trends in Sub-Saharan Africa: Divergence, Determinants and Consequences* (New York, NY: United Nations Development Programme, 2017), iii, 2.

2 Although definitions vary slightly, state fragility is generally assessed based on "the combination of exposure to risk and insufficient coping capacities of the state, system and/or communities to manage, absorb or mitigate those risks" (OECD, 2025).

3 Emma Seery, Joab Okanda, and Max Lawson. "A Tale of Two Continents: Fighting Inequality in Africa," Oxfam Briefing Paper. Oxford, UK: Oxfam International, September 2019, 2, 3.

4 Giovanni Andrea Cornia, "Income Inequality Levels, Trends and Determinants in Sub-Saharan Africa: An Overview of the Main Changes Since the Early 1990s," in *Income Inequality Trends in Sub-Saharan Africa: Divergence, Determinants and*

Consequences, ed. Ayodele Odusola, Giovanni Andrea Cornia, Haroon Bhorat, and Pedro Conceição et al. (New York, NY: United Nations Development Programme, 2017), 40, citing Frances Stewart, "Justice, Horizontal Inequality, and Policy in Multi-Ethnic Societies," in *Towards Human Development: New Approaches to Macroeconomics and Inequality*, ed. Giovanni Andrea Cornia and Frances Stewart (Oxford, UK: Oxford University Press, 2014), 122–147.

5 Paul Collier and Anke Hoeffler, "Greed and Grievance in Civil War," *Oxford Economic Papers* 56, no. 4 (October 2004): 571.

6 That being said, the World Bank's annual Country Policy and Institutional Assessment for 2024 suggests two notable trends that are expected to stimulate private sector development: digitization, inasmuch as the expansion of information technology will allow structural improvements across economic activities, increasing employment opportunities and output growth per worker; and the opportunities that the African Continental Free Trade Area will create, including foreign direct investment inflows, technology transfers, economic diversification, and improved productivity (World Bank, 2024).

7 World Bank, "Governance at a Glance," accessed April 15, 2024, https://www.worldbank.org/en/topic/governance; World Bank, "Governance: Overview," accessed April 15, 2024, https://www.worldbank.org/en/topic/governance/overview.

Bibliography

Acemoglu, Daron, and James A. Robinson. "Why Is Africa Poor?" *Economic History of Developing Regions* 25, no. 1 (June 2010): 21–50, https://doi.org/10.1080/20780389.2010.505010.

Adegbami, Adeleke, and Charles I. N. Uche. "Ethnicity and Politics: An Impediment to Political Development in Nigeria." *Public Administration Research* 4, no. 1 (2015): 59–67, https://doi.org/10.5539/par.v4n1p59.

African Development Bank (ADB), "Income Inequality in Africa," accessed April 16, 2024, https://www.afdb.org/fileadmin/uploads/afdb/Documents/Generic-Documents/Revised-Income%20inequality%20in%20Africa_LTS-rev.pdf.

Afzal, Naeem, and Minah Harun. "News Framing of the Arab Spring Conflict from the Lens of Newspaper Editorials." *International Journal of English Linguistics* 10, no. 1 (2020). 352–63, https://doi.org/10.5539/ijel.v10n1p352.

Alfa, Shaban Abdur Rahman. "Profile: Angola's Eduardo dos Santos—Guerilla Fighter to Democratic President." *AfricaNews* (Lyon, France), September 26, 2017, https://www.africanews.com/2017/09/26/profile-angolas-eduardo-dos-santos-guerilla-fighter-to-democratic-president.

Alvaredo, Facundo, Denis Cogneau, and Thomas Piketty. "Income Inequality Under Colonial Rule: Evidence from French Algeria, Cameroon, Tunisia, and Vietnam and Comparisons with the British Colonies 1920–1960." *Journal of Development Economics* 152 (September 2021), Article no. 102680. https://doi.org/10.1016/j.jdeveco.2021.102680.

Amnesty International. "Zimbabwe: One Year On, No Justice for Those Killed by Soldiers in Post-Election Demonstrations." *News Release*, August 1, 2019, https://www.amnesty.org/en/latest/press-release/2019/08/zimbabwe-one-year-on-no-justice-for-those-killed-by-soldiers-in-post-election-demonstrations.

Amnesty International UK. "Zimbabwe: Elections Marred by Voter Intimidation, Arrests and Internet Shutdowns." *News Release*, August 24, 2023, https://www.amnesty.org.uk/press-releases/zimbabwe-elections-marred-voter-intimidation-arrests-and-internet-shutdowns.

Associated Press/Agence France Presse/Reuters. "Zimbabwe Court Orders Government to Restore Internet Access." *Deutsche Welle*, January 21, 2019, https://www.dw.com/en/zimbabwe-high-court-orders-government-to-restore-internet-access/a-47170880.

Banerjee, Vasabjit. "Even After Mugabe, Zimbabwe's Elections Do Not Appear Free or Fair." *The Washington Post*, August 22, 2018, https://www.washingtonpost.com/news/monkey-cage/wp/2018/08/23/post-mugabe-zimbabwes-elections-still-look-irregular-much-as-rhodesias-once-did.

Barro, Robert J. "Rule of Law, Democracy and Economic Performance." In *Index of Economic Freedom 2000*, edited by Gerald P. O'Driscoll, Kim R. Holmes, and Melanie Kirkpatrick, 31–51. Washington, DC: Heritage Foundation and Dow Jones & Company, 2000.

Beegle, Kathleen, et al. *Poverty in a Rising Africa*. Washington, DC: World Bank Group, 2016, https://hdl.handle.net/10986/22575.

Bhorat, Haroon, Karmen Naidoo, and Kavisha Pillay. "Growth, Poverty and Inequality Interactions in Africa: An Overview of Key Issues." UNDP Regional Bureau for Africa Working Paper Series, Vol. 1, no. 1. New York, NY: United Nations Development Programme, July 2016, https://www.undp.org/africa/publications/growth-poverty-and-inequality-interactions-africa-overview-key-issues.

Bøås, Morten. "Liberia and Sierra Leone: Dead Ringers? The Logic of Neopatrimonial Rule." *Third World Quarterly* 22, no. 5 (October 2001): 697–723, https://doi.org/10.1080/01436590120084566.

Brady, David, Agnes Blome, and Hanna Kleider. "How Politics and Institutions Shape Poverty and Inequality." In *The Oxford Handbook of the Social Science of Poverty*, Vol. 1, edited by David Brady and Linda M. Burton, 117–40. New York, NY: Oxford University Press, 2017.

Brinks, Daniel M. "Inequality, Institutions, and the Rule of Law: The Social and Institutional Bases of Rights." Kellogg Working Paper No. 351. Notre Dame, IN: Kellogg Institute for International Studies, August 2008, https://kellogg.nd.edu/sites/default/files/old_files/documents/351_0.pdf.

Brophy, Kathleen, and Peter Wandera. "Keeping Corruption in Check in Uganda's Oil Sector? Uganda's Challenge to Let Everybody Eat, and Not Just the Lucky Few." CRPD Working Paper No. 59. Leuven, Belgium: Centre for Research on Peace and Development, December 2018, https://soc.kuleuven.be/crpd/files/working-papers/crpd-no-59-brophy-wandera-full.pdf.

Bulut, Abdulkadir, and Ali Tarkan Çavuşoğlu. "Pros and Cons of Corruption to Income Inequality: An Extensive Literature Survey." *Hitit Sosyal Bilimler Dergisi* 16, no. 2 (2023): 582–600, https://doi.org/10.17218/hititsbd.1330997.

Cammack, Diana. "The Logic of African Neopatrimonialism: What Role for Donors?" *Development Policy Review* 25, no. 5 (September 2007): 599–614, https://doi.org/10.1111/j.1467-7679.2007.00387.x.

Campbell, John. "Farmer Herder Clashes in Chad Follow Familiar Pattern." *Africa in Transition* (blog), Council on Foreign Relations, May 21, 2019, https://www.cfr.org/blog/farmer-herder-clashes-chad-follow-familiar-pattern.

Canen, Nathan, and Leonard Wantchekon. "Political Distortions, State Capture, and Economic Development in Africa." *Journal of Economic Perspectives* 36, no. 1 (Winter 2022): 101–24, https://doi.org/10.1257/jep.36.1.101.

Chancel, Lucas, et al. "Income Inequality in Africa, 1990–2019: Measurement, Patterns, Determinants." *World Development* 163 (March 2023), Article no. 106162. https://doi.org/10.1016/j.worlddev.2022.106162.

Chong, Alberto, and César Calderón. "Institutional Quality and Income Distribution." *Economic Development and Cultural Change* 48, no. 4 (July 2000): 761–86, https://doi.org/10.1086/452476.
Collier, Paul, and Anke Hoeffler. "Greed and Grievance in Civil War." *Oxford Economic Papers* 56, no. 4 (October 2004): 563–95, https://doi.org/10.1093/oep/gpf064.
Cornia, Giovanni Andrea. "Income Inequality Levels, Trends and Determinants in Sub-Saharan Africa: An Overview of the Main Changes Since the Early 1990s." In *Income Inequality Trends in Sub-Saharan Africa: Divergence, Determinants and Consequences*, edited by Ayodele Odusola et al., 23–51. New York, NY: United Nations Development Programme, 2017, https://www.undp.org/sites/g/files/zskgke326/files/migration/africa/undp-rba_Income-Inequality-in-SSA_Chapter-2.pdf.
Cornia, Giovanni Andrea. "Sub-Saharan Africa's Diversifying Inequality Trends, 1991–2011: A Structuralist Interpretation." *Revue d'économie du développement* 27, no. 2 (2019): 9–43, https://doi.org/10.3917/edd.332.0009.
Crocker, Chester. "African Governance: Challenges and Their Implications." In *Governance in an Emerging New World: Africa in an Emerging World.* Winter Series, no. 199, edited by Anthony Carroll, Chester Crocker, Mark Giordano, Jack A. Goldstone, George Moose, and Andre Pienaar, 23–29. Stanford, CA: Hoover Institution, 2019, https://www.hoover.org/sites/default/files/issues/resources/africa_governance.pdf.
D'Arcy, Michelle, and Agnes Cornell. "Devolution and Corruption in Kenya: Everyone's Turn to Eat?" *African Affairs* 115, no. 459 (April 2016): 246–73, https://doi.org/10.1093/afraf/adw002.
de Waal, Alex. *The Real Politics of the Horn of Africa: Money, War, and the Business of Power*. Cambridge, UK: Polity Press, 2015.
Dolan, Kerry A. "The Inside Story of How the Daughter of José Eduardo Dos Santos Looted Angola's Riches." Forbes, July 8, 2022, https://www.forbes.com/sites/kerryadolan/2022/07/08/the-inside-story-of-how-the-daughter-of-jos-eduardo-dos-santos-looted-angolas-riches.
Easterly, William. "Can Institutions Resolve Ethnic Conflict?" *Economic Development and Cultural Change* 49, no. 4 (July 2001): 687–706, https://doi.org/10.1086/452521.
Easterly, William, and Ross Levine. "Africa's Growth Tragedy: Policies and Ethnic Divisions." *The Quarterly Journal of Economics* 112, no. 4 (November 1997): 1203–50, https://doi.org/10.1162/003355300555466.
Fagbemi, Fisayo, and Adeyemi Fajingbesi. "Political Violence: Why Conflicts Can Result from Sub-Saharan Socioeconomic Conditions." *Journal of Business and Socio-Economic Development* 2, no. 2 (2022): 153–64, https://doi.org/10.1108/JBSED-12-2021-0178.
Fakir, Adnan M. S., et al. "The Comparative Effect of Corruption and Piketty's Second Fundamental Law of Capitalism on Inequality." *Economic Analysis and Policy* 55 (September 2017): 90–105, https://doi.org/10.1016/j.eap.2017.04.006.
Fombad, Charles Manga. "An Overview of the Crisis of the Rule of Law in Africa." *African Human Rights Law Journal* 18, no. 1 (2018): 213–43, https://doi.org/10.17159/1996-2096/2018/v18n1a11.
Fosu, Augustin Kwasi. "Governance and Development in Africa: A Concise Review." GDI Working Paper No. 2017–008. Manchester, UK: Global Development Institute, University of Manchester, January 2017, https://hummedia.manchester.ac.uk/institutes/gdi/publications/workingpapers/GDI/GDI_WP2017002_Fosu.pdf.
Gavin, Michelle. "Zimbabwe's Flawed Election Results Meet with Regional Skepticism." Council on Foreign Relations, August 28, 2023, https://www.cfr.org/in-brief/zimbabwes-flawed-election-results-meet-regional-skepticism.

Gelb, Stephen. "Inequality in South Africa: Nature, Causes and Responses." Presented at the "African Development and Poverty Reduction: The Micro-Macro Link" Conference, Somerset West, South Africa, October 13–15, 2004, https://www.tips.org.za/files/Gelb_Inequality_in_SouthAfrica.pdf.

Gillwald, Alison. "Beyond Access: Addressing Digital Inequality in Africa." CIGI Working Paper Series, No. 48. Waterloo, Canada: Centre for International Governance Innovation, March 2017, https://africaportal.org/wp-content/uploads/2023/06/GCIG_no.48_0.pdf.

Gradstein, Mark, Branko Milanovic, and Yvonne Ying. "Democracy and Income Inequality: An Empirical Analysis." Poverty and Human Resources Policy Research Working Paper No. 2561. Washington, DC: World Bank Development Research Group, March 2001, https://hdl.handle.net/10986/19685.

Gupta, Sanjeev, Hamid Davoodi, and Rosa Alonso-Terme. "Does Corruption Affect Income Inequality and Poverty?" IMF Working Paper No. WP/98/76. Washington, DC: International Monetary Fund, May 1998, https://doi.org/10.5089/9781451849844.001.

Gyimah-Brempong, Kwabena. "Corruption, Economic Growth, and Income Inequality in Africa." *Economics of Governance* 3, no. 3 (2002): 183–209, https://doi.org/10.1007/s101010200045.

Harsch, Ernest. "Combating Africa's Inequalities: Obscene Disparities—New UNDP Study Highlights Chasm Between Rich and Poor." *Africa Renewal*, December 2017–March 2018, https://www.un.org/africarenewal/magazine/december-2017-march-2018/combating-africa's-inequalities.

Harsch, Ernest. "Combating Inequality in Africa: Lessen Inequities to Reduce Poverty and Reach MDGs, Says UN." *Africa Renewal*, July 2006, https://www.un.org/africarenewal/magazine/july-2006/combating-inequality-africa.

Hassan, Mai. "New Insights on Africa's Autocratic Past." *African Affairs* 121, no. 483 (April 2022): 321–33, https://doi.org/10.1093/afraf/adac002.

Heldring, Leander, and James A. Robinson. "Colonialism and Development in Africa." In *The Oxford Handbook of Politics and Development*, edited by Carol Lancaster and Nicolas van de Walle, 295–327. New York, NY: Oxford University Press, 2018.

Hillesund, Solveig. "Choosing Whom to Target: Horizontal Inequality and the Risk of Civil and Communal Violence." *Conflict Resolution* 63, no. 2 (2019): 528–54, https://doi.org/10.1177/0022002717734286.

Hindriks, Jean, Michael Keen, and Abhinay Muthoo. "Corruption, Extortion and Evasion." *Journal of Public Economics* 74, no. 3 (December 1999): 395–430, https://doi.org/10.1016/S0047-2727(99)00030-4.

Human Rights Watch. "DR Congo: Voter Suppression, Violence." January 5, 2019, https://www.hrw.org/news/2019/01/05/dr-congo-voter-suppression-violence.

International Monetary Fund (IMF). "Six Charts Explain South Africa's Inequality." *IMF Country Focus*, January 30, 2020, https://www.imf.org/en/News/Articles/2020/01/29/na012820six-charts-on-south-africas-persistent-and-multi-faceted-inequality.

IMF. "South Africa: Bridging the Income Divide." *IMF Blog*, International Monetary Fund, February 7, 2020, https://www.imf.org/en/Blogs/Articles/2020/02/07/south-africa-bridging-the-income-divide.

IMF. *Sub-Saharan Africa: Recovery amid Elevated Uncertainty*. New York, NY: International Monetary Fund, April 2019, https://www.imf.org/en/Publications/REO/SSA/Issues/2019/04/01/sreo0419.

Irobi, Emmy Godwin. "Ethnic Conflict Management in Africa: A Comparative Case Study of Nigeria and South Africa." Beyond Intractability Project, Conflict Information

Consortium, University of Colorado, May 2005, https://www.beyondintractability.org/casestudy/irobi-ethnic.

Johnston, Michael. "Corruption, Inequality, and Change." In *Corruption, Development, and Inequality*, edited by Peter M. Ward, 13–37. London, UK: Routledge, 1989.

Khan, Mohsin, and Karim Mezran. "Aftermath of the Arab Spring in North Africa." Issue brief, Atlantic Council, October 31, 2016, https://www.atlanticcouncil.org/in-depth-research-reports/issue-brief/aftermath-of-the-arab-spring-in-north-africa.

Kukurigo. "Ex-Health Minister Obadiah Moyo Acquitted as US$60 Million Trial Collapses, Says 'God Is Faithful.'" *The Zimbabwean*, August 10, 2021, https://www.thezimbabwean.co/2021/10/ex-health-minister-obadiah-moyo-acquitted-as-us60-million-trial-collapses-says-god-is-faithful.

La Porta, Rafael, et al. "The Quality of Government." *The Journal of Law, Economics, and Organization* 15, no. 1 (March 1999): 222–79, https://doi.org/10.1093/jleo/15.1.222.

Latif, Hany Abdel, and Mahmoud El Gamal. "How Distrust of Government by Marginalized People Fuels Conflict in Africa." *IMF Blog*, International Monetary Fund, January 25, 2024, https://www.imf.org/en/Blogs/Articles/2024/01/25/how-distrust-of-government-by-marginalized-people-fuels-conflict-in-africa.

Leibbrandt, Murray, and Timothy Shipp. "Reducing Inequalities in South Africa: Progress on Equality Thwarted by Slow Growth and Success of Top Earners." Economics Research Policy Brief, United Nations University World Institute for Development Economics Research (UNU-WIDER), Helsinki, Finland, May 2019, https://www.wider.unu.edu/publication/reducing-inequalities-south-africa.

Li, Hongyi, Lixin Colin Xu, and Heng-fu Zou. "Corruption, Income Distribution, and Growth." *Economics and Politics* 12, no. 2 (July 2000): 155–82, https://doi.org/10.1111/1468-0343.00073.

Luyt, Derek. "Governance, Accountability and Poverty Alleviation in South Africa." Presented at the 2008 United Nations Social Forum, Geneva, Switzerland, September 2008, https://www2.ohchr.org/english/issues/poverty/docs/sforum/spresentations/d.luyt.pdf.

Mauro, Paolo. "Corruption and Growth." *The Quarterly Journal of Economics* 110, no. 3 (August 1995): 681–712, https://doi.org/10.2307/2946696.

Mavhinga, Dewa. "Dispatches: Malawi's Chaotic Vote Threatens Violence." *Human Rights Watch*, May 24, 2017, https://www.hrw.org/news/2014/05/27/dispatches-malawis-chaotic-vote-threatens-violence.

Mavhinga, Dewa. "Still No Justice for Zimbabwe's 2018 Post-Election Violence." *Human Rights Watch*, August 2, 2021, https://www.hrw.org/news/2021/08/02/still-no-justice-zimbabwes-2018-post-election-violence.

Murunga, Godwin R., and Shadrack Wanjala Nasong'o. "Bent on Self-Destruction: The Kibaki Regime in Kenya." *Journal of Contemporary African Studies* 24, no. 1 (2006): 1–28, https://doi.org/10.1080/02589000500513713.

Mutsaka, Farai. "Zimbabwe's Health Minister Charged in COVID-19 Graft Case." *Associated Press*, June 20, 2020, https://apnews.com/article/health-zimbabwe-financial-markets-virus-outbreak-international-news-fde2679be079b94950b2048e2e5cabc1.

Ndulu, Benno J., and Stephen A. O'Connell. "Governance and Growth in Sub-Saharan Africa." *Journal of Economic Perspectives* 13, no. 2 (Summer 1999): 41–66, https://doi.org/10.1257/jep.13.3.41.

Neureiter, Katharina. "Reserving Judgement on Tanzania's Natural Gas Discoveries." *Global Policy Forum*, September 24, 2012, https://archive.globalpolicy.org/security-council/dark-side-of-natural-resources/other-articles-analysis-and-general-debate/51917-reserving-judgement-on-tanzanias-natural-gas-discoveries.html.

Nwankwor, Chiedo. "Priorities for Advancing Women's Equal Political Leadership in the Coming Year." *Brookings Institution*, February 23, 2022, https://www.brookings.edu/articles/priorities-for-advancing-womens-equal-political-leadership-in-the-coming-year.

Nygård, Håvard Mokleiv, et al. *Inequality and Armed Conflict: Evidence and Data*. Olso, Norway: Peace Research Institute Olso, 2017, https://www.prio.org/publications/10538.

Odusola, Ayodele, et al., eds. *Income Inequality Trends in Sub-Saharan Africa: Divergence, Determinants and Consequences*. New York, NY: United Nations Development Programme, 2017, https://www.undp.org/sites/g/files/zskgke326/files/migration/africa/undp-rba_Income-Inequality-in-SSA_Chapter-1.pdf. (Full book available for download at https://digitallibrary.un.org/record/3799401/files/Income.pdf.).

Organization for Economic Co-operation and Development (OECD), "What Is Fragility?," accessed February 11, 2025, https://www.oecd.org/en/blogs/2022/09/what-is-fragility.html.

Ostry, Jonathan D., Andrew Berg, and Charalambos G. Tsangarides. *Redistribution, Inequality, and Growth*. IMF Staff Discusson Note. New York, NY: International Monetary Fund, April 2014, https://www.imf.org/en/Publications/Staff-Discussion-Notes/Issues/2016/12/31/Redistribution-Inequality-and-Growth-41291.

Posner, Richard A. "Equality, Wealth, and Political Stability." *The Journal of Law, Economics, and Organization* 13, no. 2 (1997): 344–65, https://www.jstor.org/stable/765095.

Ramakhula, Thabang. "In but Out in Lesotho: Women's Representation Dilemma." Briefing, Centre for International Governance Innovation and South African Institute of International Affairs Policy, August 2019, https://doi.org/10.13140/RG.2.2.29452.74887.

Seery, Emma, Joab Okanda, and Max Lawson. "A Tale of Two Continents: Fighting Inequality in Africa." Oxfam Briefing Paper. Oxford, UK: Oxfam International, September 2019, https://hdl.handle.net/10546/620856.

Shimeles, Abebe, and Tiguene Nabassaga. "Why Is Inequality High in Africa?" AFDB Working Paper, No. 246. Abidjan, Côte d'Ivoire: African Development Bank Group, January 2017, https://www.afdb.org/en/documents/document/working-paper-246-why-is-inequality-high-in-africa-94074.

Siapno, Jacqueline Aquino. *Gender, Islam, Nationalism and the State in Aceh: The Paradox of Power, Co-Optation and Resistance*. London, UK: Routledge, 2002.

Siollun, Max. *What Britain Did to Nigeria: A Short History of Conquest and Rule*. London, UK: Hurst, 2021.

Şit, Ahmet, et al. "Rethinking of Government Institutions and Governance Quality Indicators on Economic Growth in Sub-Saharan African Countries." *Journal of the Knowledge Economy* 15 (June 2024): 20883–905, https://doi.org/10.1007/s13132-024-02040-6.

Statista, "20 Countries with the Biggest Inequality in Income Distribution Worldwide in 2023, Based on the Gini Index," accessed March 23, 2025, https://www.statista.com/statistics/264627/ranking-of-the-20-countries-with-the-biggest-inequality-in-income-distribution.

Stewart, Frances. "Justice, Horizontal Inequality, and Policy in Multi-Ethnic Societies." In *Towards Human Development: New Approaches to Macroeconomics and Inequality*, edited by Giovanni Andrea Cornia and Frances Stewart, 122–47. Oxford, UK: Oxford University Press, 2014.

Taylor, Rupert. "South Africa: The Role of Peace and Conflict-Resolution Organizations in the Struggle Against Apartheid." In *Mobilizing for Peace: Conflict Resolution in Northern Ireland, South Africa, and Israel/Palestine*, edited by Benjamin Gidron, Stanley N. Katz, and Yeheskel Hasenfeld, 69–93. New York, NY: Oxford University Press, 2002.

Tsikata, Dzodzi. "Understanding and Addressing Inequalities in the Context of Structural Transformation in Africa: A Synthesis of Seven Country Studies." *Development* 58, nos. 2–3 (June 2015): 206–29, https://doi.org/10.1057/s41301-016-0002-8.

United Nations (UN). "Root Causes of Conflicts in Africa Must Be Addressed Beyond Traditional Response, Special Adviser Tells Security Council Debate on Silencing Guns: Speakers Highlight Link Between Durable Peace, Inclusive Development Policies." UN Security Council Meeting No. 9299 on Peace and Security in Africa, News Release SC/15249, March 30, 2023, https://press.un.org/en/2023/sc15249.doc.htm.

UN. *Transforming Our World: The 2030 Agenda for Sustainable Development*. New York, NY: United Nations, 2015, https://sdgs.un.org/2030agenda.

United Nations Development Programme (UNDP). *Humanity Divided: Confronting Inequality in Developing Countries*. New York, NY: UNDP Bureau for Development Policy, November 2013, https://www.undp.org/sites/g/files/zskgke326/files/publications/HumanityDivided_Full-Report.pdf.

UNDP. *International Cooperation at a Crossroads: Aid, Trade and Security in an Unequal World*. UNDP Human Development Report 2005. New York, NY: United Nations Development Programme, 2005, https://hdr.undp.org/system/files/documents/human-development-report-2005-english.human-development-report-2005-english.

UNDP. *Rethinking the Role of Law and Justice in Africa's Development: An Edited Volume of Discussion Papers*. Addis Ababa, Ethiopia: United Nations Development Programme, June 2013, https://www.undp.org/publications/rethinking-role-law-and-justice-africas-development.

United Nations Office of the High Commissioner for Human Rights (UNOHCHR). "Mozambique: Post-Election Violence and Repression Must Stop, Say UN Experts." *News Release*, November 15, 2024, https://www.ohchr.org/en/press-releases/2024/11/mozambique-post-election-violence-and-repression-must-stop-say-un-experts.

Waldorf, Lars. "Legal Empowerment and Horizontal Inequalities After Conflict." *Journal of Development Studies* 55, no. 3 (2019): 437–55, https://doi.org/10.1080/00220388.2018.1451635.

World Bank. "Circumstances at Birth Are Important Drivers of Inequality in South Africa." *News Release*, July 24, 2012, https://www.worldbank.org/en/news/press-release/2012/07/24/circumstances-birth-important-drivers-inequality-south-africa.

World Bank. *CPIA Africa, June 2024: Structural Reforms for a Vibrant Private Sector*. Washington, DC: World Bank Group, 2024, https://hdl.handle.net/10986/41830.

World Bank. *Poverty and Shared Prosperity 2016: Taking on Inequality*. Washington, DC: World Bank Group, 2016, https://hdl.handle.net/10986/25078.

World Bank. *Poverty and Shared Prosperity 2020: Reversals of Fortune*. Washington, DC: World Bank Group, 2020, https://hdl.handle.net/10986/34496.

World Bank, "Worldwide Governance Indicators—Frequently Asked Questions," accessed February 11, 2025, https://www.worldbank.org/en/publication/worldwide-governance-indicators/frequently-asked-questions.

World Bank DataBank, *Metadata Glossary*, s.v. "Gini Index," accessed April 14, 2024, https://databank.worldbank.org/metadataglossary/world-development-indicators/series/si.pov.gini.

World Justice Project. *World Justice Project Rule of Law Index 2016*. Washington, DC: World Justice Project, 2016, https://worldjusticeproject.org/our-work/publications/rule-law-index-reports/wjp-rule-law-index-2016-report.

World Justice Project. *World Justice Project Rule of Law Index 2021*. Washington, DC: World Justice Project, 2021, https://worldjusticeproject.org/our-work/publications/rule-law-index-reports/world-justice-project-rule-law-index-2021.

Xu, Guangdong. "The Role of Law in Economic Growth: A Literature Review." *Journal of Economic Surveys* 25, no. 5 (December 2011): 833–71, https://doi.org/10.1111/j.1467-6419.2011.00691.x.

You, Jong-Sung, and Sanjeev Khagram. "A Comparative Study of Inequality and Corruption." *American Sociological Review* 70, no. 1 (February 2005): 136–57, https://doi.org/10.1177/000312240507000107.

Zhuang, Juzhong, Emmanuel de Dios, and Anneli Lagman-Martin. "Governance and Institutional Quality and the Links with Economic Growth and Income Inequality: With Special Reference to Developing Asia." ADB Economics Working Paper No. 193. Manila, Philippines: Asian Development Bank, February 2010, https://doi.org/10.2139/ssrn.1619116.

Zimbabwe Democracy Institute. *ZANU PF/Military Deterrence of the Village Vote: Perceptions on the 2018 Election Environment*. Harare, Zimbabwe: Zimbabwe Democracy Institute, 2018, https://kubatana.net/wp-content/uploads/2018/07/zdi_zanupf_military_village_vote_180710.pdf.

10

ETHNIC DIVERSITY, SOCIOECONOMIC INEQUALITY, AND CONFLICT IN NIGERIA

The Case for Political and Financial Restructuring

Titiloye Ademola Oyejide and Adebowale M. Adeleke

Introduction

Nigeria is the third-most ethnically and linguistically diverse country in the world, after New Guinea and Indonesia (Blench, 2003).[1] In comparison with other countries on the African continent, Nigeria's ethnic fragmentation is at the extreme end of the spectrum. In general, ethnically diverse countries tend to face considerable challenges in terms of meaningfully addressing inter-ethnic inequality and poor social and economic performance, resolving ethnic conflicts, and creating a unifying national identity—the latter of which is known to foster social cohesion and inclusion and alleviate ethnic violence and civil strife (Smith, 2023).[2] This chapter investigates the linkages between ethnic diversity, existing political and financial allocation frameworks, socioeconomic inequality, and conflict in Nigeria in this context. More specifically, it examines the part that ethnic fragmentation plays in the occurrence and persistence of hostilities; it assesses the role of political structuring in reducing ethnic violence and building a strong national identity; and it evaluates whether and to what extent a reformed political structure and a fiscal federalism approach can effectively reduce socioeconomic inequality in Nigeria.

Underlying this set of objectives is the following line of thought. Inasmuch as ethnic diversity tends to be associated with significant ethnic conflicts (as is well established), which may in turn widen socioeconomic inequality in a country (Bleaney & Dimico, 2017; Kanbur, Rajaram, & Varshney, 2011), political and financial restructuring may be required to reduce inequality, abate ethnic conflicts, and build national identity. Political restructuring can mean state creation (which, as discussed later in this chapter, will not inherently solve ethnolinguistic or ethnoreligious divides, largely because any new state's economic viability can be a major obstacle). Political restructuring (or reform) can also mean redefining the

DOI: 10.4324/9781003357025-13

role of state governments vis-à-vis the federal government and/or implementing mechanisms to repair dysfunctional government writ large. Speaking to Nigeria's case specifically, financial restructuring/reform refers to the need to reassess the country's fiscal federalism model to reduce state governments' dependence on the federal government, ensure that states can meet their fiscal obligations, and adequately address the socioeconomic and political inequalities that continue to impede the country's economic growth and development. It is our view that effectively implemented political and financial reform will go a long way toward fostering socioeconomic equality, reducing ethnic conflict, and promoting national identity, stability, and economic growth in Nigeria.

Accordingly, this chapter proceeds as follows. After a review of the literature related to these issues, we provide an overview of Nigeria's ethnogeography, paying particular attention to climate and other geographical differences among the country's six geopolitical zones. We then examine how Nigeria's political structure has evolved since independence, with special focus on public finance arrangements, followed by a look at socioeconomic inequality in the country. After examining the extent to which the various dimensions of socioeconomic inequality have either converged or diverged over time, we turn our attention to the links between ethnic diversity and conflict, assessing their nature, their distribution across the geopolitical zones, and their impacts.

A large body of literature on the issues addressed in this chapter covers both theoretical and empirical analyses in general as well as specific applications to Nigeria. As a starting point, Rotimi Suberu lays out several key definitions that our investigation relies on. Suberu defines an *ethnic group* as a social collective whose members share not only objective characteristics such as language, core territory, ancestral myths, culture, religion, and/or political organization, but also "some subjective consciousness or perception of common descent or identity," the latter of which almost always develops in the context of other ethnic groups. *Ethnic pluralism*, according to Suberu, results when two or more ethnic groups coexist within a territorial society or political community, usually a nation-state. These two definitions, then, frame *ethnicity* as "the mobilization and politicization of ethnic group identity in situations of competitive or conflictual ethnic pluralism" (Suberu, 1996).[3]

Based on these definitions, Alberto Alesina and Elaina La Ferrara (and others) have pointed to the negative impact of ethnic fragmentation on various aspects of economic performance in developing countries (Alesina & La Ferrara, 2005; Easterly & Levine, 1997; Alesina et al., 2003; Okediji, 2011). On the other end of the spectrum, Tom Kirk, Danielle Stein, and Annette Fisher have challenged the idea that diversity is detrimental to development, proffering the notion of a "diversity paradox," wherein initial increases in diversity lead to unwanted effects called "diversity debits," with "diversity dividends" arising longer term as different ethnic groups mix over generations (Kirk, Stein, & Fisher, 2018).[4] However, several studies on Nigeria have found that inequality across ethnic groups in Nigeria has remained remarkably persistent (Mustapha, 2006; Langer & Stewart, 2015; Archibong, 2018). This result is one of the central findings that this chapter seeks to revisit.

Nigeria's Ethnogeography and Climate

As defined above, an ethnic group is typically located within a core territory. Looking at ethnogeography is therefore a relevant first step in examining the interplay between ethnic diversity, political structure, socioeconomic inequality, and conflict in Nigeria, as climate and other geographic features of particular locations can greatly influence the economies of those who live there. Our thinking is that an exploration of the geographical loci of various ethnic groups may shed light on the roots of ethnic inequality, given that linguistic groups tend to reside in distinct land endowments. In this sense, various geographic attributes across ethnic homelands may well constitute strong predictors of ethnic inequality.

Shortly after assuming the role of military head of state in 1993, General Sani Abacha divided Nigeria into six geopolitical zones—north-central, northeast, northwest, southeast, south-south, and southwest—to better reflect the country's economic, political, and cultural realities. Official justifications for the compositions of each of these six zones centered around grouping regions with common histories, ethnicities, cultures, languages, and religions under the same geopolitical banner as much as possible (although for administrative purposes, resource allocation, and power-sharing were likely motivations as well) (Nwala, 1997). As such, a mix of geographical, political, and ethnolinguistic and ethnoreligious considerations determined both the locations and the compositions of each zone; the fact that there are exactly three zones in the north and three in the south reflects an attempt to balance the north-south divide.[5] In looking at the six zones, two distinct demographic patterns emerge: Zones with a single dominant ethnicity and language include the northeast (Kanuri), northwest (Hausa), southwest (Yoruba), and southeast (Igbo), while the north-central and south-south zones have more diverse ethnolinguistic compositions (Nwala, 1997).

Nigeria is situated entirely within the earth's tropical zone, between latitudes 4 degrees and 14 degrees north of the equator (and between longitude 30 and 15 degrees east), where two seasonal wind systems influence the land: The southwesterly winds bring rain, and the northwesterlies bring the dry and dusty harmattan winds from the Sahara Desert. The Federal Ministry of Environment divides the country into four main climatic zones—equatorial, tropical hinterland, tropical continental, and montane or plateau-type.

The equatorial climate zone extends from the coast to about 150 kilometers inland. Its wet season lasts from March to October, and its dry season extends from November to March. Rainfall in the equatorial climate is between 1,500 and 3,000 millimeters per annum. The average temperature is between 17 and 24 degrees Celsius (62.6–75.2 degrees Fahrenheit); relative humidity is between 60 and

TABLE 10.1 Features of Nigeria's Climate Zones

Characteristics	*Equatorial Climate Zone*	*Tropical Hinterland Climate Zone*	*Tropical Continental Climate Zone*	*Montane/ Plateau-Type Climate Zone*
Wet season	March–October	April–October	June–September	May–October
Dry season	November–March	November–March	October–May	November–April
Average temperature	17–24°C (62.6–75.2°F)	21–25°C (69.8–77°F)	25–30°C (77–86°F)	5–20°C (41–68°F)
Rainfall (mm)	1,500–3,000	1,000–1,500	250–1,000	1,400–4,000
Relative humidity (%)	60–90	50–80	20–40	30–90
Major cities	Lagos, Port Harcourt	Ibadan, Enugu	Kano, Sokoto, Maiduguri, Yola	Adamawa, Jos

Source: FMSMD (2016); Edokpa et al. (2024); "Nigeria's Climate and Vegetation" (2020).

90 percent. Prominent Nigerian cities in this climatic zone include Port Harcourt and Lagos. The tropical hinterland climate zone lies between 150 and 240 kilometers north of the coast. Rainfall is between 1,000 and 1,500 millimeters per annum. Temperatures range from 21 to 25 degrees Celsius (69.8–77 degrees Fahrenheit), and relative humidity is between 50 and 80 percent. The dry season in the tropical hinterland lasts for four months, from November to March; the wet season is from April to October. Prominent cities within this climate zone include Ibadan and Enugu. The tropical continental climate zone has the lowest annual rainfall (between 250 and 1,000 millimeters), the lowest relative humidity (between 20 and 40 percent), and the longest dry season (from October to May); its wet season is only from June through September. Its average temperatures fall between 25 and 30 degrees Celsius (77–86 degrees Fahrenheit). Prominent cities within this zone include Kano, Sokoto, Maiduguri, and Yola. The montane/plateau-type climate zone has average temperatures ranging between 5 and 20 degrees Celsius (41–68 degrees Fahrenheit), rainfall between 1,400 and 4,000 millimeters per annum, and relative humidity between 30 and 90 percent. Its wet season lasts from May through October, and its dry season is from November through April. Adamawa and Jos are the prominent cities in Nigeria's montane/plateau-type climate zone (FMSMD, 2016; Edokpa et al., 2024) (Table 10.1).

Nigeria's Political Structure

Nigeria became a colony of the British Empire on January 1, 1914, with the amalgamation of the northern and southern protectorates. Fiscal necessity and administrative convenience motivated the amalgamation: Whereas the southern protectorate was self-financing, the northern protectorate could not balance its budget and thus relied on British taxpayers to bear a large share of the cost of its administration (Ajayi, 2022; Mohammed, 2013). Chapters 1 and 2 detail the colonial legacies of the amalgamation and indirect rule and how they set the stage for the ethnic tensions that continue to roil Nigeria today; for the present discussion, suffice it to say that the coalescence of the northern and southern protectorates was an assimilation of unequals, essentially creating a social and economic dualism between north and south and forging an ethnopolitical rivalry that has persisted in post-independence Nigeria.

The next significant change in Nigeria's governance structure came about by way of the 1946 Richards Constitution (the second of four constitutions under British rule) (Elaigwu et al., 2001), which divided the country into three regions—north, west (or southwest), and east (or southeast). A central legislature based in Lagos administered the whole country, while each region had a regional assembly to advise the federal legislature on region-specific issues. The MacPherson Constitution of 1951 retained the three regions and further enhanced their powers relative to the federal government by establishing regional public service, judiciary, and commodity marketing boards. After Nigeria won political independence in 1960, the "Independence Constitution" instituted a federal form of the Westminster-style parliamentary system of governance (Okon, 2004). The first restructuring of the federal system carved out a fourth midwestern region from the original western region in 1963. Abubakar Tafawa Balewa, Nigeria's first (and only) post-independence prime minister, found the country confronted with long-standing stresses, including ethnic competitiveness, educational inequality, and economic imbalance; he saw the new region as a way to stave off ethnic conflict. The midwestern region has been called "the only geo-political unit created based on the will of the people expressed in a popular referendum"—in other words, the only one created democratically (Bah, 2004; Komolafe, 2023).

Four years later, on the eve of Nigeria's devastating civil war, General Yakubu Gowon, the new military head of state, dissolved the four regions (along with their respective regional governments) and replaced them with twelve states. The move was ostensibly designed to give more autonomy to the people in the previous regions, to devolve power from the federal government, and, more broadly, to dilute the power of the large ethnic groups (although decades later, Gowon stated that his intent was "to prevent any one region from becoming too powerful and threatening the country's unity") (Directorate of Intelligence, 1970).[6] An alternate view is that the creation of the twelve states was designed to weaken Igbo hegemony and the influence of the Biafran separatist movement in the eastern region by confining the Igbo to only one of three new eastern states. Chapter 2 goes into more detail on the conflicts underlying—and arising from—Nigeria's evolving state divisions and its civil war (Bah, 2004; Osaghae, 1992; Klein, 2022; Directorate of Intelligence, 1970; Alechenu, 2024).[7]

In 1976, General Murtala Muhammed, who had assumed power a year earlier when Gowon was overthrown, created seven additional states, bringing the total to nineteen. According to *The New York Times*, Muhammed stated that the aim was "to bring government nearer to the people and to insure [*sic*] political stability," and also to remedy "bad government at the state level." According to a report by the panel that recommended the new political divisions, the creation of the seven additional states was intended to "reduce minority problems, accelerate development and provide for a stronger federal structure." According to an article published in Nigeria's *The Guardian* newspaper four decades later, in 2016, "it remains uncertain if the goals for which the states were created are achieved." From nineteen in 1976, Ibrahim Babangida established eleven new states between 1987 and 1991, and Sani Abacha created an additional six states in 1996, bringing the total to today's thirty-six (Bah, 2004; Nigeria to Get a New Capital and Seven Additional States, 1976; Amzat et al., 2016; Omipidan, 2015; Ota, Ecoma, & Wambu, 2020).[8]

These changes all sought to manage Nigeria's ethnic tensions, mitigate ethnic hegemony over ethnic minorities, reduce regional disparities, promote political participation, and enhance national unity. What began as a radical move in 1967—replacing the regional system with multiple states, arguably (at least in part) as a strategy to isolate the Igbo by gaining the support of the minority ethnic groups in the eastern region, who had long agitated for self-rule—eventually produced a more balanced multistate federal system by devolving power from the federal government to state governments and conferring autonomy on the indigenes in the various states.

Perhaps the pinnacle of these efforts was General Muhammed's 1976 establishment of the Federal Capital Territory (FCT) in central Nigeria, and the concurrent relocation of the nation's capital from Lagos to Abuja. In so doing, Nigeria joined the ranks of other developing countries, including Brazil, Botswana, Malawi, Pakistan, and Tanzania, in transferring its seat of government. Lagos had become the center of government by virtue of its convenience and utility to the colonial government, but by 1976, its conditions—poor infrastructure, overpopulation, and congestion; peripheral location (and potential vulnerability both to sea level rise and military attack); uneven patterns of development; and dominance by a single ethnic group (the Yoruba)—made relocation seem like an obvious step toward the objectives outlined above. In announcing the new capital, Muhammed proclaimed,

> [Abuja] is not within the control of any of the major ethnic groups in the country. . . . The new capital created on such virgin lands. . . will be for all Nigerians a symbol of their oneness and unity. [It] will belong to all Nigerians.

In sum, the FCT was to be a means of uniting a nation recently divided by a terrible civil war—a truly neutral capital city in which everyone could coexist in harmony, free of the historical legacies imposed on them (Moore, 1984; Quinn, 2006).

In the same vein, the federal military government's 1975 announcement of the transition to democratic rule was the impetus for the landmark 1979 constitution, which introduced a presidential system modeled on that of the United States. The new governance framework included several regulatory elements aimed at ensuring a wider distribution of political power and more equitable access to economic opportunities across ethnic groups. Among the key elements was that, in order to be elected, a presidential candidate had to obtain a majority of the vote—and more than 25 percent of the total in at least twenty-four of the thirty-six states (Suberu, 2019, 2022).

The new constitution also introduced the "federal character" principle, which mandated that no one ethnic or religious group or region predominate in the federal government or any of its agencies, and it prohibited ethnic-based political parties. It required that the federal cabinet be representative of the various parts of the country, with at least one cabinet member from each state. In terms of the legislative branch, the 360 members of the House of Representatives (or Green Chamber)—the lower chamber of Nigeria's bicameral National Assembly—are allocated to states based on population; each state is equally represented by three members in the Senate (or Red Chamber), with one senator representing the FCT. Although power-sharing is not constitutionally mandated per se, the country's main political parties inaugurated a tradition during the 1999 elections to present south/north—and Christian/Muslim—balanced candidates for the presidency and vice presidency. Furthermore, the constitution institutionalized an affirmative action program based on the federal character principle that provides the educationally disadvantaged states with a quota system and proportional admission requirements for federal educational institutions to widen access to education (Okeke, 2019).

Despite the wide range of policies, programs, and initiatives established and implemented to manage ethnic tensions in Nigeria, many challenges remain. In reality, some of the mechanisms that were intended to ameliorate these tensions have created additional problems. For instance, affirmative action policies designed to rectify socioeconomic disparities inevitably benefit some people at the expense of others, effectively ignoring merit—as is the case with the federal character principle's application and the aforementioned quota system. More broadly, the multistate state system also has inherent drawbacks: While the crescive increase in the number of states has reduced the agitation for some states, it certainly has not eliminated ethnic tensions. The state system is based on the geopolitical zone structure, and none of the zones—or states, for that matter—are entirely homogeneous in ethnic composition. In particular, in the more ethnically heterogeneous south-south and north-central zones, the larger ethnic groups tend to dominate and oppress the smaller ones (Ota, Ecoma, & Wambu, 2020; Eze, Elimian, & Chinwuba, 2015).

Moreover, the internal resources available to each of the thirty-six states differ widely. The process of state creation failed to factor in financial and management capacity, causing some of the state's serious and persistent sustainability challenges. Some scholars warned that the creation of additional states would reduce states' resource bases and potentially render them unviable. Indeed, the eastern region's bifurcation into three states (Rivers, South-Eastern, and East-Central) eroded its resource base: The region accounted for 65 percent of the country's oil output in 1967, but that percentage reduced from 65.4 percent to 2.8 percent with the creation of the new states. A related issue around state creation in Nigeria's federal system is that when one state is divided into two, federal resources are allocated to the area on the criteria of 50 percent federal equity and 50 percent based on population. From an economics point of view, a newly created state's entitlement to federal resources leaves existing states with less than they had previously (Okwesili, 2014; Oji, 1995).

Neither does the multistate system solve the problem of inter-ethnic competition for resources, which invariably leads to tensions—and often conflicts—for two reasons. First, some ethnic groups are just too small to constitute a state with a reasonable chance of efficiently providing public goods, which requires economics of scale. Second, such a state would also lack an adequate base of internal resources to ensure financial viability. One solution for states with heterogeneous ethnic compositions would be to adopt some of the arrangements currently used by the federal government to reduce ethnic tensions. In other words, such states could benefit from a set of "state character" principles, along with a carefully designed and broadly acceptable system of rotation for important political offices.

Fiscal Federalism, Nigerian Style

A federal system of government generally consists of three levels of political authority: federal (or central), state, and local. *Fiscal federalism* refers to the institutional arrangement that guides both the allocation of functions and resources across the federal, state, and local levels of government and the provision of revenue that enables each level to fulfill its expenditure obligations (Ekpo & Englama, 2008). Typically, the federal government is responsible for ensuring equitable distribution of income across the country, maintaining macroeconomic stability, and providing public goods that are national in character, such as defense, security, and monetary policy. The lower levels of government are required to provide statewide and local public goods, such as public education, sanitation, and infrastructure maintenance (e.g., roads, bridges, and streetlights). The notion behind this division of functions is that vesting the lower levels of government with administering public goods materializes ample benefits. In particular, it promotes more efficient provision of public services, it ensures better alignment of costs and benefits among a diverse citizenry, and it more effectively responds to local needs and preferences. Importantly, though, when jurisdictional spillovers occur, as is associated with some local public goods, it becomes the responsibility of the federal government to step in and provide appropriate and targeted grants to cover such spillovers (Oshawa &Yang, 2022).

As it is in other federations, the Nigerian constitution specifies the distribution of functions across the federal, state, and local governments, dividing these functions into so-called exclusive and concurrent legislative lists. The exclusive list consists of functions over which either the federal or state government has undivided legislative authority; the concurrent list consists of the functions for which both have authority to legislate (Brickmans Law, 2021). In effect, functions assigned to the states are residual powers not assigned to the federal government. When it comes to revenue collection and administration, fiscal federalism dictates that two key factors should determine how tax-raising powers are apportioned among the levels of government: administrative efficiency and fiscal independence. That is to say, the power to raise taxes should be designated to the level of government that will administer them most efficiently at minimum cost. Fiscal independence requires that each level of government be able to raise adequate resources to meet its needs and assigned responsibilities (Adamolekun, 1991). A true fiscal federalism approach would benefit a large multiethnic country like Nigeria with persistent inequalities (Williams & Orokpo, 2014; Ewetan, 2012).

Furthermore, there are three distinctions made in the apportionment of taxing powers: legislative power, administration and collection, and the right to revenue. Since most taxes are national in coverage, the federal government makes and implements the relevant laws, administers those laws, and collects taxes, absorbing the majority of the proceeds to go toward federation expenditures. The state governments legislate, administer, collect, and retain all taxes that are applicable exclusively within their jurisdictions. They are obliged to share designated portions of the revenue with their constituent local governments, which also have the power to impose, collect, and limit local taxes (Adamolekun, 1991).

Two competing principles govern Nigeria's revenue allocation system: fiscal centralization and fiscal decentralization. Generally, fiscal centralization applies to the vertical level, while fiscal decentralization (or *equity*) applies to the horizontal level. Fiscal centralization reflects the idea that the federal government—which bears responsibility for ensuring political, social, and economic stability, ideally along with economic growth—should rightly absorb the greater proportion of national revenue for use to achieve even development across the country. Conversely, fiscal decentralization holds that the states and local governments should have larger shares of national revenue because their activities directly impact the citizenry (Tom & Ataide, 2021).

In practice, trends in Nigeria's revenue allocation system reveal marked swings between these two principles over time. Fiscal centralization prevailed up to 1955, but when the three regional governments were granted self-governance in 1956, the federal government lost its ascendancy over the regions. As a result, the regional share of total national revenue rose from 24 percent to 50 percent. Since 1970, however, the trend toward fiscal centralization has reemerged, as the federal government has consistently allocated to itself more than 50 percent of total national revenue. As of 2022, the percentage share of each of the three tiers of government is as follows: federal, 52.68 percent; states, 26.72 percent; and local governments, 20.60 percent.[9]

Two primary criteria guide the share of federation revenues allocated to states and local governments: population and equity. The equity criterion signifies that each state has a minimum responsibility to sustain a basic set of public functions and institutions irrespective of its geographical size, population, or fiscal capacity. During the period from 1970 to 1980, these two criteria carried equal weight. More recently, two other criteria that have emerged are landmass/terrain and social development (which captures allocations for primary education, health, water, and sanitation). Since 1990, the criteria used and their shares are as follows: equity of states, 40 percent; population, 30 percent; landmass/terrain, 10 percent; and social development, 20 percent (Musa & Ajibade, 2016; Ohiomu & Oluyemi, 2019).

Emerging Challenges

There are clear indications that the state governments are dissatisfied with their share of total national revenue based on the above-described revenue allocation formula. In 2006, many state governments complained about their inability to absorb revenues derived from the increased national minimum wage of ₦5,500 per month, brought about by the Labor Act of 2004 (and subsequently increased to ₦18,000 per month in 2010).[10] The same complaints arose in 2019 regarding the new national minimum wage of ₦30,000 per month (Igbadumhe et al., 2020; Oyeyemi, 2019; Nigeria—Minimum Wages, 2024).[11] Due to the fall in world crude oil price between 2014 and 2016, which pushed the Nigerian economy into recession as government oil revenue collapsed (World Bank, 2019), about 75 percent of the states became unable to meet their salary obligations to their workers and pensioners in full. The federal government had to step in with bail-out packages, and those states had challenges meeting their payroll obligations through 2020. A 2019 report by BudgIT, a Nigeria-based civic group committed to government transparency, revealed that only three state governments (Lagos, Akwa Ibom, and Rivers) could finance their recurrent expenditures without assistance from the federal government. In 2021, the federal government announced that these loans were due for repayment (Odegbaroye, 2020; Adegboyega, 2019; Ailemen, 2021; Aina & Adaji, 2024).

Allocations of national revenue do not constitute the totality of the revenue available to the states. They also have access to what is called internally generated revenue (IGR), which refers to critical income derived from local taxes and levies for financing activities and state government projects. However, IGR has not yielded sufficient revenue for the state and local governments to attain the level of fiscal independence that the general principles of fiscal federalism recommend (Oseni, 2013). A 2021 paper by Fidelia Onuigbo identified the major challenges of IGR, some of which suggest lack of capacity on the part of state and local governments (Onuigbo, 2021). Among the study's findings were that many legitimate sources of revenue remain unexploited; that procedures for revenue collection lack efficiency and lead to avoidable leakages; that revenue collection approaches stifle instead of promote business growth; and that no database exists to identify taxpayers and their business ventures for taxation. As a result of these deficiencies, the study found that the IGR is insufficient to finance either the recurrent or the capital expenditures of state governments (Khemani, 2001).

Nigeria's Socioeconomic Performance

One of the main challenges that ethnically diverse countries face relates to attempts by different ethnic groups to capture the largest share of public goods possible, rather than working to expand available resources and distribute them equitably among all groups. An analysis of socioeconomic inequality helps reveal the extent to which this capture occurs. In the Nigerian case, one way to investigate this phenomenon is to evaluate inequality over a range of socioeconomic dimensions. Based on the broadly accepted core welfare indicators (namely, economic performance, inequality, poverty rate), we sought to assess the degree of inequality observed over relevant indicators in each of Nigeria's six geopolitical zones. The analysis below focuses on economic, health, education, and social services issues. We utilized three indicators of economic performance to examine the extent of inequality across the six zones: poverty rate, rate of unemployment, and IGR. Figure 10.1 shows poverty level and unemployment rate by geopolitical zone as of 2019.

The figure illustrates considerable differences in the levels of poverty and unemployment across the geopolitical zones. Poverty levels were consistently higher in the northern zones than in the southern ones, while unemployment was highest in the south-south zone. Only one zone showed markedly lower unemployment than the national rate of 23.1 percent: the southwest (at 14 percent); the northeast and south-east zones were marginally lower at 22 and 23 percent, respectively. However, unemployment rates were higher than the national rate in the northwest zone (24 percent), the north-central zone (27 percent), and the south-south zone (32 percent). In order to understand why, we examined the differences in the economic structures across the geopolitical zones, which may have created significant disparities within the same national market. The findings from this investigation may also suggest appropriate policies for building a more integrated national economy and market (NBS, 2013).

IGR is another principal indicator of economic activities. Table 10.2 shows the relative performance of IGR among the six geopolitical zones as of 2019. The table reveals that most of Nigeria's states did not generate enough internal revenue to

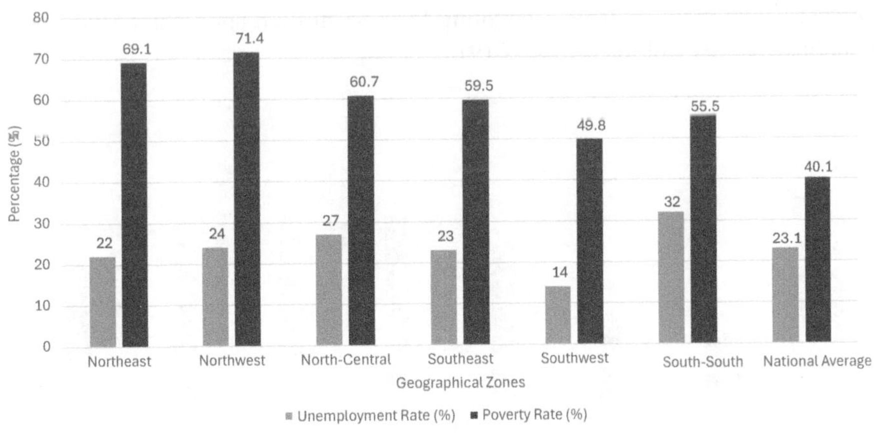

FIGURE 10.1 Poverty and Unemployment Rates by Geopolitical Zone

Source: NBS (2019) (for Individual Zones' Data); NBS (2013) (for National Averages); Otekunrin et al. (2019).

TABLE 10.2 Internally Generated Revenue by Geopolitical Zone

Zone	*PAYE (billion ₦)*	*Direct Assessments (billion ₦)*	*Road Taxes (billion ₦)*	*MDA Revenues (billion ₦)*	*Other Taxes (billion ₦)*	*Total Revenue (billion ₦)*
Northeast	336.17	8.72	10.05	119.78	38.85	513.58
North-Central	1229.97	52.94	24.35	303.70	184.58	1795.54
Northwest	567.55	40.38	38.97	354.46	486.27	1487.62
Southeast	522.77	26.50	31.38	273.03	103.90	957.59
South-South	2079.05	97.51	69.53	287.90	523.87	3057.87
Southwest	4735.52	226.05	174.28	1338.88	1337.47	7812.20

Source: NBS (2019).

Note: PAYE denotes "pay as you earn," which refers to a tax system in Nigeria wherein employers deduct income tax from employees' salaries and submit it to the government on their behalf, thus ensuring that employees meet their tax obligations and promoting a steady flow of revenue to the government Adebisi (2024). MDA stands for ministries, departments, and agencies. At the end of 2019, the naira to dollar conversion rate was ₦307/$1 CBN (2020).

perform their statutory responsibilities of providing security for and improving the welfare of their residents. In other words, most state governments relied heavily on federation account allocations to augment their IGR and finance their activities.

Next, we evaluated education using four indicators: primary school enrollment, secondary school enrollment, and youth and adult literacy rates in English. Figure 10.2 presents data on gross primary and secondary school enrollment. Across the geopolitical zones, those that recorded the lowest primary and secondary enrollment rates in 2016 were the northeast zone (at 67.4 and 45.0 percent, respectively) and the northwest zone (at 64.3 and 41.6 percent, respectively). In terms of values, total gross national secondary school enrollment stood at over 3.56 million students, with male students accounting for 1.95 million and female students accounting for 1.61 million (NBS, 2019).

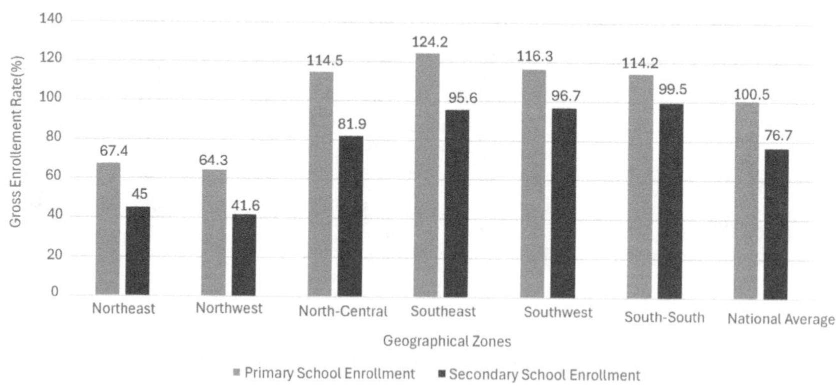

FIGURE 10.2 Gross Primary and Secondary School Enrollment by Geopolitical Zone

Source: NBS (2016).

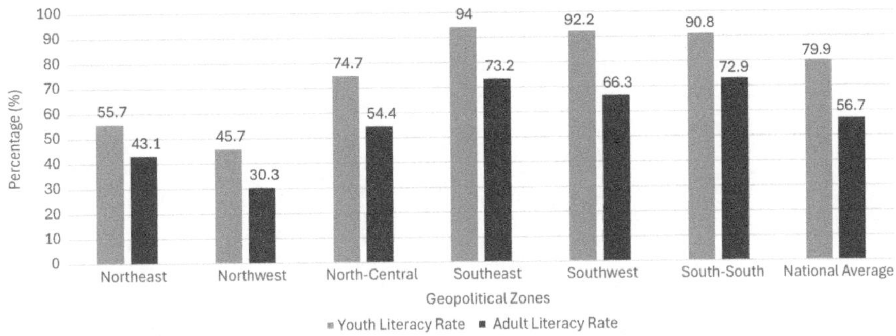

FIGURE 10.3 Youth and Adult English Language Literacy Rates by Geopolitical Zone

Source: NBS (2016).

Figure 10.3 graphs youth and adult literacy rates in English. These education indicators reveal a higher rate for youths than for adults across every geopolitical zone. The figure repeats the trend evident for the gross primary and secondary school enrollment indicators in Figure 10.2: Both youth and adult English literacy rates were higher in the southern zones than in the northern ones as of 2016. Within the southern zones, youth literacy rates in the 90th percentile range contrast sharply with those in the northern zones, which ranged from 45.7 percent in the northwest zone to 74.7 percent in the north-central zone. Youth literacy rates were higher than adult literacy rates across the country, with the northwest zone showing the lowest adult literacy rate (30.3 percent) and the southwest zone showing the highest (73.2 percent). Following the general trend, adult literacy rates were higher in the southern zones (between 66.3 and 73.2 percent) than the northern ones (between 30.3 and 54.4 percent). Among the three northern zones, the north-central zone showed the highest literacy rates for both youths and adults; the southeast zone performed the best in both indicators among the southern zones.

On health inequality across the six geopolitical zones, Figure 10.4 depicts the health access and delivery of children by health professionals and other health-related indicators as of 2015. The figure shows that both access to health and births attended by a health professional follow the same pattern as the other indicators: The southern zones enjoyed better health access than their northern counterparts. The fact that poverty is more prevalent in the northern part of the country (see Figure 10.2) partly explains these observed differences. Specifically, in the southwest zone, about 73.1 percent of residents had access to health, compared with 67.1 percent in the southeast zone, 65.9 percent in the south-south zone, 61.1 percent in the north-central zone, 55.3 percent in the northwest zone, and 48.4 percent in the northeast zone. The percentage of children under five years old who were delivered by a health care professional was low in the northeast and northwest zones (24 and 21 percent, respectively), but higher in the north-central zone (50.2 percent).

Figure 10.4 also presents another set of health services indicators: the percentage of women using family planning and the percentage of children less than one year old who were not immunized. For the country as a whole, only 5.77 percent of

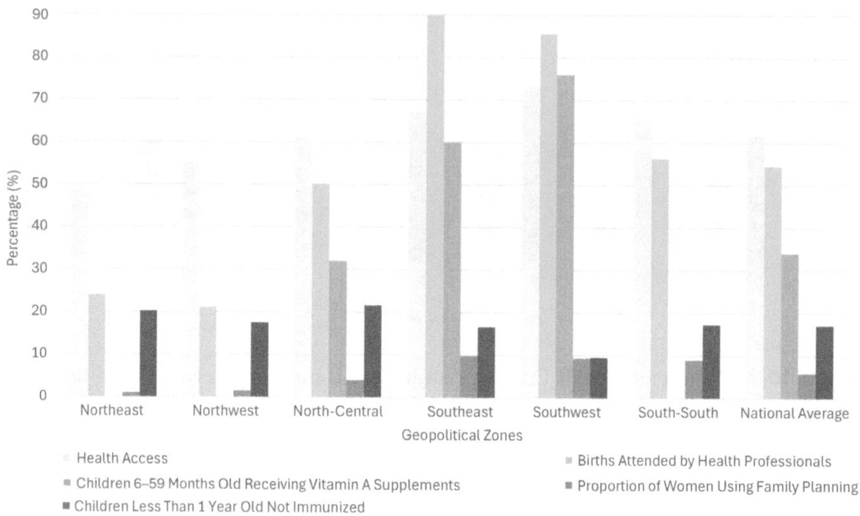

FIGURE 10.4 Health, Family Planning, and Unimmunized Children by Geopolitical Zone

Source: NBS (2015).

women were using family planning. All three northern zones showed percentages less than that average, and all three southern zones showed higher percentages, denoting poor performance health-wise in the north relative to the south. In the case of children less than a year old remaining unimmunized, the national average was 17.11 percent. Interestingly, the trend there did not follow the general pattern of poorer performance in the north versus the south: All three northern zones had higher percentages of children immunized than all three southern zones, with the north-central and northeastern zones both exceeding the 20 percent mark. By contrast, in the south, only the south-south zone exceeded the national average (and only by a very small margin); the southwest zone had the lowest percentage of children immunized (9.54 percent) out of all six zones.

To measure inequality in the provision of certain social services, we use similar cutoff points (or targets) to those used by the General Household Survey (GHS) panels conducted by the World Bank in cooperation with Nigeria's National Bureau of Statistics. Table 10.3 presents three of these indicators: access to safe water, safe sanitation (i.e., sanitary human waste and refuse disposal), and electricity. In the case of safe water sources, the zones with asterisks exceed the average cutoff points, signifying better performance relative to other zones. The better-performing zones are the southwest zone (at 75.6 percent), the northwest zone (at 50.6 percent), and the north-central zone (at 48.9 percent). Put simply, these numbers mean that roughly 75, 50, and 49 percent of people living in those zones, respectively, have access to basic drinking water services (i.e., clean water), whereas more people in northeast, southeast, and south-south zones are presumed to be drinking contaminated water at home.[12]

With respect to safe sanitation, three zones meet and surpass the target: the southeast zone (at 69.6 percent), the southwest zone (at 62.1 percent), and the northwest zone (at 61.6 percent), while people living in the other zones are presumably still practicing open defecation and refuse disposal at higher rates. Finally, three zones meet and surpass the electricity supply target: the southwest zone (at 79.1 percent), the southeast zone (at 65.4 percent), and the south-south zone (at 62.2 percent). In aggregate, only the southwest zone meets the target for safe water and safe sanitation; only the southeast zone satisfies the target for safe sanitation and electricity supply. None of the other zones satisfy more than one target: The north-central zone meets only the safe water target; the south-south zone meets only the electrify supply target; and the northwest zone meets only the safe sanitation target. The northeast zone is unable to satisfy any of the three targets.

Looking at the big picture, data derived from Nigeria's six geopolitical zones suggests a gradual shift away from the prevalent understanding of socioeconomic inequality patterns across Nigeria's geopolitical zones, suggesting that the standard assumption of a sharp, age-old, and enduring north-south divide inherited from Nigeria's colonial past may not be as entrenched as previously thought. Our analysis shows that while evidence of this pattern remains in some areas, recent developments reflect several shifts. For one, progress in the north-central zone seems to indicate a drift away from the other northern geopolitical zones such that it is beginning to resemble more closely the southern zones, especially in terms of the patterns of socioeconomic inequality inherited from colonial rule.

Yet, as Table 10.2 shows, states in all six zones have struggled to find sustainable ways of financing their governmental commitments through IGR—a fundamental problem. Generally, states have sought to alleviate this shortcoming by attempting to persuade the federal government to restructure the federation revenue allocation formula in their favor, with mixed results. However, there is another option that deserves careful study. It asks whether salaries and other conditions of service must necessarily be uniform across all governments, given the sharp

TABLE 10.3 Access to Safe Water, Safe Sanitation, and Electricity

Zone	*Safe Water (%)*	*Safe Sanitation (%)*	*Electricity Supply (%)*
Northeast	30.7	45.4	30.7
Northwest	50.6*	61.6*	37.7
North-Central	48.9*	46.6	44.6
Southeast	40.8	69.6*	65.4*
Southwest	75.6*	62.1*	79.1*
South-South	45.9	55.0	62.2*
Target	48.8	56.7	53.3

Source: NBS (2015).

disparities in the internal revenue—raising capacities among different states. Other federations around the world have debated and resolved this predicament. For instance, Canada devolved more administrative responsibilities to local governments but retained essential regulatory functions such as rectifying regional disparities and imbalances in the provision of public services (Chuangchit, 2015).

In terms of promoting equity and economic growth and creating a strong sense of national identity in Nigeria, another important question is the extent to which the challenges posed by ongoing conflicts may hinder forward momentum. Conflicts between nomadic Fulani herders and sedentary farmers of other Indigenous ethnic groups have touched every geopolitical zone to varying degrees, and the Boko Haram insurgency's stranglehold on the northeast zone continues to thwart economic growth and stymie progress relative to the other zones. The next section focuses first on the main drivers and manifestations of conflict in Nigeria, and then the chapter moves on to locate conflicts across the country's geopolitical zones, noting their relative prevalence and effects.

Ethnoreligious Diversity and Conflict in Nigeria

As previous chapters in this volume have discussed, conflict in Nigeria (as elsewhere) has numerous dimensions, including geography broadly and competition over access to land and resources more specifically, as well as ethnicity, ethnopolitics, and ethnoreligious contention. Needless to say, historical hostilities—and the myriad factors that underlie them—can also factor centrally in modern-day conflicts. Moreover, these dimensions are often overlapping; rare is a conflict over land access, for example, that does not also reflect ethnic, ethnopolitical, or (most often) ethnoreligious rivalries, at least to some degree. To this effect, it is helpful to look briefly at the history behind Nigeria's present ethnoreligious dynamics.

Traditional or Indigenous religions were the main form of spirituality in Nigeria before Christianity and Islam took hold. They encompass a variety of traditional beliefs that are unique to ethnic groups and involve different kinds of rituals and worship. According to Jacob Olupona, a professor of African religious traditions at Harvard Divinity School, "indigenous African religions are by nature plural, varied, and usually informed by one's ethnic identity, where one's family came from in Africa" (Olupona, 2015). Islam arrived in Nigeria in the eleventh and twelfth centuries through trade and migration between the Kanem-Bornu Empire and North Africa. It gained a foothold in Yorubaland (modern-day southwestern Nigeria) in the fourteenth century and made its way to Hausaland (modern-day northern Nigeria) in the fourteenth and sixteenth centuries (Fafunwa, 1974; Britannica, 2024; Badruddeen, 2023; Ngbea & Achunike, 2014). Although the Portuguese attempted to introduce Christianity to Nigeria (in the form of Roman Catholicism) in the fifteenth century, their initial missionary efforts were unsuccessful. In the nineteenth century, other Christian missionaries arrived in Nigeria from England, France, Scotland, and the United States. The Church Missionary Society (originally the Society for Missions in

Africa and the East, formed by Evangelical clergy of the Church of England in 1799) established churches in Yorubaland, particularly in Abeokuta, Ibadan, Lagos, and Benin. By 1885, the Roman Catholic Church had established itself in Abeokuta, Ibadan, Lagos, and Lokoja, and by 1920 Roman Catholic missions appeared in Igboland (in present-day southeastern Nigeria) (Diara & Nche, 2013).

Eight decades later, the end of military rule in 1999 induced a spike in ethnoreligious conflict in Nigeria, especially in the north-central zone (also known as the Middle Belt), which lies between the Muslim north and the Christian south and is home to people divided primarily along ethnoreligious lines. When the country transitioned from centralized military rule to a decentralized democratic government, the primary cause of conflict in the Middle Belt was competition over political appointments and competition for public resources (Ducrotoy et al., 2016).

Two major conflicts in Nigeria in recent years have garnered the most scholarly and media attention: the ongoing clashes between nomadic herders and sedentary farmers and the Boko Haram insurgency. Both conflicts are sources of great concern for Nigeria's leadership and citizenry alike. Unsurprisingly, given that Nigeria is a multiethnic and multireligious country, both of them include elements of ethnic and religious tensions. Importantly, though, neither is fundamentally driven by ethnoreligious concerns. Below, we look at these two conflicts in some detail. We then discuss numerous conflicts in Nigeria that *have* been purely or largely ethnoreligiously motivated, after which we break down the incidence and impact of conflicts by geopolitical zone.

* * *

According to the International Crisis Group, herders and farmers in Nigeria historically enjoyed a symbiotic and peaceful relationship, with the herders' cattle fertilizing the farmers' land in exchange for grazing rights. Mark Davidheiser and Aniuska Luna have shown that, prior to colonial rule, herders and farmers coexisted and mutually benefitted from one another through this cooperative system of land use. Colonial rule was the pivotal moment that changed the relationship between these two groups by sabotaging the informal network that had existed between them long before colonialism. The divide-and-rule tactics instituted during British rule and the resulting policies that altered land access and ownership created a tenuous and ultimately tumultuous relationship between the farmers and the herders. After independence, urbanization—and the inevitable encroachment that it engendered—intensified the tensions and conflicts between them in the competition for access to land (International Crisis Group, 2017; Davidheiser & Luna, 2008; Njoku, 2021).

Thus, the herder-farmer conflict in Nigeria was borne out of the scarcity of grazing land for the nomadic herders' livestock, resulting in violent confrontations as they encroached on sedentary farmers' land, primarily in the north-central and southern states. Though the root cause was and is contention over land, however, it is important to understand the ethnoreligious undercurrents of the conflict: The herders, mostly members of the Fulani ethnic group, are Muslims, while most of the non-Fulani farmers are from other ethnic groups and are also Christians. These differences in religious and cultural backgrounds, traditions, languages, and identity have contributed significantly to the conflict, especially in the Middle Belt and the predominantly Christian southern states.

A reduction in available pastureland—largely the result of a series of droughts in the northwest and northeast zones between 1972 and 1974—forced Fulani herders to shift their migratory routes further south in search of water and land for grazing, setting the stage for what has become a bitter and ongoing battle over land and water sources. (Migrations to the south occurred prior to this period, but this was one of the most severe droughts.) The shift created a competitive relationship between the growing population of sedentary farmers in the north-central and southern zones, many of whom had worked the same land for years if not generations, and the increasingly sedentary population of herders, triggering intensifying disputes over land and water use.

The federal government had started creating grazing reserves in the 1960s in an attempt to provide the Fulani with secure land tenure. For example, the Kachia Grazing Reserve was established in 1967 in Kaduna state (in the northwest zone) under the Grazing Reserve Act of 1964 to settle Fulani nomads and reduce conflict between nomads and farmers. However, many states were discouraged from establishing reserves due to the high levels of land compensation recommended by the Federal Land Use Act of 1978 (Waters-Bayer & Taylor-Powell, 1986; Awogbade, 1987; Ingawa, Tarawali, & von Kaufmann, 1989). Compounding the crisis, most of the four hundred-plus grazing reserves established in the 1960s have been lost due to a variety of factors—including poor government policies, mismanagement, and droughts—which has greatly reduced the availability of land and forced herders to seek pasture elsewhere (International Crisis Group, 2017).

The Nigeria Security Tracker, a project created by the Council on Foreign Relations to catalog and map violent incidents related to political, economic, and social grievances, revealed that of the 6,274 total cases of violence in Nigeria between 2014 and 2019, 309 related to herder-farmer clashes, leading to 3,087 deaths and representing roughly 5 percent of violent conflicts in Nigeria during that time period. States in the northeast zone (Adamawa and Taraba), the north-central zone (Benue, Kogi, Nasarawa, and Plateau), and the northwest zone (Kaduna) accounted for 77 percent of herder-farmer conflicts between 2014 and 2019, and 71 percent of fatalities during the period (Adigun, 2022; Brottem, 2021; Fayomi et al., 2021; Adichie, 2021).

Notwithstanding all the atrocities detailed above, Nigeria's herder-farmer crisis pales in comparison to the Boko Haram insurgency. Boko Haram is a militant Sunni Islamic sect organized in the late 1990s under the Muslim cleric Mohammed Yusuf. Its members are mostly of the Kanuri ethnic group, which dominates the region where most of Boko Haram's adherents originated—Borno state in the northeast geopolitical zone. They do not recognize any other religion other than

Islam, and their goal is to Islamize Nigeria. Specifically, the group's stated purpose is to overthrow the Nigerian government and institute a regime based on *Sharia* (or Islamic law). It is opposed to any form of Western influence in society: The name "Boko Haram" translates to "Western education is forbidden," although the group prefers to be known by its Arabic name, Jama'atu Ahlis Sunna Lidda'awati Wal-Jihad (which translates to "People Committed to the Propagation of the Prophet's Teachings and Jihad"). Governments and institutions around the world classify Boko Haram as a terrorist organization (Adibe, 2014; USNCC, 2025; Ross, 2015; Cook, 2012; USCIRF, 2024).[13]

Boko Haram operates out northeastern Nigeria. It launched its armed rebellion against the government of Nigeria in 2009. Following the deaths of scores of police officers, a joint police and military task force responded by killing hundreds of Boko Haram members and arresting Yusuf, who later died in police custody (Reuters, 2009). The group pulled off a quick resurgence in 2010 and perpetrated a spate of deadly bombings and brazen kidnappings—the most publicized of which was the April 2014 abduction of almost three hundred female students—mostly Christians—from a school in Borno state in Nigeria's northeast geopolitical zone (Brechenmacher, 2019; USNCC, 2025). As of April 2024, Amnesty International reported that eighty-two of those students remained in captivity (Amnesty International, 2024). But that atrocity was not an isolated incident: According to the United Nations Children's Fund, more than twenty-four hundred incidents of violence affecting close to seven thousand children have occurred since 2014 in Nigeria's northeast zone alone. Untold numbers of girls have been forced to marry and bear children for Boko Haram fighters, and as many as ten thousand boys have been forced to fight alongside their militant captors (Alhattab & Akau, 2023; Warren, 2017).

A coalition of military forces from Nigeria, Chad, Cameroon, and Niger began a counterinsurgency against Boko Haram in 2015. On December 24, 2016, Nigerian President Muhammadu Buhari declared that Boko Haram had been ousted from its last territorial stronghold in the Sambisa Forest in northeast Nigeria, where the group is known to have held many of its kidnapping victims (Kayode, 2014; International Crisis Group, 2020; Campbell, 2016). Although the counterinsurgency effectively degraded its territorial holdings, Boko Haram maintains an extensive capacity to carry out attacks. The Carnegie Endowment for International Peace has called the group "remarkably adaptable in its tactics," citing evidence that its relative decline since the crackdown has been uneven (Brechenmacher, 2019). The Reuters news agency reported in 2021 that Boko Haram was spreading into Niger state in the north-central zone, and as recently as January 2025 Amnesty International condemned an attack on farming communities in Borno state that killed forty people (Reuters, 2021; Amnesty International, 2025). In the words of the British Broadcasting Corporation, the Nigerian government's declarations that Boko Haram has "been 'technically defeated' is ringing increasingly hollow" (Khalid, 2021). The Islamist group continues to pose a major threat to the region, including the neighboring countries of Chad, Niger, and Cameroon. Between 2011 and 2023, Boko Haram attacks killed more than thirty-eight thousand people, the majority of them in northeastern Nigeria.[14] According to the U.S. National Counterterrorism Center, as of October 2022, Boko Haram had also displaced more than two and a half million people (USNCC, 2022).

Although both the Boko Haram insurgency and the violent clashes between herders and farmers have received more attention, Nigeria has faced a long list of strictly ethnoreligious conflicts in the years since independence: the Maitatsine religious riots in parts of Kano and Maiduguri in the early 1980s; the Kaduna Polytechnic Muslim-Christian skirmishes in 1981 and 1982; the Bulumkutu and Usman Danfodio University Sokoto Muslim-Christian riots in 1982; the Jimeta-Yola religious schisms in 1984; the so-called cross versus the crescent conflict at the University of Ibadan between 1981 and 1985; the Muslim-Christian clash during a Christian Easter procession in Ilorin in Kwara state in 1986; the Muslim-Christian riots at Kafanchan College of Education in 1987; the Zangon Kataf crises in Kaduna state in 1992; and the protests over students wearing hijabs in Kwara state in March 2021 (Isichei, 1987; Yusuf, 2007; Salawu, 2010; Garkuwa & Samuel, 2023; Eyeh, 2020; Akinyemi, 2022; Balogun, 2022). This litany of clashes demonstrates that ethnically diverse societies are inherently less likely to agree on religion—particularly when the types of religious beliefs and practices involved are based on rigid and dogmatic ideologies—and polarization and conflict are often the result. In Nigeria, a vast, ethnically and religiously diverse population coexists and competes for resources, often within boundaries (themselves a mapped legacy of colonial administrative delineations that disregarded existing social structures and norms) that incline particular regions to conflict. Unfortunately, the combined fault lines of ethnicity and religion in Nigeria make ethnoreligious conflict all but inevitable (Ukiwo, 2007; Ifeyinwa, 2002).

As described above, contentions around conventional sources of conflict—the most common being land rights, access to resources, and representation (or lack thereof) in governance and public institutions—can very easily take on ethnic or religious dimensions. In Nigeria, this conflation is all too common, especially given the ethnogeographical factors described earlier in this chapter. It is therefore unsurprising that the long list of ostensibly ethnoreligious conflicts in Nigeria also reflects issues around real or perceived inequities, competition for scarce resources, frontiers and boundaries, and indigene-settler issues. Regardless of the underlying (or overt) frictions that have driven these conflicts, the ethnoreligious element has served to amplify their divisiveness and their destructiveness.

It is also unsurprising that all these conflagrations and the circumstances surrounding them have given rise to numerous ethnic activist movements, the histories of which offer more insights into the interplay of ethnic diversity, politics, socioeconomic inequality, and conflict in Nigeria. One, the O'odua People's Congress, is a nationalist group in Nigeria's southwest geopolitical zone. It was formed in 1994 by members of the Yoruba ethnic group demanding self-determination in response to perceived marginalization in political affairs after the annulment of the 1993 presidential election results. (By all accounts, Moshood Kashimawo Abiola, a Yoruba from the southwest, won what is widely recognized as the freest and fairest election in Nigeria's history, beating Bashir Tofa, a Kanuri from the northwest. General Ibrahim Babangida, then the head of the military government—who was from the north-central zone—annulled the election; he cited voting irregularities, though it was widely known that the northern elites did not want to cede power to the south.) (Lawal, 2023; Aye, 2022; Tertsakian, 2003).

Another activist movement, the Ijaw Youth Council (IYC), is a political movement founded in 1998 in the south-south zone. After the death of Sani Abacha, the new military head of state Abdulsalami Abubakar's less repressive approach encouraged the Ijaw, Nigeria's fourth-largest ethnic group, to stand up to the political and economic marginalization and environmental degradation they had suffered since oil was discovered in commercial quantities in the Niger Delta in 1958, on their historical homelands. The IYC demanded self-determination, resource control, political restructuring, and regional autonomy within a true federal framework (Osaghae et al., 2011; Saint, 2022).

The Movement for the Actualization of the Sovereign State of Biafra (MASSOB) started in 1999 in the southeast zone with a goal of establishing a sovereign Biafra state comprising Nigeria's southeast and south-south regions. Ethnic tension is a key driver of the movement's separatist goal: The region is economically weak, and its residents feel politically marginalized and economically sidelined by northerners dating back to the civil war in 1967 (see Chapter 2). According to the European Union Agency for Asylum, although MASSOB defines itself as a nonviolent movement, it has been involved repeatedly in clashes with the police, and it was banned by Nigerian authorities in 2001 (Waddington, 2013; EUAA, 2019). Other activist movements that have served as the executors of Nigeria's manifold ethnoreligious agendas, exacerbating the deep divides between the country's various ethnic and religious groups, are the Igbo People's Congress, the Arewa People's Congress, the Bakassi Boys, the Egbesu Boys, and the Ohanaeze Ndigbo (Salawu, 2010).

Incidence and Impact of Conflicts by Geopolitical Zone

Below, we outline conflicts by geopolitical zone. In zooming in on the relative prevalence of conflicts in each of Nigeria's six geopolitical zones and their impacts, it is useful to group the six zones into two blocs. The first bloc consists of the northeast, north-central, and south-south zones. Studies by the World Bank and the Institute for Peace and Conflict Resolution have found those three zones to be epicenters of the most persistent and violent conflicts with the gravest effects. By comparison, conflicts in the remaining three geopolitical zones (northwest, southeast, and southwest) have generally been milder and more sporadic and had substantially less harmful consequences overall (IPCR, 2017; Azad & Kaila, 2018; Azad, Crawford, & Kaila, 2018; NBS, 2021).[15]

Northeast Zone

Nigeria's northeast zone includes the states of Adamawa, Bauchi, Borno, Gombe, Taraba, and Yobe. Economically, the region is known for producing crops and livestock (particularly sheep, cattle, and goats), along with minor mining activities. The major ethnic groups are the Hausa and the Fulani, who practice Islam. The region, which struggles with socioeconomic issues including high levels of poverty, illiteracy, and unemployment, is rife with poor governance and corruption. As of 2022, it had a Multidimensional Poverty Index (MPI) of 0.324, which is relatively high (Olumidey, 2024; NBS, 2021).

The northeast zone is the most severely affected by conflict of any of Nigeria's geopolitical zones in recent years. It has experienced a range of inter-group conflicts, from indigene-settler disputes and herder-farmer schisms to ethnoreligious clashes and communal land and boundary skirmishes (Azad, Crawford, & Kaila, 2018). It is known for being the birthplace of the Boko Haram insurgency, which accounts for more than two-thirds of the higher-order conflicts in the northeast zone (Adibe, 2014). Boko Haram remains concentrated there, although it is responsible for human rights abuses across Nigeria, Chad, Cameroon, and Niger (UNGA, 2015. The ongoing insurgency has affected almost fifteen million people since 2009 (Felbab-Brown, 2018). Although the conflict levels peaked in 2014, they spiked again from 2017 to 2020. Between 2010 and 2017, 49 percent of households in the northeast zone had experienced at least one instance of violence against a household member—72 percent of which were related to the Boko Haram insurgency (Azad, Crawford, & Kaila, 2018; IOM, 2018).[16]

Displacement is another huge problem in the northeast zone—again, largely a result of Boko Haram's activities. According to the International Organization for Migration, all six states in the northeast zone are affected by displacement. The overall percentages of internally displaced persons (or IDPs) in the northeast zone show a dramatic acceleration: 1 percent was displaced before 2014, and in 2014 the number rose to 2.6 percent; by 2015–16, 27 percent of the population was displaced from their homes. Although the percentage of IDPs declined somewhat to 19 percent in 2017, the sheer numbers are staggering: As of December 2017, the Boko Haram insurgency had displaced 1,702,680 people, and the number had jumped by 4.5 percent by February 2018 to reach 1,782,490. As of February 2018, IDP percentages were distributed across the northeast states as follows: Borno, 77 percent; Adamawa, 9 percent; Yobe, 6 percent; Bauchi, 3 percent; and Taraba, 3 percent (IOM, 2018).

North-Central Zone

Strategically situated in the middle of the country straddling the north and the south, the north-central zone (or Middle Belt) consists of the FCT (including the capital city, Abuja) as well as six states: Benue, Kogi, Kwara, Nasarawa, Niger, and

Plateau. The dominant ethnic groups include the Nupe, the Gwari, and the Hausa, but a large concentration of minority ethnic groups makes it the most ethnically heterogeneous and culturally diverse geopolitical zone in the country. The Middle Belt is rich with vegetation and conditions favor both agriculture and husbandry, making it attractive to the transhumant herders from northern Nigeria and the Sahel countries to the north and west. The main economic activities include farming, fishing, and mining (in tin, columbite, gold, iron ore, and limestone), along with hydroelectric power via the Kainji Dam. Endowed with irrigated and arable land, rich pastureland, forest reserves, and bodies of water, the zone is Nigeria's food basket. Nevertheless, the north-central zone is a poor region: Its 2022 MPI was 0.272 (Olumidey, 2024; NBS, 2021).

The north-central zone confronts a variety of conflicts that, as with the other zones, are primarily resource-based in nature. The most intractable among them is the herder-farmer conflict discussed above. According to the Global Centre for the Responsibility to Protect, population growth in recent decades (and since 2015 in particular) has led to increased areas earmarked for farming, leaving less land available for cattle grazing. As described above, competition over land use in the Middle Belt states is amplified, as the fault lines between farmers and herders often overlap with ethnic and religious divisions. Climate change and increasing desertification in the north has also exacerbated tensions as the loss of grazing land has driven many Fulani Muslim herders southward into areas farmed by settled communities of predominantly Christian farmers (GCRP, 2025).

Violent clashes between these herders and farmers, which typically entail attacks by one group and subsequent retaliation by another, have seen houses and farmland destroyed and cattle slaughtered. These skirmishes over access to arable and pasturable land, amplified by ethnic and religious undertones, have negatively affected food security in the north-central zone. According to the UN World Food Programme, more than thirteen million people in northern Nigeria are facing hunger (Asadu, 2022; Nnaji et al., 2022). In the north-central zone specifically, as of 2018, 71 percent of households reported not having enough food or enough money to buy food (Azad & Kaila, 2018).[17]

The number of conflicts in the north-central zone rose dramatically between 2010 and 2013 (Azad, Crawford, & Kaila, 2018; Azad & Kaila, 2018).[18] According to the International Crisis Group, one report estimated that, in 2013, more than 64,750 cattle were stolen and close to 3,000 herders were killed in states across the zone. Escalating conflicts continued to exact a steep humanitarian toll, with thousands killed and tens of thousands displaced. The governor of Benue, one of the hardest-hit states, reported that more than 1,878 people were killed there between 2014 and 2016. The economic toll is heavy as well: One ethnic association estimated that its communities in Benue state had lost ₦65 billion in property (roughly $251 million) during the early 2016 herder attacks. Community leaders interviewed by the International Crisis Group reported that "the loss of large cattle herds, crops (due to population displacements and damage to irrigation facilities), as well as increases in transport and labour costs in post-conflict environments all increase poverty and food insecurity in affected communities—and beyond" (International Crisis Group, 2017).

According to a 2018 World Bank report on conflict and violence in Nigeria, 25 percent of households in the north-central zone had experienced some type of conflict event between 2010 and 2017; 33 percent of households affected by conflict had at least one member displaced as a result; and 55 percent of all reported conflict events were caused by disputes over access to land or resources (Azad, Crawford, & Kaila, 2018).[19] While armed bandit groups motivated largely by criminal motives are a notorious problem in the Middle Belt, many bandits are ethnic Fulani who prey on settled Christian farming communities, exacerbating existing ethnoreligious tensions. The Boko Haram insurgency in the northeast has compounded these challenges by driving herders into the Middle Belt (GCRP, 2025). Making matters worse, the Boko Haram insurgency had started to spread into Niger state in the north-central zone around 2021 (Reuters, Boko Haram Spreading into North-Central Nigeria, 2021).

South-South Zone

The south-south zone, home to the Niger Delta, encompasses six states: Akwa Ibom, Bayelsa, Cross River (formerly South-Eastern), Delta, Edo, and Rivers. It is ethnically diverse with a population that is predominantly Christian. The major economic activity is farming (mainly cocoa, palm oil, kola nut, and rubber). The south-south zone also contains vast oil and natural gas reserves that account for 80 percent of federal government revenues, essentially making it the economic mainstay of the country. Although this zone is the source of Nigeria's oil wealth, that wealth has not measurably improved the lives of most of the zone's inhabitants: The south-south is one of the poorest regions in Nigeria. It lacks adequate infrastructure, and a vast majority of people are economically destitute. The zone's MPI was 0.250 as of 2022. Extreme inequality is evident between the local population and the employees of the oil companies, and the zone suffers from socioeconomic ills ranging from oil spills to high rates of youth unemployment (Olumidey, 2024; NBS, 2021; Nigeria @ 61, 2021). This extreme poverty (21.28 percent of the population in 2020) (Adeyeye, 2020) has contributed to the rise of protest movements such as the IYC and the Movement for the Survival of the Ogoni People (MOSOP).

The striking dichotomy of dire poverty in the midst of riches in Nigeria's south-south zone has triggered what one article published in the *International Journal of Development and Public Policy* termed "resource control agitations"—public demands for resource control "necessitated by the neglect and deprivation suffered by the people of the region." The Ogoni crisis was arguably the most salient example of this phenomenon in the south-south zone. The Ogoni people are a minority ethnic group that lives in the Niger Delta region, where oil was discovered in commercial quantities in 1958. The resulting exploitation by Shell Oil Company (through its subsidiary, Shell Petroleum Development Company of Nigeria), and the ensuing pollution and environmental degradation, devastated the Ogoni, their livestock, their farmland, their health, and their overall quality of life (Nwankwo Jr. et al., 2021; Nnadozie, 2004; Brudney, 2023).

Despite the fact that the oil exports from the region accounted for up to 90 percent of federal government revenues, the Ogoni people endured abject poverty and underdevelopment, minimal infrastructure, and extremely limited socioeconomic opportunities. In response to more than thirty years of these deplorable conditions, in 1990, the Ogoni mobilized to form the MOSOP to protest Shell's exploitation and devastation of their homeland and assert their right to a clean environment, self-determination, and control over resources on their land. In October 1990, under the leadership of Dr. Ken Saro-Wiwa, MOSOP presented the Ogoni Bill of Rights to the federal government of Nigeria, calling for

> political autonomy to participate in the affairs of the Republic as a distinct and separate unit. . .; the right to control and use a fair proportion of Ogoni economic resources for Ogoni development; adequate representations, as of right, in all Nigerian national institutions, and the right to protect the Ogoni environment and ecology from further degradation.
>
> *(World Bank, 2023; Nwankwo Jr. et al., 2021; Nnadozie, 2004; Brudney, 2023; MOSOP, 1992)*

MOSOP organized nonviolent protests to draw national and international attention to the socioeconomic and environmental atrocities of Shell Oil in the region and to demand an appropriate allocation of oil funds. One such march, on January 3, 1993, mobilized three hundred thousand people to march against Shell—at a time when the total Ogoni population was estimated to be about 500,000. According to court documents released in 2009, Shell paid the Nigerian military to put down MOSOP's peaceful protests and subvert MOSOP's activities, but by mid-1993 the movement's persistence succeeded in driving Shell out of Ogoniland after more than thirty years of oil drilling. Unfortunately, it came at a huge cost: The federal military government executed nine MOSOP officials in 1995, including the movement's founder, Dr. Saro-Wiwa, based on bogus charges. Today, the ramifications of the ecological disaster remain in Ogoniland (Nwankwo Jr. et al., 2021; Nnadozie, 2004; Vidal, 2011).

Nor did Shell's exit from Ogoni areas mean a respite for the entire south-south zone (or for all of Nigeria, for that matter) (Gaughran, 2024). Amid the aforementioned rampant inequality and social unrest in the Niger Delta region, several militia groups emerged and began carrying out attacks against oil installations and even kidnapping foreign oil workers and executives after the transition from military rule to civilian rule in 1999. In the first such case, youth militants from Bayelsa state in 2002 abducted ten expatriate Shell employees. Ultimately, the militants were paid a ransom of ₦3 million (about $22,000) to secure the release of the workers. Ransom kidnappings of foreign oil workers and executives soon became common occurrences in the region, as did oil siphoning rackets and incidences of sabotage on oil installations by criminal gangs and militants. Among the most active militant groups in the south-south zone were the Niger Delta People's Volunteer Force (NDPVF) and the Movement for the Emancipation of the Niger Delta (MEND), both of which were more or less Ijaw-aligned and both of which recruited impoverished and often unemployed youths who felt economically marginalized and exploited because they had not benefitted economically from the oil revenues generated by their region. Whereas the NDPVF's overarching goals were more equitable distribution of oil revenues, increased employment opportunities for Niger Delta youths, and the right to delf-determination, MEND's also included "resource control" and two specific aims: receipt of half of all Delta oil revenues and the withdrawal of all government troops from the Niger Delta region (Albert, Danjibo, & Albert, 2020; Rise, 2009; Francis, Lapin, & Rossiasco, 2011; Hazen & Horner, 2007; Hanson, 2007).

The government attempted to crack down on the militants by deploying a joint military task force, which resulted in untold atrocities and displacements among the local population but did little to discourage the militants' destruction of the oil companies' infrastructure. As a result of this militancy, the Nigerian government and the multinational oil companies—both deeply invested in the Niger Delta region and the oil revenue it generated—incurred severe economic losses. Oil production dropped dramatically, crippling the Nigerian economy. It became painfully obvious that something had to be done to quell the unrest and halt the destruction of oil-producing facilities that was costing the federal government more than ₦1.08 billion ($120 million) per day. So, on June 25, 2009, President Umaru Musa Yar'Adua announced an amnesty arrangement in an attempt to "restore peace, human and environmental security in the Niger Delta so as to create an enabling environment for accelerated and sustainable development." In return for relinquishing all illegal arms in their possession and ceasing all hostilities, the militants would receive unconditional pardons and cash payments (Ogege, 2011; Rise, 2009; Francis, Lapin, & Rossiasco, 2011; Mohammed, Robinson, & Aliyu, 2014; Oyandogha, 2009).

The amnesty program formally ended in 2015, discontinued by incoming President Buhari, although he reinstated it in 2017 after renewed militant violence. Regardless, the Niger Delta region remains fragile. As long as environmental degradation, socioeconomic inequality, unemployment, and poverty persist in the south-south zone, citizens will have cause for distress and militants will have cause for action. Perhaps unsurprisingly, neither the amnesty program nor its termination ended the prevalence of conflict. In fact, conflict events ticked up between 2010 and 2016. In February of 2016, a new militant group, the Niger Delta Avengers (NDA), emerged with the same goals as MEND—namely, running the oil companies out of the Niger Delta, giving the people who live there as much control over (and revenue from) oil operations as possible, and staving off environmental destruction. Although smaller than MEND, NDA was heavily armed and succeeded at hitting strategic, high-value targets such as Shell's Forcados oil pipeline, Chevron's Okan platform, and ExxonMobil's Qua Iboe terminal (Nigeria's largest) (Magill, 2023; Ogege, 2011; Oyandogha, 2009; Oluwaniyi, 2011; Hallmark, 2017; FPPIND, 2017).

These attacks once again crippled Nigeria's economy, bringing daily oil production from 2.2 million barrels per day down to 1.4 million—the lowest level in twenty-five years. With more than 95 percent of Nigeria's export earnings derived from petroleum oil, and given that the Niger Delta is the poorest and most underdeveloped region in the country, the detrimental effects on the local economy and on livelihoods at the household level were felt acutely in the south-south zone. According to the World Bank, 22 percent of households were directly affected by violence related to the conflict, and 37 percent of conflict-affected households had at least one member who was displaced or migrated. A study published in the *International Affairs Review* found that a major factor behind youth discontentment was an increase in the youth unemployment rate from 21 percent in 2009 to 24 percent in 2016—which would logically have served to make joining a militia movement all the more palatable. Furthermore, during that period, the proportion of households affected by violence rose steadily: A 2017 report published in the *International Journal of Advanced Academic Research* showed that low income and unemployment contribute significantly to higher levels of frustration, strife, and aggression toward female partners as well as intimate partner violence (Hallmark, 2017; Persson, 2018; Azad, Crawford, & Kaila, 2018; Udoyen, Ufot-Akpabio, & Ifeanacho, 2017). Although the NDA's last known attack took place that year, the group threatened to resume attacks on oil infrastructure in 2021 due to disagreements over the share of oil revenues among communities (Reuters, "Nigeria's 'Delta Avengers' Threaten Oil Installation Attacks," 2021).

Northwest Zone

The northwest zone comprises the states of Jigawa, Kaduna, Kano, Katsina, Kebbi, Sokoto, and Zamfara, as well as Nigeria's second-largest city, Kano. It is the largest geopolitical zone in Nigeria and is home to 25 percent of the country's population. With ample fertile land for agriculture and animal husbandry, its population is composed predominantly of farmers, but herders and those engaged in commerce represent large segments as well. Like the northeast zone, the northwest zone had an MPI of 0.324 as of 2022. The Indigenous majority population is Hausa and Fulani, although several ethnic minorities hail from southern Kaduna, including the Gwari, the Adara, the Ham, the Atyab, and the Gwong, most of whom are Christians.

This ethnic combination breeds multifarious ethnoreligious conflicts—notably but not exclusively between Fulani indigene herders and Hausa farmers as the herders are driven further and further to the south in pursuit of pastureland (Olumidey, 2024; NBS, 2021). The escalation of violence has led to a full-scale humanitarian crisis due to the displacement of farmers from their farmland and the resulting food insecurity in the region. The violence has mainly occurred in rural areas and has spread from the epicenter in Zamfara state to Kano, Kaduna, Katsina, and Kebbi states. According to the International Crisis Group, at least eight thousand deaths were recorded between 2011 and 2020 (ICG, Violence in Nigeria's North West, 2020).

Compounding the situation in the northwest zone is the proliferation of criminal gangs that perpetrate kidnappings for ransom, cattle rustling, armed robbery, and other nefarious activities. The criminal gangs are mostly comprised of Fulani, Hausa, and members of other ethnic groups seeking to enrich themselves. A third dimension of the violence in the northwest zone involves direct confrontations between government security forces and jihadist groups linked to Boko Haram that are increasingly active in the region (ICG, Violence in Nigeria's North West, 2020; ICG, 2021; Onapajo, 2023).

Southeast Zone

The southeast zone is home to Abia, Anambra, Ebonyi, Enugu, and Imo states. (Anambra and Imo were created from the former East-Central state in 1976; part of Imo became Abia state in 1991, the same year that part of Anambra became Enugu state.) The southeast is the smallest geopolitical zone and the coldest relative to the rest of the country. The main economic activities include farming (in crops such as palm oil, rubber, yams, kola nut, rice, and cassava) and mining (in coal, petroleum, and limestone). The people in Abia and Anambra states are also heavily involved in trading and local manufacturing. The region has the lowest poverty ratio in Nigeria; its 2022 MPI was 0.183 (Olumidey, 2024; European Commission, 2024; NBS, 2021; Emewu, 2023).

The vast majority of the southeast zone falls in Igboland, and the Igbo make up the largest proportion of the people in the region. The Igbo population today still simmers from the effects of Nigeria's 1967–70 civil war, and the political marginalization that many Igbo view as a direct result of the Biafra secessionist movement in the 1960s (which itself has roots in the forced amalgamation of the northern and southern protectorates) is a mobilizing factor. Several political organizations—most notably the MASSOB and the Indigenous People of Biafra (IPOB)—continue to agitate for self-determination and conduct civil protests for the realization of the Biafra, which lost its bid for independence after the civil war. These movements are more than just expressions of civil discontent; they are active campaigns for self-determination and autonomy based on decades of marginalization in the southeast zone. This marginalization is evidenced by dilapidated infrastructure (including road networks and bridges), outrageous ethnic inequality (particularly in federal civil service employment opportunities), general exclusion from federal projects, and myriad other social, economic, and political inequalities. These long-standing and chronically ill-addressed issues have spawned Indigenous organizations like MASSOB and IPOB, among others, aimed at giving voice to—and finally rectifying—the grievances of the Igbo nation (Ibe, 2021).

Other intra- and inter-state land disputes, indigene-settler conflicts, and chieftaincy and commercial leadership tussles plague the southeast zone as well. Confirming what we have seen described throughout Nigeria's geopolitical zones, Nzube Chukwuma describes the causes of subethnic conflicts in Nigeria's southeast as linked to disputes over land, chieftaincy squabbles, inter-elite competition, and indigene-settler contentions. Chukwuma uses a case study of the Oruku and Umuode subethnic communities to illustrate the power struggle in decision-making to influence the traditional institution of kingship—which existed before colonial rule and remains very influential in rural communities in Igboland. Prior to independence, traditional rulers played a large role both in garnering public acceptance for political elites and colonialists in rural communities and in mediating communal conflict. As such, a major catalyst to post-independence communal conflict in the southeast zone was the 1976 reform to the 1963 federal constitution that stripped traditional rulers of their powers. The 1960 and 1963 constitutions had previously established the council of chiefs (the traditional institution), and some chiefs in the southeast had become regional governors. The vacuum created when the traditional system was vacated led to corrupt practices by elites and intensified ethnic rivalries (Chukwuma, 2023).

A recurrence of herder-farmer disputes—especially in Enugu state, spilling over from the north-central zone—also impacts the security of the southeast zone. Although herder-farmer clashes are a relatively new phenomenon in the southeast zone, they have the potential to worsen if not adequately addressed. The northern Fulani herders' migration to the southeast threatens the region's stability, especially as the southeast is already grappling with criminal gangs preying on local communities. These gangs tend to camp in forests alongside herders, often making the two groups indistinguishable. Former President Buhari (himself a Fulani) seemed unwilling or unable to address the herder-farmer clashes, which have increasingly escalated to violence in recent years (Okibe, 2022). Buhari's successor, President Bola Tinubu, who took office in 2023, has attempted to advance his administration's Pulaku initiative (essentially, a Fulani code of conduct aimed at implementing a "cultural and ethical value system specific to the Fulani. . . designed to engineer 'a large-scale resettlement programme' to address the root causes of the conflict" in seven northern states). However, one Nigerian national newspaper, *The Nation*, expects the southeast zone to eschew any involvement with the initiative altogether, in large part due to its land shortage. Another, *The Guardian*, reported that IPOB has warned that it will never condone the "ceding or selling of any part of our ancestral land to terrorists and bandits for whatever reason" (Ade-Adeleye, 2024; Editorial Board, 2024).

Southwest Zone

Along with Ekiti, Lagos, Ogun, Ondo, Osun, and Oyo states, the southwest zone holds Nigeria's first- and third-largest cities, Lagos and Ibadan (respectively). The Yoruba are the zone's ethnic majority, and the dominant religion is Christianity, although there is also a sizable Muslim population in Lagos city. The southwest zone's major economic activities are farming, especially tree crops (including rubber, kola nut, and oil palm), and raising livestock (including pigs and chickens). Other commercial activities include textile industries, plastics, and agro-allied industries. Some of the major urban and commercial centers (namely, Ibadan, Lagos, and Abeokuta) are located in this zone, which has the lowest poverty rate in the country and an MPI of 0.151 (Olumidey, 2024; NBS, 2021).

The southwest zone has experienced several incidences of indigene-settler conflicts in the past, typically associated with Yoruba versus non-Yoruba ethnic groups, as well as Christians versus Muslims. Conflicts between herders and farmers represent the most prominent, recent, and ongoing violent conflicts in several of the zone's states. As in other zones, these altercations manifest primarily as land encroachments and transgressions by itinerant herders over sedentary farmers' lands, and they also typically involve sub- and inter-ethnic and Muslim-Christian clashes. Although Muslim Fulani herders have migrated to the southwest since the 1950s, pronounced conflicts with predominantly Christian Yoruba farmers did not occur until the 1980s and 1990s due to land grabs by members of both ethnic groups (Arowosegbe, 2017).

Violent land-based conflicts in the southwest zone occurred between 1999 and 2015 in Ondo state (between Arogbo-Ijaw and Ilaje communities), in Osun state (between Ife and Modakeke communities), and in Oyo state (between Saki-Iseyin and Hausa-Fulani communities). There has also been an uptick in violent conflicts between Fulani herders and Yoruba farmers during the same sixteen-year period: twenty-one in Ekiti state, twenty-four in Lagos state, forty-two in Ogun state, twenty-one in Ondo state, fifteen in Osun state, and forty-one in Oyo state, for a total of 164. Untold thousands were killed (Arowosegbe, 2017). In addition, since at least 2021, violence in the southwest zone has transcended the herder-farmer dynamic to encompass armed robberies, kidnappings, and attacks on religious worshippers. Ondo state has been cited as the most violent in the southwest zone, closely followed by Ogun and Oyo states (UNOCHA, 2022).

Conclusion

This chapter confirms the overall consensus in the existing literature that ethnic diversity is correlated with the occurrence and persistence of conflicts when it is instrumented—that is, when it is employed or manipulated as a basis for political power and resource distribution (i.e., access to land/land rights, provision of public infrastructure, access to economic resources, and distribution of revenues from strategic natural resources). Ethnic and ethnoreligious colorations almost universally underlie and often exacerbate the long progression of conflicts in post-independence Nigeria, even when the primary causes or drivers are neither ethnic nor ethnoreligious in nature. Compounding this conflation, agitators often couch hostilities in terms of ethnic or religious contentions in order to rally coethnics and religious compatriots to their cause. This is certainly the case for Nigeria's two most dire and enduring conflicts: the Boko Haram insurgency and the ongoing herder-farmer crisis.

Too often, efforts to resolve these conflicts and restore harmony and order miss the mark. And as long as fitting and lasting solutions remain elusive, societal harms persist, including human displacements (often on a massive scale), destruction of property and critical resources (infrastructural and otherwise), and loss of livelihoods, food insecurity, and mounting casualties. These far-reaching societal harms in turn squander opportunities for economic growth and development, thereby further diminishing trust in government and public institutions, perpetuating existing socioeconomic inequalities, and creating new dimensions to further entrench the disparities that plague Nigerian society.

Political restructuring has most frequently been the instrument of choice to deal with the many challenges associated with managing Nigeria's large, ethnoreligiously and socioeconomically diverse federal republic—namely, resolving inveterate conflicts and rebuilding both trust and infrastructure in their aftermaths; reducing socioeconomic inequality by promoting equity and opportunities for growth; ensuring fair and equitable representation and distribution of national resources; and building a strong national identity. These challenges should all be viewed as targeted objectives. (The latter especially creates a deeper and more engrained sense of national allegiance and de-emphasizes ethnic consciousness, which fosters greater social cohesion and a sense of equality among all citizens.) (Onyibor, 2016). And indeed, over the decades since independence, various heads of state have sought to meet these objectives through political and financial restructuring, as described earlier in this chapter.

Each of these focus areas requires concerted government attention, bearing in mind that neither political nor financial restructuring is a panacea; they can create unintended consequences rather than effectively solving existing issues. First, given the sheer number of ethnic groups in Nigeria and the deep-seated ethnolinguistic and ethnoreligious divides that exist, there is a limit to how much state creation can achieve if each new state is to be economically self-sustaining. Second, it is not realistic to insist that every state must offer the same uniform conditions of service to its employees. Third, the share of federation revenues distributed to state (and local) governments is based on criteria that can result in dramatically disparate allocations. And fourth, the current system of federal revenue allocation unduly enriches the federal government at the expense of the states, even as the individual states shoulder the responsibility for the core provision of welfare services, such as public health, including hospitals and health care; highways, roads, and railways; and primary, secondary, and tertiary schools.

If the goal of Nigeria's federalism is ultimately to promote national unity and to retrench generations of conflict wrought by ethnic fragmentation and socioeconomic inequality, then the government must contend with the root causes that continue to perpetuate these core challenges and impede the country's growth and development. Philip Vande has recommended the devolution of political and economic power from the central government to the states through a constitutional arrangement that ensures accountability and transparency (Vande, 2021). Emmanuel Ibiam Amah has called for amending the constitution to fundamentally transform Nigerian federalism (and society as a whole), prioritizing national unity over ethnic identity, guarding against control of the center by any one ethnic group, and restructuring revenue and resource distribution (Amah, 2017). One way or another, for Nigerian federalism to overcome the socioeconomic and political inequalities that continue to incite ethnic and ethnoreligious conflict and impede Nigeria's development, national policies must be enacted that overhaul the country's political structure and financial allocation formula to reduce state governments' reliance on the federal government, address regional and ethnic disparities, foster social cohesion and an enduring national identity, and promote lasting stability and economic growth.

Notes

1 Roger Blench, "The Dimensions of Ethnicity, Language and Culture in Nigeria," position paper prepared for the United Kingdom Department for International Development, Abuja, Nigeria, November 2003, 2.

2 Katie Smith, *Polarization, Social Cohesion, and Atrocities: Approaches for a Safer World* (Washington, DC: Search for Common Ground, 2023), 21.

3 Rotimi T. Suberu, *Ethnic Minority Conflicts and Governance in Nigeria* (Ibadan, Nigeria: IFRA-Nigeria [Institut Français de Recherche en Afrique/French Institute for Research in Africa], 1996), 4.

4 Tom Kirk, Danielle Stein, and Annette Fisher, "The Relationship Between Ethnic Diversity and Development: A Diversity Dividend?" (London, UK: Konung International, 2018), 2, 18, 33. Kirk, Stein, and Fisher identify *diversity debits* as unwanted effects, including ethnic clientelism, that exacerbate corruption among the elites, difficulty in agreeing to the provision of public goods and difficulty of market transactions or political bargaining; and *diversity dividends* as benefits from the interaction of ethnic groups in the long run that strengthen informal institutions, producing and promoting a greater level of trust among ethnic groups that can promote development. Id.

5 The north-south divide refers in part to Nigeria's religious dichotomy between Muslims, who reside predominantly in the northern part of the country, and Christians, who mostly reside in the south. The proportion of the population that is Christian and Muslim is evenly split. The north-south dichotomy also denotes stark socioeconomic differences: The south has vast reserves of oil in the Niger Delta. Additionally, although Abuja became the national capital in 1976, Lagos (which is in the southwest) is considered the economic and commercial capital of the country. By contrast, the north is poorer than the south, and its citizens have a broadly inferior quality of life than their counterparts in the south (Olumidey, 2024).

6 Directorate of Intelligence, "Special Report: Nigeria After the War," *U.S. Central Intelligence Agency*, Washington, DC, May 28, 1970, 5 (declassified, issued by the U.S. Department of State, April 21, 2005).

7 See also Chapter 2.

8 Similarly, the number of local government authorities (or LGAs) increased from 301 in 1976 to 775 in 1996. Nigeria's central government comprises three tiers: federal, state, and local. Each state is divided into LGAs. These divisions were created to devolve power to the local level and promote development. Since 1999, there have been 774 LGAs (Ojo & Adebayo, 2008; Okolo & Osimerah, 2017).

9 See Statista, "Share of Federation Accounts Allocation Committee (FAAC) Allocation in Nigeria as of 2022, by Entity," accessed December 9, 2024, https://www.statista.com/statistics/1337053/faac-revenue-share-in-nigeria-by-entity.

10 On average, the conversion rate of naira to dollar in 2006 was ₦127/$1 (CBN, 2020).

11 The ₦30,000 per month minimum wage became effective in Nigeria on April 18, 2019, at which time the naira to dollar conversion rate was ₦307/$1 (CBN, 2020).

12 See World Bank Microdata Library, GHS, Panel 2018–2019, Wave 4 (Nigeria, 2018–19), https://microdata.worldbank.org/index.php/catalog/3557.

13 In addition to Boko Haram's widespread recognition as an Islamist terrorist organization, it has also been accused of ethnic cleansing. Although this avenue has not been widely explored in the literature, its early attacks at least targeted mostly non-Kanuri ethnic groups living in and around northeastern Nigeria. An analysis published by the U.S. Naval Institute of more than two hundred Boko Haram attacks in Borno state between May 2013 and August 2014 suggested that non-Kanuri ethnicity rather than religion was the dominant factor determining Boko Haram's victims (Ross, 2015).

14 See Statista, "States Most Affected by Boko Haram's Deadly Attacks in Nigeria from 2011 to 2023," accessed January 28, 2025, https://www.statista.com/statistics/1197570/deaths-caused-by-boko-haram-in-nigeria.

15 The United Nations Development Programme's MPI is "a means to capture the complexity of poverty that considers dimensions of well-being beyond just monetary poverty." It measures the percentage of households in a given country that are deprived along three dimensions—monetary poverty, education, and basic infrastructure services—in order to convey "a more complete picture of poverty" (World Bank, 2024. A country's index is measured on a scale of zero to one, with higher values indicating higher levels of poverty (OPHI, 2025).

16 See also Statista, "Number of People Kidnapped in Terrorist Attacks in Nigeria from 2017 to 2019," accessed December 19, 2024, https://www.statista.com/statistics/1198407/people-kidnapped-in-terrorist-attacks-in-nigeria.

17 Abul Azad and Heidi Kaila, *Food Insecurity in Conflict Affected Regions in Nigeria: Results from the North East, North Central, and South South Zones* (Washington, DC: World Bank Group, 2018), 12.

18 Abul Azad, Emily Crawford, and Heidi Kaila, *Conflict and Violence in Nigeria: Results from the North East, North Central, and South South Zones* (Washington, DC: World Bank Group, 2018), 18, 28; Azad & Kaila, *Food Insecurity in Conflict Affected Regions in Nigeria*, 7.

19 Azad, Crawford, & Kaila, *Conflict and Violence in Nigeria*, 5.

Bibliography

Adamolekun, Ladipo. "Federalism in Nigeria." Publius: The Journal of Federalism 21, no. 4 (Fall 1991): 1–11, https://doi.org/10.1093/oxfordjournals.pubjof.a037961.

Ade-Adeleye, Adekunle. "How Not to End Farmers-Herders Conflict." *The Nation* (Lagos State, Nigeria), March 17, 2024, https://thenationonlineng.net/how-not-to-end-farmers-herders-conflict.

Adebisi, Oluwapelumi. "Demystifying Pay as You Earn (PAYE) in Nigeria." Nigeria Tax Weekly, September 2, 2024, https://www.linkedin.com/pulse/demystifying-pay-you-earn-paye-nigeria-oluwapelumi-adebisi-imoff.

Adegboyega, Ayodeji. "Only Three of Nigeria's 36 States Can Survive Without Federal Allocation—BudgIT." *Premium Times* (Abuja, Nigeria), October 29, 2019, https://www.premiumtimesng.com/news/top-news/359295-only-three-of-nigerias-36-states-can-survive-without-federal-allocation-budgit.html.

Adeyeye, Paul. "Nigeria's Poverty Crisis and the Nigerian Living Standards Survey." Dataphyte, June 4, 2020, https://dataphyte.com/latest-reports/development/nigerias-poverty-crisis-and-the-nigerian-living-standards-survey.

Adibe, Jideofor. "Explaining the Emergence of Boko Haram." Brookings Institution, May 6, 2014, https://www.brookings.edu/articles/explaining-the-emergence-of-boko-haram.

Adichie, Gloria Adaeze. "Religion as a Transformative Agent in the Conflict Between Farmers and Fulani Herders in Nigeria." African Journal of Emerging Issues 3, no. 4 (2021): 58–69, https://ajoeijournals.org/sys/index.php/ajoei/article/view/191.

Adigun, Olalekan W. "Analysing the Patterns and Dominant Narrative(s) of Nigeria's Farmer-Herder Conflicts." ACCORD Policy and Practice Brief No. 056. African Centre for the Constructive Resolution of Disputes, Durban, South Africa, July 2022, https://www.accord.org.za/publication/analysing-the-patterns-and-dominant-narratives-of-nigerias-farmer-herder-conflicts.

Ailemen, Anthony. "Nigeria Approves N656b for States to Repay Bailout Funds." *Business Day* (Lagos, Nigeria), November 19, 2021, https://businessday.ng/news/article/nigeria-approves-n656b-for-states-to-repay-bailout-funds.

Aina, Damilola, and Daniel Adaji. "31 States Owe CBN N340bn Bailout Funds." *The Punch* (Lagos, Nigeria), March 24, 2024, https://punchng.com/31-states-owe-cbn-n340bn-bailout-funds.

Ajayi, David Olayinka. "British Colonial Policies and the Challenge of National Unity in Nigeria, 1914–2014." Southern Journal for Contemporary History 47, no. 1 (October 2022): 27–50, https://doi.org/10.18820/24150509/SJCH47.v1.3.

Akinyemi, Demola. "Hijab Crisis: Kwara Reopens Oyun Baptist High School." Vanguard (Lagos, Nigeria), June 2, 2022, https://www.vanguardngr.com/2022/06/hijab-crisis-kwara-reopens-oyun-baptist-high-school.

Albert, Isaac Olawale, Nathaniel Danjibo, and Olumayowa Albert. "Back to the Past: Evolution of Kidnapping and Hostage Taking in the Niger Delta, Nigeria." Beijing Law Review 11, no. 1 (March 2020): 211–26, https://doi.org/10.4236/blr.2020.111015.

Alechenu, John. "Why We Broke Nigeria into 12 States—Gowon." Vanguard (Lagos, Nigeria), November 28, 2024, https://www.vanguardngr.com/2024/11/why-we-broke-nigeria-into-12-states-gowon.

Alesina, Alberto, and Elaina La Ferrara. "Ethnic Diversity and Economic Performance." Journal of Economic Literature 43, no. 3 (September 2005): 762–800, https://doi.org/10.1257/002205105774431243.

Alesina, Alberto, et al. "Fractionalization." Journal of Economic Growth 8, no. 2 (June 2003): 155–94, https://doi.org/10.1023/A:1024471506938.

Alhattab, Sara, and Safiya Akau. "'Devastating Reality': 9 Years After Chibok Abductions, Children in Northeast Nigeria Continue to Suffer the Brutal Consequences of Conflict." UNICEF News Release, April 14, 2023, https://www.unicef.org/press-releases/devastating-reality-9-years-after-chibok-abductions-children-northeast-nigeria.

Amah, Emmanuel Ibiam. "Federalism, Nigerian Federal Constitution and the Practice of Federalism: An Appraisal." Beijing Law Review 8, no. 3 (September 2017): 287–310, https://doi.org/10.4236/blr.2017.83017.

Amnesty International. "Nigeria: Boko Haram Must End Vicious Killing Spree." News Release, January 15, 2025, https://www.amnesty.org/en/latest/news/2025/01/nigeria-boko-haram-must-end-vicious-killing-spree.

Amnesty International, "Nigeria: Decade After Boko Haram Attack on Chibok, 82 Girls Still in Captivity." News Release, April 14, 2024, https://www.amnesty.org/en/latest/news/2024/04/nigeria-decade-after-boko-haram-attack-on-chibok-82-girls-still-in-captivity.

Amzat, Ajibola, et al. "The States Murtala Created. . . 40 Years After." *The Guardian* (Lagos, Nigeria), February 5, 2016, https://guardian.ng/features/the-states-murtala-created-40-years-after.

Archibong, Belinda. "Historical Origins of Persistent Inequality in Nigeria." Oxford Development Studies 46, no. 3 (2018): 325–47, https://doi.org/10.1080/13600818.2017.1416072.

Arowosegbe, Jeremiah O. "Ethnic Minorities and Land Conflicts in Southwestern Nigeria." African Peacebuilding Network Working Paper No. 14. Brooklyn, NY: Social Science Research Council, 2017, https://www.ssrc.org/publications/ethnic-minorities-and-land-conflicts-in-southwestern-nigeria.

Asadu, Chinedu. "Hunger Crisis Looms in Nigeria amid Conflict Between Farmers, Herders." AfricaNews (Lyon, France), February 2, 2022, https://www.africanews.com/2022/02/02/hunger-crisis-looms-in-nigeria-amid-conflict-between-farmers-herders.

Awogbade, Moses O. "Grazing Reserves in Nigeria." *Nomadic Peoples* 23 (1987): 19–30, https://www.jstor.org/stable/43123287.

Aye, Baba. "The Shadow of June 12: June 12, the Left and Nigeria's Democratic Revolution." *The Republic* (Lagos, Nigeria), February 14, 2022, https://republic.com.ng/february-march-2022/the-shadow-of-june12.

Azad, Abul, Emily Crawford, and Heidi Kaila. Conflict and Violence in Nigeria: Results from the North East, North Central, and South South Zones. Washington, DC: World Bank Group, 2018, https://documents.worldbank.org/curated/en/111851538025875054.

Azad, Abul, and Heidi Kaila. Food Insecurity in Conflict Affected Regions in Nigeria: Results from the North East, North Central, and South South Zones. Washington, DC: World Bank Group, 2018, https://documents.worldbank.org/curated/en/747391538026440063.

Badruddeen, Mutiah. "Islam in Nigeria [Part I]: A History." MuslimMatters, February 9, 2023, https://muslimmatters.org/2023/02/09/islam-in-nigeria-a-history-part-i.

Bah, Abu Bakarr. "Approaches to Nation Building in Post-Colonial Nigeria." Journal of Political and Military Sociology 32, no. 1 (Summer 2004): 45–60, https://www.jstor.org/stable/45371634.

Balogun, Adeyemi. "Why the Hijab Controversy Persists in Nigeria's Public Schools." The Conversation (Waltham, MA), July 26, 2022, https://theconversation.com/why-the-hijab-controversy-persists-in-nigerias-public-schools-187192.

Bleaney, Michael, and Arcangelo Dimico. "Ethnic Diversity and Conflict." Journal of Institutional Economics 13, no. 2 (June 2017): 357–78, https://doi.org/10.1017/S1744137416000369.

Blench, Roger. "The Dimensions of Ethnicity, Language and Culture in Nigeria." Position paper prepared for the United Kingdom Department for International Development, Abuja, Nigeria, November 2003, https://www.rogerblench.info/Development/Nigeria/Economic%20development/Ethnicity%20Position%20Paper%20Blench%20short.pdf.

Brechenmacher, Saskia. "Stabilizing Northeast Nigeria After Boko Haram." Working Paper. Washington, DC: Carnegie Endowment for International Peace, May 2019, https://carnegieendowment.org/2019/05/03/stabilizing-northeast-nigeria-after-boko-haram-pub-79042.

Brickmans Law. "The Exclusive Legislative List and the Concurrent Legislative List: A Case for Restructuring or Constitutional Defect?" Mondaq, November 28, 2021, https://www.mondaq.com/nigeria/constitutional-administrative-law/1135644/the-exclusive-legislative-list-and-the-concurrent-legislative-list-a-case-for-restructuring-or-constitutional-defect.

Britannica, "Church Missionary Society," last updated December 11, 2024, https://www.britannica.com/topic/Church-Missionary-Society.

Brottem, Leif. "The Growing Complexity of Farmer-Herder Conflict in West and Central Africa." Africa Security Brief No. 39, Africa Center for Strategic Studies, Washington, DC, July 12, 2021, https://africacenter.org/publication/growing-complexity-farmer-herder-conflict-west-central-africa.

Brudney, Allie. "Thirty Years Later: The Silence of the Ogoni." Corporate Accountability Lab, Chicago, IL, May 11, 2023, https://corpaccountabilitylab.org/calblog/2023/5/11/thirty-years-later-the-resilience-of-the-ogoni.

Campbell, John. "The Truth About Boko Haram in Nigeria's Sambisa Forest." *Africa in Transition* (blog), Council on Foreign Relations, December 30, 2016, https://www.cfr.org/blog/truth-about-boko-haram-nigerias-sambisa-forest.

Central Bank of Nigeria (CBN). "Statistical Bulletin." Vol. 31, December 2020, https://www.cbn.gov.ng/Out/2021/STD/2020%20Statistical%20Bulletin_Explanatory%20Notes_Final_Modified.pdf.

Chuangchit, Utamarangsee. "Toward Fiscal Responsibility in Thai Local Government: Lessons Learned from Local Fiscal Management Practices in Canada, France, Japan, South Korea, and United States." Journal of African and Asian Local Government Studies 4, no. 1 (2015): 53–70.

Chukwuma, Nzube A. "Communal Conflicts in Southeast Nigeria: Explaining the Elites' Character in the Oruku and Umuode Sub-Ethnic Conflicts of Enugu State." Socialscientia: Journal of the Social Sciences and Humanities 8, no. 1 (March 2023): 23–46, https://journals.aphriapub.com/index.php/SS/article/view/2034/1887.

Cook, David. "Boko Haram Escalates Attacks on Christians in Northern Nigeria." CTC Sentinel 5, no. 4 (April 2012): 8–10, https://ctc.westpoint.edu/boko-haram-escalates-attacks-on-christians-in-northern-nigeria.

Davidheiser, Mark, and Aniuska M. Luna. "From Complementarity to Conflict: A Historical Analysis of Farmer-Fulbe Relations in West Africa." African Journal on Conflict Resolution 8, no. 1 (July 2008): 77–103, https://doi.org/10.4314/ajcr.v8i1.39421.

Davidson, Frank P., and Kathleen Lusk Brooke. Building the World: An Encyclopedia of the Great Engineering Projects in History, Vol. 2. Westport, CT: Greenwood Press, 2006, https://blogs.umb.edu/buildingtheworld/founding-of-new-cities/the-founding-of-abuja-nigeria.

Diara, Benjamin Chinedu D., and George Christian Nche. "European and American Christian Missions and Nigeria's National Development (1840–1960)." Journal of Educational and Social Research 3, no. 10 (December 2013): 89–99, https://doi.org/10.5901/jesr.2013.v3n10p89.

Directorate of Intelligence. "Special Report: Nigeria After the War." Central Intelligence Agency, Washington, DC, May 28, 1970, 5. Declassified, issued by the U.S. Department of State, April 21, 2005, https://static.history.state.gov/frus/frus1969-76ve05p1/pdf/d194.pdf.

Ducrotoy, Maria Julie, et al. "Fulani Cattle Productivity and Management in the Kachia Grazing Reserve, Nigeria." Pastoralism: Research, Policy and Practice 6, no. 25 (2016): 1–19, https://doi.org/10.1186/s13570-016-0072-y.

Easterly, William, and Ross Levine. "Africa's Growth Tragedy: Policies and Ethnic Divisions." The Quarterly Journal of Economics 112, no. 4 (November 1997): 1203–50, https://doi.org/10.1162/003355300555466.

Editorial Board. "Tinubu's Plan to End Farmers-Herders' Conflict." *The Guardian* (Lagos, Nigeria), March 25, 2024, https://guardian.ng/opinion/tinubus-plan-to-end-farmers-herders-conflict.

Edokpa, David O., et al. "The Nigeria Climate Zones: Variability, Trends and Analysis from Era-Interim Data (2010–2015)." International Journal of Climate Research 8, no. 1 (2024): 1–24, https://doi.org/10.18488/112.v8i1.3804.

Ekpo, Akpan H., and Abwaku Englama. "Fiscal Federalism in Nigeria: Issues, Challenges and Agenda for Reform." In Economic Policy Options for a Prosperous Nigeria, edited by Paul Collier, Chukwuma Soludo, and Catherine Pattillo, 221–43. London, UK: Palgrave Macmillan, 2008.

Elaigwu, Jonah Isawa, Erin Odey Erim, Godfrey Nwanoruo Uzoigwe, and Rafiu, Ayoola Akindele. Foundations of Nigerian Federalism. Jos, Nigeria: Institute of Governance and Social Research, 2001.

Emewu, Ikenna. "South East Has Lowest Poverty Ratio in Nigeria, as North East Is Worst—Research." *Africa China Economy* (Lagos, Nigeria), September 23, 2023, https://africachinapresscentre.org/2023/09/03/south-east-has-lowest-poverty-ratio-in-nigeria-as-north-east-is-worst-research.

European Commission, "Climate in South East Nigeria," last modified June 2024, https://www.worlddata.info/africa/nigeria/climate-south-east.php.

European Union Agency for Asylum (EUAA), "Members of Separatist Movements and Individuals Perceived as Supporting Them," last updated February 2019, https://euaa.europa.eu/country-guidance-nigeria/23-members-separatist-movements-and-individuals-perceived-supporting-them.

Ewetan, Olabanji Olukayode. "Fiscal Federalism in Nigeria: Theory and Practice." International Journal of Development and Sustainability 1, no. 3 (2012): 1075–87, https://isdsnet.com/ijds-v1n3-33.pdf.

Eyeh, Emmanuel Torty. "Violent Religious Conflicts in Nigeria, 1980–2019: Causes, Mitigation and Management Strategies." The International Journal of Humanities and Social Sciences 8, no. 6 (June 2020): 216–23, https://doi.org/10.24940/theijhss/2020/v8/i6/HS2006-128.

Eze, Okonkwo C., Alexander Elimian, and Uchenna G. Chinwuba. "The Politics of State Creation and National Integration in Nigeria." Journal of Politics and Law 8, no. 1 (2015): 113–21, https://doi.org/10.5539/jpl.v8n1p113.

Fafunwa, Babatunde Aliu . "The Coming of the Missionaries." In History of Education in Nigeria. 1st ed. London, UK: Routledge, 1974.

Fayomi, Oluyemi, et al. "Dissection of Hazardous Climate and Farmer-Herder Conflicts in Nigeria." African Journal of International Affairs and Development 25, no. 1 (2021): 17–46, https://www.journals.lcu.edu.ng/index.php/AJIAD/article/view/1030.

Federal Ministry of Solid Mineral Development (FMSMD). Environmental and Social Management Framework Final Report: Nigeria Mineral Sector Support for Economic Diversification Project. Abuja, Nigeria: Federal Ministry of Solid Mineral Development, December 2016, https://documents1.worldbank.org/curated/en/280551481614032707/pdf/SFG2754-EA-P159761-Box396337B-PUBLIC-Disclosed-12-9-2016.pdf.

Felbab-Brown, Vanda. "In Nigeria, We Don't Want Them Back." Brookings Institution, May 2018, https://www.brookings.edu/articles/in-nigeria-we-dont-want-them-back.

Francis, Paul, Deirdre Lapin, and Paula Rossiasco. Securing Development and Peace in the Niger Delta: A Social and Conflict Analysis for Change. Washington, DC:

The Wilson Center, 2011, https://www.wilsoncenter.org/publication/securing-development-and-peace-the-niger-delta-social-and-conflict-analysis-for-change.

Fund for Peace and Partnership Initiatives in the Niger Delta (FPPIND). "History Never Quite Repeats: Militancy in the Niger Delta." Niger Delta Partnership Initiative Briefing, February 2017, https://fundforpeace.org/2017/02/01/history-never-quite-repeats-militancy-in-the-niger-delta.

Garkuwa, Abdulazeez Nuhu, and Opayemi Iroye Samuel. "Ethno Religious Conflicts and Management Strategies in Bauchi State Nigeria." Al Hickmah Journal of Arts and Sciences Education 5, no. 2 (2023): 6–10.

Gaughran, Audrey. Selling Out Nigeria: Shell's Irresponsible Divestment. Amsterdam, Netherlands: SOMO (Stichting Onderzoek Multinationale Ondernemingen/Centre for Research on Multinational Corporations), 2024, https://justice-project.org/wp-content/uploads/2024/04/Selling-out-Nigeria.pdf.

Global Centre for the Responsibility to Protect (GCRP), "Nigeria: Populations at Risk," last updated March 14, 2025, https://www.globalr2p.org/countries/nigeria.

Hallmark, Terry. "Oil and Violence in the Niger Delta Isn't Talked About Much, But It Has a Global Impact." *Forbes*, February 13, 2017, https://www.forbes.com/sites/uhenergy/2017/02/13/oil-and-violence-in-the-niger-delta-isnt-talked-about-much-but-it-has-a-global-impact.

Hanson, Stephanie. "MEND: The Niger Delta's Umbrella Militant Group." Council on Foreign Relations, March 21, 2007, https://www.cfr.org/backgrounder/mend-niger-deltas-umbrella-militant-group.

Hazen, Jennifer M., and Jonas Horner. "Annexe 6: Niger Delta People's Volunteer Force (NDPVF)." In Small Arms, Armed Violence, and Insecurity in Nigeria: The Niger Delta in Perspective, 127–29. Occasional Paper No. 20. Geneva, Switzerland: Small Arms Survey, Graduate Institute of International Studies, December 2007, https://www.jstor.org/stable/resrep10752.21.

Ibe, Eric Chigozie. "Agitations of the Indigenous People of Biafra and the Right to Self-Determination." Madonna University, Nigeria Faculty of Law Journal (MUNFOLL) 8 (August 2021): 27–38, https://journals.ezenwaohaetorc.org/index.php/MUNFOLLJ/article/view/1819.

Ifeyinwa, Mbakogu. "Socio-Cultural Factors and Ethnic Group Relationships in Contemporary Nigerian Society." The African Anthropologist 9, no. 2 (2002): 117–37, https://doi.org/10.4314/aa.v9i2.23063.

Igbadumhe, Abaye Friday, et al. Minimum Wage Implementation in Nigeria: Issues and Prospects. Proceedings of Seventh International Conference on Education and Social Sciences, Dubai, United Arab Emirates, January 20–22, 2020, 1308–18, https://eprints.covenantuniversity.edu.ng/id/eprint/14050.

Ingawa, Salisu Ahmed, Tarawali, Gabi, and Ralph von Kaufmann. "Grazing Reserves in Nigeria: Problems, Prospects and Policy Implications." Africa Livestock Policy Analysis Network Paper No. 22. Addis Ababa, Ethiopia: International Livestock Centre for Africa, 1989, https://openknowledge.fao.org/server/api/core/bitstreams/2264ad3d-d693-43d5-80a3-83f187301b5b/content/x5516e.htm.

Institute for Peace and Conflict Resolution (IPCR). 2016 Strategic Conflict Assessment of Nigeria: Consolidated and Zonal Reports. Abuja, Nigeria: Institute for Peace and Conflict Resolution, 2017, https://www.undp.org/nigeria/publications/strategic-conflict-assessment-nigeria-2016.

International Crisis Group (ICG). "Halting the Deepening Turmoil in Nigeria's North West." EU Watch List, May 26, 2021, https://www.crisisgroup.org/africa/west-africa/nigeria/halting-deepening-turmoil-nigerias-north-west.

ICG. Herders Against Farmers: Nigeria's Expanding Deadly Conflict. Africa Report No. 252. Brussels, Belgium: International Crisis Group, September 2017, https://www.crisisgroup.org/sites/default/files/252-nigerias-spreading-herder-farmer-conflict.pdf.

ICG. Violence in Nigeria's North West: Rolling Back the Mayhem. Africa Report No. 288. Brussels, Belgium: International Crisis Group, May 2020, https://www.crisisgroup.org/africa/west-africa/nigeria/288-violence-nigerias-north-west-rolling-back-mayhem.

ICG. What Role for the Multinational Joint Task Force in Fighting Boko Haram? Africa Report No. 291. Brussels, Belgium: International Crisis Group, July 2020, https://www.crisisgroup.org/africa/west-africa/291-what-role-multinational-joint-task-force-fighting-boko-haram.

International Organization for Migration (IOM). Displacement Tracking Matrix: Round XXI Report—February 2018. Geneva, Switzerland: International Organization for Migration, February 2018, https://dtm.iom.int/es/reports/nigeria-—-displacement-report-21-february-2018.

Isichei, Elizabeth. "The Maitatsine Risings in Nigeria 1980–85: A Revolt of the Disinherited." Journal of Religion in Africa 17, no. 3 (1987): 194–208, https://doi.org/10.1163/157006687X00136.

Kanbur, Ravi, Prem Kumar Rajaram, and Ashutosh Varshney. "Ethnic Diversity and Ethnic Strife: An Interdisciplinary Perspective." World Development 39, no. 2 (February 2011): 147–58, https://doi.org/10.1016/j.worlddev.2009.11.034.

Kayode, Bodunrin. "Inside Nigeria's Sambisa Forest, the Boko Haram Hideout Where Kidnapped School Girls Are Believed to Be Held." *The Guardian*, April 29, 2014, https://www.theguardian.com/world/2014/apr/29/nigeria-sambisa-forest-boko-haram-hideout-kidnapped-school-girls-believed-to-be-held.

Khalid, Ishaq. "Nigeria's Boko Haram Militants: Six Reasons They Have Not Been Defeated." BBC News, May 16, 2021, https://www.bbc.com/news/world-africa-57117296.

Khemani, Stuti. "Fiscal Federalism and Service Delivery in Nigeria: The Role of States and Local Governments." Paper prepared for the Nigerian PER Steering Committee Meeting, Abuja, Nigeria, July 2001, https://studylib.net/doc/18414904/fiscal-federalism-and-service-delivery-in-nigeria.

Kirk, Tom, Danielle Stein, and Annette Fisher. "The Relationship Between Ethnic Diversity and Development: A Diversity Dividend?" London, UK: Konung International, June 2018, https://www.gov.uk/research-for-development-outputs/the-relationship-between-ethnic-diversity-development-a-diversity-dividend.

Klein, Gabriel. "Determination Met with Marginalization: A Case Study on the Nigerian Civil War." edited by Isha Shahane and Justin Weir. FLUX: International Relations Review 12, no. 11 (2022): 55–61, https://fluxirr.mcgill.ca/article/view/104.

Komolafe, Kayode. "The Arrival of Midwest." ThisDay (Lagos, Nigeria), August 30, 2023, https://www.thisdaylive.com/index.php/2023/08/30/the-arrival-of-midwest.

Langer, Arnim, and Frances Stewart. Regional Imbalances, Horizontal Inequalities, and Violent Conflicts: Insights from Four West African Countries. Washington, DC: World Bank, 2015, https://hdl.handle.net/10986/22514.

Lawal, Wale. "June 12: Freest and Fairest of Them All." *The Republic* (Lagos, Nigeria), November 10, 2023.

Magill, John R. "Nigeria's Presidential Amnesty Program: Successes, Failures, and Economic Incentives." Thesis, Naval Postgraduate School, Monterey, CA, June 2023.

Marotta, Phillip, Bandy X. Lee, Morkeh Blay-Tofey, Clara H. Kim, Kelsey K. Schuder, Grace Lee, and James Gilligan. "Government Political Structure and Violent Death Rates: A Longitudinal Analysis of Forty-Three Countries, 1960–2008." Aggression and Violent Behavior 47 (July–August 2019): 101313.

Mohammed, Suleiman B., Jackson Onome Robinson, and Isiaka Hassan Aliyu. "From Conflict to Peace Building and Post Conflict Reconstruction: A Critical Reflection on the Nigeria Niger Delta Amnesty." International Letters of Social and Humanistic Sciences 30 (June 2014): 81–95.

Mohammed, Usman. "International Political Economy of Nigerian Amalgamation Since 1914." European Scientific Journal 9, no. 29 (October 2013): 429–57, https://test.eujournal.org/index.php/esj/article/view/1937.

Moore, Jonathan. "The Political History of Nigeria's New Capital." The Journal of Modern African Studies 22, no. 1 (March 1984): 167–75, https://doi.org/10.1017/S0022278X00056846.

Movement for the Survival of the Ogoni People (MOSOP). *Ogoni Bill of Rights*. Port Harcourt, Nigeria: Saros International Publishers, June 1992, https://bebor.org/wp-content/uploads/2012/09/Ogoni-Bill-of-Rights.pdf.

Musa, Phillip, and Olalekan Eyitayo Ajibade. "Local Government and Challenges of Revenue Allocation in Nigeria (A Study of Yewa South Local Government, Ogun State)." Journal of Public Administration, Finance and Law 10 (2016): 55–66, https://www.jopafl.com/uploads/issue10/LOCAL_GOVERNMENT_AND_CHALLENGES_OF_REVENUE_ALLOCATION_IN_NIGERIA.pdf.

Mustapha, Abdul Raufu. "Ethnic Structure, Inequality and Governance of the Public Sector in Nigeria." Democracy, Governance and Human Rights Programme Paper No. 24. Geneva, Switzerland: United Nations Research Institute for Social Development, November 2006, https://assets.publishing.service.gov.uk/media/57a08c97ed915d3cfd0014aa/wp18.pdf.

National Bureau of Statistics (NBS). Annual Abstract of Statistics 2013. Abuja, Nigeria: National Bureau of Statistics, 2013.

NBS. Annual Abstract of Statistics 2015. Abuja, Nigeria: National Bureau of Statistics, 2015.

NBS. Annual Abstract of Statistics 2016. Abuja, Nigeria: National Bureau of Statistics, 2016.

NBS. Annual Abstract of Statistics 2019. Abuja, Nigeria: National Bureau of Statistics, 2019.

NBS. 2021 Nigeria's Multidimensional Poverty Index (MPI): Statistical Snapshots. Abuja, Nigeria: National Bureau of Statistics, 2021, https://ngfrepository.org.ng:8080/jspui/handle/123456789/5411.

Ngbea, Gabriel Terwase, and Hilary Chukwuka Achunike. "Religion: Past and Present in Nigeria." International Journal of Sciences: Basic and Applied Research 17, no. 2 (2014): 156–74, https://www.gssrr.org/index.php/JournalOfBasicAndApplied/article/view/1942.

"Nigeria to Get a New Capital and Seven Additional States." The New York Times, February 4, 1976, 4, https://timesmachine.nytimes.com/timesmachine/1976/02/04/82620019.html.

"Nigeria—Minimum Wages," Countryeconomy.com, accessed December 11, 2024, https://countryeconomy.com/national-minimum-wage/nigeria.

"Nigeria's Climate and Vegetation." Tansi International College, Awka, Nigeria, August 5, 2020, https://tansicollege.edu.ng/content/nigeria%E2%80%99s-climate-and-vegetation.

"Nigeria @ 61: South-South, Golden Egg, Poor Infrastructure." Vanguard (Lagos, Nigeria), October 5, 2021, https://www.vanguardngr.com/2021/10/nigeria-61-south-south-golden-egg-poor-infrastructure.

Njoku, Chukwudi Gbadebo. "Farmer-Herder Relations in Nigeria: Historical Antecedents and the Way Forward for Social Cohesion." Building Blocks for Peace Foundation, May 2, 2021, https://bbforpeace.org/blog/2021/05/02/farmer-herder-relations-in-nigeria-historical-antecedents-and-the-way-forward-for-social-cohesion.

Nnadozie, Emanuel. "The Curse of Oil in Ogoniland." Case Study, University of Michigan, August 15, 2004, https://websites.umich.edu/~snre492/cases_03-04/Ogoni/Ogoni_case_study.htm.

Nnaji, Amaka, et al. "Farmer-Herder Conflicts and Food Insecurity: Evidence from Rural Nigeria." Agricultural and Resource Economics Review 51, no. 2 (August 2022): 391–421, https://doi.org/10.1017/age.2022.9.

Nwala, Timothy Uzodinma. Nigeria, Path to Unity and Stability: Abuja National Constitutional Conference (1994–95)—Background, Issues and Personal Reminiscences. Nsukka, Nigeria: Niger Books and Publishing Co., 1997.

Nwankwo, Sabastine, Jr., et al. "The Politics of Resource Control Agitation and Its Effects on the Socio-Economic Development of the Niger Delta Region of Nigeria." International Journal of Development and Public Policy 1, no. 5 (October 2021): 258–67, https://openaccessjournals.eu/index.php/ijdpp/article/view/495.

Odegbaroye, Oluwatoyin. "Here's Why 33 States May Be Unable to Pay Salaries from May." Dataphyte, May 7, 2020, https://dataphyte.com/latest-reports/economy/heres-why-33-states-may-be-unable-to-pay-salaries-from-may.

Ogege, Samuel Omadjohwoefe. "Amnesty Initiative and the Dilemma of Sustainable Development in the Niger Delta Region of Nigeria." Journal of Sustainable Development 4, no. 4 (August 2011): 249–58, https://doi.org/10.5539/jsd.v4n4p249.

Ohiomu, Sylvester, and Sunday Ade Oluyemi. "Resolving Revenue Allocation Challenges in Nigeria: Implications for Sustainable National Development." The American Economist 64, no. 1 (March 2019): 142–53, https://doi.org/10.1177/0569434518775324.

Oji, Richard Okechukwu. "Nigerian Politics and Government from 1960." Lecture notes, Department of Political Science, Enugu State University of Science and Technology, Enugu, Nigeria, 1995, cited in Aloysius-Michaels Okolie and Jide Chime, "State and Crises of Political Legitimacy in Africa," African Journal of Politics and Administrative Studies 6, no. 1 (March 2014): 1–17, https://www.ajol.info/index.php/ajpas/article/view/246861.

Ojo, Emmanuel, and Adebayo, Peter Folorunsho . "The Politics of States', Local Governments' Creation and Nigeria's Search for Geo-Political Balancing." African Research Review 2, no. 3 (2008): 334–67, https://doi.org/10.4314/afrrev.v2i3.41078.

Okediji, Tade O. "Social Fragmentation and Economic Growth: Evidence from Developing Countries." Journal of Institutional Economics 7, no. 1 (March 2011): 77–104, https://doi.org/10.1017/S1744137410000251.

Okeke, Chika Edwin. "Implementation and Enforcement of the Federal Character Principle in Nigeria." Nnamdi Azikiwe University Journal of International Law and Jurisprudence 10, no. 2 (2019): 174–85, https://www.ajol.info/index.php/naujilj/article/view/183698.

Okibe, Hyginus Banko. "Herder-Farmer Conflicts in South East Nigeria: Assessing the Dangers." Southern Voices Network for Peacebuilding Research Paper No. 34. Washington, DC: The Wilson Center, September 2022, https://www.wilsoncenter.org/publication/svnp-research-paper-okibe.

Okolie, Aloysius-Michaels, and Jide Chime. "State and Crises of Political Legitimacy in Africa." African Journal of Politics and Administrative Studies 6, no. 1 (March 2014): 1–17, https://www.ajol.info/index.php/ajpas/article/view/246861.

Okolo, Philips O., and Charles Osimerah. "The Politics of Local Government Creation: Implications for National Development in Nigeria." South East Journal of Political Science 3, no. 1 (2017): 285–99, https://journals.aphriapub.com/index.php/SEJPS/article/view/792.

Okon, Anthony O. "Nigeria and a People's Constitution: The Imperative of Democracy and Change." Constitution: A Journal of Constitutional Development 4, no. 1 (2004): 11–36, https://hdl.handle.net/10520/AJA15955753_57.

Okwesili, Nkwede Joseph. "Federalism and State Creation in Nigeria." African Journal of Politics and Administrative Studies 6, no. 1 (March 2014): 89–101, https://www.ajol.info/index.php/ajpas/article/view/246889.

Olumidey. "Economic Activities of the Six Geo-Political Zones of Nigeria." *Steemit* (blog), accessed December 12, 2024, https://steemit.com/wafrica/@olumidey/economic-activities-of-the-six-geo-political-zones-of-nigeria.

Olupona, Jacob K. "The Spirituality of Africa." Interview by Anthony Chiorazzi. The Harvard Gazette, October 6, 2015, https://news.harvard.edu/gazette/story/2015/10/the-spirituality-of-africa, https://news.harvard.edu/gazette/story/2015/10/the-spirituality-of-africa.

Oluwaniyi, Oluwatoyin O. "Post-Amnesty Programme in the Niger Delta: Challenges and Prospects." Conflict Trends 10, no. 4 (January 2011): 46–54, https://au.int/sites/default/files/documents/39221-doc-175._the_post-amnesty_programme_in_the_niger_delta._challenges_and_prospects.pdf.

Omipidan, Teslim Opemipo. "How Nigeria Got to 36 States (Timeline of State Creation in Nigeria)." OldNaija: Home of Nigerian History and Cultures (blog), July 26, 2015.

Onapajo, Hakeem. "Conflict and Peacebuilding in Northwest Nigeria: A Perspective on 'The Bandit Warlords of Zamfara.'" Kujenga Amani, African Peacebuilding Network, Social Science Research Council, September 15, 2023, https://kujenga-amani.ssrc.org/2023/09/15/conflict-and-peacebuilding-in-northwest-nigeria-a-perspective-on-the-impact-of-bbc-africas-documentary-on-the-bandit-warlords-of-zamfara.

Onuigbo, Fidelia Nebechi. "Internally Generated Revenue in Nigeria: Prospects and Challenges." Journal of Social Sciences 6, no. 2 (2021): 287–96.

Onyibor, Michael Ikechukwu Sunday. "National Identity and Crisis of Integration in Multi-Ethnic Nigeria: An Existentialist Perspective." Open Journal of Philosophy 6, no. 1 (February 2016): 1–12, https://doi.org/10.4236/ojpp.2016.61001.

Osaghae, Eghosa E. "Government and Politics." In Nigeria: A Country Study, edited by Helen Chapin Metz, 203–51. Washington, DC: U.S. Government Printing Office, 1992, https://www.marines.mil/Portals/1/Publications/Nigeria%20Study_3.pdf.

Osaghae, Eghosa E., et al. Youth Militias, Self-Determination and Resource Control Struggles in the Niger-Delta Region of Nigeria. CODESRIA Research Report No. 5. Dakar, Senegal: Council for the Development of Social Science Research in Africa, March 2011, https://publication.codesria.org/index.php/pub/catalog/book/108.

Oseni, Michael. "Internally Generated Revenue (IGR) in Nigeria: A Panacea for State Development." European Journal of Humanities and Social Sciences 21, no. 1 (2013): 1050–66, https://www.researchgate.net/publication/328346885.

Oshawa, Toshikazu, and Tong Yang. "Productive Effects of Public Spending, Spillovers, and Optimal Matching Grant Rates." Humanities and Social Sciences Communications 9, no. 366 (December 2022): 1–8, https://doi.org/10.1057/s41599-022-01378-z.

Ota, Ejitu N., Chinyere S. Ecoma, and Chimela Godwin Wambu. "Creation of States in Nigeria, 1967–1996: Deconstructing the History and Politics." American Research Journal of Humanities and Social Sciences 6, no. 1 (2020): 1–8, https://www.arjonline.org/papers/arjhss/v6-i1/5.pdf.

Otekunrin, Olutosin Ademola, et al. "How Far Has Africa Gone in Achieving the Zero Hunger Target? Evidence from Nigeria." Global Food Security 22 (September 2019): 1–12, https://doi.org/10.1016/j.gfs.2019.08.001.

Oxford Poverty and Human Development Initiative (OPHI, 2025), "The Global Multidimensional Poverty Index," accessed February 12, 2025, https://ophi.org.uk/global-mpi.

Oyandogha, Samuel. "Amnesty for Militants as Political Solution to Niger Delta Crisis." Vanguard (Lagos, Nigeria), June 28, 2009.

Oyeyemi, Tunji. "Why Each State Must Determine Its Minimum Wage." Federal Ministry of Information and National Orientation, Abuja, Nigeria, February 1, 2019, https://fmino.gov.ng/why-each-state-must-determine-its-minimum-wage.

Persson, Jennie. "Opportunity for Residents in the Niger Delta: A Problem-Driven Political Economy Analysis." The International Affairs Review, June 15, 2018, https://www.iar-gwu.org/print-archive/fj8yy35dkvsh543lfuslvxionpq5q0.

"Poorest States in Nigeria—2022." *Nairametrics Digest* (Lagos, Nigeria), November 22, 2022, https://www.linkedin.com/pulse/poorest-states-nigeria-2022-nairametrics.

Quinn, Zoe. "The Founding of Abuja, Nigeria." *Building the World* (blog), July 10, 2012. Published in Frank P. Davidson and Kathleen Lusk Brooke. Building the World: An Encyclopedia of the Great Engineering Projects in History, Vol. 2, 733–59. Westport, CT: Greenwood Press, 2006, https://blogs.umb.edu/buildingtheworld/founding-of-new-cities/the-founding-of-abuja-nigeria.

Reuters. "Boko Haram Spreading into North-Central Nigeria, Officials Say." Voice of America, October 23, 2021, https://www.voanews.com/a/boko-haram-spreadin-into-north-central-nigeria-officials-say/6255608.html.

Reuters. "Nigerian Islamic Sect Leader Mohammed Yusuf Killed in Detention." France 24, July 30, 2009, https://www.france24.com/en/20090730-nigerian-islamic-sect-leader-mohammed-yusuf-killed-detention-.

Reuters. "Nigeria's 'Delta Avengers' Threaten Oil Installation Attacks." Reuters, June 26, 2021, https://www.reuters.com/business/energy/nigerias-delta-avengers-threaten-oil-installation-attacks-2021-06-26.

Rise, Xan. "Nigeria Begins Amnesty for Niger Delta Militants." *The Guardian*, August 6, 2009, https://www.theguardian.com/world/2009/aug/06/niger-delta-militants-amnesty-launched.

Ross, Kirk. "Essay: Boko Haram's Campaign of Ethnic Cleansing." *USNI News* (United States Naval Institute), February 11, 2015, https://news.usni.org/2015/02/11/essay-boko-harams-campaign-ethnic-cleansing.

Saint, Ekpali. "Timeline: Half a Century of Oil Spills in Nigeria's Ogoniland." Al Jazeera, December 21, 2022, https://www.aljazeera.com/features/2022/12/21/timeline-oil-spills-in-nigerias-ogoniland.

Salawu, Bashiru. "Ethno-Religious Conflicts in Nigeria: Causal Analysis and Proposals for New Management Strategies." European Journal of Social Sciences 13, no. 3 (2010): 345–53.

Smith, Katie. Polarization, Social Cohesion, and Atrocities: Approaches for a Safer World. Washington, DC: Search for Common Ground, 2023, https://documents.sfcg.org/wp-content/uploads/2023/07/Polarization-Social-Cohesion-Atrocities-FINAL.pdf.

Suberu, Rotimi T. "Ethnic Inequality, the Federal Character Principle, and the Reform of Nigeria's Presidential Federalism." WIDER Working Paper No. 2022/113. Helsinki, Finland: United Nations University World Institute for Development Economics Research, October 2022, https://doi.org/10.35188/UNU-WIDER/2022/247-8.

Suberu, Rotimi T. Ethnic Minority Conflicts and Governance in Nigeria. Ibadan, Nigeria: IFRA-Nigeria (Institut Français de Recherche en Afrique/French Institute for Research in Africa), 1996, https://doi.org/10.4000/books.ifra.748.

Suberu, Rotimi T. "Nigeria's Permanent Constitutional Transition: Military Rule, Civilian Instability and 'True Federalism' in a Deeply Divided Society." Forum of Federations Occasional Series Paper No. 34. Ottawa, Ontario, Canada: Forum of Federations, 2019, https://constitutionnet.org/sites/default/files/2019-06/Nigeria_35.pdf.

Tertsakian, Carina. The O'odua People's Congress (OPC): Fighting Violence with Violence. New York, NY: Human Rights Watch, February 2003, https://www.hrw.org/sites/default/files/reports/nigeria0203.pdf.

Tom, Edet Joshua, and Harrison Otuekong Ataide. "Revenue Allocation in Nigeria: Issues, Challenges and Prospects." Journal of Public Administration and Governance 11, no. 2 (June 2021): 229–45, https://doi.org/10.5296/jpag.v11i2.18682.

Udoyen, Grace, Akpabio Ufot-Akpabio, and Ifeanacho, Martin Ikechukwu. "Socio-Economic Factors and Intimate Partner Violence in Selected States of the Niger Delta Region of Nigeria." International Journal of Advanced Academic Research 3, no. 3 (March 2017): 58–73, https://www.ijaar.org/articles/Volume3-Number3/Arts-Humanities-Education/ijaar-ahe-v3n3-m17-pp8.pdf.

Ukiwo, Ukoha. "Education, Horizontal Inequalities and Ethnic Relations in Nigeria." International Journal of Educational Development 27, no. 3 (May 2007): 266–81, https://doi.org/10.1016/j.ijedudev.2006.10.016.

United Nations General Assembly (UNGA). Violations and Abuses Committed by Boko Haram and the Impact on Human Rights in the Countries Affected. Annual Report of the United Nations High Commissioner for Human Rights, Human Rights Council, Thirteenth Session, Geneva, Switzerland, December 9, 2015, https://digitallibrary.un.org/record/819031.

United Nations Office for the Coordination of Humanitarian Affairs (UNOCHA). "Torrents of Violence." OCHA News Release, June 7, 2022, https://reliefweb.int/report/nigeria/torrents-violence.

United States Commission on International Religious Freedom (USCIRF), "Did You Know. . . . Boko Haram in Nigeria," accessed December 11, 2024, https://www.uscirf.gov/publications/did-you-knowboko-haram-nigeria.

United States National Counterterrorism Center (USNCC), "Foreign Terrorist Organizations: Boko Haram," last updated October 2022, https://www.dni.gov/nctc/ftos/boko_haram_fto.html.

USNCC, "Terrorist Groups: Boko Haram," Counter-Terrorism Guide, accessed March 26, 2025, https://www.dni.gov/nctc/groups/boko_haram.html.

Vande, Philip T. "Fiscal Federalism and the Politics of Revenue Allocation in Nigeria." Zamfara Journal of Politics and Development 2, no. 1 (2021): 1–19, https://zjpd.com.ng/index.php/zjpd/article/view/18.

Vidal, John. "Shell Oil Paid Nigerian Military to Put Down Protests, Court Documents Show." The Guardian, October 2, 2011, https://www.theguardian.com/world/2011/oct/03/shell-oil-paid-nigerian-military.

Waddington, Conway. "MASSOB and Security in South-East Nigeria—Although Peaceful, This Biafran Secessionist Movement Should Not Be Ignored." Africa Conflict Monthly Monitor 2013, no. 9 (2013): 2–85, https://hdl.handle.net/10520/EJC141696.

Warren, James. "New York Times and Nonprofit Team Up for Chilling Exposé." Poynter Institute, June 23, 2017, https://www.poynter.org/newsletters/2017/times-and-nonprofit-team-for-chilling-expose-update.

Waters-Bayer, Ann, and Ellen Taylor-Powell. "Population and Land Use in the Subhumid Zone of Nigeria." In Livestock Systems Research in Nigeria's Subhumid Zone, edited by R. von Kaufman, S. Chater, and R. Blench, 37–58. Proceedings of the Second ILCA/NAPRI (International Centre for Livestock/National Animal Product Research Institute) Symposium, Kaduna, Nigeria, October 29–November 2, 1984. Addis Ababa, Ethiopia: International Centre for Livestock, 1986, https://hdl.handle.net/10568/50034.

Williams, Ejeh Adoyi, and Ogbole F. E Orokpo. "Fiscal Federalism in Nigeria: An Analysis of Issues and Challenges." International Journal of Peace and Conflict Studies 2, no. 1 (2014): 37–45, https://journals.rcmss.com/index.php/ijpcs/article/view/133.

World Bank. Jumpstarting Inclusive Growth: Unlocking the Productive Potential of Nigeria's People and Resource Endowments. Washington, DC: World Bank Group, 2019, https://hdl.handle.net/10986/32795.

World Bank, "Multidimensional Poverty Measure," brief, last updated October 2024. https://documents.worldbank.org/en/publication/documents-reports/documentdetail/099014010212439664

World Bank. "Nigeria." In Sub-Saharan Africa: Macro Poverty Outlook—Country-by-Country Analysis and Projections for the Developing World, 68–69. Washington, DC: International Bank for Reconstruction and Development/World Bank, 2023, https://thedocs.worldbank.org/en/doc/77351105a334213c64122e44c2efe523-0500072021/related/mpo-sm23-ssa.pdf.

Yusuf, Hajiya Bilkisu. "Managing Muslim-Christian Conflicts in Northern Nigeria: A Case Study of Kaduna State." Islam and Christian-Muslim Relations 18, no. 2 (2007): 237–56, https://doi.org/10.1080/09596410701214118.

11

IDENTITY, INEQUALITY, AND COLONIAL OVERHANG

Law and Continuing Legacies of Divide and Rule in Nigeria

Olufunmilayo B. Arewa

Introduction

Political fragmentation and ethnic strife are endemic across post-independence Africa. These realities and their root causes are underpinned by the legacies of colonialism and the British imperial heritage. Colonial powers facilitated external control in Africa by fragmenting and disrupting existing institutions and relations. British colonial policies actively fostered divisions by drawing ever-finer distinctions around various identity categories and criteria, including region, language, religion, ethnicity, and skin color. At the same time, colonial administration artificially homogenized disparate groups of people into convenient political units. The multiethnic states that resulted from these conditions and the ethnopolitical fragmentation baked into them

> all derive in no small measure many of their problems from the British colonial attempt to divide the population into distinct groups. . . . Boundary lines drawn on the ground in colonial times have been remarkably difficult to erase in the post-colonial era.
>
> *(Christopher, 1988)*[1]

During the colonial period, such distinctions—even those that existed prior to sustained contact with Europeans—could take on different meanings, owing in part to colonial administrators' assumptions and activities. For instance, in the Horn of Africa, Somalis were divided into French Somaliland, British Somalia, Italian Somalia, and the Somali region of northern Kenya. Similarly, the Afar people of Ethiopia were divided among Ethiopia, Eritrea, and Djibouti. The Egba, a Yoruba ethnic group in southwestern Nigeria, were divided across three countries: Nigeria,

DOI: 10.4324/9781003357025-14

Benin, and Togo; Benin and Togo are former French colonies, while Nigeria is a former British colony (Gashaw, 2017; Christensen & Laitin, 2019). These artificial groupings have had long-lasting adverse effects on African communities by altering their sense of identity and cultural way of life.

Colonial-era missionary activity also intensified ethnic cleavages and set the stage for enduring inequalities. The penetration of Christian missionaries in southern Nigeria during colonial rule led to the building of schools and the introduction of Western education, which in turn fostered urbanization and economic growth. The north, on the other hand, lacked access to Western education, as the predominance of Islam precluded Christian missionary activity. Missionary schools and access to Western education became the pipeline for intellectual pursuits, access to civil service jobs, and a more educated polity, ultimately creating both a middle class and a class of political elites in the south that have dominated Nigeria's political structure since independence. Meanwhile, the north's lag both in urbanization and economic growth has persisted if not grown more pronounced (Afigbo, 1991).

Divergent treatment of different groups during colonialism, oftentimes enshrined in law, laid the foundation for profound and continuing inequalities in Nigeria and other former British colonies. This carving up of communities and societies was central to the colonial strategy of *divide and rule*, a system that intentionally co-opted and weakened Indigenous power structures and institutions, dividing Indigenous populations and rendering them less able to mount effective opposition to colonial authority.[2] The repercussions of divide and rule—and the hybrid legal systems that accompanied and enabled it—continue to resonate today. Even long after the formal end of colonialism, colonial-era ethnoregional and ethnopolitical boundaries and fragmented jurisprudence have been stubbornly persistent.

Evidence of colonial overhang abounds in law on the continent. Customary law has long been conceived of and implemented in ways that emphasize ethnic, ethnoregional, ethnolinguistic, and other differences, resulting in deeply embedded ethnic divisions throughout the African legal corpus. Colonial-era policies of division effectively weaponized difference by reinforcing and even creating bases for separating populations into groups that were more manageable and better administrable from the colonial authorities' perspective. Divide and rule, the creation and co-option of local elites (as earlier chapters describe in detail), and the presence of European settlers in some colonies not only facilitated colonial control, but they also became major elements in post-colonial internal competition—for resources, access, representation, prestige, and power. In Nigeria, these processes of elite formation that accompanied colonialism—and the hierarchical assumptions and applications that undergirded them—have entrenched inequality, hampered economic growth, and fostered chronic underdevelopment.

To unpack these correlations, this chapter examines the nexus of colonialism, identity, inequality, and law in Nigeria under British rule. It seeks to evaluate how patterns and policies established under conditions of external domination have contributed to continuing inequality and divisions by ethnicity. It also considers the role of law in reflecting and reinscribing ethnic and other bases of division and inequality. Ultimately, it concludes that until and unless these avenues of colonial overhang are addressed—and the fragmentation and dissonance inherited by modern-day African jurisprudence are resolved—the legacy of divide and rule will continue to perpetuate inequality and stifle prospects for equitable growth and development.

Customary Law and the Construction of "Native" and "Non-Native" Identities

Law was an essential tool of colonialism in both the international and local contexts. Colonial authorities used local or customary law to justify colonial oppression, dispossession, and violence, while colonial powers used European law to provide legal justifications for varied colonial incursions (Unobe, 1987; Anghie, 2005). Law was also a basis for organizing both the global and the local along hierarchical lines (Arewa, 2021). External understandings of what local and national legal systems should comprise were key considerations in the construction of African legal systems, which borrowed extensively from external frameworks and external laws, usually to further the interests of external actors. As a result, despite "the well-established British colonial policy of preserving, as far as was compatible with imperial rule, the laws and institutions of colonised territories" (Boparai, 1982),[3] African legal systems have long reflected models that fail to account for local needs or peoples (Arewa, 2021).

This tendency toward external determination was apparent from the earliest adoption of laws in territories within the British sphere of influence. Indeed, British domination in Nigeria and other colonies relied in large part on courts applying English law to disputes involving Westerners in local African contexts. The adoption of legal frameworks based on English law was designed to give British interests an advantage in commercial disputes. At the same time, the driving force behind British colonial legal structures was the sine qua non that English law would apply to any disputes, commercial and otherwise, with local people. This impetus predated formal colonialism: In the pre-colonial period, the courts were "a form of legal imperialism that reflected the extraterritorial reach of Britain prior to formal colonialism."[4]

Modes of external legal domination established prior to colonialism were further developed during the colonial era, as colonizers put in place hybrid legal systems derived from European law (English law in the case of British colonies) and local customary laws (i.e., those which grew out of cultural and social practices within particular communities) (Postema, 2007). Various factors determined which laws applied to which people in which types of cases. The racial, ethnic, religious, and regional identities of participants in a case or dispute, along with the area of law involved, determined which law or laws would be applicable. Yet, rules for determining which laws might apply in any given case were not always clear-cut and were, as with many aspects of colonial administration, subject to considerable discretion by colonial authorities. Customary law was primarily applied to interpersonal relationships among those categorized as "natives," including in matters involving land transactions, marriage and divorce, inheritance, and succession. Customary law was applicable only "where in the opinion of the court it was not contrary to equity and good conscience,. . . it was not contrary to an existing imperial enactment, and it was provable by evidence as a fact" (Amankwah, 1970).[5] European law, on the other hand, was almost universally applied in matters involving non-Indigenous colonialists (i.e., settlers and colonial authorities). This combination of hybridity and ambiguity precariously situated law and its application—a state of instability that remains a key element of continuing colonial overhang today.

The local legal systems that the British established in Africa were explicitly conceived and implemented based on racial, ethnic, religious, and regional identity categories, along with other cultural and traditional markers that reflected local realities. Importantly, though, these categories were framed by the colonizers' inherently external understandings of local populations. Consequently, legal frameworks implemented by colonizing powers tended to be based at least in part on how colonial authorities conceptualized and legally constructed various markers of identity. One of the principal ways that this identity framing played out involved the overarching category of "native" as contrasted with "non-native," the former of which generally applied to Africans while the latter typically denoted Europeans. Categories used to construct "native" identity for legal purposes were based on ethnicity, religion, region, or other factors, alone or in combination. Falling into the "native" category usually determined which set of laws would apply in any given legal circumstance—in terms of European versus local laws—as well as which specific local customary laws might be applicable. Questions around "native" versus "non-native" definitions could arise when people fell outside of established identity-based legal categories or fell into multiple categories, which could and did introduce ambiguity in the application of either category (Postema, 2007). However, despite these and other complexities—including how to categorize people who were neither European nor African—colonial administrators rarely problematized the application of identity-based legal categories.

The contrast between Europeans and non-Europeans was a central organizing ethos of British colonial legal systems, and courts were an important arena for the application of identity-based legal frameworks. The hierarchical frameworks developed for Indigenous courts and customary laws were expressly designed to elevate European law—and European people—over all things African. British colonizers intentionally subordinated local or Indigenous customary law to English law, treating customary law "as a foreign law in the higher courts" (Adewoye, 1973).[6] Nonetheless, the authority of Indigenous courts over Europeans was an issue much discussed among colonial administrators, as was the extension of Indigenous court jurisdiction to non-Europeans who were not locals, and the jurisdiction of Islamic courts in the northern region "over persons of other creeds and subject to other systems of law" (Native Courts (Amendment) Ordinance 1930 and Native Authority (Amendment) Ordinance 1930). These discussions about the jurisdiction of Indigenous courts reflected hierarchies of power and law.

The outcome of this patchwork of legal structures and applications in colonial Africa was that English law overlapped with varied customary law frameworks, which also intersected with one another. Customary law in and of itself comprised hundreds of different sets of laws that varied by ethnic group, religion, and region, even at the village level (Rahmatian, 1996).[7] Which law would apply depended largely on the identities of the participants in a case or dispute. Moreover, these identity categories could determine case outcomes, as an obscure case from 1929, *Ernest Carr v. Suleman Karim*, exemplifies. The case, which took place in the British protectorate of Nyasaland (today the country of Malawi), illustrates how ambiguity over questions of identity—that is to say, legal definitions of who was and was not a "native"—arose in the legal context. The case also reflects how outcomes could differ based on which identities were the basis for decisions regarding which laws should apply to a particular person in a particular case (Lee, 2005).[8]

Carr v. Karim involved a dispute over a loan given to purchase a Ford lorry. Ernest Carr, a local agent with the African Guarantee and Indemnity Co. Ltd. in the commercial hub of Blantyre, sold the truck to Suleman Abdul Karim, who lived in a neighboring town. The parties entered into a written contract that established a monthly installment payment schedule. After making two payments, Karim defaulted on the third and failed to pay the agreed-upon insurance premium. He did not return the vehicle to Carr, who brought a claim before the High Court of Nyasaland. For reasons unknown, Karim sought "non-native" status—despite the fact that had he claimed and been granted "native" status, he would have been protected from prosecution: Carr would have been in violation of the Credit Trade with Natives Ordinance 1926, which prohibited giving credit to "natives." The court determined that Karim held "non-native" status as a "half-caste Indian. . . of Indian origin," and Karim was deemed responsible for the debt, plus court fees (Lee, 2005).[9]

This case highlights the implications of "native" versus "non-native" identity in British colonial legal systems in Africa, as well as the legal ramifications of falling (or not falling) within a particular identity category. It also draws attention to questions about race, legal status, and uniformity in colonial legal contexts, underscoring core points of tension in hybrid colonial legal systems (Lee, 2005, 2011).[10] In discussing the meaning of the "native" category, the court noted:

> Defendant states that he does not wish to take the defense that he is a native. The Court however must consider this, and I therefore ask him who were his parents. He says his father was an Indian and his mother a native. . . . By the Credit Trade with Natives Ordinance 1926. . . a native is defined as a native of Africa not being of European or Asiatic race or origin; accordingly for this Ordinance a native means a native of Africa who is not of European or Asiatic race or origin,

> and all others are non-natives. . . . A person's race or origin does not depend on where he or she is born, just as being born in a manger does not make a person a cow, or a child of European parents being born in India or China is not therefore an Indian or a Chinaman.
>
> *(Lee, 2005)*[11]

As news of the case's outcome made its way to British colonial administrations throughout Africa and to the Colonial Office in London, *Carr v. Karim* ultimately became the basis for addressing issues on race, legal status, and legal uniformity in British colonial Africa. According to Olufunmilayo Arewa, "the case provides important insight into colonial state formation and state power, specifically the ambiguities, contradictions and organic, improvisational nature of their existence" (Arewa, 2021).[12] It demonstrated how African colonial administrators constructed legal systems around assumptions about identity, law, and governance that conceptualized "natives" as being governed by customary law, which was thought to be static and unchanging. As anthropologist Sally Falk Moore notes in her classic ethnographic study of customary law among the Chagga in Tanzania, customary law is "itself a cultural construct with political implications":

> The term sounds as if it designates a straightforward set of traditional rules. But the entity to which it refers is a set of ideas embedded in relationships that are historically shifting. The label "customary law" has its own history in colonial and postcolonial worlds.
>
> *(Moore, 1986)*[13]

As Moore illustrates, conveying customary law as static and unchanging was a tactic employed to delegitimize traditional African legal systems by portraying them as backward and ill-equipped in order to justify the imposition of European legal systems as a means of subjugating the Indigenous populations (Moore, 1986).[14]

The *Carr v. Karim* case illuminates two major and interrelated shortcomings that identity-based colonial legal frameworks failed to account for: conflict of law issues and opportunities for jurisdictional arbitrage. *Conflict of law* describes the question of which law (or body of laws) applies when multiple bodies of law interact. *Jurisdictional arbitrage* refers to the strategic exploitation of laws in different jurisdictions to obtain a benefit (Arewa, 2021).[15] In British colonial Africa, people realized that, given a choice of legal framework with which to engage—as in, customary versus European (and, within the former, whether to identify as a "native" or a "non-native")—they could seek to negotiate preferential outcomes. Furthermore, identity-based legal frameworks did not give sufficient attention to conflict of law principles aside from those based on identity. For example, according to T. W. Bennett, an individual who "could prove sufficient change in cultural attributes" could petition colonial authorities for application of European civil law over customary law. Additionally, Bennett suggests that "life-style" and "domicile" were factors that might permit an individual to "select his legal status without state interference" (Bennett, 1980). The overreliance on identity in constructing colonial legal systems remains an important colonial overhang in that it instilled conflict of law and jurisdictional arbitrage issues that carried over into post-independence African legal corpora in ways explored later in this chapter (Arewa, 2021).

Hierarchies of Law, Elite Formation, and Inequality

As the previous section describes, colonial authorities created hybrid legal systems in Africa that incorporated elements of European law and customary law. Identity was fundamental to the application of law to indigenes, Europeans, and those who did not fall clearly into either category. Colonial legal systems were constructed such that customary law was applied mostly to "natives," while Europeans would typically be subject to European law (English law in the case of British colonies). Applying these categories could be tricky, particularly in cases involving elite indigenes, who could be subject to English law, and those involving people who fell into multiple categories or who did not fit neatly within the "native" category. The discussion of what it meant to be a "native" in the *Carr v. Karim* case highlights the difficulties and tensions intrinsic in the legal construction of Indigenous and non-Indigenous identity in British colonial Africa.

Hierarchies surrounding race, identity, and other markers of status (such as educational attainment and land ownership) coalesced around colonialist assumptions that as "tribal" (i.e., ostensibly primitive) African societies evolved into "enlightened" communities, they would necessarily "destroy. . . tribal institutions" (such as customary law) in favor of civilized ones based on English or European models (Native Authority Ordinance, 1932). These hierarchies played a critical role in structuring colonial legal systems and making determinations about legal rights. In British colonies, English law was at the apex of these hierarchies, and anything African existed and operated at a lower level. This approach left little space for local customary law to evolve and operate other than on a fragmented basis. Western-centered ideas about law and society informed colonialist hierarchies, suffusing colonial institutions with external conceptions and assumptions that introduced and then reinforced inequality and constrained opportunity.

The British style of colonial governance in Africa relied on a system that came to be known as *indirect rule*, wherein local rulers became political intermediaries—essentially, agents of the colonial administration (Siollun, 2021).[16] British colonial authorities wielded power by relying extensively on these local intermediaries, which initiated a process of elite formation that created new hierarchies and inequalities. To administer colonialism at the local level, local chiefs became cogs in the colonial administrative machine. They and their families and cohorts received privileged access to educational and other opportunities, and their communities benefitted through colonialist investment in schools, hospitals, roads, and other vital infrastructure. Because this structure of governance involved selection and preferential treatment of members of certain ethnic groups over others, it created a class of ethnic political elites that has persisted in post-independence Nigeria. The identification and selection of such local chiefs was designed to serve the colonial leaders' interests, but the elite formation that resulted bred deep social schisms and entrenched socioeconomic inequality (Lawrance, Osborn, & Roberts, 2006; Sharkey, 2003; Siollun, 2021).[17] (See Chapters 1 and 2 for more on indirect rule and its lasting legacy.)

In northern Nigeria (as elsewhere), indirect rule strengthened the power of traditional rulers. Indirect rule in fact began in northern Nigeria, where traditional Muslim rulers called emirs carried out colonial administrative functions. The implementation of indirect rule was less challenging in the north than in other regions of the country, largely because the existing political structure among the Hausa-Fulani Muslims—with the emirs at the apex, along with a strong judicial system based on Muslim theocracy—made for a relatively smooth transition: People already accepted the authority of the emirs and the traditional legal structures. The British simply built on top of these existing political structures by co-opting them as agents and frameworks, respectively, of the colonial government (Larkin, 2008; Siollun, 2021).[18]

Outside of northern Nigeria, indirect rule was problematic because it distorted traditional pre-colonial political structures and social orders. In the diverse Middle Belt region between northern and southern Nigeria, the British employed a slightly different form of indirect rule known as *native alien subcolonialism*. According to Moses Ochonu, this less common iteration relied on "native aliens" (or "non-indigenous, presumably 'progressive' Africans from proximate 'civilized' ethno-religious communities") to administer the Indigenous, non-Muslim Africans of the Middle Belt, whom both the British and the Hausa-Fulani considered "backward" and "benighted tribesmen" (Ochonu, 2014).[19] These "native alien" proxies were Hausa-Fulani Muslims as in the north—a choice that ultimately made the implementation of indirect rule in the Middle Belt region a failure. For one thing, Middle Belt ethnic groups such as the Tiv and the Idoma were unaccustomed to established political hierarchies such as those in northern Nigeria. Moreover, installing Hausa Muslims to oversee predominantly non-Muslims was a catastrophic miscalculation on the part of the colonial authorities. These factors greatly exacerbated ethnoreligious tensions among the ethnic groups in the Middle Belt (Siollun, 2021).

Southern Nigeria also lacked the formal, top-down political structures that characterized the north. In implementing indirect rule there, the British granted chieftaincy power more strategically, which, according to Obaro Ikime, was "tantamount to granting whosoever was appointed to the office arbitrary paramountcy over a large area" (Ikime, 1965).[20] In the southeast, this strategy wreaked havoc on Indigenous societies and essentially destroyed traditional rule. Before colonization, southeastern Nigeria was made up of independent, politically autonomous villages—which made implementing indirect rule a thorny challenge. The colonial government's answer was to institute the *warrant chief* system: Individuals thought to be influential or presumed to have leadership qualities were issued warrants appointing them as local chiefs on an ad hoc basis. These so-called big men were given oversight over tax collection as well as judicial powers. The introduction of money as a means of transaction turned these "big men" into political elites (and, all too often, rent-seeking agents). This newly created artificial power dynamic bifurcated and eroded the existing sociopolitical structure in southeastern Nigeria (Siollun, 2021).[21]

Indirect rule was somewhat less pernicious in the southwest, where the colonial administration co-opted traditional Yoruba rulers called *obas* rather than ordinary citizens as proxies. Checks and balances in the traditional system of rule meant that the obas were not absolute like the emirs in the north, and the system of taxation that existed in Yorubaland before colonial rule made the payment of taxes during indirect rule easier to administer than in the southeast. All the same, the tax collection and judicial oversight authorities created a perverse incentive for obas to aspire to be "big men" similar to the warrant chiefs in the southeast (Siollun, 2021).[22] Additionally, many villages found themselves governed by chiefs from rival villages, which led to "resistance and ethnic tension as the populace felt misrepresented by these appointed leaders. This frustration was compounded by the perceived indifference to their grievances, prompting violent reactions against the colonial authorities" (Ukpe, 2024).[23]

Once in power, chiefs chosen or supported by the British often faced insufficient constraints to their exercise of power and authority. In particular, colonial officials frequently did little to curb extractive behaviors (such as nepotism, rent-seeking, and graft) that many local chiefs viewed as a de facto bonus granted to British-appointed rulers (Arewa, 2021).[24] Expediency was the guiding principle of British colonial governance, which was centered around three overarching priorities: land acquisition, resource extraction, and the exploitation of labor. Indirect rule and the warrant chief system were based on British conceptions of sovereignty that derived from absolute rule; by design, they politically and economically empowered those appointed to positions of proxy power, largely based on ethnicity, who in turn were able to enrich themselves through rent-seeking behavior with the introduction of a currency economy. In this way, indirect rule created a class of political elites during colonial rule, the members of which benefitted long past independence because they were already situated to be at the helm of governance. It was these colonial legacies of ethnic group preference and divide and rule that led to the elitism and inequality that persisted in post-independence African societies—in Nigeria and elsewhere (Ochonu, 2013; Ocheni & Nwankwo, 2012; Murray, 1967).

Alongside the local rulers selected by colonizers, Africans with access to Western educational opportunities became a core part of the elite category in Nigeria and other British colonies. In Nigeria at independence, 87 percent of college-educated people were employed by the government, primarily in senior service positions (Barnes, 1986).[25] Within the African (or "native") category, educated Africans were elevated above others during colonialism, a distinction that persisted after independence. Returning to the question of law and its application, this distinction meant that those individuals were potentially excluded from the jurisdiction of Indigenous courts. The Native Authority Ordinance of 1932 made plain that those courts—and the customary law that they adjudicated—were viewed as wholly inferior to English jurisprudence. The ordinance explicitly stated "that a Native Court in Nigeria [is] composed of uneducated and illiterate natives," and that

> throughout the greater part, if not the whole, of the Southern Provinces there are a great many educated and other Africans who do not resort to or use the Native Courts and are allowed by custom to make free use of the Provincial Courts.

It continued,

> It [native society] has no natural culture of its own and there is no culture which it can acquire except from the Europeans; unless it comes under Moslem influence, a contingency so remote that it can be disregarded. We may therefore expect the natives concerned gradually to acquire a European type of education, reading and writing English; that indeed, is the aim of our educational policy except that not everyone will attain the same proficiency in English (which will almost certainly become the common language of the south).
>
> *(Native Authority Ordinance, 1932)*

In short, as the level of Western education increased among the Indigenous people in colonized Africa, they came to favor English law. Customary courts became the exclusive domain of the non-elite Indigenous (that is, the uneducated, at least by Western standards); British law was used for transactions between the educated Indigenous class and the British, as well as for other commercial transactions. As the introduction of Western education elevated the status of certain ethnic groups in Nigeria (particularly the Yoruba and the Igbo) and opened up opportunities for them to engage in commercial activities, it effectively elevated them to elite status in local society, both politically and economically.

Notably, the same sociopolitical structures that eased the introduction of indirect rule in northern Nigeria also precluded the penetration of Western education there, which ultimately set the north and the south on dramatically divergent development paths. Whereas the north was resistant to Western instruction in favor of Islamic teachings, the south was open to Western education, culture, language, and other European norms. As a result, Western education took hold in southern Nigeria (albeit with preferential access), affording wider access to civil service jobs and significantly more building of infrastructure, including schools, roads, hospitals, and institutions of commerce, while the north did not benefit nearly as much from investment in infrastructure. The more direct approach that the British were able to take in southern Nigeria was the single-greatest contributing factor to the post-independence ethnic and regional inequalities that are still evident today (Okonwo, 2023).

Law, Identity, Conflict of Law, and Colonial Overhang

Hybrid legal and governance systems formalized during colonialism—and a lack of foresight into the challenges that they would engender—bred opportunities for manipulative and solipsistic approaches to law and governance. Such strategies, born of colonial-era identity-based legal distinctions that endured after independence in many African states, typically involve using conflicting provisions of different customary law frameworks or a conflation of customary law and English law. People seeking to employ one or another legal framework for a perceived advantage is the embodiment of jurisdictional arbitrage: the strategic use of law, often in different jurisdictions, to receive a benefit or preferential outcome (Arewa, 2021).[26] More broadly, hybrid colonial legal systems were rife for conflict of law issues.

In colonial Nigeria, the dual implementation of English law and customary law operating in jurisdictional concurrence was fraught from the outset. This duality encapsulates the British colonial enterprise's lack of forethought as to how these different systems should and would interact (Arewa, 2021; Yakubu, 2005),[27] at least on a basis other than through use of markers of identity. This oversight wove substantial instability in terms of "changing relations of authority and conflicting interpretation of rules. . . into the fabric of colonial rule" (Berry, 1993).[28] The literature has not sufficiently addressed jurisdictional arbitrage and other strategic uses of law in Nigeria and other former British colonies. The parallel legal systems established during colonialism—which continue to operate side-by-side in Nigeria today—reflect different concepts of and approaches to law that remain unreconciled, and in some cases incompatible. In large part, this failure to reconcile the conflicting elements of hybrid British colonial legal systems underscores hierarchical assumptions about the evolution of society and the development of law. In other words, colonial administrators assumed that as "tribal" African societies (i.e., primitive, in the eyes of the British) progressed along a path toward becoming "enlightened communit[ies]" (Native Authority Ordinance, 1932), customary law was destined to be supplanted by systems modeled on and molded by English law. As stated in the Native Authority Ordinance, 1932:

> [T]here is no prospect. . . that native law and custom in those places will develop out of its own inherent qualities a code of native law and custom that will satisfy a more enlightened community; and this means, surely, that as time goes on it must borrow more and more from the statute law. It may be said that if this development does take place tribal institutions must be destroyed and the answer to that seems. . . to be that if tribal institutions cease to be acceptable to an enlightened community they must be destroyed.
>
> *(Native Authority Ordinance, 1932)*

Inheritance Disputes and Conflict of Law

The hierarchical approach to customary law that remains embedded in post-colonial African legal systems, in the form of past (and enduring) power dynamics and conceptions of relationships based on identity categories, exemplifies the colonial overhang that persists in post-independence Nigeria. This overhang manifests today in sticky legal issues around conflict of law relating to inheritance disputes. English law was imposed in Nigeria on January 1, 1900, and with it came the Wills Act 1837 and the Wills Amendment Act 1852 (Wills Act 1837; Wills Amendment Act 1852). Since independence, Nigerian courts have confronted conflicts that inevitably arose between laws inherited from England on the one hand and Nigerian common law and Islamic law on the other (the former, of course, rooted in both colonial and pre-colonial customary law) (Chiroma, 1993). For instance, the case of Adesubokan v. Yunusa, (1971) involved a man in northern Nigeria who made bequests to one son through a will and gave property to two other sons outright (Adesubokan v. Yunusa, 1971). The High Court trial judge ruled that the distribution of the deceased's assets should comply with Islamic law, which favors equal distribution. The Court of Appeal noted that the trial court's view "clearly violated the provisions of the Wills Act 1837 under which a testator can dispose of his properties—real or personal—as he pleases," and that the "[p]rovisions of the Maliki Moslem Law were undoubtedly incompatible with s. 3 of the Wills Act, 1837" (Boparai, 1982; Tom & Abdulrahman, 2020).[29] The Federal Supreme Court overturned the High Court judge's decision and noted that Islamic law can only apply to the extent that it does not conflict with the Wills Act, a decision that unequivocally reinforced the lingering primacy of English law in Nigeria's legal corpus:

> [T]he High Court Law can only apply such Moslem Law which is not incompatible with the Wills Act. It was therefore clear that the Moslem Law which the trial Judge applied in this case was incompatible with the Wills Act. Consequently, he was clearly in error in setting aside the probate dated 2nd June, 1966 granted to the defendant/appellant under the Will of the testator. . . . [N]othing in the High Court Law shall deprive any person of the benefit of any native law or custom including Moslem Law, which is not incompatible directly or by implication with any law for the time being in force, and in the present case the Wills Act 1837.
>
> *(Adesubokan v. Yunusa, 1971)*

Similarly, the case of Lawal-Osula v. Lawal-Osula (1995) concerned a conflict between customary law and English law over succession and the disposition of assets. In that case, the Nigerian Supreme Court unanimously upheld the primogeniture system of the Bini (or Edo) people in southwestern Nigeria that had been enshrined in customary law for centuries (Lawal-Osula v. Lawal-Osula, 1995). *Lawal-Osula* established that a will cannot dispose of the customary law principle of *Igiogbe*, which originated as a "medium of worship between the ancestors and their living descendants" (Oluya, 2012).[30] Under *Igiogbe*, which translates to "ancestral home" or "family seat," a deceased father's eldest surviving son exclusively inherits the family's ancestral home (Okoli, Yekini, & Oamen, 2023). Prior to the twentieth century, house-building patterns and practices led to few disputes about *Igiogbe*; it was only after people began building more than one home—and began adopting the English law-inspired practice of writing wills—that litigation over *Igiogbe* started to arise (Oluya, 2012).[31]

Lawal-Osula was not the only point of tension between customary law and English law around *Igiogbe*. In the case of Idehen v. Idehen (1991), the Nigerian Supreme Court held that two houses of the deceased could constitute *Igiogbe*, which some scholars have argued is not reflective of Bini customary law (Idehen v. Idehen, 1991). Another case, Egharevba v. Oruonghae (2001), paved the way for first sons to lay claim not just to the family home(s) but also to the personal effects of their fathers by claiming the entire estate as *Igiogbe* (Egharevba v. Oruonghae, 2001; Tom & Abdulrahman, 2020). Contention within families surrounding *Igiogbe* (and the ensuing litigation) are at least in part a consequence of social changes wherein eldest sons may no longer undertake the obligations that traditionally accompanied *Igiogbe*—namely, the responsibility to support their late fathers' dependents, among them younger siblings (including those born to wives other than their mothers) (Oserogho et al., 2019). Under current judicial treatment of *Igiogbe*, an eldest son is free to sell or gift any inherited assets during his lifetime and not assume the responsibilities once considered an essential part of *Igiogbe* (Okoli, Yekini, & Oamen, 2023).

Issues of internal contestation, transition, and change arise in legal treatment of customary practices perhaps more so than in other areas of law because of customary law's asserted connection to traditional practices considered to be age-old and immutable. In their considerations, courts are cognizant of how these contestations affect the social fabric.

In ruling on *Lawal-Osula*, the Nigerian Supreme Court justified *Igiogbe* as necessary to avert social and political unrest that would detrimentally affect governance and societal cohesion (Lawal-Osula v. Lawal-Osula, 1995).[32] Yet, some commentators on judicial treatment of *Igiogbe* have noted that continuation of this practice may fuel "greater unrest. . . because the philosophy behind the practice is no longer upheld" (Oserogho et al., 2019). Regardless of where one comes down on the issue, the conflict of law resulting from colonial overhang is undeniable: The introduction of English law imbued within the Nigerian legal system a discordance with customary law to be played out in the courts.

Marriage Law and Jurisdictional Arbitrage

Contested space and jurisdictional arbitrage have been apparent since the early implementation of English law-derived legal frameworks in colonial Africa, and marriage law is no exception. In Malawi, women who sought to divorce their husbands flooded newly established customary law courts. These divorce cases underscored competing views about marriage and the role of women—who, prior to the formalization of the colonial court structure, had no avenue through which to contest marriages (which may or may not have been entered into consensually). Colonial officials weighed in to resolve this contestation by agreeing with men that "women were getting out of control" and stepping outside the bounds of traditional roles and norms (Chanock, 1978).[33] Hybrid colonial legal and governance thus located power to define this contested area squarely with men over women.

Marriage law in Nigeria is not unified and contains a problematic duality. This lack of unification highlights ways that English law and customary law have not been reconciled, creating thorny legal issues in contemporary Nigerian society. The duality arises in that both customary and Islamic law allow for polygamous marriage, whereas English law explicitly and unequivocally defines marriage as monogamous (Boparai, 1982). Marriage, therefore, exists today in Nigeria under three distinct classifications: statutory, Islamic, and customary. Under statutory marriage, a man can have only one wife; under Islamic law, the maximum number of wives is four; and under customary law, a man can have an unlimited number of wives. Notably, a statutory marriage is considered legally void if either party is already married under customary law to any person other than the person involved in the statutory marriage (Marriage Act of 1990; Marriages [Validation] Act of 1990).[34] In actual practice, however, spouses routinely combine statutory and customary marriages (Boparai, 1982; Umezuruike, 2024).

Statutory marriage in Nigeria is based on ideas about marriage and family that originated with Christian missionaries and derive from colonial legislation based on English law (Rahmatian, 1996).[35] The colonial-era law around statutory marriage (the Marriage Act of 1914) remained largely unaltered for nearly a century (when it was amended with the Marriage Act of 2004) (Marriage Act of 1914; Marriage Act of 2004). The Matrimonial Causes Act of 1970 (which regulates the dissolution of marriages) is too, "curiously enough, the product of a long evolution of English, and not of Nigerian divorce law." It follows almost to the letter the English Divorce Reform Act of 1969 and the Australian Matrimonial Causes Act 1959 and "adopt[s] exactly their principles concerning the ground for divorce" (Matrimonial Causes Act of 1970; Divorce Reform Act of 1969; Australian Matrimonial Causes Act 1959; Rahmatian, 1996).[36]

Although some African nations (notably, Côte d'Ivoire, Kenya, and Tanzania) have attempted to unify marriage law, Nigeria has not done so, despite the manifest conflicts and the acknowledged need for marriage law reforms (Law of Marriage Act; Rahmatian, 1996; Prinsloo, 1990).[37] Statutory marriage and divorce laws in Nigeria have been criticized on multiple grounds, including their use of cut-and-paste legal drafting approaches that blindly copy foreign statutes, their lack of consideration for traditional values, and their failure to address conflicts of law problems (Rahmatian, 1996).[38] For example, although the provision is rarely enforced, the Marriage Act provides for five years' imprisonment for any person in a statutory marriage to then "contract[ ] a marriage in accordance with customary law" (Marriage Act of 1990).[39] The Nigerian Supreme Court, in Jadesimi v. Okotie-Eboh (1996), noted that

> it is matter of common knowledge that in spite of the punishment provided under Section 47 of the Marriage Act against any of the parties entering another customary marriage, the malefolk in particular observe the restriction more in breach than obedience, with impunity.
>
> *(Jadesimi v. Okotie-Eboh, 1996)*

In other words, men already married under statutory law more often subsequently marry under customary law than women.

About 31 percent of women ages 15–49 in Nigeria have a husband or partner who has other wives, while 13 percent of men of the same age have more than one wife.[40] Polygamous households are more prevalent in rural than urban settings, and polygamy rates are higher in northern Nigerian states, which tend to observe Islamic law. Insofar as polygamy is demonstrably widespread and "[b]igamy is carried out openly," the current system of marriage law in Nigeria inevitably leads to noncompliance with statutory marriage law (National Population Commission, 2019; Chinwuba, 2016).[41] Critics of the present system have argued for discarding legal penalties for bigamy in Nigerian marriage law under the circumstances. In 2004, the Nigerian Family Law Reform Commission proposed removing bigamy from the law. That recommendation did not receive a response from the legislature (Chinwuba, 2016).[42] In 2011, Lagos became the only southern state to decriminalize bigamy; twelve northern states permit polygamous marriage. However, Nigerian law contains no national provision allowing bigamy to be recognized (Lateef & Adegbite, 2017). Section 370 of the Nigerian Criminal Code Act states:

> Any person who, having a husband or wife living, marries in any case in which such marriage is void by reason of its taking place during the life of such husband or wife, is guilty of a felony, and is liable to imprisonment for seven years.
>
> *(Nigerian Criminal Code Act of 1990)*

A number of cases have addressed questions about the interrelationship between statutory and customary marriage in Nigeria. These cases, among which M.O. v. R.O. and Anor (2013) is perhaps the most prominent, demonstrate the lack of reconciliation between statutory and customary law, and the resulting uncertainty for both courts and for litigants. *M.O. v. R.O.* involved litigation in both London and Lagos, complicating matters even more. M.O. claimed that she was married to R.O. in a customary marriage ceremony in Nigeria in 1977. R.O., the alleged husband, had been married previously, in 1967. His first wife, Mary, had separated from him and remarried in 1977. M.O. and R.O. lived together for decades in

England, where M.O. had actually assumed the identity of R.O.'s first wife Mary (adding yet another level of complexity). M.O. and R.O. had two children together, and they also raised R.O.'s four children by Mary. The English court reviewed thirteen hundred pages of documentation in the case before reaching the conclusion that a customary marriage had not taken place. The court in Lagos also issued a declaration that no marriage had taken place (M.O. v. R.O. and Anor, 2013; M.O. v. R.O. and Rig Ltd., 2013).

Although this case was about the validity of a marriage, it had implications for M.O.'s occupancy of a property in London. M.O. claimed that R.O. owned the property, while R.O. claimed that the property was owned by the company of which he was a director. The case also had ramifications for M.O.'s financial status and her claims for financial provision upon divorce. R.O. had locked M.O. out of the property where she had lived; the finding of no marriage eliminated any marriage-based financial claims, presumably leaving M.O. in dire straits. Cases like this one also have implications for children born into such relationships, who become illegitimate upon a court finding of no marriage. Legitimacy is yet another concept whose understanding, context, and treatment differ significantly under English law and customary law. *M.O. v. R.O.* reveals how questions about valid marriage under existing marriage laws in Nigeria have implications that extend far beyond marriage itself.

Treatment of marriage by Nigerian courts illustrates the inherent difficulties of maintaining separate and at times incompatible legal frameworks for marriage. Although early cases involving marriage decided during the colonial era may no longer be good law, these cases underscore long-standing tensions amid the competing notions of marriage that underlie marriage law in Nigeria. They also reflect areas of considerable incompatibility between the legal systems that govern marriage. The essential requirements for a valid marriage are different under the Marriage Act and customary law, as are requirements for capacity and allowed and prohibited degrees of relationships (such as restrictions on marriages between close relatives to avoid incestuous unions). The nature of marriages under customary and statutory law also differs. At least twenty different forms of customary marriage exist in Nigeria. Marriage as conceptualized under customary law is a contract between two families—not in terms of a formal legal contract, but in adherence to the traditions and cultural rites of a particular ethnic community, which requires parental and familial consent and thus reflects the union of extended families (1st Attorneys, 2024).

Customary law marriages are potentially polygamous. (Customary law also provides for levirate and sororate marriages, which are beyond the scope of this chapter.) (Boparai, 1982; Chinwuba, 2016) A statutory marriage under the Marriage Act is based on English law and cannot be polygamous. The landmark case of *Hyde v. Hyde*, decided by the English Court of Probate and Divorce in 1866, defined the institution of marriage as "a voluntary union involving one woman and one man for life and to the exclusion of all others" (Boparai, 1982; Chinwuba, 2016; Hyde

v. Hyde and Woodmansee, 1866). The relatively common and abiding tradition of polygamous marriage in Nigeria must therefore be governed by customary law, because English law and norms alike preclude a contract of marriage for someone who is already married. In terms of marriage dissolution, only the High Court—which is derived from English law practice—has jurisdiction to terminate a statutory marriage, while a customary marriage may be legally terminated by customary courts or area courts.[43]

The pronounced lack of a unified marriage law represents a missed opportunity during and after colonialism to customize the Nigerian legal system to better fit local contexts. Such a reconciliation of English and customary law could have engendered modifying both frameworks to create more cohesive and coherent legal systems. Instead, the contemporary divergence of customary marriage laws and those laws derived from English jurisprudence invites jurisdictional arbitrage. Specifically, it brings to the fore points of contestation that litigants can strategically employ in ways that can be detrimental to the operation of law itself. The current system allows individuals (particularly men) to select the laws they desire to be bound by. This strategic use of law (again, usually by men) raises legal questions related to paternity, inheritance, and succession matters. Critically, it also reduces men's accountability to those involved in relationships with them, which can have grave impacts on women and children.

Conclusion

Customary law in Africa was conceptualized and constructed in ways that tracked British colonialist notions of ethnicity—notions that at best only partially represented the realities of ethnic identification on the continent. The system of ethnic identification that underlies customary law thus limited jurisdiction to particular cultural boundaries (i.e., it applied only to certain segments of the population) and constituted "the possession and right of a restricted ethnic group" (Kiye, 2015).[44] As a result, customary law existed and operated on a fragmented basis, which fit well with the colonial policy of divide and rule. Customary law as it has evolved in the post-independence period retained this fragmentary nature, often placing it in conflict with itself and with the body of English law imported by colonial powers.

Unpacking just how this fragmentation arose requires seeing colonialism for what it was: an unabashed endeavor to exploit new lands and peoples in furtherance of imperial aims. The hierarchies that arose—or, in fact, were actively instituted—in concert with the colonial enterprise necessitated a particular brand of externalism that manifested in the application of Western-centric ideas of ethnicity, primitivity, and modernity, especially as they related to governance and law. The external determinism underscoring these hierarchies guided the development of legal frameworks in Africa that were by their very nature fragmented and bound to be in conflict.

In Nigeria (as elsewhere), British officials presented the rule of law as one of the major benefits of colonialism and used it to justify colonial rule. However, the legal systems implemented in colonial Africa were less about bringing the rule of law and the benefits of modernity to ostensibly primitive cultures and more about elevating British interests legally and commercially. Colonial African legal frameworks were conceived and organized around "native" versus "non-native" identity categories—and notions of "native" identity that did not always reflect local conditions or historical realities. Underpinning these frameworks, and the indirect rule methodology more broadly, was the colonialist view that development required destruction of the local and the African.

Contemporary African legal systems echo with patterns of borrowing that reflect external determination and demonstrate in their applications the extent and persistence of colonial overhang—legacies that continue to cast a shadow over countries that were once colonies. In Nigeria, patterns and policies established during British rule have amplified ethnic divisions and created new ones, the result of which is the persistent inequality that plagues the country today. For so long as the ongoing failure to address the present legal system's colonial overhang endures, the prospects for equitable development and growth in Nigeria will remain bleak. Vanquishing the ghosts of colonialism requires concerted attention to the local, systematic elimination of opportunities and incentives for jurisdictional arbitrage, and greater focus on conflict of law issues and legal outcomes.

Notes

1 Anthony John Christopher, "'Divide and Rule': The Impress of British Separation Policies," *Area* 20, no. 3 (September 1988): 233, 239.
2 *Cambridge Advanced Learner's Dictionary and Thesaurus*, s.v. "Divide and Rule," accessed May 13, 2024, https://dictionary.cambridge.org/us/dictionary/english/divide-and-rule.
3 Harinder Boparai, "The Customary and Statutory Law of Marriage in Nigeria," *Rabels Zeitschrift für ausländisches und internationales Privatrecht/The Rabel Journal of Comparative and International Private Law* 46, no. 3 (1982): 531.
4 Olufunmilayo B. Arewa, *Disrupting Africa: Technology, Law, and Development* (Cambridge, UK: Cambridge University Press, 2021): 112, 241.
5 Harrison A. Amankwah, "Ghanaian Law: Its Evolution and Interaction with English Law," *Cornell International Law Journal* 4, no. 1 (Fall 1970): 40.
6 Omoniyi Adewoye, "Review: *Law and Social Change in Nigeria*, by T. O. Elias," *Journal of the Historical Society of Nigeria* 7, no. 1 (December 1973): 149.
7 Andreas Rahmatian, "Termination of Marriage in Nigerian Family Laws: The Need for Reform and the Relevance of the Tanzanian Experience," *International Journal of Law, Policy and the Family* 10, no. 3 (December 1996): 283.
8 Christopher Joon-Hai Lee, "The 'Native' Undefined: Colonial Categories, Anglo-African Status and the Politics of Kinship in British Central Africa, 1929–38," *The Journal of African History* 46, no. 3 (November 2005): 456 (citing Ernest Carr v. Suleman Abdul Karim (1929) Nyasaland).
9 Lee, "'Native' Undefined," 456 (citing *Carr v. Karim*).

10 Lee, "'Native' Undefined," 457; Christopher J. Lee, "*Jus Soli* and *Jus Sanguinis* in the Colonies: The Interwar Politics of Race, Culture, and Multiracial Legal Status in British Africa," *Law and History Review* 29, no. 2 (May 2011): 499.

11 Lee, "'Native' Undefined," 456 (citing *Carr v. Karim*).

12 Arewa, *Disrupting Africa*, 30.

13 Sally Falk Moore, *Social Facts and Fabrications: "Customary" Law on Kilimanjaro, 1880–1980* (Cambridge, UK: Cambridge University Press, 1986), xv.

14 Moore, *Social Facts and Fabrications*, 172–73.

15 Arewa, *Disrupting Africa*, 28, 241.

16 Max Siollun, *What Britain Did to Nigeria: A Short History of Conquest and Rule* (London, UK: Hurst, 2021), 284. In contrast, other colonial powers, such as France, favored a *direct rule* style of governance, in which colonial officials had direct authority over local rulers and local populations alike (Kehinde, 2024). Classification of Belgian and Portuguese colonial rule, respectively, as direct or indirect rule is a matter of some scholarly debate. See Zajaczkowski, 1984; Havik, 2010.

17 Benjamin N. Lawrance, Emily Lynn Osborn, and Richard L. Roberts, "Introduction: African Intermediaries and the 'Bargain' of Collaboration," in *Intermediaries, Interpreters, and Clerks: African Employees in the Making of Colonial Africa*, ed. Benjamin N. Lawrance, Emily Lynn Osborn, and Richard L. Roberts (Madison: University of Wisconsin Press, 2006), 9–10; Heather J. Sharkey, *Living with Colonialism: Nationalism and Culture in the Anglo-Egyptian Sudan* (Berkeley: University of California Press, 2003), 1; Siollun, *What Britain Did to Nigeria.*

18 Brian Larkin, *Signal and Noise: Media, Infrastructure, and Urban Culture in Nigeria* (Durham, NC: Duke University Press, 2008), 21–25; Siollun, *What Britain Did to Nigeria.* The term *indirect rule* is believed to have been coined based on the pre-colonial frameworks of the Hausa-Fulani Muslims in northern Nigeria. Siollun, *What Britain Did to Nigeria*, 295.

19 Moses E. Ochonu, *Colonialism by Proxy: Hausa Imperial Agents and Middle Belt Consciousness in Nigeria* (Bloomington: Indiana University Press, 2014), 3, 8.

20 Obaro Ikime, "Chief Dogho: The Lugardian System in Warri, 1917–1932," *Journal of the Historical Society of Nigeria* 3, no. 2 (December 1965): 314.

21 Siollun, *What Britain Did to Nigeria*, 281–97.

22 Siollun, *What Britain Did to Nigeria*, 281–97.

23 Essien Ukpe, "Ethnocentrism as a Colonial Relic in Africa," Chapter 14 in *Relics of Colonialism: An Introduction to African Politics* (Uyo, Nigeria: Robertminder International, 2024), 86–92.

24 Arewa, *Disrupting Africa*, 240–45.

25 Sandra T. Barnes, *Patrons and Power: Creating a Political Community in Metropolitan Lagos* (London, UK: Routledge, 1986), 14.

26 Arewa, *Disrupting Africa*, 241. To use a contemporary example, multinational corporations and wealthy individuals commonly use jurisdictional arbitrage today to minimize taxes. Ronen Palan and Giovanni Mangraviti, "Troubling Tax Havens: Multi-Jurisdictional Arbitrage and Tax Footprint Reduction," in *Handbook on Wealth and the Super-Rich*, ed. Iain Hay and Jonathan V. Beaverstock (Cheltenham, UK: Edward Elgar, 2016), 422.

27 Arewa, *Disrupting Africa*, 241; John Ademola Yakubu, "Colonialism, Customary Law and the Post-Colonial State in Africa: The Case of Nigeria," *Africa Development* 30, no. 4 (2005): 201–20.

28 Sara Berry, *No Condition Is Permanent: The Social Dynamics of Agrarian Change in Sub-Saharan Africa* (Madison: University of Wisconsin Press, 1993), 32.

29 Boparai, "Customary and Statutory Law of Marriage in Nigeria," 530; Patricia Izuka Tom and Saka Toyin Abdulrahman, "Effect of Will on Those Subject to Customary Law in Nigeria," *International Journal of Law* 6, no. 3 (2020): 61–69.

30 Donatus Sunday Oluya, "Bini Customary Law of Inheritance: Shift in 'Igiogbe' as a Case Study" (master's thesis, Dalarna University, Falun, Sweden, June 2012), 8, 33.
31 Oluya, "Bini Customary Law of Inheritance," 9.
32 *Lawal-Osula v. Lawal-Osula*, paragraphs H-A.
33 Martin Chanock, "Neo-Traditionalism and the Customary Law in Malawi," *African Legal Studies* 16 (1978): 88.
34 Marriage Act of 1990, Ch. 218, Laws of the Federation of Nigeria; Marriages (Validation) Act of 1990, Ch. 219, Laws of the Federation of Nigeria, § 33(1).
35 Rahmatian, "Termination of Marriage in Nigerian Family Laws," 289.
36 Matrimonial Causes Act of 1970, Cap. M7, Laws of the Federation of Nigeria; Divorce Reform Act of 1969, c. 55 (Eng.); Australian Matrimonial Causes Act 1959 (Cth), No. 104 (Austrl.); Rahmatian, "Termination of Marriage in Nigerian Family Laws," 289.
37 Law of Marriage Act, 1971 (LMA) (Tanzania) (Cap 29 R.E 2002) (attempted to unify marriage law); Rahmatian, "Termination of Marriage in Nigerian Family Laws," 283, 297–98; Prinsloo, Marthinus Wilhelm, "Pluralism or Unification in Family Law in South Africa," *The Comparative and International Law Journal of Southern Africa* 23, no. 3 (November 1990): 324–36, https://hdl.handle.net/10520/AJA00104051_577.
38 Rahmatian, "Termination of Marriage in Nigerian Family Laws," 283.
39 Marriage Act of 1990, §§ 35, 47.
40 The percentage of women in polygamous unions has declined over the past thirty years from 41 percent in 1990 to 33 percent in 2013. National Population Commission, *Nigeria Demographic and Health Survey 2018* (Abuja, Nigeria: National Population Commission and ICF International, 2019): 80.
41 National Population Commission, *Nigeria Demographic and Health Survey 2018*; Nwudego N. Chinwuba, "Interaction of Customs and Colonial Heritage: Their Impact on Marriage and Children in Nigeria," *Anthropos* 111, no. 1 (2016): 51.
42 Chinwuba, "Interaction of Customs and Colonial Heritage," 52.
43 Area courts were established after the first military government in Nigeria revoked the earlier orders and laws related to native and customary courts and issued edicts that led to the formation of new customary court systems in some states. In states in the northern region, the existing Indigenous court system was abolished and replaced by the area court system (Nwogugu, 1976).
44 Mikano E. Kiye, "The Repugnancy and Incompatibility Tests and Customary Law in Anglophone Cameroon," *African Studies Quarterly* 15, no. 2 (March 2015): 86.

Bibliography

1st Attorneys. "Understanding Statutory and Customary Marriages Under the Marriage Act: Essential Requirements and Legal Implications." *Law Articles* (blog), June 24, 2024, https://1stattorneys.com/articles/2024/06/24/understanding-statutory-and-customary-marriages-under-the-marriage-act-essential-requirements-and-legal-implications.

Adesubokan v. Yunusa (1971) 1 All NLR 225, 227, Court of Appeal, Nigeria, https://www.lawglobalhub.com/timothy-tanloju-adesubokan-vs-rasaki-yunusa-1971-lljr-sc.

Adewoye, Omoniyi. "Review: Law and Social Change in Nigeria, by T. O. Elias." Journal of the Historical Society of Nigeria 7, no. 1 (December 1973): 149–59, https://www.jstor.org/stable/41856993.

Afigbo, Adiele E. "Background to Nigerian Federalism: Federal Features in the Colonial State." Publius: The Journal of Federalism 21, no. 4 (Fall 1991): 13–29, https://doi.org/10.1093/oxfordjournals.pubjof.a037965.

Amankwah, Harrison A. "Ghanaian Law: Its Evolution and Interaction with English Law." Cornell International Law Journal 4, no. 1 (Fall 1970): 37–57, https://scholarship.law.cornell.edu/cilj/vol4/iss1/3.

Anghie, Antony. Imperialism, Sovereignty and the Making of International Law. Cambridge, UK: Cambridge University Press, 2005.

Arewa, Olufunmilayo B. Disrupting Africa: Technology, Law, and Development. Cambridge, UK: Cambridge University Press, 2021.

Australian Matrimonial Causes Act 1959 (Cth), No. 104 (Austrl.).

Barnes, Sandra T. Patrons and Power: Creating a Political Community in Metropolitan Lagos. London, UK: Routledge, 1986.

Bennett, Thomas W. "The Interpersonal Conflict of Laws: A Technique for Adapting Social Change in Africa." The Journal of Modern African Studies 18, no. 1 (March 1980): 127–34, https://doi.org/10.1017/S0022278X00009472.

Berry, Sara. No Condition Is Permanent: The Social Dynamics of Agrarian Change in Sub-Saharan Africa. Madison: University of Wisconsin Press, 1993.

Boparai, Harinder. "The Customary and Statutory Law of Marriage in Nigeria." Rabels Zeitschrift für ausländisches und internationales Privatrecht/The Rabel Journal of Comparative and International Private Law 46, no. 3 (1982): 530–57, https://www.jstor.org/stable/27876669.

Chanock, Martin. "Neo-Traditionalism and the Customary Law in Malawi." African Legal Studies 16 (1978): 80–90, https://commission-on-legal-pluralism.com/system/commission-on-legal-pluralism/volumes/16/chanock-art.pdf.

Chinwuba, Nwudego N. "Interaction of Customs and Colonial Heritage: Their Impact on Marriage and Children in Nigeria." Anthropos 111, no. 1 (2016): 49–68, https://doi.org/10.5771/0257-9774-2016-1-49.

Chiroma, Isa H. "Conflict Between Islamic Law and Common Law on the Testamentary Powers [Waṣiyyah]: The Attitude of Nigerian Courts." Islamic Studies 32, no. 3 (Autumn 1993): 339–49, https://www.jstor.org/stable/20840135.

Christensen, Darin, and David D. Laitin. African States Since Independence: Order, Development, and Democracy. New Haven, CT: Yale University Press, 2019.

Christopher, Anthony John "'Divide and Rule': The Impress of British Separation Policies." Area 20, no. 3 (September 1988): 233–40, https://www.jstor.org/stable/20002624.

Divorce Reform Act of 1969, c. 55 (Eng.).

Egharevba v. Oruonghae (2001) 11 NWLR, pt. 724, 318, Court of Appeal, Nigeria, https://www.lawglobalhub.com/emmanuel-osaheni-egharevba-v-mrs-comfort-oruonghae-2001-lljr-ca/#google_vignette.

Ernest Carr v. Suleman Abdul Karim (1929) Nyasaland.

Gashaw, Tasew Tafese. "Colonial Borders in Africa: Improper Design and Its Impact on African Borderland Communities." The Wilson Center, November 17, 2017, https://www.wilsoncenter.org/blog-post/colonial-borders-in-africa-improper-design-and-its-impact-on-african-borderland-communities.

Havik, Philip J. "'Direct' or 'Indirect' Rule? Reconsidering the Roles of Appointed Chiefs and Native Employees in Portuguese West Africa." Africana Studia 15 (January 2010): 29–56, https://ojs.letras.up.pt/index.php/AfricanaStudia/article/view/7337/6722.

Hyde v. Hyde and Woodmansee (1866) LR 1 PD 130, Court of Probate and Divorce, United Kingdom, https://vlex.co.uk/vid/hyde-v-hyde-and-805460993.

Idehen v. Idehen (1991) 6 NWLR 387, Supreme Court of Nigeria, https://www.lawglobalhub.com/joseph-osemwegie-idehen-ors-vs-george-otutu-idehen-ors-1991-lljr-sc.

Ikime, Obaro. "Chief Dogho: The Lugardian System in Warri, 1917–1932." Journal of the Historical Society of Nigeria 3, no. 2 (December 1965): 313–33, https://www.jstor.org/stable/41971166.

Jadesimi v. Okotie-Eboh (1996) All NLR 385, Supreme Court of Nigeria, https://www.lawglobalhub.com/mrs-alero-jadesimi-v-mrs-victoria-okotie-eboh-ors-1996-lljr-sc.

Kehinde, Tola Benjamin. "French Colonial Policies in West Africa: Power Dynamics, Cultural Impositions and Economic Legacies." International Journal of Advances in Social Sciences and Humanities 3, no. 1 (February 2024): 8–17, https://doi.org/10.56225/ijassh.v3i1.248.

Kiye, Mikano E. "The Repugnancy and Incompatibility Tests and Customary Law in Anglophone Cameroon." African Studies Quarterly 15, no. 2 (March 2015): 85–101, https://journals.flvc.org/ASQ/article/view/136157.

Larkin, Brian. Signal and Noise: Media, Infrastructure, and Urban Culture in Nigeria. Durham, NC: Duke University Press, 2008.

Lateef, Misbau Alamu, and Nathaniel Kehinde Adegbite. "Bigamy and Dearth of Prosecution in Nigeria." OAU Journal of Public Law 1, no. 1 (2017): 91–117, https://doi.org/10.2139/ssrn.3412119.

Law of Marriage Act (Tanzania), (LMA) 1971 (Cap 29 R.E 2002).

Lawal-Osula v. Lawal-Osula (1995), 9 NWLR, pt. 419, 259–72, Supreme Court of Nigeria, https://www.lawglobalhub.com/lydia-modupe-lawal-osula-ors-v-chief-saka-lawal-osula-ors-1995-lljr-sc.

Lawrance, Benjamin N., Emily Lynn Osborn, and Richard L. Roberts. "Introduction: African Intermediaries and the 'Bargain' of Collaboration." In Intermediaries, Interpreters, and Clerks: African Employees in the Making of Colonial Africa, edited by Benjamin N. Lawrance, Emily Lynn Osborn, and Richard L. Roberts, 3–34. Madison: University of Wisconsin Press, 2006.

Lee, Christopher J. "Jus Soli and Jus Sanguinis in the Colonies: The Interwar Politics of Race, Culture, and Multiracial Legal Status in British Africa." Law and History Review 29, no. 2 (May 2011): 497–522, https://doi.org/10.1017/S073824801100006X.

Lee, Christopher Joon-Hai. "The 'Native' Undefined: Colonial Categories, Anglo-African Status and the Politics of Kinship in British Central Africa, 1929–38." The Journal of African History 46, no. 3 (November 2005): 455–78, https://doi.org/10.1017/S0021853705000861.

Marriage Act of 1914, Act No. 18, Laws of the Federation of Nigeria.

Marriage Act of 1990, Ch. 218, Laws of the Federation of Nigeria.

Marriage Act of 2004, Cap. M6, Laws of the Federation of Nigeria.

Marriages (Validation) Act of 1990, Ch. 219, Laws of the Federation of Nigeria.

Matrimonial Causes Act of 1970, Cap. M7, Laws of the Federation of Nigeria.

M.O. v. R.O. and Anor (2013), EWHC 392 (Fam), High Court of Justice, Family Division, United Kingdom, https://www.casemine.com/judgement/uk/5a8ff76c60d03e7f57eac557.

M.O. v. R.O. and Rig Ltd. (2013), EWHC 392, High Court of Justice, Family Division, United Kingdom, https://vlex.co.uk/vid/mo-v-ro-first-792555313.

Moore, Sally Falk. Social Facts and Fabrications: "Customary" Law on Kilimanjaro, 1880–1980. Cambridge, UK: Cambridge University Press, 1986.

Murray, David J. "Britain's Influence in Africa." Current History 52, no. 309 (May 1967): 276–81, https://www.jstor.org/stable/45311694.

National Population Commission. Nigeria Demographic and Health Survey 2018. Abuja, Nigeria: National Population Commission and ICF International, 2019, https://www.dhsprogram.com/pubs/pdf/FR359/FR359.pdf.

Native Authority Ordinance 1932. British National Archives, CO 583/183/13, Kew, UK.

Native Courts (Amendment) Ordinance 1930 and Native Authority (Amendment) Ordinance 1930. British National Archives, CO 583/175/5, Kew, UK.

Nigerian Criminal Code Act of 1990, Ch. 32, § 370, Laws of the Federation of Nigeria.

Nwogugu, Edwin Ifeanyinchukwu "Abolition of Customary Courts—the Nigerian Experiment." Journal of African Law 20, no. 1 (Spring 1976): 1–19, https://doi.org/10.1017/S0021855300006689.

Ocheni, Stephen, and Basil C. Nwankwo. "Analysis of Colonialism and Its Impact in Africa." *Cross-Cultural Communication* 8, no. 3 (2012): 46–54, https://doi.org/10.3968/j.ccc.1923670020120803.1189.

Ochonu, Moses. "African Colonial Economies: Land, Labor, and Livelihoods." History Compass 11, no. 2 (February 2013): 91–103, https://doi.org/10.1111/hic3.12031

Ochonu, Moses E. Colonialism by Proxy: Hausa Imperial Agents and Middle Belt Consciousness in Nigeria. Bloomington: Indiana University Press, 2014.

Okoli, Chukwuma Samuel Adesina, Abubakri Yekini, and Philip Oamen. "The Igiogbe Custom as a Mandatory Norm in Conflict of Laws: An Exploration of Nigerian Appellate Court Decisions." African Journal of International and Comparative Law 31, no. 3 (August 2023): 396–415, https://doi.org/10.3366/ajicl.2023.0455.

Okonwo, Ogechukwu. "The Making of Modern Nigeria: British Imperialism and the Political Evolution of Nigeria." *The Republic* (Lagos, Nigeria), September 29, 2023, https://republic.com.ng/october-november-2023/the-making-of-nigeria.

Oluya, Donatus Sunday. "Bini Customary Law of Inheritance: Shift in 'Igiogbe' as a Case Study." Master's thesis, Dalarna University, Falun, Sweden, June 2012, https://du.diva-portal.org/smash/get/diva2:601048/FULLTEXT01.

Oserogho, Akhigbe, et al. "Nigeria." In Private Wealth and Private Client Review. 8th ed. edited by John Riches, 363–75. London, UK: Law Business Research, 2019.

Palan, Ronen, and Giovanni Mangraviti. "Troubling Tax Havens: Multi-Jurisdictional Arbitrage and Tax Footprint Reduction." In Handbook on Wealth and the Super-Rich, edited by Iain Hay and Jonathan V. Beaverstock, 422–42. Cheltenham, UK: Edward Elgar, 2016.

Postema, Gerald J. "Custom in International Law: A Normative Practice Account." In The Nature of Customary Law: Legal, Historical, and Philosophical Perspectives, edited by Amanda Perreau-Saussine and James Bernard Murphy, 279–306. Cambridge, UK: Cambridge University Press, 2007.

Rahmatian. Andreas. "Termination of Marriage in Nigerian Family Laws: The Need for Reform and the Relevance of the Tanzanian Experience." International Journal of Law, Policy and the Family 10, no. 3 (December 1996): 281–316, https://doi.org/10.1093/lawfam/10.3.281.

Sharkey, Heather J. Living with Colonialism: Nationalism and Culture in the Anglo-Egyptian Sudan. Berkeley: University of California Press, 2003.

Siollun, Max. What Britain Did to Nigeria: A Short History of Conquest and Rule. London, UK: Hurst, 2021.

Tom, Patricia Izuka, and Saka Toyin Abdulrahman. "Effect of Will on Those Subject to Customary Law in Nigeria." International Journal of Law 6, no. 3 (2020): 61–69, https://www.lawjournals.org/assets/archives/2020/vol6issue3/6-2-32-361.pdf.

Ukpe, Essien. "Ethnocentrism as a Colonial Relic in Africa." Chapter 14. In Relics of Colonialism: An Introduction to African Politics, 86–92. Uyo, Nigeria: Robertminder International, 2024.

Umezuruike, Chima. "The Concept of 'Double-Decker' Marriages in Nigeria." The Barrister Group, August 23, 2024, https://thebarristergroup.co.uk/blog/the-concept-of-double-decker-marriages-in-nigeria.

Unobe, Ejembi Anefu. "Class-Formation, State Construction and Customary Law in Colonial Nigeria." Presented at the National Conference on Nigeria in the Twenty-First Century, Ahmadu Bello University, Zaria, Nigeria, May 4–9, 1987, https://journals.codesria.org/index.php/ad/article/view/2815/2721.

Wills Act 1837, 1 Vict. c. 26, United Kingdom.

Wills Amendment Act 1852, 15–16 Vict. c. 24, United Kingdom.

Yakubu, John Ademola. "Colonialism, Customary Law and the Post-Colonial State in Africa: The Case of Nigeria." Africa Development 30, no. 4 (2005): 201–20, https://www.jstor.org/stable/24483841.

Zajaczkowski, Andrej. "Belgian Congo: Between Indirect and Direct Rule." Hemispheres: Studies on Cultures and Societies 1 (1984): 259–70.

EPILOGUE

There is no gainsaying that ethnicity plays a role in sub-Saharan Africa's prospects for long-term economic performance; that enduring legacy of European colonization has plagued the subcontinent since independence. Though colonialism obviously did not *create* ethnic identity in Africa, imperial governance structures amplified and problematized it by carving out colonial states as amalgamations of ethnic identities—or, in reality, based on European notions, assumptions, and conflations about ethnicity (and driven, of course, by the overarching principle and driving force of colonialism: expediency, in terms of land acquisition, resource extraction, and the exploitation of labor). In the case of British colonial rule, these artificial constructs subsumed minority ethnic groups under the hegemony of larger ones, conferring disproportionate benefits on particular ethnic groups through the pernicious system of indirect rule, under which members of preferred ethnics became surrogates of the colonial state. After independence, members of those favored ethnic groups became the new political elites. In Africa, as elsewhere, it is well established that political power begets economic power, which incentivizes ethnic patronage. This dynamic encapsulates how colonial rule entrenched inequality in post-colonial states in sub-Saharan Africa.

Colonialism also spawned uneven regional development by way of Indigenous populations' disparate contact with Europeans. By and large, those living in proximity to the loci of the colonial apparatus benefitted disproportionately from its by-products. Settler colonialism necessitated the building of infrastructure, including Western-style educational institutions: Not only did the colonizers "come to stay" (progeny often in tow),[1] but a major component of the colonial project—and its incumbent erasure of Indigenous communities and traditional ways of life—was the introduction of new societal structures that replicated European cultural values and promoted a Western-centric order. Successful implementation of those structures required a population that (a) spoke English and (b) spoke the same language, so to speak (i.e., understood the Western way of life and was demonstrably willing to emulate it). Importantly, and perhaps ironically, the composition of the classes of educated Indigenous elites that arose during the colonial period was skewed in favor of the ethnic groups that had the most contact with settler colonial institutions and infrastructure. It was also skewed in favor of regions that availed from the establishment of settler colonial, Western-style educational institutions, and those that enabled Christian missionary expansion, and thus Christian schools.

For example, in Kenya, colonial rule inaugurated a class of Indigenous political elites that has largely dominated post-independence political and socioeconomic affairs. The Kikuyu ethnic group's early and comparatively extensive contact with settler colonial capitalism offered its numbers significant political and economic advantages over other ethnic groups in terms of access to education, resources, position, and opportunity. After independence, these advantages translated to hegemony in national politics. As described in these pages, the traditional Kikuyu heartland encompassed the so-called White Highlands settled by the British during colonization. The region's infrastructural advantages, along with substantial post-independence allocation of state resources, made it the country's most economically developed region and the epicenter of the Kenyan economy, cementing Kikuyu dominance in the country's political and socioeconomic hierarchy. The resulting structural inequalities between ethnic groups created ethnic tensions that continue to flare to this day.[2]

In Nigeria, the proliferation of Christian missionary activity in the south brought about considerably more modern (i.e., Western-oriented) infrastructure development—including the construction of schools and institutions of higher learning—relative to the north, which was predominantly Muslim and shunned Western and Christian influence. As detailed in this volume, the resulting modernization in the south and the institutions and societal frameworks that came with it accelerated the growth of human capital and enterprise, creating a post-independence corps of educated elites in the south with better access to civil service jobs at the federal government level. These and other socioeconomic dichotomies sparked (and continue to stoke) north-south and ethnoreligious rivalries that have been ingrained in Nigeria's political and socioeconomic fabric since independence.[3]

Although this volume focuses heavily on the Kenyan and Nigerian experiences, other sub-Saharan African countries have had similar experiences. In Rwanda during colonial rule, the Belgians favored the Tutsi over the Hutu majority, and the Belgian colonial administration employed the Tutsi to rule over the Hutu and other minority groups. Hutu chiefs were deposed in favor of the Tutsi, and only the Tutsi had access to Western-style education, which was the training ground for employment in the colonial administration. This ethnic favoritism bred structural inequalities in Rwandan society that persisted after independence; the long-standing Hutu-Tutsi hostility ultimately led to the Rwandan genocide in 1994.[4]

In Ghana, colonial rule created structural inequalities between the north and the south. Viewing the north as "backward and inferior," the British colonial administration willfully neglected the region, relegating it to little more than a labor source to support the building of infrastructure while investing in and modernizing the south. This policy inevitably wrought socioeconomic disparities and structural inequality between the south and the north as the south became more prosperous and politically influential than the north. Despite some notable government efforts to bridge this development gap since independence, significant socioeconomic disparities endure, fueling tensions between northern and southern Ghana.[5]

The chapters in this volume reach a consensus on two very clear imperatives for the mission to ameliorate inequality and poverty in sub-Saharan Africa. First, good governance—as in, transparent, accountable, democratic governance that actively promotes equitability, inclusion, and the rule of law—is essential for driving economic growth and eliminating structural inequalities across the subcontinent. Such governance must address the plight of marginalized and disenfranchised ethnic groups and regions by actively committing to inclusionary and corrective strategies. In other words, governments must enact policies that effectively grapple with persistent socioeconomic inequities between regions and between ethnic groups. Good governance can cultivate a sense of nationhood, foster political stability, and advance socioeconomic development and long-term growth. But it requires commitments on the part of leaders at the national level.

The second imperative is for countries to embrace the African Continental Free Trade Agreement (AfCFTA). If properly managed and implemented, AfCFTA is poised to unlock sub-Saharan Africa's substantial potential for prosperity. Eliminating trade barriers, connecting economies, taking advantage of economies of scale, and creating a global African market will enable the continent as a whole to "take-off," achieving high growth and industrialization, as described in W. W. Rostow's third stage of economic growth.[6] The mobility of capital and labor across borders, along with heightened foreign investment, will catalyze entrepreneurial spirit and generate employment opportunities through intra-industry trade. Big picture, these economic activities can reduce poverty and inequality in the long durée and reverse the course of the subcontinent's development crisis—so long as governments provide institutional and leadership commitments to ensure AfCFTA's viability and success.

The woeful colonial legacies that set the stage for sub-Saharan Africa's decades-long quagmire of embedded ethnic inequality and calamitous underdevelopment are well studied. Likewise, economic development literature is replete with studies that analyze the effects of ethnic diversity on economic growth, and the scholarly consensus is that ethnic diversity impedes the prospects of long-term economic performance in sub-Saharan Africa. But lacking in the literature is a critical framework grounding ethnic fragmentation as a principal factor in underdevelopment: There remains a dearth of development studies on the link between ethnicity, inequality, and economic performance on the subcontinent.

The chapters in this volume have sought to provide a base for that framework by offering a more holistic analysis of those interrelationships, examining the impact of ethnic diversity on structural inequality and economic development on the subcontinent from multidisciplinary perspectives. Those perspectives, from authors across social science disciplines, allow the book to present a more robust approach to the complex relationship among the variables. More specifically, the book's country studies and macro analyses dissect both the direct and indirect mechanisms through which ethnic fragmentation affects socioeconomic inequality and, subsequently, long-term economic performance in sub-Saharan Africa.

Proposing coherent socioeconomic policies to address the long-standing structural inequalities in sub-Saharan Africa requires a broad-based intellectual framework firmly rooted in a historical context. The studies in this volume have aimed to deconstruct deeply impacted societal realities and suggest policies that can engender meaningful change. That change can only come in the form of top-down socioeconomic strategies to ameliorate the endemic ethnoregional disparities and structural inequalities across sub-Saharan Africa and unlock the subcontinent's economic potential in the twenty-first century and beyond.

Notes

1 Patrick Wolfe, *Settler Colonialism and the Transformation of Anthropology: The Politics and Poetics of an Ethnographic Event* (London, UK: Cassell, 1999), 2.

2 Rok Ajulu, "Politicised Ethnicity, Competitive Politics and Conflict in Kenya: A Historical Perspective," *African Studies* 61, no. 2 (2002): 252–68, https://doi.org/10.1080/0002018022000032947.

3 Adiele E. Afigbo, "Background to Nigerian Federalism: Federal Features in the Colonial State," *Publius: The Journal of Federalism* 21, no. 4 (Fall 1991): 13–29, https://doi.org/10.1093/oxfordjournals.pubjof.a037965.

4 United States Holocaust Memorial Museum, "Rwanda: Divided by Ethnicity," last updated September 2021, https://www.ushmm.org/genocide-prevention/countries/rwanda/divided-by-ethnicity; Colette Braeckman, "Belgium's Role in Rwandan Genocide," *Le Monde diplomatique*, June 2021, https://mondediplo.com/2021/06/11rwanda; Luc de Heusch, "Rwanda: Responsibilities for a Genocide," *Anthropology Today* 11, no. 4 (August 1995): 3–7, https://doi.org/10.2307/2783105.

5 Ali Yakubu Nyaaba and George M. Bob-Milliar, "The Economic Potentials of Northern Ghana: The Ambivalence of the Colonial and Post-Colonial States to Develop the North," *African Economic History* 47, no. 2 (January 2020): 45–67, https://doi.org/10.3368/aeh.47.2.45; Isaac Abotebuno Akolgo, "Afro-Euphoria: Is Ghana's Economy an Exception to the Growth Paradox?," *Review of African Political Economy* 45, no. 155 (March 2018): 146–57, https://www.jstor.org/stable/48540818.

6 Walt Whitman Rostow, "The Five Stages-of-Growth—A Summary," Chapter 2. in *The Stages of Economic Growth: A Non-Communist Manifesto* (Cambridge, UK: Cambridge University Press, 1990), 4–16.

INDEX

Note: **Bold** page numbers refer to tables; *italic* page numbers refer to figures and page numbers followed by 'n' refer to notes.

For Product Safety Concerns and Information please contact our EU representative GPSR@taylorandfrancis.com Taylor & Francis Verlag GmbH, Kaufingerstraße 24, 80331 München, Germany